PRINCIPLES OF ELECTRON TUBES

PRINCIPLES

OF

ELECTRON TUBES

Understanding and Designing Simple Circuits

BY

HERBERT J. REICH, Ph.D.
Professor of Electrical Engineering
University of Illinois

Audio Amateur Press
Publishers
Peterborough, New Hampshire

FIRST REPRINT EDITION
1995

Distribution Agents

Old Colony Sound Lab
PO Box 243   305 Union Street
Peterborough, New Hampshire 03458-0243 USA

Library of Congress Card Catalog Number: 95-075528
ISBN: 1-882580-07-9

Printed in the United States of America

PREFACE

The increasing importance of electron tubes in fields of engineering other than communication has necessitated the development of courses offered primarily for students who do not intend to specialize in communication. Experience has also shown the value of an introductory course for those who do specialize in this field. The need for a text suitable for such courses has been apparent for some time. "Principles of Electron Tubes," which is essentially an abridgement of "Theory and Applications of Electron Tubes," is designed to meet this need. It should also prove suitable for home study by students who have not had an introductory course on electron tubes.

As in "Theory and Applications of Electron Tubes," the author has attempted to present fundamental principles together with discussions of representative practical circuits. He believes that the material included in this book can be adequately covered in a three-hour one-semester course, and that such a course will enable the student to understand typical industrial and laboratory applications of electron tubes and to design simple circuits to meet specific needs.

The student who studies electron tubes for the first time is likely to be confused and discouraged by the large number of symbols necessitated by the fact that electron tubes are non-linear circuit elements. In order to reduce the number of symbols required, therefore, several simplifying assumptions are made in Chaps. 3 and 4. The importance of these assumptions is, however, pointed out, and the interested student is referred to rigorous treatments. The derivation and use of equivalent circuits are emphasized. The problems on equivalent circuits should tie in nicely with material presented in courses on a-c circuit theory.

Because of the present great interest in frequency modulation, even on the part of the layman, a brief treatment of the subject is included. The entire chapter on modulation and detection may be omitted without loss of continuity if the instructor feels

v

that this material belongs only in courses designed for students majoring in communication.

Since the symbols used in this book are included in those used in the unabridged edition, the student who wishes to proceed to an advanced course in electron tubes will experience no difficulty in changing to the unabridged edition.

The author wishes to acknowledge the helpful suggestions and criticisms of Prof. Hugh A. Brown and Dr. Gilbert H. Fett of the Department of Electrical Engineering; and of Mr. A. James Ebel, chief engineer of radio station WILL, University of Illinois. The author is also indebted to the Allis-Chalmers Manufacturing Company, the Clough-Brengle Company, the General Electric Company, the General Radio Company, the Ken-rad Tube and Lamp Corporation, the Radio Corporation of America, and the Westinghouse Electric & Manufacturing Co. for valuable information, photographs, and diagrams.

HERBERT J. REICH.

URBANA, ILL.,
August, 1941.

CONTENTS

CHAPTER 6

CHAPTER 7

CHAPTER 10

CONTENTS

CHAPTER 11

CHAPTER 12

LIST OF SYMBOLS

The following list gives the pages on which each symbol used with a particular connotation is defined. It does not include many of the special symbols for electrode voltages and currents listed on pages 77–78, symbols used only in a single figure, or well-known standard symbols such as π and the vector operator j.

PRINCIPLES
OF ELECTRON TUBES

CHAPTER 1

PHYSICAL CONCEPTS

An *electron tube* is a device consisting of a number of electrodes contained within a totally or partly evacuated enclosure. The usefulness of such a device arises from its capacity to pass current, the magnitude of which may be controlled by the voltages of the electrodes. As suggested by the term *electron tube*, the operation of all types of electron tubes is dependent upon the movement of *electrons* within the tubes. The electron, which is the smallest known particle, has a mass of 9.03×10^{-28} g and a negative charge of 16×10^{-20} coulomb. The operation of many types of electron tubes also depends upon the separation and motion of other elementary particles of which matter is composed. For this reason a brief discussion of the fundamental processes governing the behavior of these elementary particles is of value in the study of electron tubes and their applications.

1-1. Excitation, Ionization, and Radiation.—The mass of the electron is greatly exceeded by that of an atom, the lightest atom, hydrogen, having a mass approximately eighteen hundred times that of the electron. The major portion of the mass of an atom is accounted for by the *nucleus*, a stable assemblage of charged and neutral particles having a net positive charge equal to the atomic number of the element. The atom also contains relatively loosely bound electrons, normally equal in number to its atomic number. The normal atom is therefore neutral.

Experiments show that in addition to possessing kinetic energy, an atom is capable of absorbing energy internally. The internal energy appears to be associated with the configuration of the particles of which the atom is composed. The internal energy can be altered only in discrete quantities, called *quanta*, and hence the atom can exist only in definite stable *states*, which are characterized by the internal energy content.   Under ordinary conditions an atom is most likely to be in that state in which the internal energy is a minimum, known as the *normal state*.   If the internal energy of the atom exceeds that of its normal state, it is said to be *excited*.   Excitation may be caused in a number of ways, among which is collision of the atom with rapidly moving positive or negative particles, which may give up some or all of their kinetic energy to the atom during the collision.   A limiting case of excitation is *ionization*, in which the energy absorbed by the atom is sufficient to allow a loosely bound electron to leave the atom against the electrostatic force which tends to hold it within the atom.   An atom that has lost one or more electrons is said to be *ionized* and is one type of *positive ion*.   It is possible for excitation or ionization to take place in successive steps by the absorption of two or more quanta of energy.

The return of an excited atom to a state of lower energy content usually is accompanied by electromagnetic radiation.   Since the energy of the atom can have only discrete values, the radiated electromagnetic energy corresponding to a change from one given energy state to another of lower energy is always associated with the releasing of a definite quantum of electromagnetic energy, called a *photon*.   The frequency of the radiated energy is determined by the relation $W_1 - W_2 = h\nu$, in which W_1 and W_2 are the values of the internal energy of the atom in the initial and final states; h is a universal constant called *Planck's constant*, 6.55×10^{-27} erg-sec; and ν is the frequency of the radiated energy in cycles per second.   From the form of this relation it is seen that the quantity $h\nu$ is the energy of the emitted photon.   Each line of the emission spectrum of an element represents the transition of atoms of the element from some energy state to another of lower internal energy.

In interacting with atoms and molecules, photons exhibit some of the characteristics of material particles, a photon behaving as though it were a bundle of energy.   The collision of an atom with a photon whose energy is equal to the required change of internal energy may result in excitation of the atom.   If the energy of the colliding photon is equal to or greater than that necessary to remove an electron from the atom, the collision may result in ionization of the atom.

A number of attempts have been made to give a picture of the structure of atoms that will account for the phenomena of excitation, ionization, and radiation. The most successful of these, proposed by Bohr, is based upon the assumption that one or more electrons move about the central nucleus of an atom in a manner similar to the motion of the planets about the sun. To account for the observed definite values of internal energy, it was assumed that the electrons can move only in certain orbits and that the internal energy of the atom is increased when one or more electrons are abruptly displaced from given orbits to others at a greater distance from the nucleus. Radiation was assumed to result when one or more electrons jump from given orbits to others nearer to the nucleus. Any such picture is valuable principally in its ability to explain observed phenomena and to predict others. The complexity of atoms containing more than two orbital electrons limited the usefulness of the Bohr picture of the atom to the hydrogen and helium atoms.

The phenomena of excitation, ionization, and radiation are also observed in molecules. Because of the greater complexity of molecules, and the fact that their internal energy is partly associated with the vibrational and rotational motion of the atoms of which they are composed, a molecule has many more stable states than an atom of the same element.

1-2. Electron Volt.—Since the energy that a charged particle acquires in free space when accelerated by an electric field is equal to the product of the charge by the difference of potential between the initial and final positions, the difference in potential may be used as a measure of the gain in kinetic energy. Any quantity of energy may, in fact, be expressed in "electron volts." An *electron volt* is the amount of energy gained by an electron when accelerated in free space through a difference of potential of 1 volt. It is customary to express in electron volts the energy required to ionize or excite atoms or molecules.

1-3. Ionization and Excitation Potentials.—An *excitation potential* is the energy, expressed in electron volts, that must be given to an atom or molecule in order to cause a transition from a given state to one of higher internal energy. An *ionization potential* is the least energy, expressed in electron volts, that must be supplied to a normal or an ionized atom or molecule in order to remove an electron from the atom or molecule. Inasmuch as all atoms but hydrogen contain more than one electron, an atom or molecule may, in general, have more than one ionization potential. The first ionization potential applies to the removal of an electron from a normal atom or molecule; the second ionization potential applies to the removal of a second electron from an atom or molecule that has already lost one electron; etc. A less likely type of ionization is the simultaneous removal of two or more electrons. The following table lists the first ionization potentials of some of the elements that are used in electron tubes. It should be noted that when ionization or excitation potentials are expressed in electron volts they indicate the minimum voltage that must be applied between two electrodes in order to cause ionization as the result of acceleration of electrons or other singly charged particles by the resulting field between the electrodes.

TABLE 1-I.—FIRST IONIZATION POTENTIALS IN ELECTRON VOLTS

Argon	15.69	Nitrogen	14.48	Sodium	5.12
Neon	21.47	Carbon dioxide	14.4	Rubidium	4.16
Helium	24.46	Mercury	10.38	Cesium	3.87
Hydrogen	13.53	Lithium	5.37	Magnesium	7.61
Oxygen	13.55	Potassium	4.32	Barium	5.19

1-4. Ionization.—The positively charged mass resulting from the removal of one or more electrons from an atom is only one of many types of ions. In general, an *ion* is an elementary particle of matter or a small group of such particles having a net positive or negative charge. Atoms or molecules that have lost one or more electrons, or that have picked up one or more extra electrons, and simple or complex groups of a number of atoms or molecules bearing excess positive or negative charge are special examples of ions. This definition of an ion also includes such relatively simple particles as the electron and other elementary charged particles of which atomic nuclei are composed. The process of ionization, broadly defined, is the production of ions in gases, liquids, or solids. It may result from a number of causes, among which are

1. Collision of atoms or molecules with
   a. Electrons.
   b. Positive or negative ions of atomic or molecular mass.
   c. Excited atoms or molecules.

2. Collision of atoms or molecules with photons (photoelectric effect).
3. Cosmic radiation.
4. High temperatures in gases or vapors.
5. Chemical action.

1-5. Ionization by Moving Electrons.—One of the most important causes of ionization in electron tubes is the collision of rapidly moving electrons with atoms or molecules.   In order that a single moving electron may ionize an atom or molecule it is necessary that its kinetic energy shall be at least equal to the first ionization potential of the atom or molecule.   It is sometimes observed, however, that ions appear in a gas or vapor when the bombarding electrons have energy corresponding to the first excitation potential.   The explanation of this is that the atom may be ionized in steps, each successive impact by an electron supplying sufficient energy to cause a transition to a state of higher energy.   Thus, although the first ionization potential of mercury is 10.38 volts, ionization of mercury vapor by moving electrons begins when the colliding electrons have energy corresponding to the lowest excitation potential, 4.68 volts.   Other more complicated processes may produce similar results.   Precise measurements show that the voltages at which moving electrons begin to ionize a gas or vapor are very sharply defined.

1-6. Ionization by Positive Ions.—Ionization by positive ions is a more complicated phenomenon than ionization by electrons. One reason for this is that a positive ion which strikes a neutral atom or molecule is able to surrender not only its kinetic energy but also some or all of its own energy of ionization, thus reverting to a state of lower energy.   A collision in which an ionized or excited atom or molecule transfers all or part of its energy of excitation to another atom or molecule is known as a *collision of the second kind.*   The transferred energy may be used to excite or ionize the unexcited particle or may be converted into kinetic energy of one or both particles.   In a mixture of gases a bombarding positive ion of one of the gases may ionize a neutral atom or molecule of the other, the difference in energies of ionization being supplied by or added to the kinetic energies of the two particles.   Because of conservation of momentum, the large mass of the positive ion also complicates the process of ionization by positive ions.   Ionization by bombardment of positive ions requires higher accelerating potentials than by electrons, and the potentials at which ionization begins are not sharply defined.

1-7. Amount of Ionization.—The ionization potential is a measure only of the minimum kinetic energy, below which a moving ion cannot ionize a normal atom or molecule by a single collision. It does not follow that every electron that acquires this amount of energy will necessarily ionize a gas through which it moves. The likelihood of ionization, which differs for different gases, is a function of the energy of the bombarding particles. The amount of ionization produced in a gas or vapor by charges that are accelerated by electric fields in the gas may be most conveniently specified by the *ionization coefficient*. The ionization coefficient is defined as the number of ionizing collisions made by an ion per centimeter of advance through the gas. It differs for different gases and for different types of ions and is a function of the gas pressure and the electric field strength. The ionization factor varies with electric field strength because increase of field strength increases the energy acquired by an ion between collisions. It varies with gas pressure because increase of gas density increases the likelihood that an ion will strike a gas particle in a given distance, but decreases the distance it moves and hence the energy it acquires between successive collisions with gas particles. Because of these conflicting effects, the ionization factor passes through a maximum value as the pressure is raised from a low value.

1-8. Photoionization.—In its narrower sense, the photoelectric effect is the release of electrons from the surface of a solid by light or other electromagnetic radiation. In its broader sense the photoelectric effect is the ionization of an atom or molecule by collision with a photon and may take place not only at the surface of a solid, but throughout a gas, liquid, or solid. The photoelectric effect and its applications will be discussed in detail in Chap. 10. The principles that govern ionization by collision also apply to photoelectric ionization. The energy of a single incident photon $h\nu$ must be at least equal to the first ionization potential of the atom. Impact of photons with atoms results not only in ionization but also in excitation. Ionization may occur in successive steps by a rapid sequence of impacts of successive photons. Excitation by photons is the inverse process to radiation, just as collision of the second kind is the inverse phenomenon to excitation or ionization by collision. Absorption spectra are an indication of the conversion of radiant energy into energy of excitation or ionization.

The frequencies of photons capable of ionizing most elements lie outside of the visible spectrum. The exceptions to this rule are the alkali metals, which are therefore used in light-sensitive electron tubes.

1-9. Ionization by Cosmic Rays.—The exact constitution of cosmic rays is still the basis of much scientific controversy. All experiments seem to indicate, however, that the primary source is outside of the earth and its atmosphere. They appear to be either electromagnetic radiation, of very short wave length, or charged particles that move with extremely high velocity. Ionization by cosmic rays at the surface of the earth results mainly from secondary rays formed in the outer atmosphere and appears to consist of both photoelectric ionization and ionization by collision. It is of importance in connection with glow and arc discharges because it is one of the sources of initial ionization that is necessary to the formation of glows in cold-cathode discharge tubes.

1-10. Space Charge and Space Current.—A group of free charges in space is called a *space charge*. If the charge is of one sign only, or if the density of charge of one sign in a given volume exceeds that of the other sign, the charge will give rise to an electrostatic field. The relation between the net charge within a volume and the resulting electrostatic flux is given by Gauss's law, which states that the electric flux through any surface enclosing free charges is equal to 4π times the sum of the enclosed charges.[1]

The movement of free charges in space constitutes a current, called *space current*. The current per unit area is equal to the product of the charge density and the velocity normal to the area. The conventional direction of current is in the direction of motion of positive charges and opposite in direction to the motion of negative charges.

1-11. Deionization.—The rapid disappearance of the products of ionization is necessary for the proper functioning of certain types of electron tubes containing gas or vapor. The

[1] PAGE, L., and ADAMS, N. I., "Principles of Electricity," pp. 18, 41, D. Van Nostrand Company, Inc., New York, 1931.

removal of ions from a volume of gas or vapor takes place in four ways:

1. Volume recombination.
2. Surface recombination.
3. Action of electric fields.
4. Diffusion.

There is good experimental evidence that the direct recombination of electrons with positive ions is of relatively rare occurrence in electrical discharges. Volume recombination results mainly from the attachment of electrons to neutral gas molecules to form the heavier and slower-moving negative ions, which subsequently combine with positive ions. The likelihood of attachment of electrons to neutral molecules decreases with increase in temperature, decrease in pressure, and increase in field strength. The rate of recombination of positive and negative ions is proportional to the product of the two ion densities, the constant of proportionality being called the *coefficient of recombination*. The coefficient of recombination is different for different gases.

Surface recombination occurs at conducting walls of the tube that contains the ionized gas, at the electrodes, and at surfaces of any other conducting solids that project into the ionized gas. Recombination takes place as the result of charges of opposite sign which are induced on conducting surfaces or pulled out by strong fields at the surfaces. On insulating surfaces or on conductors that are electrically isolated, charges may also accumulate and build up an electric field that repels charges of the same sign and attracts those of opposite sign. Surface recombination is one of the main factors affecting deionization in glow- and arc-discharge tubes and in circuit breakers of the "deion" type.

The electric field in the vicinity of the electrodes carries ions to the electrode surfaces, where surface recombination may take place. Within the main part of the gas, the electric field can change the ion density in a given small volume only if the ion density is not uniform throughout the tube, or at least in the vicinity of the volume under consideration. If the ion density is uniform, the field will sweep as many new ions into one side of the volume as it removes from the other. If an ion density gradient does exist, the action of the field may either increase or decrease the density in the given volume. An example of deionization by electric fields is the removal of ions in glow- and arc-discharge tubes when applied potentials are reduced below the value necessary to maintain a glow or arc.

Diffusion of ions results from the fact that the ions, like the gas molecules, have a random motion which carries them from point to point. If the ion density in an element of volume is greater than in adjacent elements, then on the average more ions leave the given element than enter it; if, on the other hand, the ion density is uniform throughout the region under consideration, then on the average just as many ions enter a given element of volume in unit time as leave it. Thus, deionization by diffusion, like deionization by electric fields, is dependent upon nonuniform density. Because of surface recombination and nonuniform production of ions throughout the tube, ion density differences are set up in glow- and arc-discharge tubes which enable diffusion and electric fields to be effective deionizing agents.

1-12. Free Electrons in Metals. Electron Affinity.—Some of the electrons of metallic atoms are very loosely bound to the atoms. When groups of such atoms are massed together into solids or liquids, the loosely bound electrons can readily pass from atom to atom. Because of their random temperature velocity these *free electrons* are constantly moving about within the mass, and, although at some particular instant they may be loosely bound to particular atoms, on the average they experience no force in any particular direction. It is these electrons that make metallic conduction possible and that play indispensable roles in thermionic emission.

An electron that, in the course of its random motion, happens to pass through the surface of the metal will, while it is still close to the surface, induce on the surface of the metal a positive charge. This induced charge results in a force that tends to return the electron into the metal, the so-called *image force*. In order to escape from the metal the electron must give up a certain amount of kinetic energy. The kinetic energy that an electron loses in passing through the surface of a metal and far enough away to be beyond the range of the image forces is called the *electron affinity* of that metal and is represented by the symbol w.

The electron affinity is different for different materials and varies greatly with the condition of the surface and with impurities contained in the substance, particularly at the surface. Schottky has shown theoretically that the electron affinity should be reduced by strong electric fields at the surface and that it should vary from point to point on a given surface because of microscopic irregularities, being smaller at projections and larger in hollows.[1] Table 1-II lists representative values of electron affinity for a number of metals commonly used in electron tubes.

TABLE 1-II.—ELECTRON AFFINITY w IN ELECTRON VOLTS

Tungsten	4.52	Magnesium	2.7
Platinum	5.0	Nickel	4.0
Tantalum	4.1	Sodium	1.9
Molybdenum	4.3	Mercury	4.4
Carbon	4.5	Calcium	2.5
Copper	4.0	Barium	2.0
Thorium	3.0	Thorium on tungsten	2.63

Oxide-coated nickel....0.5 to 1.5

1-13. Contact Difference of Potential.[2]—A potential difference, called *contact difference of potential*, exists between the surfaces of two different metals that are in contact or are con-

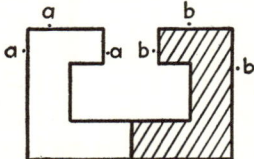

FIG. 1-1.—Production of contact difference of potential by metals of unequal electron affinities.

nected through an external circuit, as shown in Fig. 1-1. Contact difference of potential results from the fact that the electron affinities of the two metals differ. It is very nearly equal to the difference between the electron affinities divided by the charge of an electron. To prove this, suppose that an electron starts from any point a close to the surface of one of the

metals, passes into this surface, around the external circuit, and out through the surface of the second metal to any point b close to its surface. In passing into the first metal the electron does work equal to $-w_1$, the electron affinity of that metal. In crossing the junction between the metals it does a small amount of work because of the Peltier potential difference, which always exists at the junction of two different metals and which is also a function of the electron affinities of the metals. In passing out of the surface of the second metal it does work equal to w_2, the electron

[1] Schottky, W., *Physik. Z.*, **12**, 872 (1914), **20**, 220 (1919); *Ann. Physik*, **44**, 1011 (1914); *Z. Physik*, **14**, 63 (1923).

[2] An interesting discussion of contact potential and other small effective electrode voltages is given by R. M. Bowie, *Proc. I.R.E.*, **24**, 1501 (1936).

affinity of that metal.   If the small amount of energy that the electron loses as the result of impacts with atoms and molecules in the metals (I^2R loss) is neglected and the Peltier potential difference is called V_P, the total amount of work done is $\varepsilon V_P + w_2 - w_1$, where ε is the charge of an electron. εV_P may be shown to be small in comparison with $w_2 - w_1$, and so the work done is approximately $w_2 - w_1$.   Since the potential difference between two points may be defined as the work done in moving unit charge between the points, it follows that a difference of potential approximately equal to $(w_2 - w_1)/\varepsilon$ exists between any two points a and b close to the surfaces of the two metals.   If the connection between the metals is made through an external circuit containing one or more additional metals, the proof is altered only in respect to the additional Peltier potential differences, which are negligible.

Inasmuch as the various electrodes in electron tubes may be made of different metals, contact potentials may exist.   The contact potential differences may be of the order of 1 to 4 volts, as seen from Table 1-II, and must sometimes be taken into account when applied voltages are small or when high accuracy is necessary in the analysis of electron tube behavior.

1-14. Emission of Electrons and Other Ions from Solids.—The presence of ions in a given volume may result not only from ionization processes in that volume but also from the introduction of ions produced or existing elsewhere.   The mechanism by which ions are introduced may be diffusion, action of electric fields, or the emission of electrons or positive ions from the surfaces of solids or liquids.   There are five ways in which ions may be emitted from the surfaces of solids or liquids:

1. Thermionic emission.
2. Photoelectric emission.
3. Secondary emission.
4. Field emission.
5. Radioactive disintegration.

Thermionic and photoelectric emission will be discussed in detail in later chapters and therefore need no further consideration at this point.

Secondary Emission.—When ions or excited atoms impinge upon the surface of a solid, electrons may be ejected from the surface. These are called *secondary electrons*, and the phenomenon is termed *secondary emission*. Some secondary emission as the result of electron bombardment appears to take place when the energy of the impinging electrons is less than the electron affinity of the emitter. For this reason it seems likely that the energy that makes possible the escape of a secondary electron is obtained not only from the impinging electron, but also from the thermal energy of the emitter. The number of secondary electrons ejected per primary electron increases with the velocity of the primary electrons and may become great enough to have an appreciable effect upon the behavior of electron tubes at accelerating voltages as low as 5 to 10 volts. At several hundred volts the emission passes through a maximum and then continues to fall with further increase of accelerating voltage. This may be because the primary electrons penetrate farther into the solid and transfer most of their energy to electrons that are so far from the surface that they collide with atoms or molecules before reaching it. The number of secondary electrons emitted per primary electron is in general higher for surfaces having a low electron affinity. It also depends upon the condition of the emitting surface, being reduced by degassing the emitter and by carbonizing the surface. A single primary electron may eject as many as 8 or 10 secondary electrons. The primary electrons may be absorbed, reflected, or scattered by the surface. The number of secondary electrons released by a single impinging particle is less for positive-ion bombardment than for electron bombardment, and emission does not appear to take place unless the energy of the impinging ions exceeds the electron affinity of the emitter. The phenomenon of secondary emission is an important one in all types of electron tubes.

Field emission is the emission of electrons as the result of intense electric fields at a surface. It is probably an important factor in the operation of certain types of arc discharges. The field strengths required to pull electrons through surfaces at ordinary temperatures are so great that the phenomenon is difficult to produce by direct means.

The emission of alpha particles or gamma rays in the disintegration of radioactive substances is of importance in glow- and arc-discharge tubes because the presence of minute traces of radioactive materials in the tube walls and electrodes may thus produce a small amount of residual ionization which makes possible the initial flow of current.

1-15. Electron Dynamics.—The motion of ions, including electrons, is governed by the same laws as the motion of larger masses that can be observed directly. Analyses of the dynamics of masses are based primarily upon Newton's second law, which may be stated symbolically by the equation

$$f = ma \tag{1-1}$$

in which f is the force in dynes acting upon a mass of m grams and a is the resulting acceleration in centimeters per second per second. Aside from forces resulting from the collision of charged particles with other charged or uncharged masses, the forces acting upon charged particles are electrostatic and electromagnetic. An *electric* or a *magnetic field* is said to exist in a region in which electric or magnetic forces, respectively, act. The *electric intensity (electric force)* at any point is a vector quantity which is given, both in magnitude and in direction, by the force (mechanical) per unit positive charge which would act in vacuum on a charged particle placed at this point. The *magnetic intensity (magnetic force)* at a point may be defined as the vector quantity which is measured in magnitude and direction by the force (mechanical) which would be exerted on a unit magnetic pole placed at the point when the point under consideration is in vacuum.

1-16. Motion of an Electron with Zero Initial Velocity in a Uniform Electric Field.—In the simplest case commonly encountered in electron tubes, the electrostatic force acting upon an ion results from the application of a potential difference to two parallel plane electrodes whose area is large in comparison with their separation. Except near the edges, the electric intensity between such plates is constant throughout the space between them. Since difference of potential between two points may be defined as the work done in moving a unit charge between the points, it follows that the potential difference is equal to

$$E = \int_0^d F\, ds \quad \text{e.s.u. (statvolts)} = 300 \int_0^d F\, ds \quad \text{volts} \tag{1-2}$$

where F is the electric intensity in e.s.u. and d is the electrode spacing in centimeters. Since F is constant,

$$E = F \int_0^d ds = Fd \qquad \text{e.s.u.} \tag{1-3}$$

and

$$F = \frac{E}{d} \qquad \text{e.s.u.} \tag{1-4}$$

The force exerted upon an electron between two such plates is equal to the force exerted upon a unit charge times the charge of the electron:

$$f_e = \frac{E\varepsilon}{d} \qquad \text{dynes} \tag{1-5}$$

where E is expressed in e.s.u. (statvolts), ε in e.s.u. (statcoulombs), and d in centimeters. It follows from Eqs. (1-1) and (1-5) that the acceleration of the electron is

$$a_e = \frac{f_e}{m_e} = \frac{E\varepsilon}{m_e d} \qquad \text{cm/sec}^2 \tag{1-6}$$

in which m_e is the mass of the electron in grams. Since, by definition, acceleration is the rate of change of velocity, the velocity at any instant after the electron starts moving under the influence of the field is

$$v_e = \int_0^t a_e\, dt = \frac{E\varepsilon}{m_e d} \int_0^t dt = \frac{E\varepsilon t}{m_e d} \qquad \text{cm/sec} \tag{1-7}$$

The distance moved by the electron in the time t is

$$s = \int_0^t v_e\, dt = \frac{E\varepsilon}{m_e d} \int_0^t t\, dt = \frac{E\varepsilon}{2m_e d} t^2 \qquad \text{cm} \tag{1-8}$$

From Eq. (1-8) it follows that the time taken for the electron to move from one electrode to the other under the sole influence of the electric field is

$$t_d = d \sqrt{\frac{2m_e}{E\varepsilon}} \qquad \text{sec} \tag{1-9}$$

The velocity with which it strikes the positive plate is

$$v_d = \frac{E\varepsilon t_d}{m_e d} = \sqrt{\frac{2E\varepsilon}{m_e}} \qquad \text{cm/sec} \tag{1-10}$$

The energy with which it strikes and which is converted into heat in the positive electrode is

$$K.E. = \tfrac{1}{2}m_e v_d^2 = E\mathcal{E} \qquad \text{ergs} \qquad (1\text{-}11)$$

Equation (1-11) might have been obtained directly, since the difference of potential between the electrodes is the energy acquired by a unit charge moved under the sole influence of the field and, if the charge does not collide with other particles on the way, this energy can appear only in kinetic form.

1-17. Motion of an Electron in a Uniform Electric Field. Initial Velocity Parallel to the Field.—If an electron leaves one of the plates with initial velocity of v_o parallel to the field, the velocity at any instant thereafter is

$$v_e = v_o \pm a_e t \qquad \text{cm/sec} \qquad (1\text{-}12)$$

in which the minus sign is used if the direction of the electric force is such as to reduce the initial velocity. The distance moved in the time t is

$$s = \int_0^t (v_o \pm a_e t)dt = v_o t \pm \tfrac{1}{2}a_e t^2 \qquad \text{cm} \qquad (1\text{-}13)$$

If the field reduces the initial velocity, the maximum distance moved can be found by differentiating Eq. (1-13). The time taken for the electron to move through this distance is found by equating ds/dt to zero.

$$0 = \frac{ds}{dt} = v_o - a_e t_{\max} \qquad (1\text{-}14)$$

$$t_{\max} = \frac{v_o}{a_e} \qquad \text{sec} \qquad (1\text{-}15)$$

$$s_{\max} = \frac{v_o^2}{a_e} - \frac{v_o^2}{2a_e} = \frac{v_o^2}{2a_e} \qquad \text{cm} \qquad (1\text{-}16)$$

The electron will reach the second electrode if

$$s_{\max} \equiv \frac{v_o^2}{2a_e} \equiv \frac{m_e d}{2E\mathcal{E}} v_o^2 \geqq d \qquad (1\text{-}17)$$

that is, if

$$\tfrac{1}{2}m_e v_o^2 \geqq E\mathcal{E} \qquad (1\text{-}18)$$

Equation (1-18) follows directly from the law of conservation of energy, since the electron can reach the second electrode only if its initial kinetic energy $\tfrac{1}{2}m_e v_o^2$ equals or exceeds the energy it would lose in moving between the electrodes, *i.e.*, $E\mathcal{E}$.

It also follows from the law of energy conservation that energy gained by a charged particle while moving in vacuum under the action of an electric field must be supplied by the source of potential applied to the electrodes. Conversely, energy given up by an ion in moving in an electric field is returned to the source, converted into I^2R loss in conductors joining the electrodes to the source, or into heat of impact if the electron strikes an electrode or other surface.

1-18. Motion of Electrons in Nonuniform Electric Fields.— In general, the electric intensity in electron tubes is not uniform, and so the integration of Eqs. (1-7), (1-8), and (1-13) is less simple. When space charge becomes appreciable, the motion of individual electrons is also affected by the fields set up by other electrons. This important phenomenon will be discussed in detail in Chap. 2.

Inspection of the methods used in deriving Eqs. (1-5) to (1-18) shows that they may be applied to other ions than electrons by making suitable changes in the values of charge and mass.

1-19. Importance of Transit Time.—The time taken for electrons and other ions to move between electrodes is so small that it may be neglected in many analyses of the operation of electron tubes (see Probs. 1-1 and 1-2). It cannot be neglected, however, when the electrode voltages alternate at frequencies so high that the time of transit is of the same order of magnitude as the periods of the voltages. It is also of importance in the study of the deionization of gas- or vapor-filled tubes.

1-20. Electric Field Normal to Initial Direction of Motion.— Up to this point it has been assumed that the initial velocity of the electron is parallel to the electric field. Under this assumption there is no change in the direction of motion in vacuum. In cathode-ray oscillograph and television tubes, electron beams are deflected by electric fields perpendicular to the initial direction of motion.

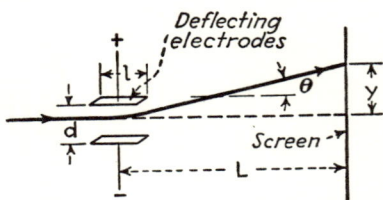

FIG. 1-2.—Deflection of electron beam by electric field.

The arrangement is essentially that shown in Fig. 1-2. Electrons enter the space between the deflecting electrodes with a velocity v_o parallel to the electrode surfaces, are deflected by the electrodes, which have a length l, a separation d, and a potential difference E, and strike a fluorescent screen placed at a distance L from the center of the deflecting plates.

The time taken for an electron to move through the deflecting field, which is assumed to be uniform between the plates and zero on either side, is l/v_o. The acceleration produced by the field is normal to the initial velocity and its magnitude is given by Eq. (1-6) as $E\varepsilon/m_e d$ cm/sec^2. The vertical displacement at the point where the electron leaves the plates is given by Eq. (1-8). It is

$$\delta = \frac{E\varepsilon}{2m_e d}\, t^2 = \frac{E\varepsilon l^2}{2m_e d v_o{}^2} \qquad \text{cm} \qquad (1\text{-}19)$$

The vertical velocity when the electron leaves the deflecting plates is given by Eq. (1-7)

$$v_y = \frac{E\varepsilon t}{m_e d} = \frac{E\varepsilon l}{v_o m_e d} \qquad \text{cm/sec} \qquad (1\text{-}20)$$

The horizontal velocity, which is unaffected by the field, is still v_o. Therefore, the final direction of motion makes an angle with the initial direction given by the relation

$$\tan \theta = \frac{v_y}{v_o} = \frac{E\varepsilon l}{v_o{}^2 m_e d} \qquad (1\text{-}21)$$

But by Eq. (1-19),

$$\frac{\delta}{\tfrac{1}{2}l} = \frac{E\varepsilon l}{m_e d v_o{}^2} = \tan \theta \qquad (1\text{-}22)$$

Examination of Fig. 1-3 shows, therefore, that after deflection the electrons move as though they had passed through a point

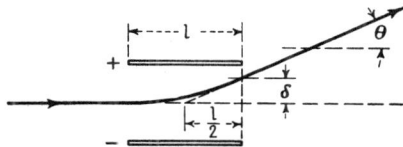

Fig. 1-3.—Deflection of electron beam by electric field.

midway between and midway along the deflecting plates. The deflection of the electron when it reaches the screen is

$$y = L \tan \theta = \frac{E\varepsilon l L}{v_o{}^2 m_e d} \qquad \text{cm} \qquad (1\text{-}23)$$

1-21. Motion of an Electron in a Magnetic Field Normal to the Initial Velocity.—Like a current-carrying conductor, an electron moving normal to a magnetic field experiences a force perpendicular to the field and to the direction of motion of the charge. The magnitude of the force is given by the relation

$$f_h = B\mathcal{E}'v \qquad \text{dynes} \qquad (1\text{-}24)$$

in which B is the flux density in gauss, $\mathcal{E}'$ is the charge of an electron in *electromagnetic* units, and v is the velocity in cm/sec.

If the electronic charge is expressed in e.s.u., Eq. (1-24) may also be written

$$f_h = \frac{B\mathcal{E}v}{3 \times 10^{10}} \qquad \text{dynes} \qquad (1\text{-}25)$$

The action of a magnetic field differs from that of an electric field in that the force on a moving charge in an electric field is always parallel to the field, whereas the force on a moving charge in a magnetic field is always at right angles to the instantaneous velocity. If an electron enters a uniform magnetic field with an initial velocity v_o normal to the field, it will be deflected at right angles to the field by the force $B\mathcal{E}'v_o$ dynes. Since the acceleration is normal to the velocity, the speed remains constant. If ρ is the instantaneous radius of curvature, the radial acceleration is v_o^2/ρ. Therefore, by Eq. (1-1),

$$B\mathcal{E}'v_o = \frac{m_e v_o^2}{\rho} \qquad (1\text{-}26)$$

and

$$\rho = \frac{v_o m_e}{B\mathcal{E}'} \qquad \text{cm} \qquad (1\text{-}27)$$

Since B is assumed to be constant, the electron moves with constant speed along a path of constant radius of curvature, *i.e.*, along a circular path, in a plane perpendicular to the field. The dependence of the radius of curvature upon the velocity and upon the mass makes possible the separation of charged particles of different velocities or masses.

If the initial velocity also has a component parallel to the field, then the electron will describe a spiral path around an axis parallel to the field. A similar spiral motion results if the initial velocity is parallel to the field, but some other force, such as repulsion between two or more electrons, produces an

acceleration normal to the field. This principle may be used
in preventing the spreading of and in focusing a beam of electrons.
Electron beams may also be focused by the use of nonuniform
electric fields such as exist between adjacent cylinders of unequal
diameter when a difference of potential exists between them.[1]
These methods are used in focusing electron beams in cathode-ray
oscillograph and television tubes and in electron microscopes (see
Sec. 12-5 and page 27).

1-22. Crossed Electric and Magnetic Fields.—If an electron is
sent through electric and magnetic
fields that are perpendicular to each
other and to the initial velocity of the
electron, as shown in Fig. 1-4, the
electron is acted upon by a force $\mathcal{E}F$
dynes caused by the electric field and
a force $B\mathcal{E}v_o/(3 \times 10^{10})$ dynes caused
by the magnetic field. These forces
are both normal to the surfaces of the
deflecting plates. If they are equal

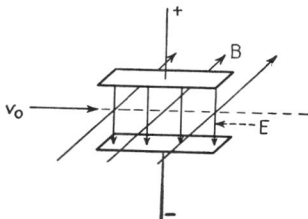

FIG. 1-4.—Path of an electron through balanced combined
electric and magnetic fields.

in magnitude and opposite in direction, the electron is undeflected.
This is true if

$$\mathcal{E}F = \frac{B\mathcal{E}v_o}{3 \times 10^{10}} \tag{1-28}$$

or

$$v_o = 3 \times 10^{10} \frac{F}{B} \qquad \text{cm/sec} \tag{1-29}$$

in which F is measured in e.s.u. and B is measured in gauss.
This phenomenon may obviously be used to measure the speed
of electrons or other charged particles.

Problems

1-1. *a.* Find the time of transit of an electron between parallel plane
electrodes having a separation of 0.2 cm and a potential difference of 250
volts. $\mathcal{E} = 4.8 \times 10^{-10}$ e.s.u.

b. Find the energy delivered to the positive electrode by the electron.

1-2. *a.* An electron at the surface of a plane electrode is accelerated
toward a second parallel plane electrode by a 200-volt battery, the polarity
of which is reversed without loss of time 10^{-9} sec after the circuit is closed.

[1] See, for instance, I. G. Maloff, and D. W. Epstein, "Electron Optics in
Television," McGraw-Hill Book Company, Inc., New York, 1939.

If the electrode separation is 1.5 cm, on which electrode will the electron terminate its flight?

b. What will become of the kinetic energy that it acquires during its acceleration?

1-3. *a.* An electron having initial kinetic energy of 10^{-9} erg at the surface of one of two parallel plane electrodes and moving normal to the surface is slowed down by the retarding field caused by a 400-volt potential applied between the electrodes. Will the electron reach the second electrode?

b. What will become of its initial energy?

Bibliography

WATERMAN, A. T.: Fundamental Properties of the Electron, *Elec. Eng.*, **53**, 3 (1934).

HUGGINS, M. L.: Structure of Atoms and Molecules, Electronic Theory of Valence, *Elec. Eng.*, **53**, 851 (1934).

BRODE, R. B.: Quantitative Study of the Collisions of Electrons with Atoms, *Rev. Modern Phys.*, **5**, 257 (1933).

COMPTON, K. T., and LANGMUIR, I.: Electrical Discharges in Gases; Part I, *Rev. Modern Phys.*, **2**, 123 (1930).

LANGMUIR, I., and COMPTON, K. T.: Electrical Discharges in Gases; Part II, *Rev. Modern Phys.*, **3**, 191 (1931).

TONKS, L.: Electrical Discharges in Gases, *Elec. Eng.*, **53**, 239 (1934).

DARROW, K. K.: Electrical Discharges in Gases—II, Ions in Dense Gases, *Elec. Eng.*, **53**, 388 (1934).

SLEPIAN, J., and MASON, R. C.: Electrical Discharges in Gases—III, Self-maintained Discharges, *Elec. Eng.*, **53**, 511 (193÷).

HULL, A. W.: Fundamental Electrical Properties of Mercury Vapor and Monatomic Gases, *Elec. Eng.*, **53**, 1435 (1934).

DARROW, K. K., *Bell System Tech. J.*, **11**, 576 (1932); **12**, 91 (1933); *Rev. Sci. Instruments*, **4**, 6 (1933); *Elec. Eng.*, **54**, 808 (1935).

Physics Staff, University of Pittsburgh: "An Outline of Atomic Physics," John Wiley & Sons, Inc., New York, 1933.

DARROW, K. K.: "Electrical Phenomena in Gases," Williams & Wilkins Company, Baltimore, 1932.

SLEPIAN, J.: "Conduction of Electricity in Gases," Educational Department, Westinghouse Electric and Manufacturing Company, East Pittsburgh, 1933.

THOMSON, J. J., and THOMSON, G. P.: "Conduction of Electricity Through Gases," Cambridge University Press, London, 1928–1932.

EMELÉUS, K. G.: "The Conduction of Electricity through Gases," E. P. Dutton & Company, Inc., New York, 1929.

TOWNSEND, J. S.: "Electricity in Gases," Oxford University Press, New York, 1915; "Motion of Electrons in Gases," 1925.

LOEB, L. B.: "Fundamental Processes of Electrical Discharge in Gases," John Wiley & Sons, Inc., New York, 1939.

CHAPTER 2

THERMIONIC EMISSION;
THE HIGH-VACUUM THERMIONIC DIODE

The operation of the majority of electron tubes is dependent upon thermionic emission. The theory of thermionic emission is therefore of great importance in the study of electron tubes. It is the purpose of this chapter to discuss the basic principles of thermionic emission, the construction of practical emitters, and the flow of electron space current in high-vacuum tubes containing two electrodes.

2-1. Theory of Thermionic Emission.—Richardson's theory of the emission of electrons from hot bodies is in many respects analogous to the kinetic theory of vaporization.[1] Heat possessed by a metal is believed to be stored not only in the kinetic energy of random motion of atoms and molecules, but also in the kinetic energy of free electrons. As a result of collisions between electrons or between electrons and atoms or molecules, the speed and direction of motion of a given electron are constantly changing. At any instant there will be, close to the surface of the metal, some electrons that have a component of velocity toward the surface of such magnitude that the corresponding kinetic energy is equal to or exceeds the electron affinity. If these electrons reach the surface without colliding with atoms, they will pass through the surface. At room temperatures the number of electrons meeting this requirement is extremely small, and hence no thermionic emission is detectable. As the temperature of the emitter is increased, however, the average velocity of the free electrons increases. The number having velocity components toward the surface sufficient to allow them to escape, therefore, increases with temperature. Reduction of electron affinity reduces the velocity toward the surface necessary to allow an electron to escape, and so increases the number

[1] RICHARDSON, O. W., *Proc. Cambridge Phil. Soc.*, **11**, 286 (1901); "Emission of Electricity from Hot Bodies," rev. ed., Longmans, Green & Company, New York, 1921.

having the requisite velocity.   Thermionic emission of electrons therefore increases with increase of temperature and with reduction of electron affinity.   Measurable emission is observed at temperatures above 1000°K.

Electrons that escape will have resultant velocities made up of the excess perpendicular to the surface, plus the original components parallel to the surface, which are not altered by the surface forces.   If the emitted electrons are not drawn away by an external field, they will form a space charge, the individual particles of which are moving about with random velocities.   Because the initial average normal velocity of the electrons after emission is away from the surface and because of the mutual repulsion of like charges, electrons drift away from the surface.   Collisions between electrons cause some of them to acquire velocity components toward the emitter, where they may reenter the surface with a gain of kinetic energy equal to the electron affinity.   Another factor responsible for the return of electrons to the emitter is the electrostatic field set up by the negative space charge and, if the emitter is insulated, by the positive charge that it acquires as the result of loss of electrons.   This field increases with the density of space charge, and equilibrium is established when only enough electrons can move away from the surface to supply the loss by diffusion of the space charge.   If diffusion can then be prevented, just as many electrons return to the metal in unit time as leave it.   Figure 2-1 gives a rough picture of the electron distribution under equilibrium conditions.

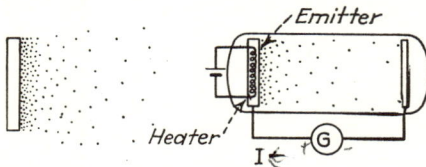

Fig. 2-1.— Distribution of electrons near an emitting surface.

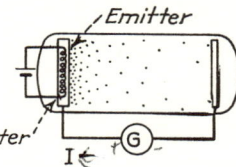

Fig. 2-2.—Flow of anode current as the result of diffusion of electrons from cathode to anode without the application of anode voltage (Edison effect).

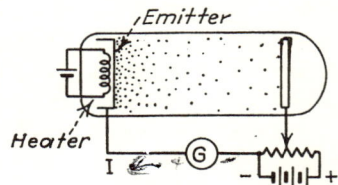

Fig. 2-3.—Use of anode voltage to increase anode current.

If a second, cold electrode is placed near the emitting surface in vacuum and connected to the emitter through a galvanometer, as shown in Fig. 2-2, the meter will indicate the small current resulting from the drift of electrons from the emitter to the second electrode.   These electrons return to the emitter through the galvanometer and prevent the emitter from becoming positively charged.   This phenomenon, first observed by Edison, is called the *Edison effect*.   When the second electrode is made positive with respect to the emitter by the addition of a battery, as shown in Fig. 2-3, the current is increased.   As the voltage is gradually raised, it is found that at any emitter temperature there is a more or less definite voltage beyond which the current is nearly constant, all emitted electrons being drawn to the collector. This current is called the *saturation current*, and the corresponding voltage, the *saturation voltage*.   The lack of increase of current beyond saturation voltage is spoken of as *voltage saturation*. Saturation current varies with the temperature and electron affinity of the emitter.   The negative emitter in Fig. 2-3 is called the *cathode;* and the positive collector, the *anode* or *plate*.   An electron tube containing only a cathode and an anode is called a *diode*.   Although the electrons move from cathode to anode, the current, according to convention, is said to flow from anode to cathode within the tube.

2-2. Richardson's Equation.—By means of classical kinetic theory, and by thermodynamic theory, Richardson derived two slightly different equations for saturation current as a function of temperature.[1]   It is not possible experimentally to determine which of Richardson's equations is correct, but this was later done theoretically by M. v. Laue, S. Dushman, and A. Sommerfeld.   The equation that is now believed to be correct is

$$I_s = A T^2 \epsilon^{-w/kT} \tag{2-1}$$

in which I_s is the saturation current per unit area of emitter, T is the absolute temperature, w is the electron affinity of the emitter, k is Boltzmann's universal gas constant, and A is a constant, probably universal for pure metals.   The value of k is 8.63×10^{-5} volt/deg and the theoretical value of A for pure metals is 60.2.   The form of the curve that represents Richardson's equation, shown in Fig. 2-4, is determined practically entirely by the exponential factor.

It is important to note that Richardson's equation holds only for the saturation current and that the anode voltage must,

[1] RICHARDSON, *loc. cit.*

therefore, be high enough at all times so that all emitted electrons are drawn to the anode. If the anode voltage is fixed at some value E_1, while the temperature is raised, then at some temperature the current will begin to be limited by space charge in a manner similar to that when there is no accelerating voltage. Further increases of temperature will then have no effect upon the current. This temperature is called the *saturation temperature*, and the failure of the current to increase at higher temperature

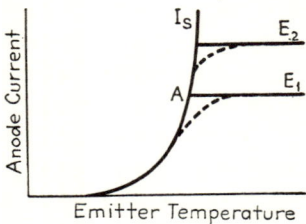

Fig. 2-4.—Curves of anode current *vs.* emitter temperature at two values of anode voltage. The left-hand curve, I_s, represents saturation emission current.

is spoken of as *temperature saturation.* If the emitter were homogeneous and the electrostatic field constant over the surface of the emitter, the advent of saturation would be abrupt, as indicated at point A. Actually, because of variations of temperature and electron affinity and of electrostatic field, saturation does not take place over the whole cathode surface at the same temperature, and so experimentally determined curves bend over gradually, as shown by the dotted curves. At higher anode voltage E_2, saturation occurs at a higher temperature. If the voltage is increased with temperature, then the current will continue to rise with temperature until the temperature becomes sufficiently high to vaporize the emitter.

Since only those electrons which have relatively high energies can escape from the metal, thermionic emission necessarily results in the reduction of the average energy of the remaining electrons and molecules, and hence of temperature of the emitter. Heat must be supplied continuously to the emitter in order to prevent its temperature from falling as the result of emission. The cooling effect of emission current is plainly visible in filaments in which the emission current is comparable with the heating current, as in the type 30 tube.

Richardson's equation shows that the emission current which can be obtained at any temperature varies inversely with the electron affinity. Because of the exponential form of the equation, small changes in temperature or electron affinity result in large changes of emission current. A 15 per cent reduction of electron affinity produces an eight- or tenfold increase of emission over the working range of temperature. The ratio of the emission current in milliamperes per square centimeter to the heating power in watts per square centimeter is called the *emission efficiency*. Emission efficiency increases with decrease of electron affinity.

A satisfactory practical source of thermionic emission must satisfy two requirements: it must have a high emission efficiency, and it must have a long life. Thermal losses can be reduced by proper design of the emitter and by reduction of emitter temperature. (Cathodes of special design, which give very low thermal losses, can be used in gaseous discharge tubes. These will be discussed in Sec. 9-14.) The life of an emitter increases with the difference between the normal operating temperature and the vaporization or melting temperatures of the metal or metals of which it is constructed. Since low operating temperature is made possible by low electron affinity, it is evident that the choice of emitters of low electron affinity is favorable to long life, as well as to high efficiency.

2-3. Pure Metallic Emitters.—Pure metals having low electron affinities, such as the alkali metals or calcium, cannot be used as emitters in electron tubes because they vaporize excessively at temperatures at which appreciable emission is obtained. Only two pure metals, tantalum and tungsten, are suitable for use as practical emitters. Although the electron affinity of tantalum is lower than that of tungsten, tantalum is more sensitive to the action of residual gases and has lower vaporization temperature. Tantalum is therefore seldom used. Pure metallic emitters are now used only in large high-voltage (above 3500 volts) power tubes, in which they are found to have longer life than the special emitters which are used successfully in small tubes.

2-4. Thoriated Tungsten Emitters.—The presence of impurities in a metal may produce a marked change in the value of its electron affinity. This is usually attributed to the formation of thin layers of these impurities at the surface. Such a layer may produce very high fields at the surface by virtue of the fact that it may be electropositive or electronegative relative to the main metal. Thus the presence of an absorbed layer of oxygen, which is electronegative with respect to tungsten, results in a field that opposes the emission of electrons and therefore increases the electron affinity of tungsten. The presence, on the other hand, of a monatomic layer of thorium atoms or ions on the surface of tungsten reduces its electron affinity remarkably. It is of interest to note that the electron affinity of thoriated tungsten may be even lower than that of pure thorium (see Table 1-II).

The reduction of the electron affinity of tungsten as the result of introduction of small amounts of thorium was first observed by Langmuir in 1914 in the course of a study of the properties of tungsten filaments.[1] Thorium oxide is introduced into tungsten during the process of manufacture in order to improve its physical properties. Subsequent high temperature converts a portion of the thorium oxide into metallic thorium, which diffuses to the surface. Investigations by Dushman, Becker, and others[2] indicated that the lowest value of w and the highest value of the constant A in Richardson's equation are obtained when the tungsten is completely, or perhaps very nearly, covered with a single layer of thorium atoms.

Thoriated tungsten shows no increase of emission over that of pure tungsten until it is *activated*. The activation process is performed after evacuation of the tube. It consists first in "flashing" the emitter for a few moments at a temperature of 2500 to 2800°K. This high temperature reduces some of the thorium oxide to thorium. The temperature is then kept for some minutes at about 2200°K, which allows the metallic thorium to diffuse to the surface. The best value of diffusing temperature is determined by the rates of diffusion of thorium to the surface, and of evaporation from the surface. If the temperature is too high, the evaporation exceeds the diffusion, resulting in deactivation. The emitter is normally operated at temperatures that do not exceed 2000°K, which is sufficiently low so that evaporation of thorium from the surface is negligible. If the emitter is accidentally operated at such a high temperature that the whole supply of thorium diffuses to the surface and evaporates, it can be reactivated by repeating the original activation process. This may be done several times before all the thorium oxide is used up.

[1] LANGMUIR, I., *Phys. Rev.*, **4**, 544 (1914).

[2] DUSHMAN, S., and EWALD, J., *Phys. Rev.*, **29**, 857 (1927); BECKER, J. A., *Trans. Am. Electrochem. Soc.*, **55**, 153 (1929).

A useful tool in the study of the phenomenon of activation is the "electron microscope."[1] This consists of the emitter and means for accelerating the electrons and for focusing them upon a screen[2] which fluoresces under the impact of electrons. It has been shown that the action of electromagnetic and electrostatic fields upon electron beams is similar to the action of lenses upon light.[3] Thus it is possible to obtain on the screen a sharp enlarged image which shows clearly the individual points of emission of the cathode.[4] Similar results are achieved by use of a straight filament at the axis of a cylindrical glass tube, the inner surface of which is covered with a fluorescent material.[5] The coated surface, which acts as the anode, is maintained at a positive potential of several thousand volts by means of a wire helix coiled inside the tube in contact with the coating. Electrons emitted by the filament are attracted radially toward the anode coating, where they produce a magnified image of the electron emission at the surface of the filament. Figure 2-5 gives a series of photographs of the screen of such a tube, showing the activation of thoriated tungsten. (The bright vertical line is caused by light from the filament, and the dark lines by the shadow of the helix.)

The presence of even small amounts of gas has a very destructive effect upon a thoriated tungsten emitter. This may result either from direct chemical action, such as oxidation, or from the removal of thorium from the surface by the bombardment of positive ions. The sensitiveness of thoriated emitters to the

[1] KNOLL, M., and RUSKA, E., *Ann. Physik*, **12**, 607 (1932). The electron microscope has many applications besides that mentioned here. Recent instruments may be used in place of ordinary microscopes in the study of matter and give higher magnification than can be attained with light. For a survey and a bibliography of this subject, see R. P. Johnson, *J. Applied Physics*, **9**, 508 (1938).

[2] See, for instance, I. G. Maloff and D. W. Epstein, "Electron Optics in Television," McGraw-Hill Book Company, Inc., New York, 1938.

[3] BUSCH, H., *Ann. Physik*, **81**, 974 (1926); MALOFF, I. G., and EPSTEIN, D. W., *Proc. I.R.E.*, **22**, 1386 (1934); EPSTEIN, D. W., *Proc. I.R.E.*, **24**, 1095 (1936); MALOFF and EPSTEIN, *loc. cit.*

[4] See, for instance, E. Brüche and H. Johannson, *Ann. Physik*, **15**, 145 (1932); M. KNOLL, *Electronics*, September, 1933, p. 243.

[5] JOHNSON, R. P., and SHOCKLEY, W., *Phys. Rev.*, **49**, 436 (1936). See also *Electronics*, January, 1936, p. 10, March, 1937, p. 23.

action of gases and the rate of evaporation of thorium may be greatly reduced by heating the emitter in an atmosphere of hydrocarbon vapor, which causes the formation of a shell of

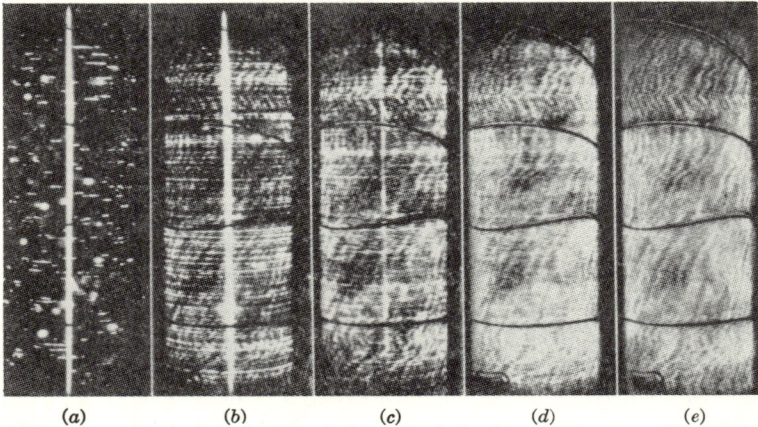

(a)   (b)   (c)   (d)   (e)

Fig. 2-5.—Typical activation behavior of thoriated tungsten. Image (a) immediately after 10 seconds at 2800°K, (b) after additional 4 minutes at 1850°K, (c) after 20 minutes at 1850°K, (d) after 30 minutes at 1850°K, (e) after 70 minutes at 1850°K. All pictures made at 1200°K. The decreasing exposure time is evidenced by reduction of apparent brilliance of the filament. (*Courtesy of R. P. Johnson.*)

tungsten carbide. Because of the reduction of the rate of evaporation of the thorium, a carbonized emitter can be oper-

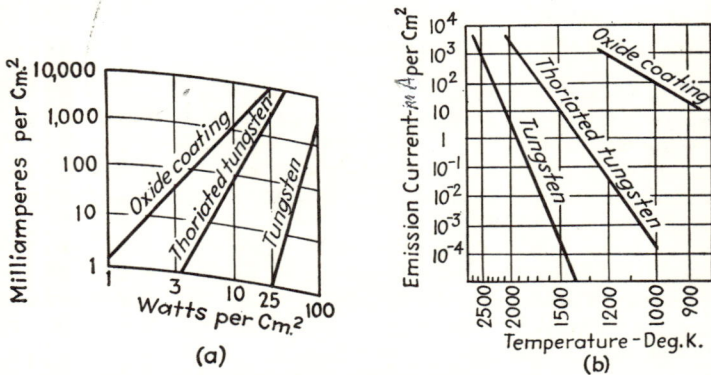

(a)

(b)

Fig. 2-6.—*a.* Curves of emission current *vs.* heating power.   *b.* Curves of emission current *vs.* emitter temperature.

ated at a much higher temperature, with consequent increase of emission current and efficiency. At this higher temperature the increase of diffusion makes possible the continuous replacement of thorium removed from the surface by the action of gas molecules or ions. Figure 2-6 shows that the emission efficiency of thoriated tungsten is much higher than that of pure tungsten and that a given emission may be obtained at a much lower temperature. Because of the lower electron affinity, higher emission efficiency, and longer life of oxide-coated emitters, thoriated tungsten emitters are now used very little in receiving tubes.

2-5. Oxide-coated Emitters.—By far the most widely used emitters in small high-vacuum tubes are oxide-coated emitters, first used by Wehnelt.[1] Although the process of manufacture of oxide-coated cathodes varies considerably, it consists, in general, in coating a core metal, usually nickel or alloys of nickel and other metals, with one or more layers of a mixture of barium and strontium carbonates. The carbonates may be suspended in water, although a binder such as collodion or a mixture of one part of Zapon varnish in 20 parts of amyl acetate is usually used. The mixture may be applied to the core by spraying or by dipping or dragging the core through the mixture. When a thick coating is desired, the mixture is applied preferably in the form of several thin coatings heated sufficiently between applications to burn out the binder. After application of the carbonate coating, the emitter is mounted in the tube, which is then evacuated, and the emitter is heated electrically to a temperature of about 1400°K. The high temperature reduces the carbonates to oxides, the liberated carbon dioxide being removed by the pumps. The temperature is then lowered somewhat and voltage is applied to the anode for some time, during which the emission builds up to its proper value. The normal operating temperature is in the range from 1000 to 1300°K.

Many experiments have been performed to determine what takes place during the activation process and from which part of the emitter electrons are emitted. Reduction of the oxides to pure metal may result from chemical reaction, from electrolysis of the oxides, or from the bombardment of positive ions formed in the gas between the anode and the emitter by electrons

[1] WEHNELT, A., *Ann. Physik*, **14**, 425 (1904). For an excellent review of the subject of oxide-coated emitters see J. P. Blewett, *J. Applied Physics*, **10**, 668 and 831 (1939).

accelerated by the applied field. Perhaps all three of these processes occur. Free metal formed throughout the oxide diffuses toward the surface. Although particles of free metal are distributed throughout the coating in a completed emitter, most recent evidence appears to indicate that the emission takes place at the outer surface.

Examination of Fig. 2-6 shows that the emission efficiency of an oxide-coated emitter is even higher than that of thoriated tungsten. The low temperature at which an oxide-coated cathode can be operated is an advantage in some applications.

The emission from oxide-coated cathodes is reduced or destroyed by the presence of gases, due to oxidation of the active metal or to removal of the active metal or even the complete coating by positive-ion bombardment. Another cause of damage to oxide-coated cathodes is the development of hot spots. Because of nonuniform activation of the emitter, emission is not uniform over the surface. The flow of emission current through the oxide coating, which has high resistance, raises its temperature. Since the temperature rise is greatest at points of the cathode at which the emission is high, the emission increases still more at these points. If the current is not limited by space charge, the action may become cumulative and the current and temperature increase to such an extent that the coating is removed. In filamentary cathodes the local rise in temperature may be so great as to melt the filament. Hot spots are most likely to occur at high anode voltages. This is one reason why oxide-coated emitters are not used in high-voltage tubes.

When full emission current is drawn from an oxide-coated emitter the current first falls rapidly and then slowly approaches a steady value. This decay of current is thought to be caused by electrolytic removal of barium from the surface or by electrolytic deposition of oxygen on the surface. The initial emission is recovered if the emitter is heated without the flow of space current. The useful life of oxide-coated emitters, which is several thousand hours, is terminated by a rather sudden decay in emission to a very low value. This may be caused by evaporation of free barium and of the supply of barium oxide that furnishes free barium during the active life of the emitter. The useful life of a vacuum tube containing an oxide-coated cathode may also be terminated by the liberation of gas from the emitter.

2-6. Cesiated Tungsten Emitters.—A fourth type of emitter, not used commercially in thermionic tubes, is produced by depositing a monatomic layer of cesium on tungsten. Because the ionizing potential of cesium vapor is less than the electron affinity of tungsten, the tungsten removes an electron from a cesium atom which strikes it, leaving a positive ion which is held to the tungsten surface by the resulting electrostatic field. The force of adhesion is even greater if the tungsten is first covered with a monatomic layer of oxygen, which is electronegative with regard to tungsten. The strong electrostatic field between the cesium ions and the tungsten or oxygen reduces the electron affinity to the comparatively low value of 0.7 electron volt or less. Because cesium melts at a temperature only slightly above room temperature, the cesium vapor is obtained by merely introducing a small amount of cesium into the evacuated tube, the subsequent vaporization being sufficient to coat the filament.

The low electron affinity of the tungsten-oxygen-cesium emitter makes possible high emission currents at a temperature of only 1000°K. This type of emitter has several disadvantages, however, which make it impractical for use in commercial tubes. As the result of the high vapor pressure of cesium at operating temperatures of the tube, the characteristics of the tube are influenced by tube temperature. Too high temperature vaporizes the cesium, causing temporary reduction in emission, or even removal of the oxygen layer with permanent reduction of emission. Except at very low anode voltages, ionization of the cesium vapor occurs, resulting in fluctuations of anode current. The presence of positive ions is also detrimental to the action of amplifier tubes for other reasons, which will be discussed (Secs. 2-8, 6-5, 10-16).

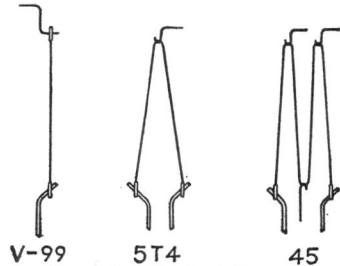

V-99   5T4   45
Fig. 2-7.—Typical filamentary cathodes. (*Courtesy of Radio Corporation of America.*)

2-7. Mechanical Construction of Cathodes.—Cathodes used in high-vacuum thermionic tubes are divided into two general classes, filamentary and indirectly heated. Figure 2-7 shows the form of typical filamentary cathodes. Early vacuum tubes used only filamentary cathodes. When filamentary cathodes are operated on alternating current, the stray alternating electrostatic field and the alternating voltage across the filament cause an alternating component of plate current that may be objectionable in amplifiers in which several tubes are used in succession. This difficulty led to the development of the indirectly heated, or *heater-type*, cathode. In addition to the unipotential emitting surface and freedom from large stray fields, the heater-type cathode has the advantage that a single source of power may be used to heat a number of cathodes between which a difference of potential must exist.

Indirectly heated cathodes used in receiving tubes consist of an oxide-coated cylindrical sleeve, usually of nickel, within which is some form of heater. The most common types of heaters are illustrated in Fig. 2-8. The 5Z4 and 25A6 heater coils are helically wound. That of the 6K7 type of cathode is wound in a reverse helix. After being wound and formed, the coils are coated with a refractory insulating material and inserted into the sleeve. The heater of the 25L6 type of cathode is covered with a refractory insulating coating of sufficient adherence to permit the wire to be bent into the desired shape after it has been coated.

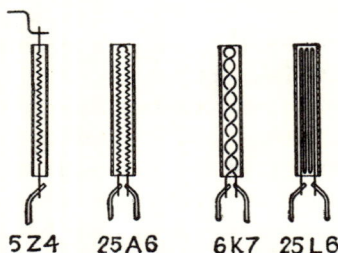

5Z4   25A6   6K7   25L6
Fig. 2-8.—Structure of typical heater-type cathodes. (*Courtesy of Radio Corporation of America.*)

Because of the small magnetic field produced by the 6K7 type of heater, there is very little 60-cycle plate-current variation, or "hum," when the heater is operated on alternating current. The return type of helical heater exemplified by the 25A6 heater and the folded type of heater used in the 25L6 cathode make possible the use of enough wire for 25-volt operation. The advantage of the 25L6 construction is its low cost. More complicated cathode structures used in arc-discharge tubes will be discussed in Chap. 9.

2-8. Effects of Gas upon Emission and Space Currents.—The deleterious effects of gas upon emitters of various types as the result of chemical action, absorption of thin layers of gas upon the surface, and positive-ion bombardment have already been mentioned. If the anode voltage is sufficiently high to produce ionization of the gas, other effects become apparent. If anode current is at first limited by space charge, the appearance of positive ions tends to neutralize the negative space charge surrounding the filament, thus increasing the anode current.   If the voltage is high enough to give saturation current initially, then increase of current occurs because the electrons and ions produced by bombardment of neutral gas molecules by the emitted electrons add to the current.   Unfortunately this increase of current is likely to be accompanied by a number of undesirable effects.   Currents through ionized gases usually fluctuate, resulting in "noise" in tubes used for amplification.   The relatively low velocity of positive and negative ions produces a lag in the response of current to changes of voltage.   Variations of gas pressure resulting from changes of temperature or from the absorption or emission of gas from the walls and electrodes may cause the characteristics of the tube to vary.   Finally, in a gassy tube, positive-ion current flows to an electrode to which a negative voltage is applied.   When the anode current is controlled by means of a negative voltage applied to an electrode through a high resistance, the flow of positive-ion current through the resistance may cause an objectionable voltage drop and, under certain circumstances, may even result in damage to the tube (see Secs. 6-5, 9-17, and 10-16).

In the manufacture of high-vacuum tubes, many precautions are taken to ensure the removal of gas from walls and electrodes. The electrodes are thoroughly cleaned and are then heated for several minutes in an atmosphere of hydrogen, which removes oxygen and water vapor.   After the tube is assembled and connected to the pumps, the electrodes are heated to about 800 or 1000°C by high-frequency induction in order to remove other occluded gases.   Residual gas is removed by the use of *getters*, which are active chemical substances such as barium, magnesium, aluminum, and tantalum, having the property of combining with gases when they are vaporized.   In glass tubes a small amount of the getter is mounted in such a position that it will be heated and vaporized or "flashed" during the inductive heating of the elements.   By proper location of the getter, the vapor can be prevented from condensing in places where it might cause electrical leakage or undesirable primary or secondary emission. The effectiveness of the getter results not only from its chemical combination with gases during flashing, but also from subsequent absorption of gases by getter that has condensed on the walls of the tube.   The action of the getter during flashing is increased by ionization of the gas by means of voltages applied between the electrodes or by the radio-frequency field of the induct on heater.   To ensure the removal of gas from the walls, tubes are baked during the process of manufacture.   On machines that exhaust and seal the tubes separately, the bulbs are heated in ovens during exhaustion.   On "Sealex" machines, the tubes are sealed and exhausted on the same machine, the heat from sealing being used to drive gases from the bulbs during exhaustion.

In tubes with metal envelopes, the shielding action of the shell makes it impossible to heat the electrodes and the getter by induction.   The electrodes may be heated by radiation from the shell, which is heated by gas flames.   Although the getter may be fastened to the inside of the shell and vaporized by heating the shell locally, another method has been developed that requires less critical control.[1]   A short length of tantalum ribbon, which connects the shell to its terminal pin in the base, is coated with a mixture of barium and strontium carbonates.   While the tube is on the pumps, the temperature of the tantalum wire is raised electrically to about 1100°C.   This converts the carbonates into oxides.   After the tube has been sealed off, the tantalum wire is heated to a temperature in excess of 1200°C.   This causes the tantalum to reduce the oxides to pure metallic barium and strontium, which vaporize.   Since the vapor moves in straight lines, it can be directed as desired by means of shields and by proper location of the tantalum wire.   This type of getter is called *batalum* [See (11) in Fig. 3-11*b*].

2-9. Limitation of Anode Current by Space Charge.—The effect of space charge in limiting space current and the increase of anode current resulting from an accelerating anode potential have already been mentioned in connection with the theory of thermionic emission.   Before proceeding to a discussion of the quantitative relation between anode current and anode potential in a two-element tube, it is of interest to discuss further the physical picture underlying the phenomenon.   The behavior of the emitted thermionic electrons is complicated by their initial velocities.   For this reason it is best first to formulate a theory

---

[1] Lederer, E. A., and Wamsley, D. H., *RCA Rev.*, **2**, 117 (1937).   This article also discusses gettering methods used in glass tubes.

on the assumption that the initial velocities are zero and then, when they are taken into consideration, to see in what manner the results should be altered.   For the present, therefore, initial velocities will be assumed to be zero.   It will be further assumed that both cathode and anode are homogeneous, constant-potential, parallel planes of large area, and hence that the electric field over the surface of the cathode may be assumed to be uniform.

Electrons that leave the cathode constitute a space charge that exerts a retarding field at the cathode.   The net field at the surface of the cathode is the difference between this retarding field and the accelerating field produced by the positive voltage of the anode.   The number of electrons in the space, and hence the retarding component of field at the cathode, increases with the anode current.   When the positive anode voltage is applied, the anode current builds up with great rapidity to such a value that the average retarding field at the cathode caused by the space charge is equal to the accelerating field caused by the anode voltage, making the average field zero at the cathode.   Increase of emission then does not raise the anode current, as the additional emitted electrons merely reenter the cathode.   If it were possible in some manner to increase the density of space charge by increasing the current beyond this equilibrium value, or if the anode voltage were reduced slightly, then the net field at the cathode would be a retarding one.   For an instant, all emitted electrons would be prevented from moving away from the cathode, and the current and space-charge density would be automatically reduced to a value that would again make the average field at the cathode zero.   An increase of anode voltage causes the accelerating field to exceed the retarding field. The number of electrons moving to the anode then increases until the retarding field again equals the accelerating field.

At first thought it may not seem plausible that there can be a steady flow of electrons to the anode when both the velocities of emitted electrons and the average electrostatic field are zero at the cathode.   It is only the *time average* field, however, that is zero at any point on the cathode.   The *instantaneous* field at any point may vary in a random manner between positive and negative values.   Immediately after one or more electrons have entered some point of the anode, the net field at a corresponding point of the cathode may be positive, causing one or more electrons to move away from the cathode.   These electrons produce a retarding field behind them which prevents the departure of more electrons from that point until the entrance of other electrons into the anode again results in an accelerating field. Many electrons are entering and leaving the space at any instant, so that the field fluctuations are rapid and haphazard.

2-10. Child's Law.—The foregoing descriptive explanation shows that, if an ample supply of electrons is available at the cathode, the anode current in a diode varies with the voltage applied between the anode and cathode. A mathematical analysis of this phenomenon was first made by Child.[1]   The equation relating the anode current and voltage is called *Child's law*.   The general derivation for electrodes of any size and shape is too difficult to yield a useful equation, and so only the relatively simple cases such as those applying to plane parallel electrodes of large area and to long concentric cylinders are ordinarily considered.   In deriving Child's law for plane parallel electrodes the following assumptions are made:

1. The cathode temperature is high enough at all points so that more electrons are emitted than are drawn to the anode; *i.e.*, the current is limited by space charge.

2. The cathode and anode are parallel plates whose area is large as compared to their spacing; *i.e.*, the electrostatic field is uniform over the surface of any plane parallel to the electrodes.

3. The surfaces of the anode and cathode are equipotential surfaces.

4. The space between the cathode and the anode is sufficiently free of gas so that electrons do not lose energy by collision with gas molecules in moving from the cathode to the anode.

5. Emitted electrons have zero initial velocity after emission.

Under these assumptions the following three equations may be written:

$$\frac{\partial^2 V}{\partial x^2} = 4\pi\rho \tag{2-2}$$

$$\varepsilon V = \tfrac{1}{2}m_e v^2 \tag{2-3}$$

$$\rho v A = i_b \tag{2-4}$$

in which V is the potential, relative to the cathode, at a distance x from the cathode; ρ is the density of electron space charge at a

[1] CHILD, C. D., *Phys. Rev.*, **32**, 498 (1911).

distance x from the cathode; ε and m_e are the charge and mass, respectively, of an electron; v is the velocity dx/dt of an electron at a distance x from the cathode; i_b is the anode current; and A is the area of the electrodes.

Equation (2-2) combines in symbolic form the definitions of potential difference and electric field. It is a special form of Poisson's equation, one of the most important fundamental laws of electrostatics, and may be derived directly from Gauss's law[1] (see Sec. 1-10). Equation (2-3) states that the energy gained by an electron in moving from the cathode to a distance x from the cathode under the influence of the electric field appears entirely in the form of kinetic energy. Equation (2-4) is a symbolic formulation of the definition of the magnitude of an electric current as the rate of flow of charge.

In the solution of the simultaneous differential Eqs. (2-2), (2-3), and (2-4), the following boundary conditions must be applied: At the cathode, the potential V, the average electric field $\partial V/\partial x$, and the velocity v are zero. At the anode, where x is equal to the cathode-to-anode spacing d, the potential is equal to e_b, the applied anode voltage. Solution of the equations and substitution of numerical values of ε and m_e give the following equation for the anode current of a diode:[2]

$$i_b = 2.34 \times 10^{-6} \frac{A e_b^{3/2}}{d^2} \quad \text{amp} \quad (2\text{-}5)$$

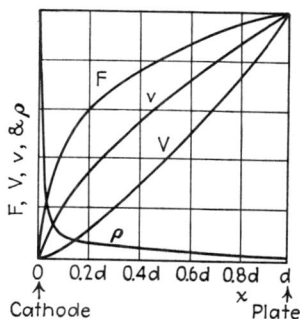

FIG. 2-9.—Variation of field strength F, potential V, electron velocity v, and space-charge density ρ with distance x from plane cathode. Zero initial velocity. Arbitrary units.

By combining Eq. (2-5) with Eqs. (2-2), (2-3), and (2-4), theoretical expressions may be derived for density of space charge, electron velocity, electric field strength, and potential as functions of distance from the cathode. Curves derived from these are shown in Fig. 2-9.

Child's law for concentric cylinders whose length is large as compared to their spacing is

[1] PAGE, L., and ADAMS, N. I., "Principles of Electricity," p. 83, D. Van Nostrand Company, Inc., New York, 1931.

[2] PAGE and ADAMS, *op. cit.*, p. 297.

$$i_b = 14.68 \times 10^{-6} \frac{h e_b{}^{3/2}}{br} \qquad \text{amp} \qquad (2\text{-}6)$$

in which r is the radius of the anode, h is the length of the electrodes, and b is a factor whose value depends upon the ratio of the radius of the anode to that of the cathode. b has the approximate value $\frac{1}{4}$ for a ratio 2, $\frac{1}{2}$ for a ratio 3, and 0.9 for a ratio 8. If the plate diameter is large as compared to that of the cathode, Eq. (2-6) reduces to the approximate form

$$i_b = 14.7 \times 10^{-6} \frac{h e_b{}^{3/2}}{r} \qquad \text{amp} \qquad (2\text{-}7)$$

Equations (2-5), (2-6), and (2-7) show the importance of close spacing between cathode and anode if large currents are desired at small anode voltages.

2-11. Deviations from Child's Law Observed in Practical Diodes.—Deviations from Child's law result from the failure of practical diodes to satisfy the assumptions made in its derivation. Since the temperature of the cathode is fixed by considerations of emission efficiency and life, there is always a saturation voltage above which the current is not limited by space charge but by filament emission. If other assumptions were satisfied, the

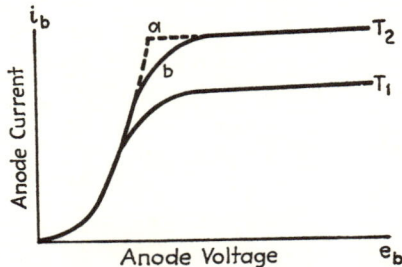

Fig. 2-10.—Curves of anode current *vs.* anode voltage at two values of emitter temperature.

saturation voltage would be quite definite and the current-voltage curve would be as shown by the dotted lines of Fig. 2-10. Because of variations in temperature, electron affinity, and field strength over the cathode surface, the anode voltage at which voltage saturation takes place is not the same for all points of the cathode. The curve of anode current *vs.* anode voltage therefore bends over gradually, as shown by the full line of Fig. 2-10. Above saturation the current is not entirely constant but continues to rise somewhat with anode voltage. This is explained by reduction of electron affinity with increase of external field (see Sec. 1-12), and lack of homogeneity of the surface of the emitter. The effect is particularly noticeable with oxide-coated cathodes.

The assumptions of uniform field and equipotential cathode are satisfied fairly closely in heater-type diodes with cylindrical plates. The voltage drop in filamentary cathodes may be shown to change Child's $\frac{3}{2}$-power law into a $\frac{5}{2}$-power law at anode voltages relative to the negative end of the filament that are less than the voltage of the positive end of the filament. This tends to make the lower part of the i_b-e_b curve steeper. The exact effect upon the curve of failure to satisfy the assumption of uniform field is complicated and impossible to predict completely.

2-12. Effect of Initial Velocities of Emitted Electrons.—Modified forms of Child's law which take into consideration the initial velocities of emitted electrons have been derived by Schottky, Langmuir, and others.[1] For the purpose of this book, a qualitative explanation of the effect of initial velocities is sufficient. Let it first be supposed that the electrons emerge with zero velocity. Under equilibrium conditions the space current and the space-charge density assume such values that the average field at the cathode is zero. The field and potential distributions in the interelectrode space are as shown in Fig. 2-9. Now let the emitted electrons suddenly have initial velocities that, for the sake of simplicity, are assumed to be the same for all electrons. Electrons that, without initial velocity, would have reentered the cathode now move toward the anode in spite of the fact that the average field is zero. As a result, the current and the space-charge density increase. The retarding field of the space charge now exceeds the accelerating field of the anode, giving a net retarding field at the cathode surface which slows up the electrons in the vicinity of the cathode. Equilibrium results when the retarding field in the vicinity of the cathode is sufficiently high so that the electrons are brought to rest in a plane a short distance s from the cathode. The average field in

[1] SCHOTTKY, W., *Physik. Z.*, **15**, 526 (1914); *Ann. Physik*, **44**, 1011 (1914). LANGMUIR, I., *Phys. Rev.*, **21**, 419 (1923). DAVISSON, C., *Phys. Rev.*, **25**, 808 (1925).

this plane is zero, but instantaneous fluctuations allow just enough electrons to pass to give the required anode current. The behavior is similar to that which would obtain if the initial velocity were zero and the cathode were moved toward the anode by the distance s. Because of the random distribution of electron velocities the phenomenon is actually more complicated than this simplified picture indicates. The simple theory shows, however, that the effect of initial velocities is to increase the anode current corresponding to any anode voltage and is therefore equivalent to that of a small increase of anode voltage. Because the electrons emerge with velocities of the order of a volt or less, the effect is appreciable only for low anode voltages. The field and potential distributions throughout the interelectrode space are plotted in Fig. 2-11. That the potential must pass through a minimum where the field is zero follows from the fact that the field at any point may be expressed as the space derivative of the potential at that point.

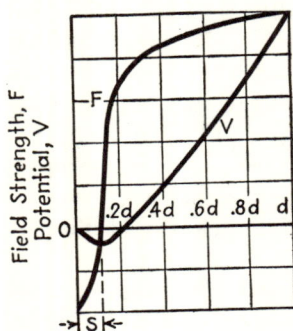

Fig. 2-11.—Variation of field strength and potential with distance from cathode for plane parallel electrodes of separation d. Initial velocities of emitted electrons considered.

The lower part of the i_b-e_b curve of Fig. 2-10 is raised slightly as the result of initial velocities of emitted electrons, and a small negative voltage must be applied in order to reduce the anode current to zero. Theoretical equations relating anode current and voltage at negative anode voltages have been derived by Schottky[1] and Davisson.[2] Because of their complicated form and because of failure to satisfy in practice the assumptions made in their derivation, these are seldom of great practical value. At negative anode voltages that are high enough to reduce the anode current to the order of 50 μa or less, the anode current of diodes with unipotential cathodes follows closely the empirical relation

$$i_b = k_1\epsilon^{k_2 e_b} \tag{2-8}$$

in which k_1 and k_2 are constants for a given tube. The current

[1] SCHOTTKY, loc. cit.; LANGMUIR, loc. cit.
[2] DAVISSON, loc. cit.

departs materially from this exponential law as the negative anode voltage is reduced in the vicinity of zero voltage, particularly at high cathode temperatures. Experimental curves corresponding to Eq. (2-8) were first obtained by Germer.[1]

Unless the plate of a highly evacuated diode becomes hot enough to emit electrons, increase of negative anode voltage beyond the value that reduces the current to zero has no further effect upon the anode current. The fact that anode current flows in one direction only is employed in the application of diodes to detection and to power rectification, which will be discussed in Chaps. 7 and 11.

2-13. Relation of Richardson's and Child's Laws.—It should be noted that Richardson's equation and Child's law apply to two different conditions of operation of two-element tubes. Richardson's equation holds only under voltage saturation, whereas Child's law applies only under temperature saturation. In most applications, vacuum tubes are used in such a manner that temperature saturation prevails.

2-14. Shot Effect.—The random motion of electrons causes rapid variations of the number of electrons that pass from the cathode to the anode in unit time, and thus produces fluctuations of anode current. This phenomenon, which may be readily detected by the use of sufficient amplification, is called the *shot effect*. It is one of the factors that limit amplification by vacuum tubes (see Sec. 6-15).

Heating of the Plate.—The kinetic energy acquired by electrons in moving from the cathode to the plate is converted into heat when the electrons strike the plate. The average current that a vacuum tube can pass is limited by the temperature of the plate at which absorbed gas is driven out of the plate or electron emission takes place from the plate. The power that is converted into heat at the plate is equal to the time integral of the product of the plate current and plate voltage. Radiation of heat from the plate is increased by blackening its outer surface.

2-15. Classification of Tubes.—Electron tubes may be classified in a number of ways. These classifications include those based upon the process involved in the emission of electrons from the cathode, the degree of evacuation, the number of elec-

[1] GERMER, L. H., *Phys. Rev.*, **25**, 795 (1925).

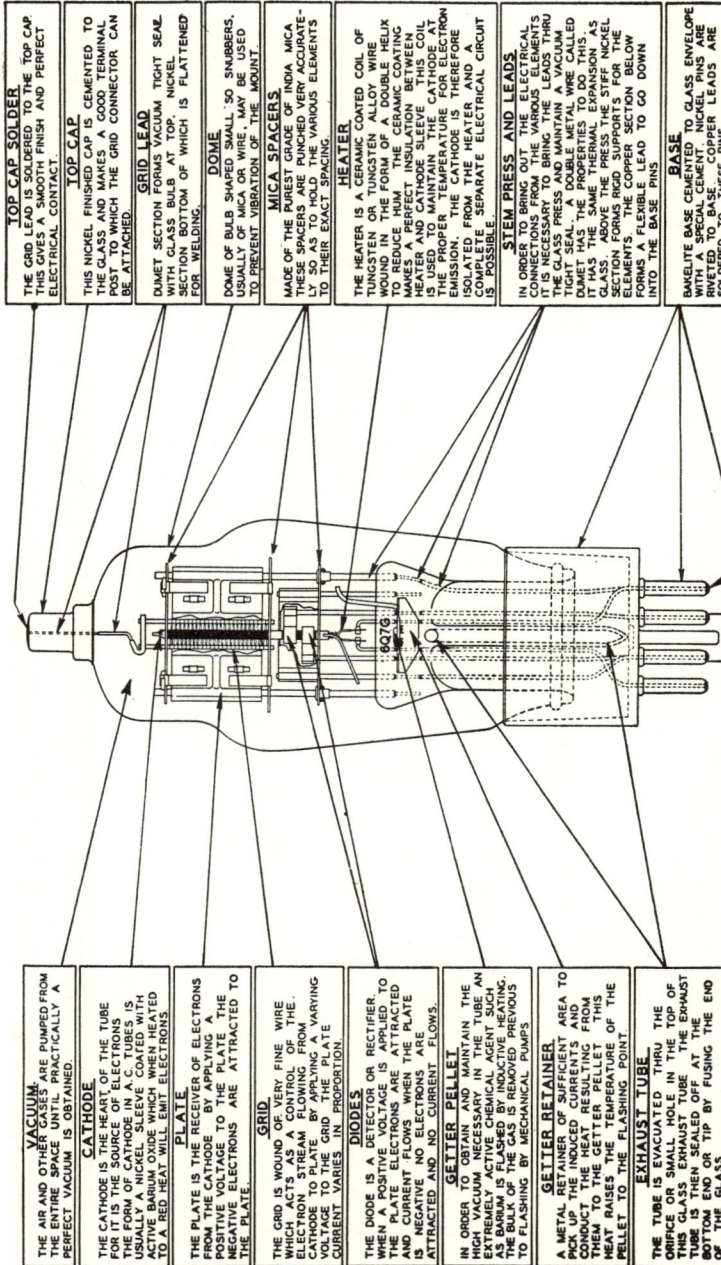

TOP CAP SOLDER
THE GRID LEAD IS SOLDERED TO THE TOP CAP. THIS GIVES A SMOOTH FINISH AND PERFECT ELECTRICAL CONTACT.

TOP CAP
THIS NICKEL FINISHED CAP IS CEMENTED TO THE GLASS AND MAKES A GOOD TERMINAL POST TO WHICH THE GRID CONNECTOR CAN BE ATTACHED.

GRID LEAD
DUMET SECTION FORMS VACUUM TIGHT SEAL WITH GLASS BULB AT TOP. NICKEL SECTION BOTTOM OF WHICH IS FLATTENED FOR WELDING.

DOME
DOME OF BULB SHAPED SMALL SO SNUBBERS, USUALLY OF MICA OR WIRE, MAY BE USED TO PREVENT VIBRATION OF THE MOUNT.

MICA SPACERS
MADE OF THE PUREST GRADE OF INDIA MICA THESE SPACERS ARE PUNCHED VERY ACCURATELY SO AS TO HOLD THE VARIOUS ELEMENTS TO THEIR EXACT SPACING.

HEATER
THE HEATER IS A CERAMIC COATED COIL OF TUNGSTEN OR TUNGSTEN ALLOY WIRE WOUND IN THE FORM OF A DOUBLE HELIX TO REDUCE HUM. THE CERAMIC COATING MAKES A PERFECT INSULATION BETWEEN HEATER AND CATHODE SLEEVE. THE HEATER IS USED TO MAINTAIN THE CATHODE AT THE PROPER TEMPERATURE FOR ELECTRON EMISSION. THE CATHODE IS THEREFORE ISOLATED FROM THE HEATER AND A COMPLETE SEPARATE ELECTRICAL CIRCUIT IS POSSIBLE.

STEM PRESS AND LEADS
IN ORDER TO BRING OUT THE ELECTRICAL CONNECTIONS FROM THE VARIOUS ELEMENTS IT IS NECESSARY TO BRING THE LEADS THRU THE GLASS PRESS AND MAINTAIN A VACUUM TIGHT SEAL. A DOUBLE METAL WIRE CALLED DUMET HAS THE PROPERTIES TO DO THIS. IT HAS THE SAME THERMAL EXPANSION AS GLASS. ABOVE THE PRESS THE STIFF NICKEL SECTION FORMS RIGID SUPPORTS FOR THE ELEMENTS. THE COPPER SECTION BELOW FORMS A FLEXIBLE LEAD TO GO DOWN INTO THE BASE PINS.

BASE
BAKELITE BASE CEMENTED TO GLASS ENVELOPE WITH A SPECIAL CEMENT. NICKEL PINS ARE RIVETED TO BASE. COPPER LEADS ARE SOLDERED TO THESE PINS.

VACUUM
THE AIR AND OTHER GASES ARE PUMPED FROM THE ENTIRE SPACE UNTIL PRACTICALLY A PERFECT VACUUM IS OBTAINED.

CATHODE
THE CATHODE IS THE HEART OF THE TUBE FOR IT IS THE SOURCE OF ELECTRONS. THE FORM OF CATHODE IN A.C. TUBES IS USUALLY A NICKEL SLEEVE COATED WITH ACTIVE BARIUM OXIDE WHICH WHEN HEATED TO A RED HEAT WILL EMIT ELECTRONS.

PLATE
THE PLATE IS THE RECEIVER OF ELECTRONS FROM THE CATHODE BY APPLYING A POSITIVE VOLTAGE TO THE PLATE THE NEGATIVE ELECTRONS ARE ATTRACTED TO THE PLATE.

GRID
THE GRID IS WOUND OF VERY FINE WIRE WHICH ACTS AS A CONTROL OF THE ELECTRON STREAM FLOWING FROM CATHODE TO PLATE. BY APPLYING A VARYING VOLTAGE TO THE GRID THE PLATE CURRENT VARIES IN PROPORTION.

DIODES
THE DIODE IS A DETECTOR OR RECTIFIER. WHEN A POSITIVE VOLTAGE IS APPLIED TO THE PLATE ELECTRONS ARE ATTRACTED AND CURRENT FLOWS. WHEN THE PLATE IS NEGATIVE, ELECTRONS ARE NOT ATTRACTED AND NO CURRENT FLOWS.

GETTER PELLET
IN ORDER TO OBTAIN AND MAINTAIN THE EXTREME VACUUM NECESSARY IN THE TUBE AN EXTREMELY ACTIVE CHEMICAL SUCH AS BARIUM IS FLASHED BY INDUCTIVE HEATING. THE BULK OF THE GAS IS REMOVED PREVIOUS TO FLASHING BY MECHANICAL PUMPS.

GETTER RETAINER
A METAL RETAINER OF SUFFICIENT AREA TO PICK UP THE HEAT RESULTING AND CONDUCT THE HEAT RESULTING FROM THEM TO THE GETTER PELLET. THIS HEAT RAISES THE TEMPERATURE OF THE PELLET TO THE FLASHING POINT.

EXHAUST TUBE
THE TUBE IS EVACUATED THRU THE ORIFICE OR SMALL HOLE IN THE TOP OF THIS GLASS EXHAUST TUBE. THE EXHAUST TUBE IS THEN SEALED OFF AT THE BOTTOM END OR TIP BY FUSING THE END OF THE GLASS.

FIG. 2-12.—Structure of a typical glass receiving tube. (*Courtesy of Ken-rad Tube and Lamp Corp.*)

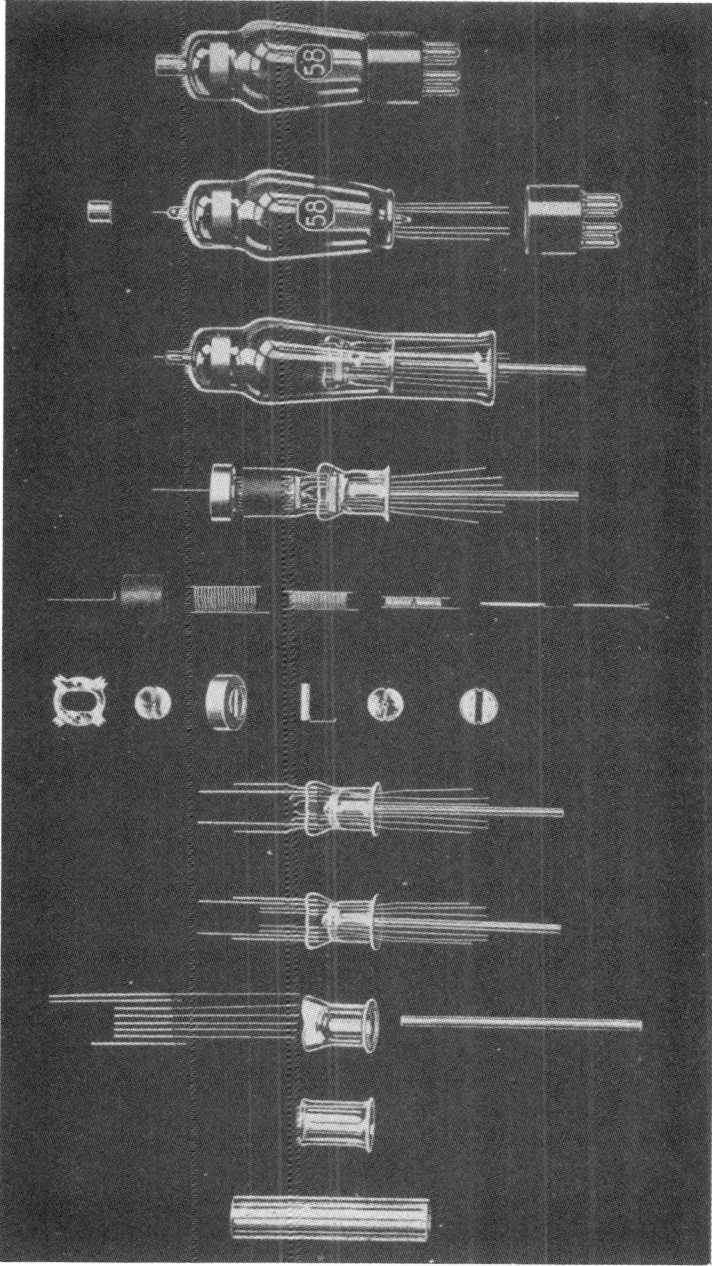

Fig. 2-13.—Assembly of a typical glass receiving tube. (Courtesy of Radio Corporation of America.)

trodes, and the type of application. Included in the first classification are the thermionic tube and the phototube. A *thermionic tube* is an electron tube in which the electron or ion emission is

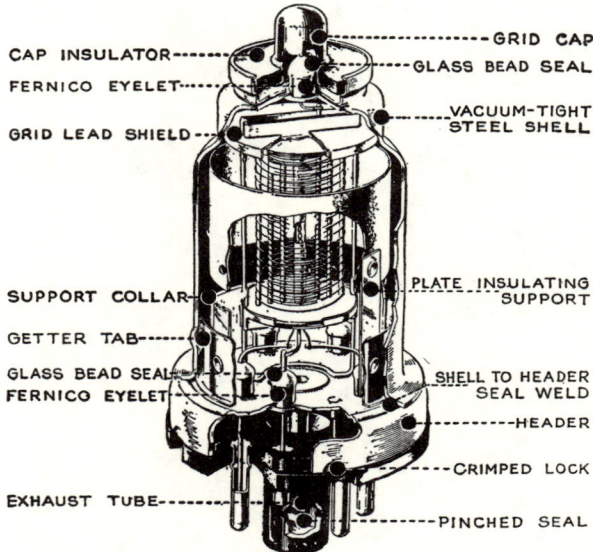

FIG. 2-14.—Structure of typical metal receiving tube.

FIG. 2-15.—Size of typical "acorn" tubes shown in comparison with a golf ball. (*Courtesy of Radio Corporation of America.*)

produced by the heating of an electrode. A *phototube* is an electron tube in which electron emission is produced directly by radiation falling upon an electrode. According to degree of evacuation, electron tubes are classified as high-vacuum tubes and gas- or vapor-filled tubes A *high-vacuum tube* (*vacuum tube* or *pliotron*) is an electron tube evacuated to such a degree that its electrical characteristics are essentially unaffected by gaseous ionization. A *gas-filled* or *vapor-filled tube* (*gas tube*) is an electron tube in which the pressure of the gas or vapor is such as to affect appreciably the electrical characteristics of the tube. According to the number of electrodes, tubes are classified as *diodes, triodes, pentodes*, etc. For convenience or economy or for reduction of space or weight, two or more sets of elements may be enclosed in a single envelope. Thus, there are duplex (double) triodes, duplex-diode pentodes, triode pentodes, etc. The diverse classification of electron tubes according to application will be made in later chapters.

2-16. Construction of Tubes.—Tubes are made with both glass and metal envelopes.[1] The principal advantages of metal tubes lie in their greater mechanical strength and in the fact that the electrodes are permanently and completely shielded without the use of an external shield. Furthermore, they do not require on the inside of the envelope the conducting coating that must be used in glass tubes to prevent the wall from acquiring a positive charge as the result of secondary emission caused by the impact of electrons that pass around the plate. A dis-

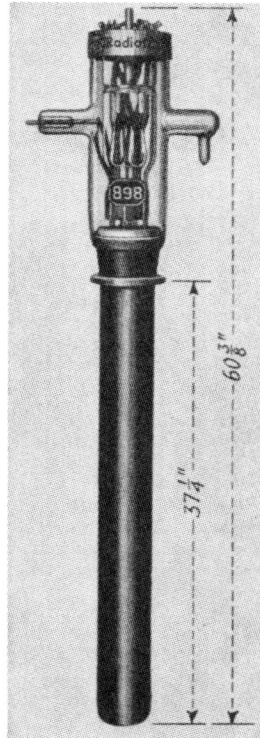

Fig. 2-16.—100-kw water-cooled transmitting tube. (*Courtesy of Radio Corporation of America.*)

advantage of metal tubes is that the shells become so hot in operation that they cannot be conveniently handled. This is of importance in the routine factory testing of radio receivers. Another minor disadvantage is the impossibility of determining visually whether the heater is in operation. Glass tubes appear to be somewhat more reliable. In rectifiers, particularly, metal

[1] Pike, O. W., and Metcalf, G. F., *Electronics*, October, 1934, p. 312. See also *Electronics*, September, 1935, p. 31.

tubes are likely to give difficulty as the result of short circuits. Figures 2-12 and 2-13 show the construction of a glass receiving tube; Figs. 2-14 and 3-11*b* show typical metal receiving tubes.

The great range in size of vacuum tubes is illustrated by Figs. 2-15 and 2-16.   Figure 2-15 shows a typical *acorn* tube, developed for use at very high frequencies, at which it is essential

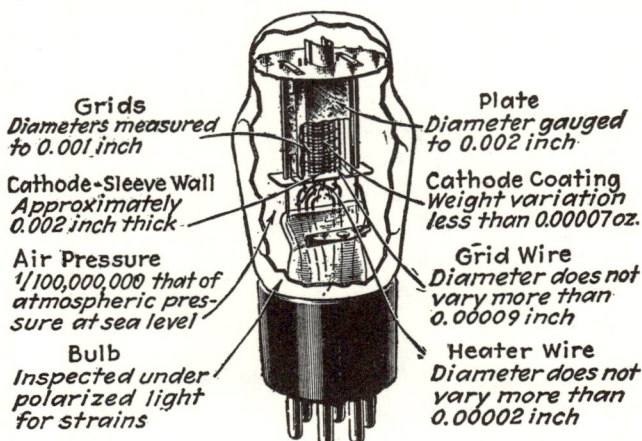

FIG. 2-17.—Materials used in typical radio receiving tubes.   The complex nature of the structure of the modern vacuum tube, and of the manufacturing processes, is well illustrated by a consideration of the materials that are used.

Gases.—Argon, carbon dioxide, chlorine, helium, hydrogen, illuminating gas, neon, nitrogen, and oxygen.

Metals and Compounds.—Alumina, aluminum, ammonium chloride, arsenic trioxide, barium, barium carbonate, barium nitrate, borax, boron, cesium, calcium, calcium aluminum fluoride, calcium carbonate, calcium oxide, carbon, chromium, cobalt, cobalt oxide, copper, iridium, iron, lead, lead acetate, lead oxide, magnesia, magnesium, mercury, misch metal, molybdenum, monel, nickel, phosphorus, platinum, potassium, potassium carbonate, silica, silicon, silver, silver oxide, sodium, sodium carbonate, sodium nitrate, tantalum, thorium, thorium nitrate, tin, titanium, tungsten, zinc, zinc chloride, and zinc oxide.

Accessories.—Bakelite, ethyl alcohol, glass, glycerine, isolantite, lava, malachite green, marble dust, mica, nigrosine, petroleum jelly, porcelain, rosin, shellac, synthetic resin, and wood fiber.

to keep lead capacitance and inductance as small as possible.[1] No base is used on the acorn type of tube, connections being made directly to the electrode leads.   Figure 2-16 shows a 100-kw water-cooled transmitting tube of a type that is used in large broadcasting stations.

Bibliography

RICHARDSON, O. W.: "Emission of Electricity from Hot Bodies," Longmans, Green & Company, New York, 1916.
DUSHMAN, S.: Thermionic Emission, *Rev. Modern Phys.*, **2**, 381 (1930).

[1] SALZBERG, B., and BURNSIDE, D. G., *Proc. I.R.E.*, **23**, 1142 (1935).

Compton, K. T., and Langmuir, I.: *Rev. Modern Phys.*, **3**, 191 (1931).

Reimann, A. L.: "Thermionic Emission," John Wiley & Sons, Inc., New York, 1934.

Stiles, W. S.: *Dept. Sci. Ind. Research (Brit.), Special Rept.* 11, London, 1932.

Dushman, S.: Electron Emission, *Elec. Eng.*, **53**, 1054 (1934).

Chaffee, E. L.: "Theory of Thermionic Vacuum Tubes," Chaps. IV, V, McGraw-Hill Book Company, Inc., New York, 1933.

Koller, L. R.: "The Physics of Electron Tubes," 2d ed., Chaps. I-IV, McGraw-Hill Book Company, Inc., New York, 1937.

McArthur, E. D.: "Electronics and Electron Tubes," Chap. III, John Wiley & Sons, Inc., New York, 1936.

CHAPTER 3

GRID-CONTROLLED HIGH-VACUUM TUBES

3-1. The greatest single advance in the development of vacuum tubes undoubtedly came with the introduction by De Forest of a control electrode between the cathode and plate of the diode.[1] The principal value of such a control electrode arises from the fact that relatively large plate current and power may be controlled by small variations of voltage of the control electrode relative to the cathode without the expenditure of

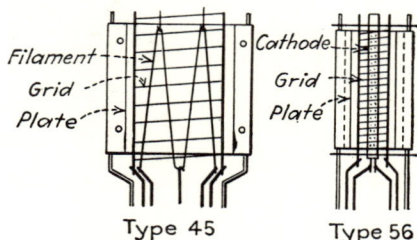

Filament
Grid
Plate

Cathode
Grid
Plate

Type 45   Type 56

Fig. 3-1.—Electrode structure of typical filamentary and heater-type triode receiving tubes.

appreciable power in the control circuit. A three-electrode vacuum tube containing an anode, a cathode, and a control electrode is called a *triode*. Figure 3-1 shows the cross sections of typical high-vacuum triodes.

The form of the control electrode in early tubes led to the use of the term *grid* for this electrode. A grid is now defined more broadly as an electrode that contains openings through which electrons or ions may pass. Many vacuum tubes contain two or more grids. In numerous applications of multigrid tubes the voltages of all but one grid are kept constant. This grid, called the *control grid*, serves to vary the plate (or other electrode) current by means of changes of voltage applied to it. The behavior of multigrid tubes with all grid voltages but that of the control grid fixed is in many respects similar to that of a triode.

[1] DE FOREST, LEE, U. S. Patent 841387 (1907); U. S. Patent 879532 (1908).

48

Standard symbols for filamentary and heater-type triodes are shown in Fig. 3-2a.[1] Often circuit diagrams can be simplified by the use of the modified forms of Fig. 3-2b. In most circuits the filament and heater connections are of secondary importance and may be omitted. Whenever possible, therefore, simplified symbols such as those of Fig. 3-2c will be used. Except for the omission of the grid, diode symbols are the same as those used for triodes. Figure 11-3 contains the symbol used for a diode with two anodes, and Fig. 12-10 shows the symbol for a tube in which a single envelope contains a diode and a triode with a common cathode connection.

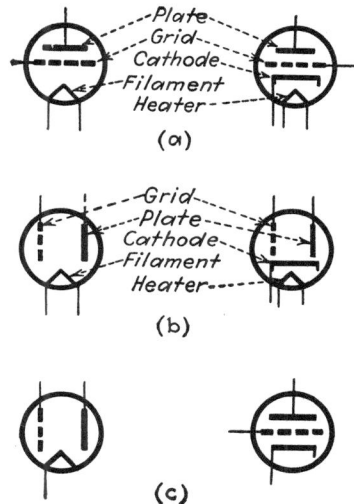

(a)

(b)

(c)

FIG. 3-2.—Symbols for filamentary and heater-type high-vacuum triodes.

3-2. Theory of Grid Action in Triodes. Equations for Plate and Grid Currents.—Electrodynamic analyses of the action of the grid in controlling the plate current of a triode have been developed.[2] For the purposes of this book it will be better to present a brief qualitative discussion of the phenomenon of grid control and to base subsequent derivations upon empirically determined facts.

In Fig. 3-3 is shown the approximate field distribution resulting from applied electrode voltages in a triode with plane cathode and anode. Lines are used in the customary manner to indicate the electrostatic field, but, contrary to convention, the arrows indicate the direction in which electrons are urged by the field.[3] The plate voltage is assumed to be positive and constant in

[1] "Standards on Electronics," p. 15, Institute of Radio Engineers, New York, 1938.

[2] See, for instance, E. L. Chaffee, "Theory of Thermionic Vacuum Tubes," Chap. VII, McGraw-Hill Book Company, Inc., New York, 1933.

[3] No special effort has been made in Fig. 3-3 to depict the field distribution accurately. Figure 3-3 is derived from more complete and carefully constructed diagrams shown on pp. 175 and 176 of "Theory of Thermionic Vacuum Tubes," by E. L. Chaffee.

value. If the grid is made sufficiently negative with respect to the cathode, all lines of force terminate on the grid, and no field exists directly between the plate and cathode. This is illustrated in Fig. 3-3a. The field at all points of the cathode is in the direction to return emitted electrons to the cathode, and so the plate current is zero. If the grid is slightly less negative, some field will extend directly from the anode to the cathode, as shown in Fig. 3-3b, and there will be a force

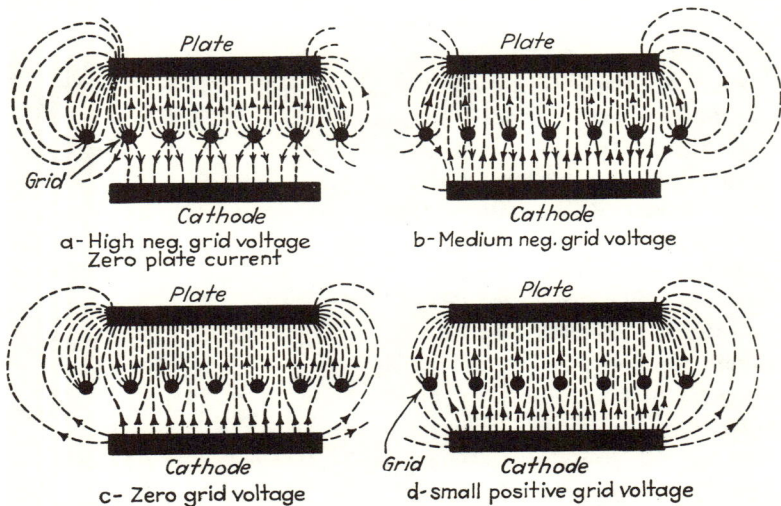

Fig. 3-3.—Approximate field distribution resulting from applied voltages in a triode with plane parallel electrodes for fixed positive plate voltage and four values of grid voltage. Arrows indicate direction of force on an electron.

tending to carry electrons from certain points of the cathode to the anode. Further decrease of negative grid potential increases the areas of the cathode over which the field tends to remove electrons and strengthens the average field over these areas. As long as the grid is negative with respect to the cathode, electrons can reach the grid only if they have sufficient kinetic energy to overcome the retarding field terminating on the grid. Because the initial velocity of emission of the electrons is small, electron current to the grid is zero until the negative grid voltage is appreciably less than a volt. If the tube contains traces of gas, there may be a small positive-ion current to the grid when the grid is negative. At zero grid potential, illustrated by Fig. 3-3c, no point of the cathode experiences a retarding field. Initial velocities cause some electrons to strike the grid, giving a small grid current. When the grid is positive, as in Fig. 3-3d, there is an accelerating field over the whole surface of the cathode. A portion of this field terminates on the grid, causing appreciable grid current to flow.

As in the diode, the net field at the cathode is actually the resultant of the retarding field produced by the space charge and the field caused by the electrode voltages. Equilibrium is established when the average net field is zero at a short distance from the cathode. Increase of applied accelerating field causes the net field to become positive and thus allows more electrons to go to the plate. The space current and space charge increase until the average net field is again zero a short distance from the cathode.

Since the field at the cathode depends upon the potential both of the grid and of the plate, the plate current is a function of both grid and plate voltages. This may be stated symbolically by the equation

$$i_b = f(e_b, e_c) \qquad (3\text{-}1)$$

in which i_b is the plate current, e_b is the plate voltage, and e_c is the grid voltage. Because of the screening action of the grid, only a portion of the field from the plate extends directly to the cathode, whereas there is nothing to intercept the field between the grid and the cathode. One is led to guess, therefore, that the plate current is affected more by changes of grid voltage than of plate voltage, *i.e.*, that the grid voltage is μ times as effective as the plate voltage in controlling the plate current, μ being a factor greater than unity. μ is not necessarily constant. The effect of initial velocity of emitted electrons is the same as though a small increase were made in either grid or plate potential. The contact potentials may either increase or decrease the effective field at the cathode. It is convenient to combine the effects of initial velocity and contact potentials into a single quantity ϵ, an equivalent voltage that would produce the same effect upon plate current as the initial velocity plus the contact potentials. ϵ is ordinarily so small in comparison with externally applied potentials that it may be neglected. This analysis leads to the assumption that the plate current is a function of $(e_b + \mu e_c + \epsilon)$.

This fact may be expressed by the functional equation

$$i_b = F(e_b + \mu e_c + \epsilon) \qquad (T_f = \text{const.}) \qquad (3\text{-}2)$$

where T_f is the temperature of the cathode.

The use of Eq. 3-2 is justified by the fact that it is verified experimentally. Sometimes it is possible to make use of the more explicit approximate law

$$i_b = A(e_b + \mu e_c)^n \qquad (3\text{-}3)$$

in which A is a constant. The exponent n varies considerably with grid and plate voltage, the values ranging roughly between 1.2 and 2.5 for negative values of e_c. When either grid or plate voltage is maintained constant, however, the variation of n is often so small that it may be assumed to be constant over certain ranges. In some analyses, n is assumed to be equal to 1.5 when $e_c = 0$, although actual values may depart appreciably from this value.

μ is called the *plate amplification factor*, or simply the *amplification factor* of the tube. It is a measure of the relative effectiveness of the grid and plate voltages in controlling the plate current. The amplification factor will be shown to be related to certain of the characteristic curves of a triode, and it will be defined mathematically on the basis of this relationship (see Sec. 3-5). The value of μ depends upon the shape and spacing of the electrodes,[1] and to some extent upon the plate current; it may also be made to vary with electrode voltages (see Sec. 3-7). Electrodynamic analysis, based upon the assumption that the electrodes are parallel and of infinite extent, that the grid wire spacing is large compared to the diameter of the grid wire, and that the space charge between electrodes is zero, yields the following approximate formula for μ:[2]

$$\mu = -\frac{2\pi p}{a \log_\epsilon \left(2 \sin \dfrac{\pi r}{a}\right)} \qquad (3\text{-}4)$$

in which p is the distance between the planes of the grid and the plate, a is the distance between adjacent grid wires, and r is the radius of the grid wire. An approximate expression for μ which

[1] KUSUNOSE, Y., *Proc. I.R.E.*, **17**, 1706 (1929).
[2] SCHOTTKY, W., *Arch. Elektrotech.*, **8**, 21 (1919).

applies to a long cylindrical anode and cathode and a helical grid is[1]

$$\mu = -\frac{2\pi \frac{\rho_g}{\rho_p}(\rho_p - \rho_g)}{a \log_\epsilon \frac{a}{2\pi r}} \tag{3-5}$$

in which ρ_p and ρ_g are the radii of the anode and grid, respectively, and a is the spacing of the grid wires.

The effect of space charge is to cause a variation of amplification factor with plate current or electrode voltages. Except in the case of "variable-mu" tubes (see Sec. 3-7), in which the grid wires are not equally spaced, the variation of μ with electrode voltages is sufficiently small so that it may often be assumed to be constant over the working range of current and voltages. At positive grid voltages, however, diversion of current from the plate to the grid lowers μ.

The grid current of a triode is also a function of the grid and plate voltages. This fact may be expressed by the functional equation

$$i_c = G(e_c - \mu_g e_b + \epsilon) \qquad (T_f = \text{const.}) \tag{3-6}$$

in which μ_g, the *grid amplification factor*, is less than unity.

3-3. Time of Transit of Electrons.—Because of its small mass, the acceleration of an electron is so rapid that the time taken for electrons to pass from the cathode to the plate may usually be neglected and the response of electrode currents to changes of electrode voltages considered to be instantaneous. At the very high frequencies corresponding to wave lengths of the order of a few meters or less, however, time of transit must be taken into consideration.[2] Since the operation of vacuum tubes at ultrahigh frequencies will not be discussed in detail in this book, the time of transit of electrons will be neglected.

3-4. Static and Dynamic Characteristics.—Theoretical and practical studies of the performance of vacuum tubes and vacuum-tube circuits are greatly facilitated by the use of curves

---

[1] ABRAHAM, H., *Arch. Elektrotech.*, **8**, 42 (1919); KING, R. W., *Phys. Rev.*, **15**, 256 (1920).

[2] BENHAM, W. E., *Phil. Mag.*, **5**, 641 (1928). LLEWELLYN, F. B., *Proc. I.R.E.;* **21**, 1532 (1933); **22**, 947 (1934); **23**, 112 (1935). CHAFFEE, J. G., *Proc. I.R.E.*, **22**, 1009 (1934). FERRIS, W. R., *Proc. I.R.E.*, **24**, 82, 105 (1936). NORTH, D. O., *Proc. I.R.E.*, **24**, 108 (1936).

relating the electrode currents and voltages, called *characteristics*. A *static electrode characteristic* is a relation, usually shown by a graph, between the voltage and current of that electrode, other electrode voltages being maintained constant. A *static transfer characteristic* is a relation, usually shown by a graph, between the voltage of one electrode and the current of another electrode, all other voltages being maintained constant. Unless otherwise specified, the term *transfer characteristic* is understood to apply to characteristics relating control-grid voltage and plate current, which are the most frequently used transfer characteristics.

Strictly, a *static* characteristic is one obtained with steady voltages, whereas a *dynamic* characteristic is one obtained with alternating voltages. Inasmuch as all voltages but one are specified to be constant in the above definitions, the characteristics obtained with alternating voltages differ from those obtained with direct voltages only when the frequency is so high that tube capacitances and electron transit time cause appreciable out-of-phase components of current. The term *dynamic transfer characteristic* has come to be applied to a transfer characteristic obtained with alternating control-grid voltage when the electrode current under consideration passes through an external imped-ance, called the *load impedance*, the supply voltage for that current being maintained constant. Voltage drops in the load impedance cause the electrode voltage to differ from the supply voltage, and the electrode voltage to vary with current. In general, IR drop in the load causes the transfer characteristic to be affected by load even when the characteristic is derived by using steady voltages. Extension of the term *dynamic transfer characteristic* to include such a characteristic may be justified by considering it to be a limiting curve obtained as the frequency of alternating voltage is made to approach zero.

There are four sets of static characteristics of triodes. They are the plate characteristics i_b vs. e_b at constant values of e_c; the grid characteristics i_c vs. e_c at constant values of e_b; the grid-plate transfer characteristics i_b vs. e_c at constant values of e_b; and the plate-grid transfer characteristics i_c vs. e_b at constant values of e_c.[1] The behavior of a triode is completely specified by either

[1] Since the static characteristics are constructed by plotting corresponding values of direct voltages and currents, the letters used in representing these voltages and currents should be capitals to be entirely in accord with the

the plate and grid families of characteristics or the two families of transfer characteristics.

In Figs. 3-4a and 3-4b are shown typical characteristics for a triode. The bending of the i_b-e_c curves of Fig. 3-4b at positive values of e_c, particularly noticeable for low values of plate voltage, is caused by diversion to the grid of electrons emitted by the cathode, and by secondary emission. When the grid voltage is less than the plate voltage, secondary electrons emitted

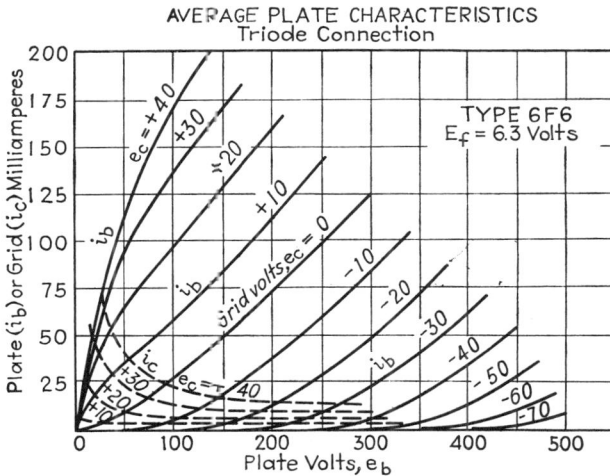

FIG. 3-4a.—Typical triode plate characteristics and plate-grid transfer characteristics.

by the grid are drawn to the plate, but secondary electrons emitted by the plate, when the grid voltage exceeds the plate voltage, are drawn to the grid and constitute a current opposite in direction to the normal plate current. Typical curves of i_b and i_c vs. e_b at large positive grid voltages are shown in Fig. 3-4c. The reversal of curvature of the plate characteristics of Fig. 3-4c between the plate voltages of 50 and 100 for grid voltages of 45 and above is also the result of secondary emission.

The points at which the characteristic curves intercept the voltage axes are called *cutoff points*, and the corresponding

system of nomenclature used in this book (Sec. 3-17). In most applications of the characteristic curves, however, the currents and voltages are assumed to vary, and so must be represented by lower-case symbols. For this reason, lower-case symbols have been used in Eqs. (3-1) to (3-6) and will be used for all characteristic curves.

voltages, the *cutoff voltages*. An approximate relation between grid and plate voltages at plate current cutoff can be derived from Eq. (3-3). When $i_b = 0$, $(e_b + \mu e_c)^n = 0$. This can be true only if $e_b = \mu e_c$. Because μ is never strictly constant, the accuracy of this relation depends upon the voltages at which μ is evaluated. Considerable error may result when the usual published value of μ is used, but the relation is often useful in making a rapid approximate determination of cutoff voltages. Because of lack of homogeneity of the emitter, voltage drops in the cathode, variation of the electric field at various points of the cathode, and distribution of initial velocities of emission, the inter-

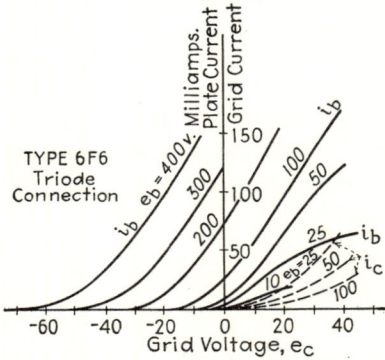

Fig. 3-4b.—Typical triode grid-plate transfer characteristics and grid characteristics (same tube as Fig. 3-4a).

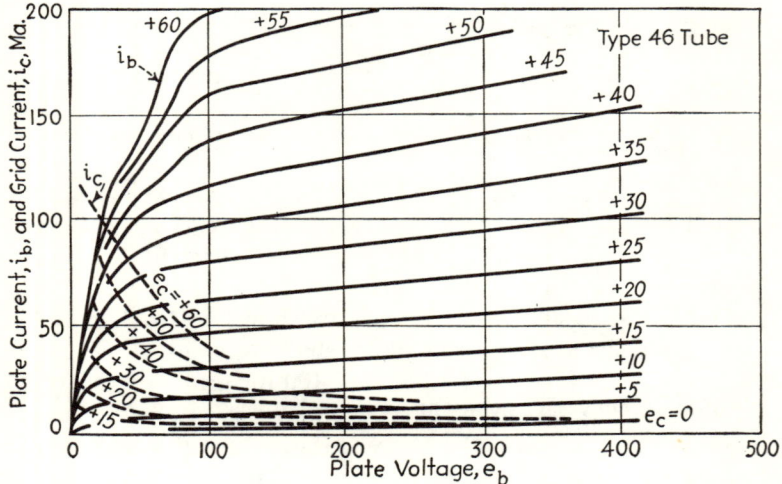

Fig. 3-4c.—Typical triode plate characteristics and plate-grid transfer characteristics at high positive grid voltages.

sections of the characteristic curves with the voltage axis at cutoff are not sharp. Although some grid current usually flows at negative grid voltages lower than half a volt to a volt, the simplifying assumption is often made that grid current cutoff occurs at zero grid voltage.

The transfer characteristics of Fig. 3-4b may be derived from the plate characteristics of Fig. 3-4a, and vice versa.   In Chap. 4 it will be shown that much essential information concerning the performance of tubes in circuits may be obtained from the plate characteristics.   It is important to note that in tubes with filamentary cathodes the grid and plate voltages are measured with respect to the negative end of the filament.

The curves of plate and grid currents against cathode temperature of a triode are similar to those of plate current against cathode temperature of a diode, but voltage at which saturation becomes apparent depends upon both plate voltage and grid voltage.   Since triodes are almost always operated above temperature saturation, these curves are of comparatively little practical value in connection with ordinary applications.

3-5. Tube Factors.—The mathematical and graphical analyses of the operation of vacuum tubes and vacuum-tube circuits require the use of certain tube *factors* whose numerical values are dependent upon the construction of the tube and upon the electrode voltages and currents, and which serve as indices of the ability of given tubes to perform specific functions.   Although only triodes have been discussed so far, it will be convenient also to present at this point general definitions which apply to tubes with more than three electrodes.

Mu-factor is the ratio of the change in one electrode voltage to the change in another electrode voltage, under the conditions that a specified current remains unchanged and that all other electrode voltages are maintained constant.   It is a measure of the relative effect of the voltages of two electrodes upon the current in the circuit of any specified electrode.   As most precisely used, the term refers to infinitesimal changes.   Symbolically, mu-factor is defined by the equation

$$\mu_{jkl} = -\frac{\partial e_j}{\partial e_k} \qquad (i_l,\ e_l,\ e_m,\ \text{etc.},\ =\ \text{const.}) \qquad (3\text{-}7)[1]$$

The most important mu-factor is the control-grid–plate mu-factor, or *amplification factor*.   Amplification factor is the

[1] Although the partial derivative implies that other variables are held constant, for the sake of emphasis it seems advisable in this and following equations to indicate the constant parameters in parentheses.

ratio of the change in plate voltage to a change in control-grid voltage under the conditions that the plate current remains unchanged and that all other electrode voltages are maintained constant. It is a measure of the effectiveness of the control-grid voltage, relative to that of the plate voltage, upon the plate current. The sign is taken as positive when the voltage changes of the two electrodes must be of opposite sign. As most precisely used, the term refers to infinitesimal changes. Symbolically, amplification factor is defined by the equation

$$\mu = -\frac{\partial e_b}{\partial e_c} \qquad (i_b = \text{const.}) \tag{3-8}[1]$$

It must be proved that the factor μ which appears in Eqs. (3-2) and (3-3) is the same as that defined by Eq. (3-8). Examination of Eq. (3-2) shows that, unless the plate current is independent of electrode' voltages, which is true in practice only when the current is zero or saturated, i_b is constant only when $e_b + \mu e_c + \epsilon$ is constant. Since tubes are seldom used continuously either with zero plate current or with saturation plate current, i_b is constant when

$$e_b + \mu e_c + \epsilon = \text{const.} \tag{3-9}$$

Differentiation of Eq. (3-9) shows that

$$-\frac{de_b}{de_c}\bigg]_{i_b = \text{const.}} = \mu \tag{3-10}$$

or

$$\mu = -\frac{\partial e_b}{\partial e_c} \tag{3-11}$$

Since Eq. (3-11) is identical with Eq. (3-8), the factor μ of Eq. (3-2) is the same as that of Eq. (3-8).

[1] The symbolic definitions of tube factors are usually written in terms of the alternating components of electrode voltages and currents, rather than in terms of the total values. Since the difference between the instantaneous value of the alternating component of a varying quantity and the instantaneous total value of the quantity is equal to the average value, the derivative of which is zero, derivatives of the alternating component and of the total quantity are equivalent. In order to show more closely the relation of the tube factors to the characteristic curves, and to simplify derivations based upon Eq. (3-2), the tube factors will be defined in terms of the total values of currents and voltages (see Secs. 3-17 and 3-18 for symbols).

Electrode conductance is the ratio of the change in the current in the circuit of an electrode to a change in the voltage of the same electrode, all other electrode voltages being maintained constant. As most precisely used, the term refers to infinitesimal changes as indicated by the defining equation

$$g_j = \frac{\partial i_j}{\partial e_j} \qquad (e_k,\ e_l,\ \text{etc.} = \text{const.}) \tag{3-12}$$

(See also Sec. 3-25.)

Electrode resistance r_j is the reciprocal of electrode conductance.

The electrode conductance that is used most frequently in the analysis of vacuum tubes and vacuum-tube circuits is the *plate conductance*

$$g_p = \frac{\partial i_b}{\partial e_b} \qquad (e_c = \text{const.}) \tag{3-13}$$

Plate resistance is the reciprocal of plate conductance.

$$r_p \equiv \frac{1}{g_p} = \frac{\partial e_b}{\partial i_b} \qquad (e_c = \text{const.}) \tag{3-14}$$

(See also Sec. 3-25.)

Transconductance is the ratio of the change in the current in the circuit of an electrode to the change in the voltage of another electrode, under the condition that all other voltages remain unchanged. As most precisely used, the term refers to infinitesimal changes as indicated by the defining equation

$$g_{jk} = \frac{\partial i_j}{\partial e_k} \qquad (e_j,\ e_l,\ \text{etc.} = \text{const.}) \tag{3-15}$$

The transconductance most frequently used in the analysis of vacuum tubes and vacuum-tube circuits is the *grid-plate transconductance* (*mutual conductance*), which is defined symbolically as

$$g_m = \frac{\partial i_b}{\partial e_c} \qquad (e_b = \text{const.}) \tag{3-16}$$

Unless otherwise specified, the term *transconductance* usually refers to control-grid-plate transconductance and will be so used in the remainder of this book.

Grid Factors.—In many applications of vacuum tubes the operating voltages are such that no conduction current flows to the control grid and all electrode voltages except those of the control grid and the plate are kept constant. Under these conditions, vacuum-tube problems and derivations can be treated by the use of only three of the factors that have been defined: μ, r_p, and g_m. If conduction current flows to the control grid, it may be necessary to make use of the corresponding control-grid factors, which are defined symbolically as follows:

$$Grid\ amplification\ factor\ \mu_g = -\frac{\partial e_c}{\partial e_b} \qquad (i_c = \text{const.}) \qquad (3\text{-}17)$$

$$Grid\ conductance\ g_g = \frac{\partial i_c}{\partial e_c} \qquad (e_b = \text{const.}) \qquad (3\text{-}18)$$

$$Plate\text{-}grid\ transconductance\ g_n = \frac{\partial i_c}{\partial e_b} \qquad (e_c = \text{const.}) \qquad (3\text{-}19)$$

Because of the effect of space charge, and because of division of the total cathode current between the grid and the plate, μ_g is not in general the reciprocal of μ.

Proof that $g_m = \mu/r_p$.— Only two of the plate factors are independent. This may be shown by taking the partial derivatives of the plate current, as expressed by Eq. (3-2).

$$g_m = \frac{\partial i_b}{\partial e_c} = \mu F'(e_b + \mu e_c + \epsilon) \qquad (3\text{-}20)$$

$$g_p = \frac{\partial i_b}{\partial e_b} = F'(e_b + \mu e_c + \epsilon) \qquad (3\text{-}21)$$

Dividing Eq. (3-20) by Eq. (3-21) gives

$$\frac{g_m}{g_p} = \mu \qquad \text{or} \qquad g_m = \frac{\mu}{r_p} \qquad (3\text{-}22)$$

A similar derivation, based on Eq. (3-6), shows that

$$g_n = \frac{\mu_g}{r_g} \qquad (3\text{-}23)$$

3-6. Relation of Tube Factors to Characteristic Curves.—The definitions state that g_p, g_m, and μ are the slopes of the i_b-e_b, i_b-e_c, and e_b-e_c curves, respectively, at points corresponding to the given voltages. Values of these factors may, therefore, be determined accurately by measuring the slopes of the static characteristics at points corresponding to the electrode voltages, and approximately by taking the ratios of small increments of current and voltage corresponding to points on the characteristics. All three factors may be determined from a single family of character-istics. The most accurate method of obtaining the three plate factors of a triode from the plate family of characteristics is to find r_p from the reciprocal of the slope of the tangent to the i_b-e_b curve at the point correspond-ing to the given electrode volt-ages, μ from the ratio of Δe_b to Δe_c at the constant current at the point, as shown in Fig. 3-5, and g_m from the ratio of μ to r_p. Curves of e_b vs. e_c at con-stant i_b for a typical triode are shown in Fig. 3-6.[1] The

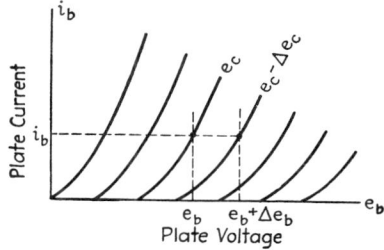

Fɪɢ. 3-5.—Method of determining triode amplification factor from plate characteristics.

practically constant slope of the curves except at low plate voltages and high positive grid voltages indicates that over the normal operating range the amplification factor is nearly con-stant. Except in tubes designed to have variable amplification

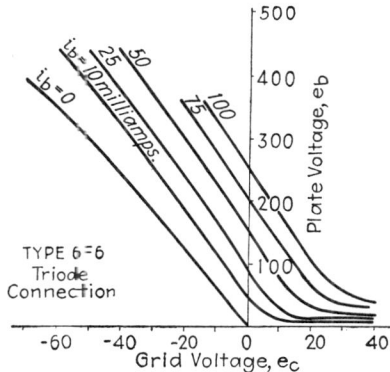

Fɪɢ. 3-6.—Typical triode e_b-e_c characteristics (derived from Fig. 3-4a).

factor, the variation of μ over the normal range of voltages does not exceed 10 to 15 per cent in triodes. Because of the small variation of μ at negative grid voltages, fairly large voltage increments may be used without great error in determining its value from the plate characteristics. Some increase in accuracy

[1] e_b-e_c curves are not usually used in the solution of vacuum-tube prob-lems and are shown here only to point out the nearly constant value of amplification factor in the normal range of voltages.

is gained by using a grid-voltage increment such that the point at which μ is desired is at the center of the increment, rather than at one side as in Fig. 3-5.

3-7. Sharp-cutoff and Remote-cutoff Grids. Variable-mu Tubes.—Thus far it has been assumed that the grid-wire spacing and diameter and the spacing of the grid from the cathode are uniform throughout the length of the grid. When this is true the field strength does not vary greatly over the cathode surface and so the negative grid voltage necessary to prevent electrons from going to the plate at any value of plate voltage is very nearly the same for all points of the cathode. The static transfer characteristic therefore approaches the grid-voltage axis relatively sharply. For this reason a grid of uniform structure is called a *sharp-cutoff grid*. If some dimension of the grid, such as the spacing between the wires, varies along the grid, on the other hand, the field at the cathode varies correspondingly at the cathode surface. A greater negative grid voltage is required to prevent electrons from leaving the cathode at points corresponding to portions of the grid where the spacing is large than to portions where the spacing is small. Cutoff consequently takes place at different values of grid voltage at different parts of the cathode and so the static transfer characteristic approaches the axis gradually. Such a grid is known as a *gradual-cutoff* or *remote-cutoff* (*super-control*) *grid*. Because the mu-factor corresponding to an elementary length of the grid varies along the grid, and because the mu-factor of the entire grid varies greatly with electrode voltages, such a grid is also termed a *variable-mu* grid. A tube that has a variable-mu control grid is called a variable-mu tube.

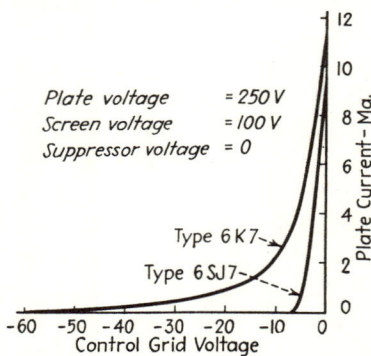

Fig. 3-7.—Comparison of transfer characteristics of similar tubes having remote-cutoff (6K7) and sharp-cutoff (6SJ7) grids.

Figure 3-7 shows the static transfer characteristics of two comparable tubes, one of which has a sharp-cutoff control grid, and the other a remote-cutoff control grid. Multigrid tubes may contain both one or more sharp-cutoff grids and one or more remote-cutoff grids. The advantages of remote-cutoff grids and tubes are discussed in Secs. 6-11 and 6-13 in connection with their use in voltage amplifiers.

3-8. Multigrid Tubes.—Many desirable characteristics can be attained in vacuum tubes by the use of more than one grid. The most common types of multigrid tubes are the tetrode and the pentode. A *tetrode* is a four-electrode type of thermionic tube containing an anode, a cathode, a control electrode, and an additional electrode, which is ordinarily a grid. A *pentode* is a five-electrode type of thermionic tube containing an anode, a cathode, a control electrode, and two additional electrodes, which are ordinarily grids.

The symbols for tetrodes and pentodes are similar to those for triodes, the various grids being shown in the relative positions that they occupy in the tubes. A special symbol, shown in Fig. 3-8b, is often used for screen-grid tetrodes.

The Screen-grid Tetrode.—One stimulus to the development of multigrid tubes was the necessity of reducing the capacitance between the grid and plate of the triode. If a vacuum tube used in a voltage amplifier has high grid-plate capacitance, the relatively large variations of plate voltage may induce appreciable variations of grid voltage. If the phase relations are correct, this induced grid voltage may add to the impressed alternating voltage in such a manner as to cause the amplifier to oscillate (see Sec. 8-3). This difficulty imposes a limit upon the amplification that can be attained in radio-frequency amplifiers. For some years the problem was solved by "neutralizing." Neutralization consists in connecting the grid through a small variable condenser to a point in the output circuit whose voltage is opposite in phase to that of the plate. The condenser may be adjusted so that the alternating grid voltage is independent of the output of the amplifier. Difficulties of adjustment, circuit complications, and the cost of patent royalties made it advantageous to solve the problem by removing the cause, rather than by counteracting it. This was accomplished by introducing between the control grid and the plate another grid, the *screen grid*, the purpose of which is to shield the grid from the plate, and thus reduce the grid-to-plate capacitance.[1] Further

[1] SCHOTTKY, W., *Arch. Elektrotech.*, **8**, 299 (1919); U. S. Patent 1537708; BARKHAUSEN, H., *Jahrb. drahtl. Tel. u. Tel.*, **14**, 43 (1919); HOWE, G. W. O.,

reduction in capacitance between the grid and plate was attained by placing the control-grid terminal at the top of the tube, instead of on the base.   The screen-grid tetrode proved to have other characteristics which are fully as important as its low grid-to-plate capacitance.

The general construction of the elements of a type 24A screen-grid tetrode is shown in Fig. 3-8a.   The screen grid consists of two cylinders of fine-mesh screening, one of which is between the plate and the control grid and the other outside of the plate. These two cylinders are joined at the top by an annular disk, which completes the shielding.   The potential of the screen is normally intermediate between the quiescent potentials of the cathode and plate.   The positive voltage of the screen draws the

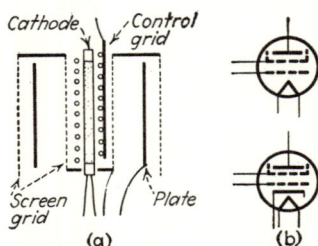

electrons away from the cathode. Some of these electrons strike the screen and result in a screen current which usually performs no useful function; the rest pass through the screen grid and into the field of the plate, which causes them to be drawn to the plate.   Since the electrostatic field of the plate terminates almost completely on the screen, the capacitance between the plate and grid is very small.   Furthermore,

Fig. 3-8.—(a) Electrode structure of heater-type screen-grid tetrode. (b) Tube symbols for filamentary and heater-type screen-grid tetrodes.

variations of plate voltage have little effect on the plate current. The control-grid voltage, on the other hand, is just as effective as in the triode.   The change in plate current resulting from a change in plate voltage at constant grid voltage is small, and the ratio of the change in plate voltage to the change in grid voltage, necessary to produce a given change in plate current, is very high.   It follows from the definitions of plate resistance and amplification factor that the screen-grid tetrode has high plate resistance and high amplification factor.   By proper choice of control-grid structure and spacing of electrodes the transconductance can also be made

Radio Rev., **2**, 337 (1921); Hull, A. W., and Williams, N. H., *Phys. Rev.*, **27**, 432 (1926); Hull, A. W., *Phys. Rev.*, **27**, 439 (1926); Warner, J. C., *Proc. I.R.E.*, **16**, 424 (1928) (with 22 references); Prince, D. C., *Proc. I.R.E.*, **16**, 805 (1928); Williams, N. H., *Proc. I.R.E.*, **16**, 840 (1928); Pidgeon, H. A., and McNally, J. O., *Proc. I.R.E.*, **18**, 266 (1930).

high. Therefore a screen-grid tetrode can be designed to have the same transconductance as that of an equivalent triode and very much higher amplification factor and plate resistance.

In Fig. 3-9 is shown a family of plate characteristics for a typical screen-grid tetrode, the type 24A. The negative slope of the characteristics at plate voltages lower than the screen voltage is the result of secondary emission from the plate. At zero plate voltage there is a small plate current which results from those electrons that pass through the screen with sufficient velocity to reach the plate. As the plate voltage is raised, more and more electrons are drawn to the plate after passing through the screen.

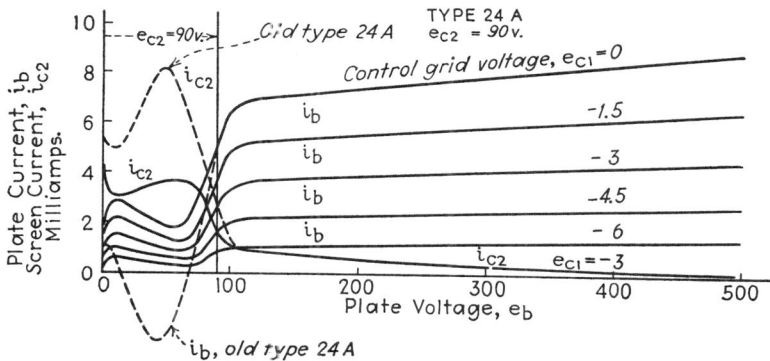

FIG. 3-9.—Plate characteristics of type 24A screen-grid tetrode at 90-volt screen voltage, e_{c2}.

The velocity with which they strike the plate increases with the plate voltage and, when e_b is about 10 volts, becomes sufficiently high to produce appreciable secondary emission from the plate. Because the screen is at a higher voltage than the plate, these secondary electrons are drawn to the screen. Since the secondary electrons move in the direction opposite to that of the primary electrons, they reduce the net plate current. If the plate is not treated to reduce secondary emission, the number of secondary electrons leaving the plate may exceed the number of primary electrons that strike the plate, and so the plate current may reverse in direction. This is shown by the dashed curve of Fig. 3-9, which is for the old type 24A tube, with untreated plate. As the plate voltage approaches the screen voltage, the field at the plate caused by the screen voltage becomes smaller, and the electrons in the space between the screen and plate partly offset this field. The number of secondary electrons drawn to the screen therefore falls off, and the plate current again increases. When the plate voltage is slightly higher than that of the screen, all the secondary electrons return to the plate. At higher voltages secondary emission from the plate has no effect upon the plate current, which is then determined almost entirely by the screen and control-grid voltages. Since very little of the plate field penetrates to the cathode, further increase of plate voltage has only a small effect upon the plate current. The small increase of plate current at plate voltages higher than the screen voltage is accounted for partly by increase in the number of secondary electrons from the screen that are drawn to the plate.

3-9. The Space-charge Tetrode.—Instead of using the inner grid of a tetrode as the control electrode and applying a positive voltage to the second grid, it is possible to operate the tube by applying a small positive voltage to the inner grid and using the second grid as the control electrode.[1] The positive voltage on the first grid overcomes the effect of the space charge in the vicinity of the cathode, and thus increases the plate current and the transconductance. Some of the electrons are drawn to the positive inner space-charge grid, but the remainder pass

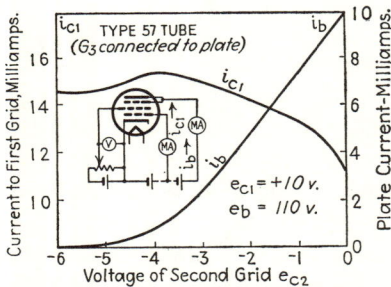

Fig. 3-10.—Characteristics showing first-grid current i_{c1} and plate current i_b of a space-charge tetrode as a function of second-grid voltage e_{c2}.

through this grid and into the region controlled by the second grid and the plate. The effect is in some respects the same as though the cathode were placed much closer to the control grid in a triode. A high negative voltage on the second grid prevents the electrons from passing to the plate and returns them to the positive space-charge grid. As the negative control-grid voltage is reduced, more electrons pass to the plate and fewer to the space-charge grid. Thus, the plate current increases, and the space-charge grid current decreases with decrease of negative voltage on the

[1] Ardenne, M. von, *Hochfrequenztech. u. Elektroakustik*, **42**, 149 (1933). See also *Wireless Eng.*, **11**, 93 (1934) (abstr.); I. Langmuir, U. S. Patent 1558437, filed Oct. 29, 1913; Warner, *loc. cit.*

control grid.   Figure 3-10 shows typical curves of plate current and of first-grid current as a function of second-grid voltage.

Although the transconductance of a space-charge tetrode is greater than that of a triode with a similar cathode, the relatively high current to the space-charge grid results in a less efficient use of the cathode current.   Because more recently developed pentodes have much better characteristics than space-charge tetrodes, space-charge tetrodes are now used only in special applications, some of which will be discussed in later chapters.

3-10. The Pentode.—For most applications the curved portions of the characteristic curves of screen-grid tetrodes at plate voltages lower than the screen voltage are undesirable.   In amplifiers, excessive distortion results if the tube is operated in this region, and, if the circuit contains inductance and capacitance, oscillation may occur (see Sec. 8-2).   Restriction of operation to the region to the right of the plate-current dip reduces the voltage or power output that can be obtained at a given value of operating voltage.

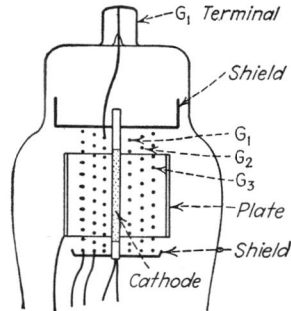

FIG. 3-11*a*.—Electrode structure of the type 57 pentode. G_1, G_2, and G_3 are normally the control, screen, and suppressor grids, respectively.

By the use of a ribbed plate and special treatment to reduce secondary emission, it is possible to design tetrodes whose characteristic curves do not have portions with negative slope. The type 48 tetrode is an example of such a tube.   The effects of secondary emission can also be reduced or eliminated by preventing the secondary electrons from the plate from going to the screen.   This can be done by placing between the screen and the plate a third grid, called the *suppressor grid*.   Figure 3-11*a* shows the arrangement of the electrodes of a typical suppressor pentode of the voltage amplifier type, the 57.   The purpose of the shield in the dome of the tube is to shield the control-grid lead and terminal from the plate.   This shield is connected internally to the cathode and shaped so as to act as the continuation of an external shield which may be placed around the tube.   In voltage pentodes of more recent design, such as that shown in Fig. 3-11*b*, special precautions in placing and shielding the leads have made it possible to connect the control grid to a base pin instead of to a terminal at the top of the tube.[1]   In power pentodes the control-grid terminal is in the base of the tube.

Figure 3-12 shows a series of plate characteristics of the 57 tube at constant control-grid and screen-grid voltages for a number of suppressor-grid voltages.   It can be seen that the secondary-

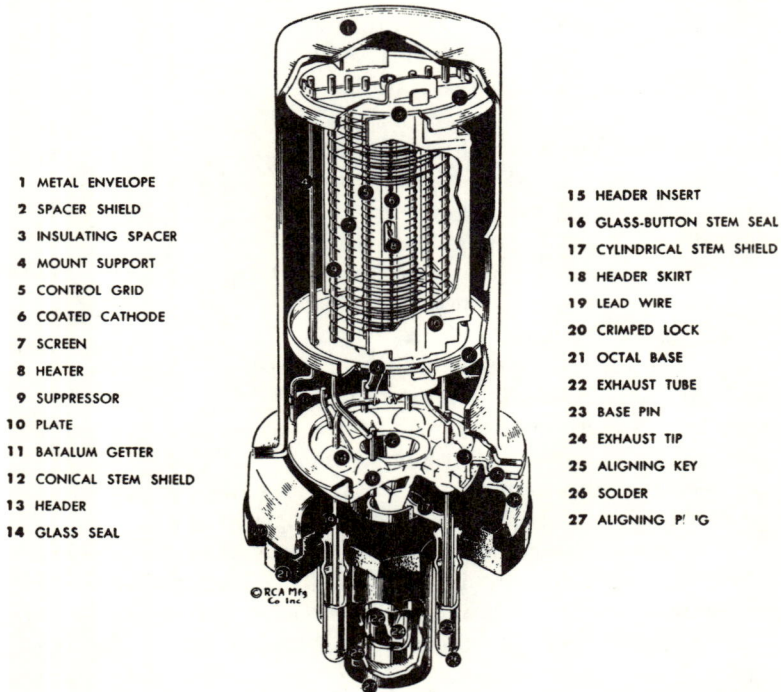

1 METAL ENVELOPE
2 SPACER SHIELD
3 INSULATING SPACER
4 MOUNT SUPPORT
5 CONTROL GRID
6 COATED CATHODE
7 SCREEN
8 HEATER
9 SUPPRESSOR
10 PLATE
11 BATALUM GETTER
12 CONICAL STEM SHIELD
13 HEADER
14 GLASS SEAL

15 HEADER INSERT
16 GLASS-BUTTON STEM SEAL
17 CYLINDRICAL STEM SHIELD
18 HEADER SKIRT
19 LEAD WIRE
20 CRIMPED LOCK
21 OCTAL BASE
22 EXHAUST TUBE
23 BASE PIN
24 EXHAUST TIP
25 ALIGNING KEY
26 SOLDER
27 ALIGNING PLUG

©RCA Mfg Co Inc

FIG. 3-11b.—Typical metal voltage-amplifier pentode in which the control-grid connection is brought out through the base.   Note conical stem shield 12. (*Courtesy of Radio Corporation of America.*)

emission dips move to the left and become less pronounced as the suppressor-grid voltage is reduced below the screen voltage. When the suppressor voltage is zero, *i.e.*, when the suppressor is connected to the cathode, the secondary-emission effects are almost entirely absent.

The explanation of the action of the suppressor is simple. When the suppressor is connected to the cathode, the field

---

[1] KELLY, R. L., and MILLER, J. F., *Electronics*, September, 1938, p. 26.

between the plate and the suppressor is always such as to move electrons toward the plate. The secondary electrons removed from the plate have sufficiently low velocity of emission so that even at low plate voltages few can permanently leave the plate against this retarding field. Velocity acquired by the primary electrons in the space between the cathode and the screen carries most of them through the screen and suppressor and thence into the field beyond the suppressor, which draws them to the plate.

The additional shielding effect of the suppressor grid results in plate resistance and amplification factor that are even greater

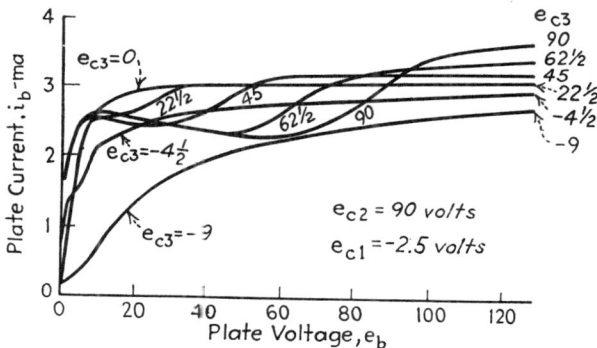

Fig. 3-12.—Plate characteristics of the type 57 pentode, showing effect of variation of suppressor voltage e_{c3} at 90-volt screen voltage e_{c2}.

than for tetrodes. It can be seen from Fig. 3-12 that the plate resistance of the suppressor pentode can be varied by means of negative suppressor voltage.

In some pentodes the suppressor is permanently connected to the cathode internally, but all three grids may have external connections in order that the grids may be used in various ways. When the second and third grids are connected to the plate, the tube has ordinary triode characteristics. When the first and second grids are used together as the control grid and the third is connected to the plate, the tube acts as a triode with very high amplification factor and low plate current. Other special applications of pentodes will be discussed in later chapters (see end of Sec. 6-1 and Secs. 6-18, 8-2, 8-10, and 12-4).

Figures 3-13 and 3-14 show the plate characteristics for two types of suppressor pentodes, the 57 and the 2A5 (see also Figs. A-7, A-9, and A-12, page 375). It will become apparent from material to be presented in this and later chapters that ideal characteristics for amplifier tubes would be straight, parallel, and equidistant for all values of plate voltage. The gradual bending of the characteristics at low plate voltages, particularly noticeable in the characteristics of pentodes designed to give

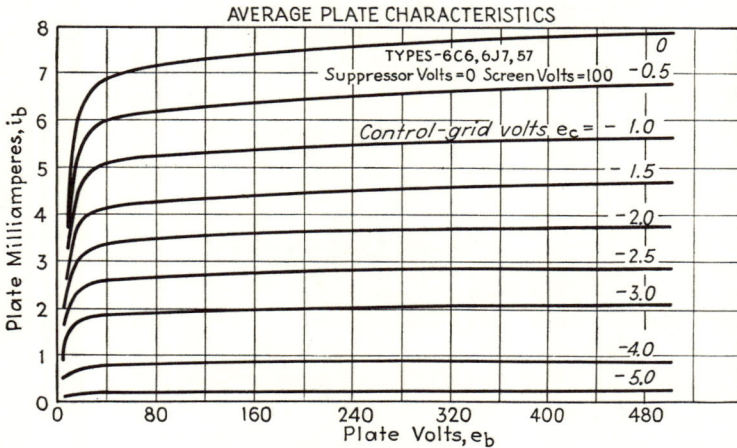

Fig. 3–13.—Plate characteristics of a typical voltage pentode.

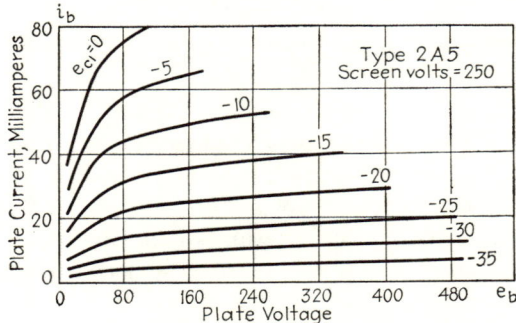

Fig. 3-14.—Plate characteristics of a typical power pentode.

large power output, such as the type 2A5, causes distortion and is therefore objectionable. It is the result of nonuniformity of the field in the plane of the suppressor grid. Saturation is obtained at different plate voltages for different sections of this plane, and so the characteristics bend gradually and have broad knees. This difficulty is avoided in the *beam power tube*.[1]

[1] Schade, O. H., *Proc. I.R.E.*, **26**, 137 (1938). See also F. Below, *Z.*

3-11. Beam Pentodes.—In the beam tube the secondary electrons are returned to the plate by the repulsion of negative space charge between the screen and the plate. This space charge is accentuated by the retarding field of the plate when the plate potential is lower than the screen potential. By proper design the space charge may be made so dense as to cause the formation of a virtual cathode (*i.e.*, a plane of zero average field and zero electron velocity) near the plate at low plate voltages. For all values of plate voltage less than the screen voltage a potential minimum is formed which may be kept sufficiently lower than the plate potential so that secondary electrons from the plate are

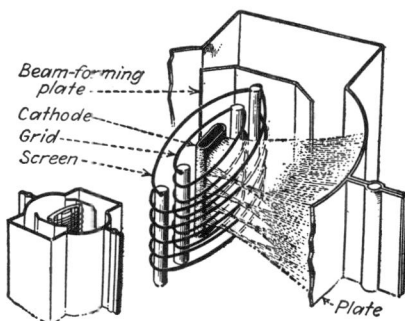

FIG. 3-15.—Electrode structure of the type 6L6 beam power pentode. (*Courtesy of Radio Corporation of America.*)

returned to the plate. The action is similar to that of a suppressor grid; but, if the density of space charge and the electron velocity at the virtual cathode are uniform and the distance of the virtual cathode from the plate is everywhere the same, then saturation takes place simultaneously at all points in the plane of the virtual cathode, and the knee of the plate characteristic is sharp. The virtual cathode and the plate act in a manner similar to a diode, the plate current being limited by space charge at low plate voltages. As in a diode, saturation at low plate voltage, *i.e.*, a low-voltage knee, requires that the virtual cathode shall be close to the plate.

In the beam power tube, of which the 6L6 is a typical example, the required electron density is achieved by confining the elec-

Fernmeldetech. **9**, 113 (1928); R. S. Burnap, *RCA Rev.*, **1**, 101 (1936); J. F. Dreyer, Jr., *Electronics*, April, 1936, p. 18; J. H. O. Harries, *Electronics*, May, 1936, p. 33; B. Salzberg and A. V. Haeff, *RCA Rev.*, **2**, 336 (1938).

trons to beams.   The homogeneity of space charge and electron velocity is attained by proper design of the contours of the cathode, grids, and plate and by correct choice of the ratio of screen-plate to screen-cathode spacing (2.9) and beam angle (approximately 60 deg).   The electrons are confined to beams by means of beam-forming plates, as shown in Fig. 3-15, which are at cathode potential.   The flattened cathode gives a larger effective area than a round cathode and so results in a higher transconductance.

The screen current of beam power tubes is much lower than that of suppressor pentodes.   The screen and control grid have

AVERAGE PLATE CHARACTERISTICS
with e_{c1} as variable

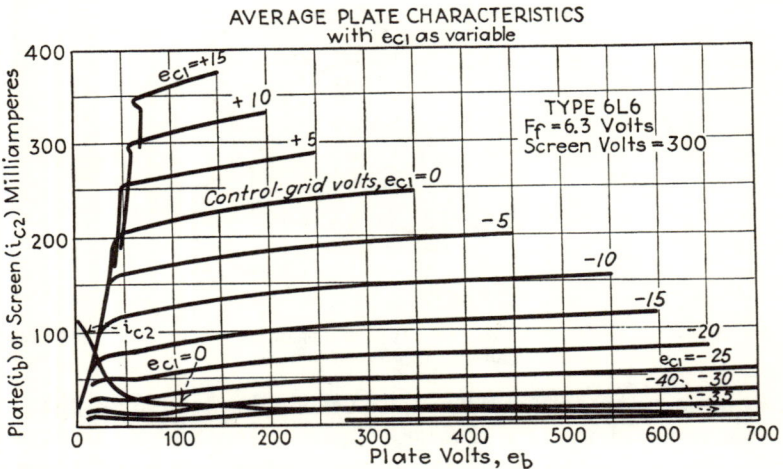

FIG. 3-16.—Plate characteristics of the type 6L6 beam power pentode.

equal pitch and are proportioned and assembled so that the screen grid is hidden from the cathode by the control grid, and the individual beam sheets formed by the control grid are focused in the plane of the screen.   Very few, therefore, of the electrons moving toward the plate can strike the screen directly. Furthermore, because of the sharpness of the beams and the uniform fields, few electrons acquire tangential velocity at the expense of velocity normal to the electrode planes.   The number of electrons that miss the plate at low plate voltage and return to the screen is therefore also small.   Low screen current results in a number of advantages, among which are low screen dissipation and consequent larger power rating without danger of electron emission from the screen because of high screen temperature, and the possibility of using low-power resistors in the voltage divider that supplies the screen voltage.

Figure 3-16 shows the plate characteristics of the 6L6. These characteristics are straight and parallel over a much greater range of plate voltage than those of suppressor pentodes, and the knees are sharper.

3-12. Equations for Plate Current of Multigrid Tubes.—Plate-current equations similar to Eqs. (3-1) and (3-2) may be written for tetrodes and pentodes. In most circuits, however, only the control-grid and plate voltages are varied, and Eqs. (3-1) and (3-2) may be applied.

3-13. Determination of Tetrode and Pentode Factors from Characteristics.—The most accurate method of determining tetrode and pentode tube factors at given voltages from the plate characteristics is to find r_p from the reciprocal of the slope of the characteristic at the point corresponding to the given voltages; g_m from the ratio of a small increment of plate current to the increment of control-grid voltage that causes it at constant plate voltage, as in Fig. 3-17; and μ from the product of r_p and g_m. Since g_m is not constant, accuracy in the values of g_m and μ found by this method is dependent upon the use of very small increments. For the sake of accuracy it is desirable, when convenient, to

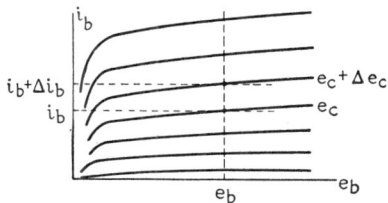

Fig. 3-17.—Graphical determination of transconductance of pentodes.

use an increment of grid voltage such that the point at which g_m is desired lies at the center of the increment, rather than at one end. If the grid voltage intervals corresponding to the available plate characteristics are large, it may be desirable to construct the static transfer characteristic corresponding to the given plate voltage and to find g_m from the slope of this characteristic at the given grid voltage.

3-13A. Duplex Tubes and Tubes with More than Three Grids.— The behavior of the individual units of duplex tubes is no different than when these units are enclosed in separate envelopes. For this reason duplex tubes require no further discussion. Special tubes having more than three grids will be treated in later chapters in connection with their applications (see Secs. 6-11, 6-18, 7-10, and 12-3).

3-14. Applied Voltages in Grid and Plate Circuits.—In most applications of vacuum tubes, one or more alternating voltages are applied to the control-grid and plate circuits, in addition to the steady voltages, as shown in Fig. 3-18. The steady applied voltages E_{cc}, E_{bb}, and E_{ff} are called the *grid supply voltage* or *C-supply voltage*, the *plate supply voltage* or *B-supply voltage*, and the *filament* or *heater supply voltage*, respectively. v_g and v_p, the applied alternating voltages in the grid and plate circuits, are called the *grid excitation voltage* and *plate excitation voltage*, respectively. Because of external circuit impedance, the electrode voltages will in general differ from the applied voltages when current flows.

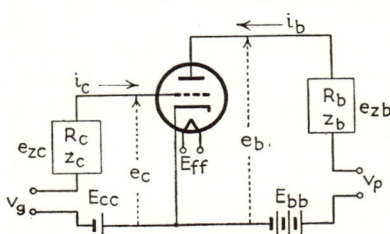

Fig. 3-18.—Triode grid and plate circuits, showing impressed voltages, electrode voltages, and voltages across grid and plate load impedances.

3-15. Form of Alternating Plate-current Wave.—Figure 3-19 shows the manner in which a sinusoidal grid voltage causes the plate current to vary when the load is nonreactive. The wave of plate current is constructed by projecting from the wave of grid voltage to the transfer characteristic at various instants throughout the cycle (see Fig. 4-12).

When the a-c resistance of the plate circuit differs from the d-c resistance, as when the load consists of a transformer with a resistance across the secondary, the current corresponding to the time axis of the wave of alternating plate current actually differs somewhat from the value I_{bo} assumed when the excitation voltages are zero. Since it is not often essential to take this fact into consideration, and since a more rigorous analysis is likely to prove confusing to a student studying the subject of electron tubes for the first time, it will be assumed throughout the remainder of this book that the current corresponding to the axis of the wave is the same as that assumed when there is no excitation. The errors resulting from this simplification in treatment are of importance mainly in the graphical analysis of pentode power amplifiers. For a rigorous analysis the student should refer to a more advanced treatment of electron tubes.[1]

Curvature of the transfer characteristic in general causes the wave of varying plate current to be asymmetrical even though the exciting voltage is sinusoidal. It will be proved in later sections that the wave of alternating plate current, measured relative to the time axis, in general contains not only a fundamental component of the same frequency as the grid excitation voltage, but also harmonics of that frequency and a steady component. The steady component of alternating plate current causes the average value of plate current to differ from the value assumed with zero excitation. When the load is nonreactive, the wave of plate voltage is of the same form as the wave of plate current.

Usually it is most convenient to measure the instantaneous value of the alternating component of plate or grid current or voltage relative to the time axis of the wave. Occasionally, however, it is necessary to measure the instantaneous value with respect to the average value. An instantaneous value measured relative to the axis differs from the value measured relative to the average in that the former contains the steady component of the alternating current or voltage, whereas the latter does not. Unless otherwise specifically stated, the terms *alternating plate current* and *alternating grid current*, and the corresponding terms for voltages, will be understood to refer to values measured relative to the time axes.

3-16. Static and Dynamic Operating Points.—The steady values of electrode voltages and currents assumed when the excitation voltages are zero are called the *quiescent* or *static operating* voltages and currents. The point on the static characteristics corresponding to given static operating voltages and currents is termed the *static operating point* (or *quiescent point*). The static operating point will be indicated on the characteristic curves by the letter O. The average values of electrode voltages and currents assumed with excitation are called the *dynamic operating* voltages and currents. The corresponding point on

[1] See, for instance, H. J. Reich, "Theory and Applications of Electron Tubes," Secs. 4-7 to 4-13, McGraw-Hill Book Company, Inc., New York, 1939.

the plate characteristics is termed the *dynamic operating point* and will be indicated by the letter A. The dynamic and static operating points coincide when the wave of plate current is symmetrical.

3-17. Symbols.—The presence of both steady and varying components in the electrode voltages and currents necessitates the use of a large number of symbols. The symbols used in this book are based upon those proposed in 1933 by the Standards

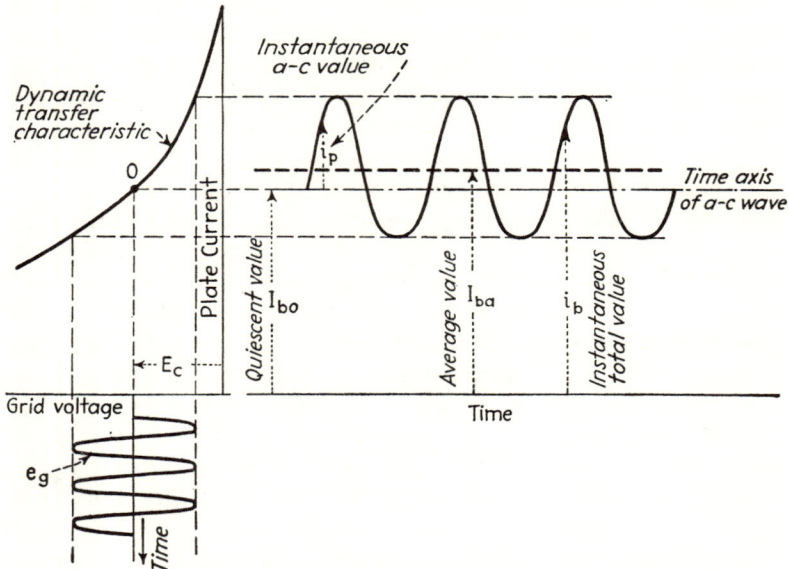

FIG. 3-19.—Plate-current relations for asymmetrical wave of plate current.

Committee of the Institute of Radio Engineers. The student will find it helpful to learn the following rules, according to which these symbols are formed:

1. The subscripts c and g refer to the grids or to the grid circuits, and the subscripts b and p to the plate or to the plate circuits.

2. Lower-case letters indicate instantaneous values of varying quantities, and capital letters indicate steady (direct) values and average, r-m-s, and crest values of varying quantities (see Figs. 3-19 and 3-20).

3. Lower-case letters with subscripts c and b indicate *total* instantaneous values of varying quantities (see Figs. 3-19 and 3-20).

4. Lower-case letters with subscripts g and p indicate instantaneous values *of the alternating components* of varying quantities.

5. Capital letters with subscripts $_c$ and $_b$ indicate direct or average values. Second subscripts $_o$ or $_a$ are added to differentiate between quiescent and average values of an asymmetrical wave of total varying plate current or voltage (see Fig. 3-19).

6. Capital letters with subscripts $_g$ and $_p$ indicate r-m-s or crest values of alternating quantities. Crest values of sinusoidal alternating quantities are distinguished from r-m-s values by the addition of the second subscript $_m$ (see Fig. 3-20).

In tetrodes and pentodes and in tubes having more than three grids, it is necessary to distinguish between the voltages and between the currents of the various grids. This is done by

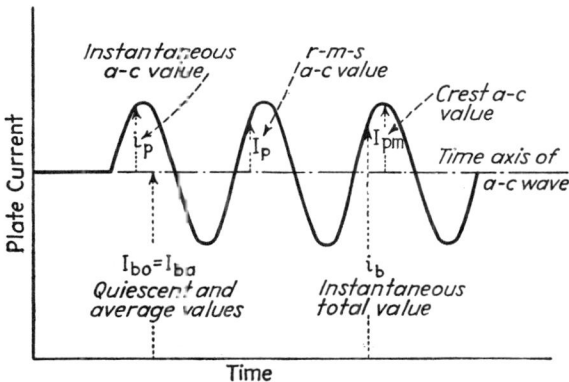

Fig. 3-20.—Plate-current relations for sinusoidal wave of plate current.

means of the addition of a number in the subscript to indicate the number of the grid. Thus e_{c1}, e_{c2}, e_{c3}, etc., indicate the instantaneous total voltages of the first, second, and third, etc., grids, grid 1 being nearest the cathode. Usually the first grid serves as the control electrode, and e_{c1} indicates the control-grid voltage. In many analyses it is necessary to speak only of the control-grid voltage. It is then convenient to omit the number in the subscript, even though the tube contains more than one grid. In the work which follows, therefore, it will be understood that, when no number appears in the subscript, reference is to the control grid and that the term *grid* refers to the control grid.

The following symbols will be used in the remainder of this book.

Control-grid supply voltage.................................E_{cc1} or E_{cc}
Screen-grid supply voltage.................................E_{cc2}

Plate supply voltage.................................E_{bb}
Filament or heater supply voltage......................E_{ff}
Instantaneous value of grid excitation voltage.............v_g
Instantaneous value of plate excitation voltage............v_p
Instantaneous total grid voltage......................e_c
Instantaneous total plate voltage.....................e_b
Instantaneous total grid current......................i_c
Instantaneous total plate current (see Fig. 3-19)..........i_b
Quiescent (zero excitation) value of grid voltage..........E_{co}
Quiescent (zero excitation) value of plate voltage..........E_{bo}
Quiescent (zero excitation) value of plate current (see Fig. 3-19)..I_{bo}
Average value of grid voltage (grid bias)...............E_c (or E_{ca})
Average value of plate voltage.......................E_{ba}
Average value of plate current.......................I_{ba}
Instantaneous value of alternating component of grid voltage...e_g
Instantaneous value of alternating component of plate voltage,
  measured relative to the time axis of the wave of alternating
  plate voltage.................................e_p
Instantaneous value of alternating component of plate current,
  measured relative to the time axis of the wave of alternating
  plate current (see Fig. 3-19).......................i_p
Effective value of alternating component of grid voltage........E_g
Effective value of alternating component of plate voltage.......E_p
Effective value of alternating component of plate current.......I_p
Crest value of sinusoidal alternating component of grid voltage
  (grid swing).................................E_{gm}
Crest value of sinusoidal alternating component of plate voltage E_{pm}
Crest value of sinusoidal alternating component of plate current I_{pm}
Impedance of the plate circuit (load impedance) at angular
  frequency ω..................................$z_b = r_b + jx_b$
Admittance of the plate circuit at angular frequency ω...$y_b \equiv \dfrac{1}{z_b} = g_b - jb_b$
D-c resistance of the plate circuit.....................R_b
Instantaneous value of the alternating voltage drop in the plate
  circuit impedance..............................e_{zb}

3-18. Current and Voltage Relations in the Grid and Plate Circuits.—The following relations are apparent from Fig. 3-18 and from Fig. 3-19 and the similar wave of plate voltage:

$$e_p = v_p + e_{zb} = v_p - i_p z_b \qquad (3\text{-}24)$$
$$i_b = I_{bo} + i_p \qquad (3\text{-}25)$$
$$e_b = E_{bo} + e_p \qquad (3\text{-}26)$$
$$E_{ba} = E_{bb} - I_{ba}R_b \qquad (3\text{-}27)$$

For the special case in which the wave of alternating plate current is symmetrical, as illustrated by the sinusoidal current wave of

Fig. 3-20, I_{ba} is identical with I_{bo}, and E_{ba} is identical with E_{bo}. For a symmetrical wave, therefore, Eq. (3-27) reduces to

$$E_{bo} = E_{bb} - I_{bo}R_b \tag{3-28}$$

Equation (3-28) also holds when the excitation is zero. In most applications of vacuum tubes, excitation voltage is applied only to the grid, and Eq. (3-24) reduces to

$$e_p = -i_p z_b \tag{3-29}$$

The amplitude of the alternating grid voltage E_{gm} is called the *grid swing*. The direct component of grid voltage is called the *grid bias* or *C bias*. Because the symbol E_c has long been used to represent the grid bias, this symbol, rather than the alternative E_{ca}, will be used throughout the remainder of this book. In all applications of electron tubes to be treated analytically in this book the grid bias is maintained sufficiently negative so that grid current does not flow, and the following relations apply:

$$E_c = E_{cc} \tag{3-30}$$
$$e_g = v_g \tag{3-31}$$

3-19. Generation of Harmonics.—If a sine wave of excitation voltage is applied to an electrode of a vacuum tube, it is found that the plate current in general contains not only an alternating component of the same frequency as that of the applied voltage but also components whose frequencies are equal to harmonics of the impressed frequency. Usually there is also a change in average plate current. If two or more sinusoidal voltages are impressed simultaneously the wave form of the alternating plate current is even more complicated, containing the applied frequencies and their harmonics and also frequencies equal to the sums and differences of the applied frequencies and their multiples. It is evident, therefore, that it is not in general possible to apply to the vacuum tube the superposition theorem, which states that the current that flows through a linear circuit element as the result of a number of simultaneously impressed voltages of different frequencies is equal to the sum of the currents that would flow if the various voltage components were applied individually.

The generation of new frequencies by a vacuum tube is associated with the fact that it is not a linear circuit element, *i.e.*, that the characteristic curves are not linear. The appearance of plate-current components of frequencies different from the impressed frequency as the result of curvature of the transfer characteristic can be readily demonstrated graphically. The transfer characteristic of Fig. 3-21 is parabolic, and the exciting voltage sinusoidal, as indicated by the curve of e_g. The wave of i_p is constructed by finding from the transfer characteristic the values of instantaneous plate current corresponding to instantaneous grid voltages at various instants of the cycle. The dotted curves show the fundamental, steady, and second-harmonic components into which the alternating plate current i_p may be resolved.

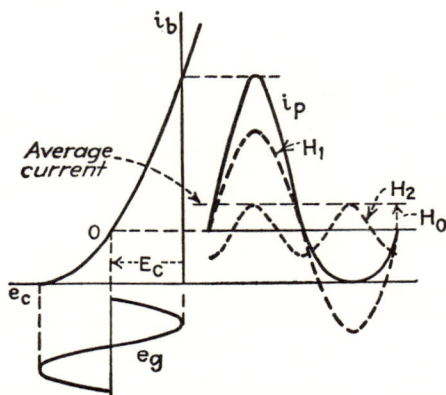

Fig. 3-21.—Generation of second-harmonic and steady components of plate current by tube with parabolic transfer characteristic.

3-20. Series Expansion for Alternating Plate Current.—Theoretically, it should be possible to predict from Eq. (3-2) and corresponding tetrode and pentode equations the form of the alternating plate current corresponding to an exciting voltage of known wave form. Practically, however, $F(e_b + \mu e_c + \epsilon)$ is so complicated in form that Eq. (3-2) is of little or no value for this purpose. The behavior of a nonlinear circuit element can in general be analyzed mathematically most readily by expressing the alternating current in the form of an infinite power series. For a two-terminal element, in which the current depends upon only one voltage, the series involves only the impressed voltage, the impedance of the element and its derivatives at the operating point, and the circuit impedance. It may be derived by the application of Taylor's expansion for a function of one variable to the functional equation of current. Because the plate current of a vacuum tube depends upon all the electrode voltages, a complete series expansion applicable to a tube with three or more electrodes must involve all electrode voltages, as well as various tube factors and their derivatives at the operating point.[1] The general series expansion for tetrodes and pentodes is complicated, therefore, particularly if control-grid current is assumed to flow and the control-grid circuit contains an impedance. When all electrode voltages except those of the control grid and the plate are constant, however, as is usually true, the action of multigrid tubes is similar to that of triodes, and the general form of the series reduces to that for a triode. The triode expansion may consequently be applied to any tube in which only the plate and control-grid voltages vary. Furthermore, most problems in which the series expansion is of value can be adequately treated by the use of the form derived under the assumption that control-grid current does not flow. A further simplification results from the assumption that μ is constant, which is approximately true in many tubes. For the general forms of the series expansion for plate current of multigrid tubes, and for the similar expansions for currents to other electrodes, the student should refer to the work of Llewellyn[2] and others.[3]

3-21. Series Expansion. *Resistance Load.*—The series expansion for the plate current of a triode with negative grid voltage for the case of constant amplification factor and nonreactive load has the following form:[4]

$$i_p = a_1 e + a_2 e^2 + a_3 e^3 + \cdots \tag{3-32}$$

where

$$
\left.
\begin{aligned}
a_1 &= \frac{\mu}{r_p + r_b} \\[2mm]
a_2 &= -\frac{\mu^2 r_p}{2(r_p + r_b)^3}\frac{\partial r_p}{\partial e_b} \\[2mm]
a_3 &= \frac{\mu^3 r_p}{6(r_p + r_b)^5}\left[(2r_p - r_b)\left(\frac{\partial r_p}{\partial e_b}\right)^2 - r_p(r_p + r_b)\frac{\partial^2 r_p}{\partial e_b^2}\right]
\end{aligned}
\right\} \tag{3-33}
$$

[1] CARSON, J. R., *Proc. I.R.E.*, **7**, 187 (1919).

[2] LLEWELLYN, F. B., *Bell System Tech. J.*, **5**, 433 (1926).

[3] BRAINERD, J. G., *Proc. I.R.E.*, **17**, 1006 (1929); CAPORALE, P., *Proc. I.R.E.*, **18**, 1593 (1930); BONER, M. O., *Phys. Rev.*, **39**, 863 (1932); BENNETT, W. R., *Bell System Tech. J.*, **12**, 228 (1933); ESPLEY, D. C., *Proc. I.R.E.*, **22**, 781 (1934); BARROW, W. L., *Proc. I.R.E.*, **22**, 964 (1934).

[4] The derivation of Eqs. (3-32) and (3-33) is outlined in Sec. 3-22 of "Theory and Applications of Electron Tubes."

and

$$e = e_g + \frac{v_p}{\mu} \tag{3-34}$$

r_p and its derivatives are evaluated at the operating point in Eqs. (3-33).

For common high-vacuum triodes, Eq. (3-32) converges rapidly enough so that the required accuracy is usually obtained with only a few terms of the series if the current amplitude is not too great. $\partial r_p/\partial e_b$ may be evaluated by plotting a curve of r_p vs. e_b determined from the static plate characteristic corresponding to the given operating grid bias. $\partial r_p/\partial e_b$ is the slope of this r_p-e_b curve at the point corresponding to the operating plate voltage. Other higher-order derivatives may be evaluated in a similar manner from curves of derivatives of the next lower order, but the accuracy rapidly decreases with increase of order of the derivative. The value of the series expansion lies not so much in the direct solution of numerical problems, as in the general analysis of the operation of vacuum tubes. Applications of the series expansion in the study of the operation of vacuum tubes and associated circuits will be made in this and later chapters.

3-22. Harmonic Generation and Intermodulation.—Before proceeding to a discussion of the more general problem of a tube with impedance load, it is necessary to show that the presence of the second- and higher-order terms of the series is associated with the production of components of alternating plate current of frequencies other than those which are contained in the applied signal. Consider, for instance, the simple case in which the excitation voltage has only a single frequency. Then

$$\left.\begin{array}{l} e = E_m \sin \omega t \\ e^2 = E_m{}^2 \sin^2 \omega t = \tfrac{1}{2}E_m{}^2 - \tfrac{1}{2}E_m{}^2 \cos 2\omega t \\ e^3 = \tfrac{3}{4}E_m{}^3 \sin \omega t - \tfrac{1}{4}E_m{}^3 \sin 3\omega t \end{array}\right\} \tag{3-35}$$

Thus the second-order term of the series gives rise to a steady component and to a second-harmonic component in the alternating plate current. The third-order term gives rise to a fundamental and a third-harmonic component of alternating plate current. The production of harmonics in the plate current has been shown graphically in Fig. 3-21 for the simple case in which the static characteristics are assumed to obey a parabolic law, $i_b = A(e_b + \mu e_c)^2$, and z_b is assumed to be zero. If r_b is zero, a_1, a_2, and a_3, as given by Eqs. (3-33), reduce to $\mu \dfrac{\partial i_b}{\partial e_b}$, $\dfrac{\mu^2}{2!} \dfrac{\partial^2 i_b}{\partial e_b{}^2}$, and $\dfrac{\mu^3}{3!} \dfrac{\partial^3 i_b}{\partial e_b{}^3}$, respectively. Similarly, any coefficient a_n reduces to $\dfrac{\mu^n}{n!} \dfrac{\partial^n i_b}{\partial e_b{}^n}$. Since $\dfrac{\partial^3 i_b}{\partial e_b{}^3}$ and higher-order derivatives of plate current with respect to plate voltage are zero when the static characteristics obey a parabolic law, the plate-current series contains only the first- and second-order terms. Consequently the alternating plate current should consist of fundamental, steady, and second-harmonic components when the excitation is sinusoidal. This is in agreement with Fig. 3-21.

If the excitation voltage contains more than one frequency, the plate current contains not only the impressed frequencies and their harmonics, but also frequencies equal to the sums and differences of the impressed frequencies and their integral multiples, as may be shown by expanding

$$(E_1 \sin \omega_1 t + E_2 \sin \omega_2 t + E_3 \sin \omega_3 t + \cdots)^n.$$

These are called *intermodulation* frequencies. *Intermodulation* is defined as the production, in a nonlinear circuit element, of frequencies equal to the sums and differences of integral (1, 2, 3, etc.) multiples of two or more frequencies which are transmitted to that element. It should be noted that the harmonic and intermodulation frequencies contained in the output are not present in the impressed excitation but are generated by the nonlinear circuit element. It will be shown in later chapters that intermodulation in vacuum-tube circuits is sometimes desirable and sometimes objectionable.

The production of intermodulation frequencies can be demonstrated in a striking manner by a simple laboratory experiment. The voltages from two audio-frequency oscillators are filtered to remove harmonics and are applied in series to the grid circuit of a vacuum tube. The voltage developed across a plate load resistance (preferably considerably smaller than the plate resistance) is applied to the input of a low-pass filter (0- to 3000-cycle, for instance), the output of which goes to headphones or, through an amplifier, to a loud-speaker. The oscillator frequencies are made high enough so that the fundamental components of the output voltage cannot pass through the filter. Various combinations of oscillator frequencies can be found at which one or more frequencies are heard in the phones, the pitch of which varies with the tuning of either oscillator. The frequencies are always found to be equal to the difference between one oscillator frequency or one of its multiples and the other oscillator frequency or one of its multiples. Since the application of the harmonics to the grid of the tube is prevented by filtering the oscillator voltages, the frequencies that are heard in the output are generated by the tube. A similar experiment, performed with a high-pass filter in the output, demonstrates the production of intermodulation frequencies equal to the sums of the oscillator frequencies and their multiples.

3-23. Series Expansion. *Impedance Load and Variable Amplification Factor.*—The series expansion for the more general case of impedance load, although similar in form to that for resistance load, is considerably more complicated. Since the coefficients of the series involve the load impedance, which depends upon the frequency, there must be a coefficient a_n for each frequency arising from the expansion of $e^n = (E_1 \sin \omega_1 t + E_2 \sin \omega_2 t + \cdots)^n$, instead of a single coefficient a_n, as with resistance load. This may be indicated by writing Eq. (3-32) in the form

$$i_p = \Sigma a_1 e + \Sigma a_2 e^2 + \Sigma a_3 e^3 + \cdots \qquad (3\text{-}36)$$

An excellent development of the series expansion for the general case of impedance load and variable amplification factor has been given by Llewellyn, who has derived the first two coefficients.[1] The first coefficient, which will be used in later chapters, is

$$a_1 = \frac{\mu}{r_p + z_b} \qquad (3\text{-}37)$$

In using Eq. (3-37) it must be kept in mind that there is one coefficient for each frequency component of the excitation voltage, z_b being evaluated at these frequencies.

No step in the derivation of Eqs. (3-32) and (3-33) restricts these equations to alternating exciting voltage. They apply equally well when e is a small charge of applied grid or plate voltage. Equations (3-36) and (3-37), on the other hand,

[1] LLEWELLYN, *loc. cit.*

involve impedances that are evaluated at specific frequencies. They cannot, therefore, be used when e is not a periodic function of time.   The sudden application of grid or plate excitation or of direct voltages will in general result in the production of transient components of plate current when the grid or plate circuits contain reactance.   The theory of the transient behavior of tube circuits is beyond the scope of this book.[1]

3-24. Relation of Series Coefficients to Tube Characteristics.— The ratio of a_2 to a_1 for the special case of resistance load and constant amplification factor is found from Eqs. (3-33) to be proportional to $r_p/(r_t + r_b)^2$.   This rapidly approaches zero as r_b is increased relative to r_p.   The ratios of a_3 and other higher-order coefficients to a_1 decrease even more rapidly with increase of r_b.   A similar analysis for the more general case of impedance load, although not quite so simple, also shows that in general the amplitudes of the second- and higher-order terms of the series are decreased relative to the amplitude of the first term by increase of load impedance and, if μ were constant, could be reduced to any desired degree by making z_b/r_p sufficiently high.

Equations (3-32) and (3-33) show that for resistance load the dynamic transfer characteristic would be a straight line if the series contained only the first term and that the presence of the higher-order terms is associated with curvature of the dynamic transfer characteristic.   If only the first term were present, a change of grid voltage Δe_c would result in a proportional change of plate current Δi_b, indicating a linear relation between i_b and e_c.   The higher-order terms of the series destroy this linearity, since contributions to Δi_b from the higher-order terms are not proportional to Δe_c.   Reduction of the higher-order terms of the series by increase of load resistance is therefore accompanied by reduction of the curvature of the dynamic transfer characteristic.

That the transfer characteristic of a triode is straightened by the introduction of plate load resistance and, hence, that the amplitudes of the second and higher terms of the series are reduced with respect to the first term can also be shown by constructing dynamic transfer characteristics for different values of load resistance.   Although the dynamic transfer character-

[1] JACKSON, W., *Phil. Mag.*, **13**, 143, 735 (1932); SCHLESINGER, K., *E.N.T.*, **38**, 144 (1931).

istics can be most readily obtained from the plate family of characteristics in a manner that will be explained in Chap. 4, it is instructive at this point to derive one from the static transfer characteristics. O represents the static operating point in

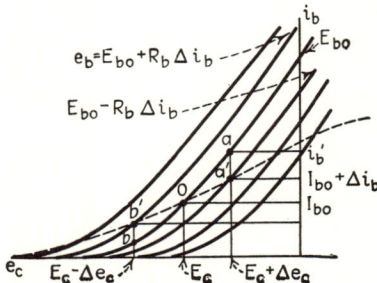

Fig. 3-22. With no external resistance in the plate circuit a change of grid voltage from E_c to $E_c + \Delta e_c$ would cause the current to change to i_b', corresponding to a new point a on the same static characteristic. With resistance in the plate circuit, however, the increase of plate current accompanying the change in grid voltage increases the IR drop in the plate circuit

Fig. 3-22.—Construction of dynamic transfer characteristic from family of static transfer characteristics.

and thus reduces the voltage of the plate to a new value $E_{bo} - R_b \Delta i_b$, corresponding to point a'. Similarly, if the grid voltage is changed to $E_c - \Delta e_c$, the point shifts to b'. By plotting corresponding values of i_b and e_c it is possible to obtain the complete

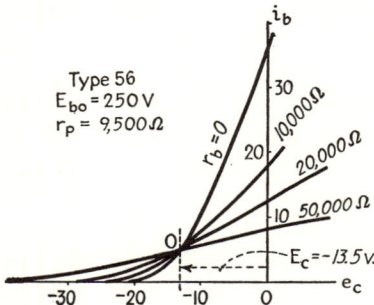

Fig. 3-23.—Dynamic transfer characteristics of the type 56 triode for four values of load resistance at fixed operating voltages. $r_b = R_b$.

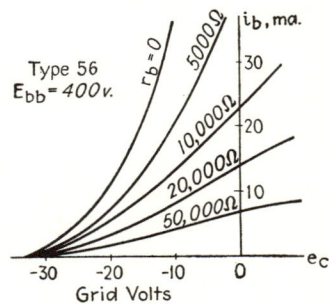

Fig. 3-24.—Dynamic transfer characteristics of the type 56 triode for five values of load resistance at fixed plate supply voltage.

dynamic transfer characteristic, shown by the dashed line. Figure 3-23 shows the dynamic transfer characteristics of a type 56 triode for various values of resistance load, the plate supply voltage being increased with R_b in such a manner as to maintain the same static operating point. Figure 3-24 shows similar curves for constant plate supply voltage.

At large values of grid excitation voltage, the amplification factor of pentodes is not constant throughout the range of operation and, although the curvature of the transfer characteristic first decreases with increase of load resistance, a value is reached beyond which curvature again increases (see Sec. 6-25).

When the load contains reactance, as well as resistance, the behavior is complicated by the phase difference between the plate voltage and plate current. If the impedance is sufficiently high, the dynamic transfer characteristic obtained with sinusoidal excitation is nearly elliptical. For lower values of impedance the dynamic transfer characteristic resembles an ellipse but has a curved axis, as shown for inductive reactance in Fig. 3-25. As the reactance is reduced, the path of operation gradually changes into the curve obtained for pure resistance (see Sec. 4-6).

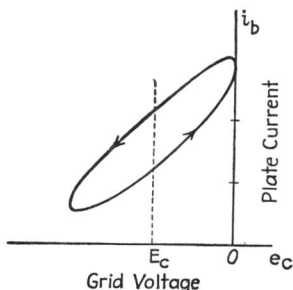

FIG. 3-25.—Typical dynamic transfer characteristic for load containing inductance.

3-25. Dynamic Plate Resistance.—The *dynamic plate resistance* is the quotient of the alternating plate voltage by the inphase component of the alternating plate current, all other electrode voltages being maintained constant. The quadrature component of current, which results from electrode capacitances and, at ultrahigh frequencies from electron transit time, is negligible at low audio frequency. The inphase component of plate current corresponding to a given alternating plate voltage when other electrode voltages are constant may be found from Eqs. (3-32), (3-33), and (3-34) by making e_g and r_b zero. When r_b is zero, $v_p = e_p$, and Eq. (3-32) becomes

$$i_p = \frac{e_p}{r_p} - \frac{e_p^2}{2r_p^2}\frac{\partial r_p}{\partial e_b} + \frac{e_p^3}{6r_p^3}\left(2\frac{\partial r_p}{\partial e_b} - r_p\frac{\partial^2 r_p}{\partial e_b^2}\right) + \cdots \quad (3\text{-}38)$$

Because of curvature of the static plate characteristics, the derivatives of the plate resistance are not zero. When the excitation voltage is high, therefore, the second- and higher-order terms of Eq. (3-38) are not negligible. Contributions of the third- and other odd-order terms to the fundamental component of plate current cause the ratio of the alternating plate voltage to the fundamental component of alternating plate current to differ from r_p, the static plate resistance. As e_p is reduced, however, the ratio of the higher-order terms to the first term decreases, and e_p/i_p approaches r_p. If the amplitude of the plate excitation voltage is small enough, the dynamic plate resistance approximates the value determined from the slope of the static characteristic at the operating point (at frequencies low enough so that the electron transit time is negligible). The static plate resistance may, therefore, be found dynamically by using a sufficiently small plate excitation voltage. In a similar manner it may be shown that the dynamic measurement of transconductance and of variable amplification factor requires the use of small excitation voltages.

Problems

3-1. From the static plate characteristics of the type 6J5 tube find the values of μ, r_p, and g_m at the point $E_b = 200$ volts, $E_c = -8$ volts.

3-2. From the static plate characteristics of the type 6SJ7 tube, find the values of μ, r_p, and g_m at the point $E_b = 200$ volts, $E_c = -2$ volts.

3-3. *a.* From the following data find approximate values of μ, r_p, and g_m at the point $E_b = 180$ volts, $E_c = -12.5$ volts. (Note that only two of these factors can be found directly from the data given.)

E_b, volts	E_c, volts	I_b, ma
180	-12.5	7.5
160	-10.0	7.5
180	-12.3	7.84

b. From the following data find approximate values of μ, r_p, and g_m at the point $E_b = 250$ volts, $E_c = -16$ volts.

E_b, volts	E_c, volts	I_b, ma
250	-16	2.0
220	-14	2.0
260	-16	3.0

3-4. Determine the frequencies of all components of alternating plate current associated with the first three terms of the plate-current series when the frequencies 60, 100, and 900 are simultaneously impressed upon the grid of a vacuum tube.

CHAPTER 4

METHODS OF ANALYSIS OF VACUUM TUBES AND VACUUM-TUBE CIRCUITS

Since the application of vacuum tubes is governed in part by the extent to which it is possible to analyze the operation of tubes and associated circuits a study of the methods of analysis is of considerable importance. This chapter will therefore present analytical and graphical methods of analysis of high-vacuum tubes and their circuits.

4-1. The Equivalent Plate Circuit.[1]—In the solution of many vacuum-tube problems, particularly when the excitation voltage is small and the load impedance high, sufficient accuracy is obtained by making use of only the first term of the series expansion for the plate current [Eqs. (3-36), (3-37)]. To a first approximation the alternating plate current is then given by the equations

$$i_p = \frac{\mu e}{r_p + z_b} = \frac{\mu e}{r_p + r_b + jx_b} \tag{4-1}$$

$$= \frac{\mu e}{\sqrt{(r_p + r_b)^2 + x_b^2}} \, \underline{/\theta} \tag{4-2}$$

where

$$e = \frac{v_p}{\mu} + e_g \qquad \text{and} \qquad \theta = -\tan^{-1}\frac{x_b}{r_p + r_b}$$

In these equations r_p is the plate resistance at the operating point, and z_b is the impedance of the plate load at the frequency of the applied voltage. The value of i_p given by Eqs. (4-1) and (4-2) is the same as that which would flow in the simple series circuit of Fig. 4-1. This *equivalent plate circuit* may, therefore, be used to find the approximate value of the fundamental com-

---

[1] MILLER, J. M., *Bur. Standards Bull.* 15, 367 (1911); *Proc. I.R.E.*, **6**, 141 (1918). VAN DER BIJL, H. J., *Phys. Rev.*, **12**, 171 (1918); *Proc. I.R.E.*, **7**, 97 (1919). CHAFFEE, E. L., *Proc. I.R.E.*, **17**, 1633 (1929). GOODHUE, W. M., *Electronics*, December, 1933, p. 341. RICHTER, W., *Electronics*, March, 1936, p. 19. LANDON, V. D., *Proc. I.R.E.*, **18**, 294 (1930).

ponent of plate current and of the currents in the various branches of the load impedance This fact may be expressed in the form of the *equivalent-plate-circuit theorem for amplification,* which states that the fundamental component of alternating plate current is approximately equal to the current that flows as the result of the application of the voltage $v_p + \mu e_g$ to an equivalent circuit consisting of the external load impedance in series with a

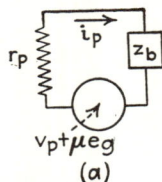

FIG. 4-1.— Series equivalent plate circuit for amplification.

constant resistance equal to the a-c plate resistance of the tube at the operating point.

A similar equivalent circuit for any other electrode may be derived from the first term of the series expansion for the current to that electrode. For applications in which the voltage of only the current electrode and of one other electrode is varied, the equivalent circuits are of the same form as that of Fig. 4-1, the subscripts and amplification factor being replaced by corresponding symbols applying to the electrodes in question. The equivalent circuit for the grid of a triode, for instance, is obtained by replacing the subscripts p, g, and b by g, p, and c, and μ by μ_g.

Equation (4-1) is based upon Fig. 3-18, in which the load impedance is assumed to be free of e.m.fs. and the plate excitation voltage v_p is assumed to be in series with z_b. The load impedance is in general made up of a number of branches that may contain other e.m.fs., in addition to or in place of the e.m.f. in series with the entire impedance. Application of the principle of superposition, which is valid under the assumption that the second- and higher-order terms of the plate current series may be neglected, shows that the presence of additional alternating e.m.fs. in z_b does not affect the currents caused by e_g or by a voltage v_p in series with z_b. The equivalent circuit will, therefore, give the correct values of currents if the additional alternating voltages are included in the equivalent circuit in the positions that they occupy in the actual circuit. The equivalent plate circuit must include all circuit elements that are conductively, inductively, or capacitively coupled to the plate. Since Eqs. (4-1) and (4-2) may also be written in terms of r-m-s or crest values, the equivalent circuit may be used to find instantaneous, r-m-s, or crest values of fundamental currents and voltages.

The use of equivalent circuits greatly simplifies the solution of many problems involving tubes and associated circuits. Once the equivalent circuit has been formed, it is not even necessary to know that a vacuum tube is involved, as currents and voltages at various points may be computed by the ordinary methods of a-c circuit analysis. The validity of the equivalent circuit in a given problem depends upon the desired accuracy. If only qualitative results are desired, it is often possible to apply the equivalent circuit even when the harmonic production is high. Where a high degree of accuracy is essential, the use of the equivalent circuit is valid only at small amplitudes. It cannot be applied when the conditions of operation are such that current ceases to flow during a portion of the cycle of exciting voltage (see Sec. 5-14). The equivalent circuit obviously gives no indication of the production of harmonics and intermodulation frequencies.

Since the grid conducts only when it is positive and since the grid characteristics are not linear, the flow of grid current through external impedance distorts the alternating grid voltage. Furthermore, the grid current varies with plate voltage. For these reasons the simple equivalent plate circuit is not applicable with accuracy when grid current flows through a grid-circuit impedance. Ordinarily, however, in circuits in which appreciable grid current is allowed to flow, the conditions of operation are such that the equivalent circuit would not be applicable even if no grid current flowed. In such circuits it is necessary to resort to graphical or experimental methods of analysis.

4-2. Construction of Equivalent Circuits.—Use of the following procedure ensures that voltage and current polarities are correct in the equivalent circuit:

1. In the actual circuit diagram, show the instantaneous grid excitation voltage v_g in such polarity as to make the grid *positive*.

2. Show the instantaneous plate current i_p flowing *into* the plate.

3. Insert the equivalent voltage μe_g, in series with the operating plate resistance r_p, between the plate and the cathode, choosing the polarity of the equivalent voltage so that it would cause i_p to flow *in the indicated direction*.

4. Assume positive directions for the other instantaneous circuit currents.

5. Delete the tube symbol (or show dotted), the batteries, and all circuit elements not coupled to the plate (such as the screen circuit).

6. Redraw the resulting equivalent circuit in the form in which it may be most readily analyzed.

The value of the instantaneous grid voltage e_g may differ from the exciting voltage v_g applied from an external source if the plate circuit is coupled in any manner to the grid circuit as, for instance, in Fig. 4-2. In general, therefore, it is necessary to evaluate e_g in terms of v_g and circuit parameters and currents before the circuit can be solved. e_g is usually most readily found from the actual circuit and is equal to the vector sum of all *alternating* voltages between the cathode and the grid along any continuous path.

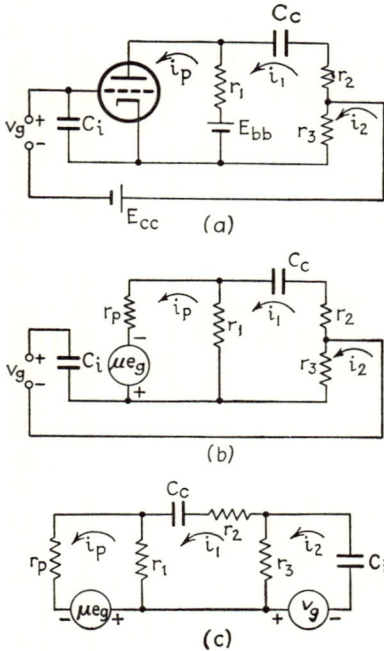

This procedure is not restricted to the plate circuit, but may be used in forming the equivalent circuit of any electrode. It is merely necessary to use in place of r_p the appropriate symbol for the resistance of the electrode for which the circuit is being formed, in place of μ the mu-factor relating that electrode and the electrode which serves as the control electrode, and for e_g the excitation voltage applied to the control electrode. If two electrodes serve as control electrodes simultaneously, then the equivalent circuit contains two equivalent voltages in series with the electrode resistance. Thus, if excitation is applied to the third grid of a pentode in order to vary the current to the second grid, the equivalent circuit of the second grid contains the equivalent voltage $\mu_{23}e_{g3}$ in series with the resistance r_{g2} of the second grid. If the excitation is applied simultaneously to the third grid and to the first grid, then the equivalent circuit

Fig. 4-2.—*a*. Tube circuit. *b*. Corresponding equivalent plate circuit. *c*. Equivalent plate circuit after rearrangement.

of the second grid contains the two equivalent voltages $\mu_{23}e_{g3}$ and $\mu_{21}e_{g1}$ in series with r_{g2}.

The method of constructing the equivalent circuit and of finding the value of e_c to be used in the equivalent circuit is illustrated by the following example. Figure 4-2a shows the circuit of an amplifier in which a portion of the output voltage is impressed in the grid circuit. Application of steps (1) to (5) of the above procedure to Fig. 4-2a gives the equivalent circuit of Fig. 4-2b, which may be rearranged into the more convenient form of Fig. 4-2c. The most direct path between cathode and grid is through C_i. The magnitude of e_g is equal to the product of i_2 and the reactance of C_i and, since increase of i_2 tends to make the grid negative relative to the cathode, the sign of e_g is opposite to that of i_2. Therefore $e_g = -i_2/j\omega C_i$. An alternative path from cathode to grid is through r_3 and v_g. Hence e_g is also equal to $v_g + (i_2 - i_1)r_3$. Either of these expressions for e_g and the three equations obtained by summing voltages in the three loops of the equivalent circuit may be solved simultaneously to find the values of the currents in terms of the circuit constants and v_g. If C_i were omitted, then i_2 would be zero and e_g would be equal to $v_g - i_1r_3$. The right-hand loop of the equivalent circuit of Fig. 4-2c would also be omitted.

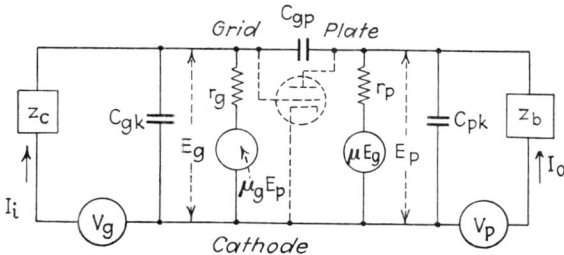

FIG. 4-3.—Complete equivalent circuit of triode with negligible leakage conductances. C_{gk}, C_{gp}, and C_{pk} are the interelectrode capacitances.

4-3. Tube Capacitances and Admittances.—The complete equivalent circuit is not so simple as that which has been presented up to this point. The small interelectrode capacitances and the conductances caused by surface leakage or by electron or ion currents between grid and cathode or grid and plate cannot always be neglected. Fortunately this does not invalidate the equivalent-circuit theorems, inasmuch as the interelectrode capacitances and conductances act the same as equal capacitances and conductances connected externally between the electrodes. It is permissible, therefore, to add them to the simple equivalent grid and plate circuits as parts of the external impedances. In modern tubes of good manufacture the leakage conductances are so small that they can usually be neglected in comparison with other tube and circuit conductances. Figure 4-3 shows the complete equivalent circuit of a triode (or any tube in which only the plate and control-grid voltages are allowed to vary) with negligible leakage conductances.

The rather involved formulas for the total grid and plate admittances which may be derived by the solution of the network of Fig. 4-3[1] are seldom useful. In most circuits in which electron grid current is allowed to flow, harmonic generation is so great that the equivalent plate circuit is not applicable. More frequently used are the somewhat less complicated formulas for the case in which the grid bias is sufficiently great to prevent the flow of thermionic grid current. Approximate forms of these formulas can be obtained by an analysis based upon the circuit of Fig. 4-4. Figure 4-3 reduces to that of Fig. 4-4 when thermionic grid current does not flow.

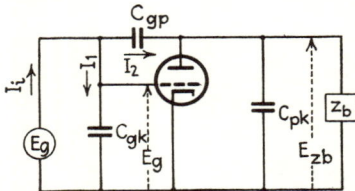

Fig. 4-4.—Circuit of triode with impedance load, showing interelectrode capacitances.

The input current I_i in the equivalent circuit of Fig. 4-4 is the vector sum of two components: I_1, which flows through C_{gk}, and I_2, which flows through C_{gp}. The voltage which causes I_1 is E_g, whereas that which causes I_2 is the vector difference between E_g and E_{zb}. Application of the equivalent-plate-circuit theorem shows that

$$E_{zb} = - \frac{\mu E_g z_b{}'}{r_p + z_b{}'} \qquad (4\text{-}3)$$

where $z_b{}'$ is the resultant impedance of the load z_b, in parallel with C_{pk} and C_{gp}.[2] The vector difference between E_g and E_{zb} is

[1] Chaffee, E. L., *Proc. I.R.E.*, **17**, 1633 (1929); Colebrook, F. M., *Wireless Eng.*, **10**, 657 (1933). See also J. M. Miller, *Bur. Standards Sci. Paper* 351 (1919); S. Ballantine, *Phys. Rev.*, **15**, 409 (1920).

[2] Actually, C_{gp} shunts z_b through E_g, so that this value of $z_b{}'$ is approximately correct only when E_{zb} is much larger than E_g, which is usually so.

$E_g + \mu E_g z_b'/(r_p + z_b')$, and the input current is

$$I_i = I_1 + I_2 = E_g j\omega C_{gk} + E_g j\omega C_{gp}\left(1 + \frac{\mu z_b'}{r_p + z_b'}\right) \quad (4\text{-}4)$$

When the load is a pure resistance r_b, which is small in comparison with the reactance of C_{pk} and C_{gp} in parallel, z_b' is approximately r_b, and the approximate input admittance is

$$Y_g = \frac{I_i}{E_g} = j\omega\left[C_{gk} + C_{gp}\left(1 + \frac{\mu r_b}{r_p + r_b}\right)\right] \quad (4\text{-}5)$$

Y_g increases with the ratio of r_b to r_p and, if the reactance of $C_{pk} + C_{gp}$ is large in comparison with r_p, approaches the limiting value $j\omega[C_{gk} + C_{gp}(1 + \mu)]$. The limiting value of effective input capacitance is

$$C_i = \frac{Y_g}{j\omega} = C_{gk} + C_{gp}(1 + \mu) \quad (4\text{-}6)$$

For pure reactance load x_b, small in comparison with the reactance of $C_{pk} + C_{gp}$, the input admittance is approximately

$$Y_g = j\omega\left[C_{gk} + C_{gp}\left(1 + \mu\frac{x_b^2}{r_p^2 + x_b^2}\right)\right] - \mu\frac{r_p x_b \omega C_{gp}}{r_p^2 + x_b^2} \quad (4\text{-}7)$$

If the reactance of $C_{pk} + C_{gp}$ is much larger than r_p, the effective input capacitance approaches the value given by Eq. (4-6) as the ratio of x_b to r_p is increased. The input conductance, given by the second term of Eq. (4-7), is zero when x_b is zero, rises to a maximum value at $x_b = r_p$, and then falls with further increase of x_b. When the load is an inductance L_b, the input conductance is negative and has an approximate maximum value

$$\text{Max } G_g = -\tfrac{1}{2}\mu\omega C_{gp} \quad (4\text{-}8)$$

It must be remembered that this analysis is an approximation and that Eqs. (4-5) to (4-8) yield sufficiently accurate results only when the reactance of $C_{pk} + C_{gp}$ is considerably larger than r_p and z_b. The effect of the capacitance $C_{pk} + C_{gp}$ is usually to decrease z_b' and thus to reduce the effective input capacitance below the value given by Eq. (4-6). This equation is, therefore, useful in indicating approximately the largest value of C_i that is likely to be obtained. At 10,000 cycles the reactance of $C_{pk} + C_{gp}$ is of the order of 1 to 3 megohms in receiving tubes and so does affect the value of Y_g of pentodes, tetrodes, and high-mu triodes even at audio frequencies.

More accurate values of input admittance may be found by laboratory measurement or by the use of equations derived by a more rigorous method.[1] It should be noted that the foregoing analysis neglects electron transit time, which has an appreciable effect upon tube admittances at ultrahigh frequencies. The approximate analysis shows that the increase of effective input capacitance over that obtained when the cathode is cold results from the action of E_{zb} in sending current through C_{gp}.

The fact that the input conductance may be negative when the plate load contains inductance is of importance because oscillation may take place when an oscillatory circuit shunts a negative resistance (see Sec. 8-2). It will be shown in Chap. 6 that the input capacitance must be taken into consideration in the analysis of vacuum-tube amplifiers at frequencies above about 2000 cycles per sec.

4-4. Graphical Methods.—Many vacuum-tube problems can be solved most readily by graphical methods based upon the plate or transfer families of characteristics.[2] In certain cases there is some advantage in the use of the transfer characteristics, but the usefulness of the plate characteristics is much broader. This results partly from the fact that with nonreactive load the locus of corresponding values of plate current and plate voltage assumed during the cycle with a given load is a straight line in an i_b-e_b diagram, and partly because certain areas of the i_b-e_b diagram are proportional to power supplied or expended in various parts of the plate circuit.

4-5. Static Load Line.—When the excitation voltages are zero, the plate current and voltage assume their quiescent values, which are related by Eq. (3-28). This equation may be written in the form

$$I_{bo} = \frac{E_{bb} - E_{bo}}{R_b} \tag{4-9}$$

If R_b is constant, Eq. (4-9) is that of a straight line intersecting

[1] See, for instance, Chaffee, *loc. cit.*, or H. J. Reich, "Theory and Applications of Electron Tubes," Sec. 4-2.

[2] WARNER, J. C., and LOUGHREN, A. V., *Proc. I.R.E.*, **14**, 735 (1926); GREEN, E., *Wireless Eng.*, **3**, 402, 469 (1926); GRÜNWALD, E., *T.F.T.*, **22**, 306 (1933); COCKING, W. T., *Wireless Eng.*, **11**, 655 (1934).

the voltage axis at the point $e_b = E_{bb}$ and having a negative slope in amperes per volt equal to the reciprocal of the d-c load resistance. Occasionally the d-c load resistance may vary with I_{bo}. Then Eq. (4-9) is that of a curve passing through the point on the voltage axis where $e_b = E_{bb}$. Static load lines for fixed and variable load resistance are illustrated in Figs. 4-5a and 4-5b. The line represented by Eq. (4-9) is the locus of all static operating points that can be assumed with the given d-c load resistance and plate supply voltage, and is called the *static load line*. From a comparison of Eqs. (3-27) and (3-28) it follows that all corresponding values of average plate current and average plate voltage assumed with excitation must also lie on the static load line.

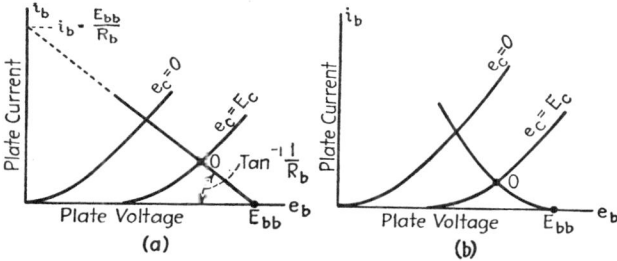

FIG. 4-5.—Static load line for (a) fixed d-c load resistance and (b) d-c load resistance that varies with current.

For constant d-c load resistance and given plate supply voltage, the static load line may be constructed by drawing a straight line through the point $e_b = E_{bb}$ on the voltage axis and through any other point whose coordinates satisfy Eq. (4-9). If the d-c load resistance is not too small, the intercept on the current axis, for which $i_b = E_{bb}/R_b$, may be conveniently used. The static operating point for a particular grid bias may then be determined from the intersection of the load line with the static characteristic corresponding to the given bias. Similarly, for a given operating point, the static load line is drawn through this point and through any other point whose coordinates satisfy Eq. (4-9). Although the required plate supply voltage may then be found from the intersection of the load line with the voltage axis, it may be determined with greater accuracy from Eq. (4-9). If the d-c load resistance is a function of the steady plate current, the static load line may be constructed by making use of the fact, shown by Eq. (4-9), that the static load line is a curve of current through the load *vs.* voltage drop through the load.   The load voltage drop is plotted in the negative direction relative to E_{bb}.

4-6. Dynamic Path of Operation.   Dynamic Load Line.—The locus of all corresponding values of instantaneous plate current and plate voltage assumed during the cycle with a given value of load impedance is called the *dynamic path of operation*.   Under the assumption that the alternating plate current is sinusoidal, the instantaneous alternating plate current and plate voltage are

$$i_p = I_{pm} \sin \omega t \qquad (4\text{-}10)$$
$$e_p = -I_{pm} z_b \sin (\omega t + \theta) \qquad (4\text{-}11)$$

(see Eq. 3-29) where

$$\theta = \tan^{-1} \frac{x_b}{r_b} \qquad (4\text{-}12)$$

Expanding $\sin (\omega t + \theta)$ and substituting Eq. (4-10) in Eq. (4-11) gives

$$-e_p = i_p z_b \cos \theta + z_b \sqrt{I_{pm}{}^2 - i_p{}^2} \sin \theta \qquad (4\text{-}13)$$

Transposing, squaring, and substituting r_b/z_b and x_b/z_b for $\cos \theta$ and $\sin \theta$ simplify Eq. (4-13) to:

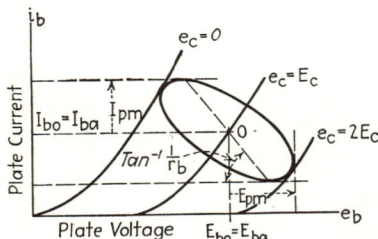

$$e_p{}^2 + 2e_p i_p r_b + i_p{}^2 z_b{}^2 = I_{pm}{}^2 x_b{}^2 \qquad (4\text{-}14)$$

This is the equation of an ellipse whose center is at the operating point.   It follows that the dynamic path of operation is an ellipse whose center is the operating point, as shown in Fig. 4-6. When $i_p = I_{pm}$, Eq. (4-14) reduces to $I_{pm}/e_p = -1/r_b$, indicating that the slope of the line joining the operating point with the points of tangency of the ellipse to the upper and lower horizontal tangents is the reciprocal of the a-c load resistance.

Fig. 4-6.—Path of operation for load containing reactance.   Distortion assumed to be negligible.

The presence of harmonics in the plate current and voltage causes the path of operation to depart from the elliptical form indicated by an analysis based only upon the fundamental component.   Graphical methods of analysis are most useful when harmonic production is not negligible.   Since the true path of operation cannot be determined until the harmonic content is known, however, and the path of operation is needed for the determination of harmonic content, graphical analysis is rather complicated when the load reactance is taken into consideration.[1] For this reason it is customary to make the assumption that the load is nonreactive. Although the results attained under this assumption are not rigorous, they are of considerable value in predicting the performance of vacuum-tube circuits. If $x_b = 0$, Eq. (4-14) reduces to

$$e_p + i_p r_b = 0 \qquad\qquad (4\text{-}15)$$

which is the equation of a straight line through the static operating point having a negative slope equal to the reciprocal of the a-c load resistance. This line, which represents the locus of all corresponding values of plate current and voltage assumed during the cycle with the given resistance load, is called the *dynamic load line*. If the a-c load resistance varies with plate current, as is usually true if the plate is coupled to the grid of a tube that passes grid current, then the dynamic load line is a curve whose slope at every point is the reciprocal of the a-c resistance corresponding to the current at that point. The dynamic load line will be indicated by the letters M-N, as in Figs. 4-7, 4-10, and 4-11.

4-7. Construction of the Load Line. Plate Diagram.—Possible confusion, caused by the fact that the slope of the load line is measured in mhos, is avoided by the use of the equivalent units, amperes per volt. The slope of the dynamic load line must be such that $\Delta e_b / \Delta i_b = r_b$ in ohms, or volts per ampere, where Δe_b and Δi_b are the differences of voltage and current of any two points on the line. Similarly, the slope of the static load line must be such that $\Delta e_b / \Delta i_b = R_b$ in volts per ampere, where Δe_b and Δi_b are the differences of voltage and current of any two points on that line.

The family of plate characteristics, together with the static and dynamic load lines, is called the *plate-circuit diagram*, or simply the *plate diagram*. In the derivations and analyses presented in the remainder of this book, the reactive component of load impedance will be neglected in the construction of plate-circuit diagrams.

[1] GREEN, *loc. cit.;* ARDENNE, M. VON, *Proc. I.R.E.*, **16**, 193 (1928); BARCLAY, W. A., *Wireless Eng.*, **5**, 660 (1928); PREISMAN, A., *RCA Rev.*, **2**, 124, 240 (1937) (with bibliography).

Figure 4-7 shows the plate diagram for a circuit in which the load is a pure resistance. Since the a-c and d-c load resistances are equal, the static and dynamic load lines coincide. In Fig. 4-7 the path of operation and the shape of the static characteristics are such that the current amplitude of the positive half cycle exceeds that of the negative. The average plate current,

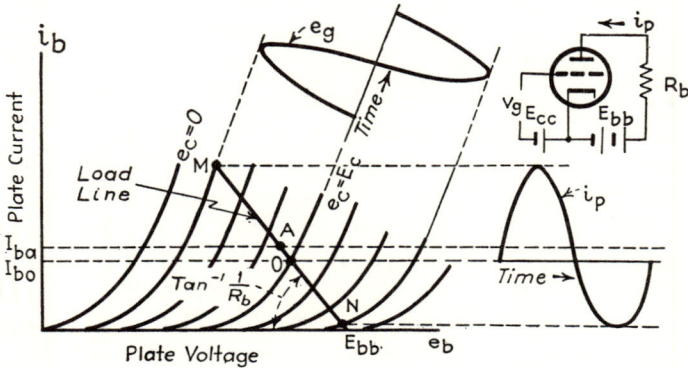

Fig. 4-7.—Triode plate diagram. Pure resistance load. $r_b = R_b$.

therefore, increases with excitation and the dynamic operating point A lies above the static operating point O. In general, the position of A relative to O depends upon the region of operation and the shape of the static characteristics.

Fig. 4-8.—Circuit in which the a-c resistance between the terminals exceeds the d-c resistance.

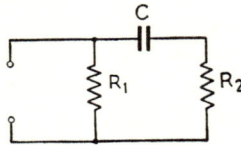

Fig. 4-9.—Circuit in which the a-c resistance between the terminals is less than the d-c resistance.

Usually the a-c resistance of the load differs from the d-c resistance. Figure 4-8 shows a circuit in which the a-c resistance exceeds the d-c resistance. The d-c resistance is merely the resistance R_1 of the transformer. The a-c resistance, however, is equal to $R_1 + \dfrac{M^2\omega^2(R_2 + R)}{(R_2 + R)^2 + \omega^2 L_2{}^2}$. For an iron-core transformer this may usually be simplified to $R_1 + \dfrac{R_2 + R}{n^2}$, where n is the turn ratio.[1] Figure 4-9 shows a circuit in which the a-c resistance is less than the d-c resistance. The d-c resistance is R_1, whereas the a-c resistance approaches that of R_1 and R_2 in parallel as the frequency is increased.

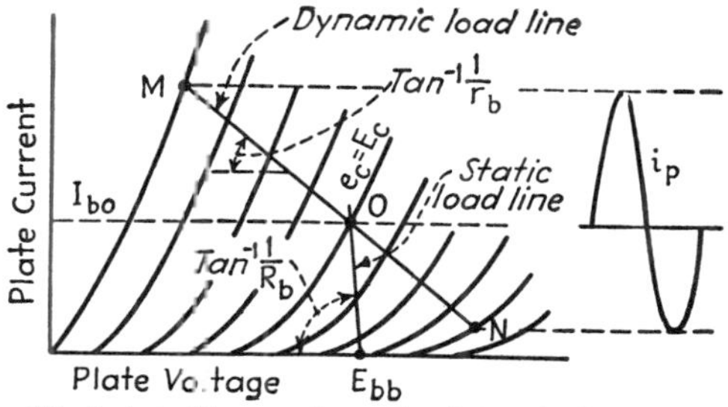

FIG. 4-10.—Simplified plate diagram for a circuit in which the a-c resistance of the load exceeds the d-c resistance.

Figure 4-10 shows a simplified plate diagram for a circuit in which the a-c resistance of the load exceeds the d-c resistance. A rigorous analysis shows that the dynamic operating point A lies above or below O on the static load line, and that the dynamic load line should pass through this point, as shown in Fig. 4-11,

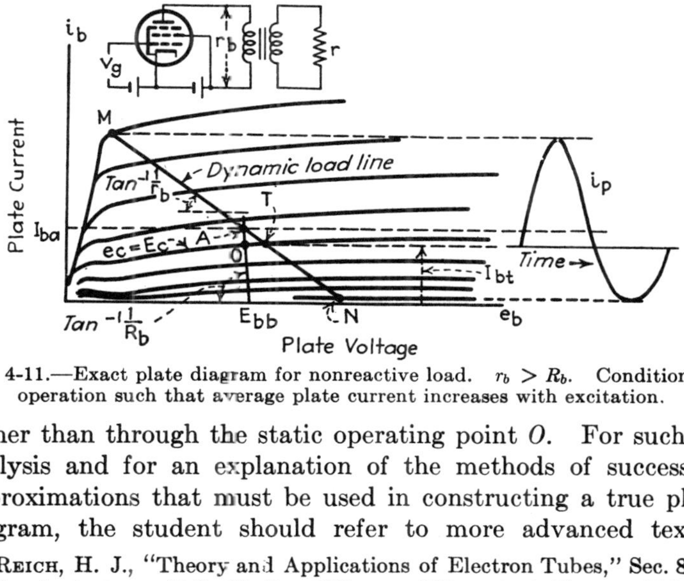

FIG. 4-11.—Exact plate diagram for nonreactive load. $r_b > R_b$. Conditions of operation such that average plate current increases with excitation.

rather than through the static operating point O. For such an analysis and for an explanation of the methods of successive approximations that must be used in constructing a true plate diagram, the student should refer to more advanced texts.[2]

[1] REICH, H. J., "Theory and Applications of Electron Tubes," Sec. 8-20.

[2] See, for instance, E. L. Chaffee, "Theory of Thermionic Vacuum Tubes," pp. 201–213, McGraw-Hill Book Company, Inc., New York, 1933; H. J. Reich, *op. cit.*, pp. 92–107.

Errors resulting from the use of the simplified plate diagram in the graphical study of vacuum-tube circuits are appreciable only when there is a relatively large change in average plate current with excitation, as there may be, for instance, in pentode circuits.

4-7A. Operating Point for Tubes with Filamentary Cathodes.— In obtaining the data for the static characteristics of a tube with a filamentary cathode, the filaments are always operated on direct voltage, and the grid and plate voltages are measured with respect to the negative end of the filament. When such a tube is operated with alternating filament voltage, the grid and plate circuits are connected to the filament through a center tap on the filament transformer or through a center-tapped resistor shunting the filament (see Sec. 5-12), and the operating grid bias is specified with respect to the center tap. Therefore the numerical value of bias used in locating the operating point graphically under a-c operation is less, by one-half the filament voltage, than the voltage specified or applied between the grid and center of the filament. In families of plate characteristics furnished by tube manufacturers, the static characteristic corresponding to specified operating voltages with respect to the center of the filament is often shown as a dotted curve. The filament voltage is ordinarily so much smaller than the plate voltage that no correction need be made in the plate voltage in locating the operating point.

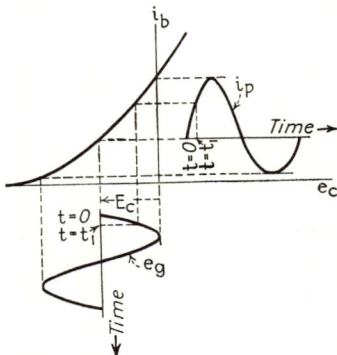

Fig. 4-12.—Use of the dynamic transfer characteristic in the graphical construction of the plate-current wave.

4-8. Applications of the Plate Diagram.—Dynamic transfer characteristics may be readily derived from the plate diagram by plotting corresponding values of i_b and e_c for the points at which the dynamic load line intersects the static characteristics. The dynamic transfer characteristic can then be used to determine the wave form of the plate current for a given wave of alternating grid voltage. From the values of instantaneous grid voltage at various points in the cycle the corresponding values of current are determined by reference to the curve, or the current wave may be constructed by projection, as in Fig. 4-12. Other applications of the plate diagram will be discussed in later sections.

It is sometimes convenient to indicate the range over which the grid voltage varies by showing the wave of alternating grid voltage on an extension of the static characteristic through the operating point, as in Fig. 4-7. It should be noted that because the static characteristics for equal intervals of grid voltage are not usually equally spaced, the wave of plate current cannot be accurately constructed by projecting from the grid-voltage wave to the load line.

4-9. Graphical Analysis of Plate Current.—Graphical methods of analyzing the plate current of a vacuum tube are based upon the assumption that for sinusoidal excitation voltage the plate current contains a finite number of frequency components, or upon the equivalent assumption that the plate current may be expressed as a finite series. If as many instantaneous values of current can be determined graphically as there are components, or terms in the series, simultaneous equations can be set up from which the amplitudes may be computed. A number of interesting and useful methods have been developed, which differ from one another mainly as to choice of the points of the cycle at which the currents are evaluated.[1] The accuracy and convenience of these methods depend upon the manner in which the selected currents are chosen. The currents may be evaluated at equal time intervals of the excitation cycle, as exemplified by the method of Lucas; they may be evaluated at equal grid-voltage intervals, as in Espley's method; or they may be evaluated at such instants as to give the highest accuracy. The advantage of the second method lies in the fact that the grid voltages at which the current is evaluated may often be made to coincide with those of the static plate characteristics, so that the currents may be read directly from the intersections of the dynamic load line with these static characteristics. Chaffee has developed a more general method which includes all three of these special methods.[2]

In the treatment that follows, it will be assumed that the load is nonreactive. The path of operation is then a straight line, and

[1] See bibliography at end of chapter.
[2] CHAFFEE, E. L., *Rev. Sci. Instruments*, **7**, 384 (1936).

evaluating the current at a given number of points on the path of operation is equivalent to evaluating at twice that number of instants in the fundamental cycle. It is sometimes convenient to differentiate between methods of analysis according to the number of instantaneous values of current that are used to determine the amplitudes of the fundamental and harmonic frequency components. Thus a five-point analysis is one in which the current is evaluated at five points of the path of operation or of the dynamic transfer characteristic, or at 10 instants in the fundamental period.

Substitution of the sinusoidal voltage $E_{gm} \sin \omega t$ for the excitation voltage e in the series expansion for i_p [Eq. (3-32)], gives

$$i_p = a_1 E_{gm} \sin \omega t + a_2 E_{gm}^2 \sin^2 \omega t + a_3 E_{gm}^3 \sin^3 \omega t \\ + a_4 E_{gm}^4 \sin^4 \omega t + \cdots \quad (4\text{-}16)$$

which may be written in the form

$$i_p = H_0 + H_1 \sin \omega t - H_2 \cos 2\omega t - H_3 \sin 3\omega t + H_4 \cos 4\omega t \\ + H_5 \sin 5\omega t - \cdots \quad (4\text{-}17)$$

in which H_n is the amplitude of the nth harmonic component of the alternating plate current and H_0 is the steady component of alternating plate current. Under the simplifying assumption, discussed in Sec. 4-7, that the dynamic load line passes through the static operating point, the axis of the wave of alternating current also passes through the static operating point, as in Figs. 4-10 and 4-13, and the total instantaneous plate current is[1]

$$i_b = I_{bo} + i_p = I_{bo} + H_0 + H_1 \sin \omega t - H_2 \cos 2\omega t - H_3 \sin 3\omega t \\ + H_4 \cos 4\omega t + H_5 \sin 5\omega t - \cdots \quad (4\text{-}18)$$

Formulas must be derived for the coefficients of Eq. (4-18) in terms of selected values of instantaneous plate current. The accuracy of these formulas for harmonic amplitudes increases with the number of points of the fundamental cycle at which the current is evaluated and also depends upon the location of these points in the cycle. The variation of the instantaneous total plate current with amplitude of a given harmonic is greatest at

[1] As shown by Fig. 4-11, the axis of the wave actually passes through the point T, determined by the intersection of the dynamic load line with the static plate characteristic for which $e_c = E_c$, and I_{bt} should be used in Eq. (4-18), in place of I_{bo}. The error resulting from the use of I_{bo} is small unless I_{ba} differs appreciably from I_{bo}, as it may in pentode circuits.

the instants at which the harmonic has its crest value.   Highest accuracy is, therefore, obtained if the currents used to determine the amplitude of a given harmonic correspond to the instants at which the harmonic has its crest value.

In order to explain the method and thus justify the use of the formulas, Espley's formulas will be derived for the simple case in which the third and higher harmonics are assumed to be negligible.   Under this assumption the alternating plate current may be expressed by two terms of the plate-current series.   Plate

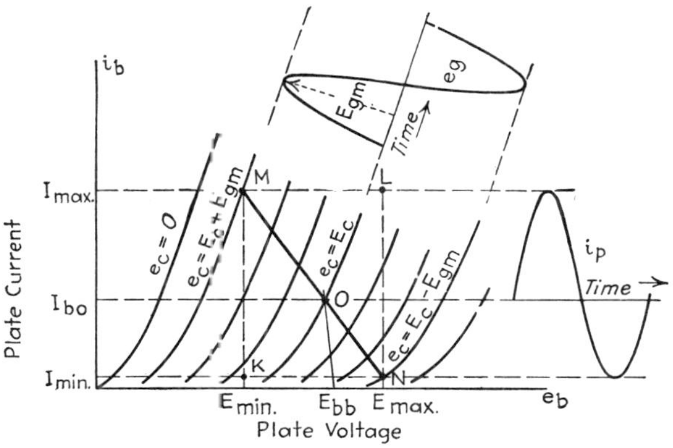

Fig. 4-13.—Diagram for use with Eqs. (4-20, 4-21, and 4-24).

excitation voltage is assumed to be zero.   The total instantaneous plate current is

$$i_b = I_{bo} + a_1 e_g + a_2 e_g^2 \tag{4-19}$$

The following relations are apparent from Fig. 4-13:

$$i_b = I_{max} \quad \text{when} \quad e_g = E_{gm} \tag{4-20}$$
$$i_b = I_{min} \quad \text{when} \quad e_g = -E_{gm} \tag{4-21}$$

Substituting Eqs. (4-20) and (4-21) in Eq. (4-19) and solving the resulting simultaneous equations gives

$$a_1 = \frac{I_{max} - I_{min}}{2E_{gm}} \qquad a_2 = \frac{I_{max} + I_{min} - 2I_{bo}}{2E_{gm}^2} \tag{4-22}$$

Substituting Eq. (4-22) in the first two terms of Eq. (4-16) and expanding $\sin^2 \omega t$ gives

$$i_b = I_{bo} + \tfrac{1}{4}(I_{max} + I_{min} - 2I_{bo}) + \tfrac{1}{2}(I_{max} - I_{min}) \sin \omega t$$
$$- \tfrac{1}{4}(I_{max} + I_{min} - 2I_{bo}) \cos 2\omega t \tag{4-23}$$

The average plate current and the amplitudes of the fundamental and second-harmonic components of plate current are

$$\left.\begin{aligned}
H_0 &= \tfrac{1}{4}(I_{\max} + I_{\min} - 2I_{bo}) \\
I_{ba} &= I_{bo} + H_0 = \tfrac{1}{4}(I_{\max} + I_{\min} + 2I_{bo}) \\
H_1 &= \tfrac{1}{2}(I_{\max} - I_{\min}) \\
H_2 &= \tfrac{1}{4}(I_{\max} + I_{\min} - 2I_{bo})
\end{aligned}\right\} \quad (4\text{-}24)$$

It is important to note that Eqs. (4-24) will give sufficiently accurate values of steady, fundamental, and second-harmonic components of plate current only when higher harmonics are negligible. If the higher harmonics cannot be neglected, it is necessary to use formulas based upon a greater number of terms of the series expansion for i_p. To derive equations that include harmonics up to the nth, n terms of the expansion are used, and the series is evaluated at $n + 1$ values of instantaneous grid voltage. Espley's method for four harmonics requires the determination of the instantaneous plate currents corresponding to $e_g = +E_{gm}$, $e_g = +\tfrac{1}{2}E_{gm}$, $e_g = 0$, $e_g = -\tfrac{1}{2}E_{gm}$, and $e_g = -E_{gm}$. These five values of current will be represented by the symbols I_1, $I_{\frac{1}{2}}$, I_{bo}, $I_{-\frac{1}{2}}$, and I_{-1}, respectively.

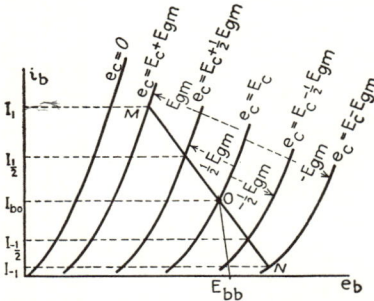

FIG. 4-14.—Use of the plate diagram in the application of Eqs. (4-25).

The following expressions give the amplitudes of the components of plate current:

$$\left.\begin{aligned}
I_{ba} &= \tfrac{1}{6}(I_1 + 2I_{\frac{1}{2}} + 2I_{-\frac{1}{2}} + I_{-1}) \\
H_1 &= \tfrac{1}{3}(I_1 + I_{\frac{1}{2}} - I_{-\frac{1}{2}} - I_{-1}) \\
H_2 &= \tfrac{1}{4}(I_1 - 2I_{bo} + I_{-1}) \\
H_3 &= \tfrac{1}{6}(I_1 - 2I_{\frac{1}{2}} + 2I_{-\frac{1}{2}} - I_{-1}) \\
H_4 &= \tfrac{1}{12}(I_1 - 4I_{\frac{1}{2}} + 6I_{bo} - 4I_{-\frac{1}{2}} + I_{-1})
\end{aligned}\right\} \quad (4\text{-}25)$$

I_1, $I_{\frac{1}{2}}$, $I_{-\frac{1}{2}}$, and I_{-1} are determined from the intersections of the dynamic load line with the static characteristics corresponding to $e_c = E_c + E_{gm}$, $e_c = E_c + \tfrac{1}{2}E_{gm}$, $e_c = E_c - \tfrac{1}{2}E_{gm}$, and $e_c = E_c - E_{gm}$, as shown in Fig. 4-14. If the static characteristics corresponding to these values of grid voltage are not available, the currents may be read from the dynamic transfer characteristic derived from the plate diagram, as shown in Fig. 4-15.

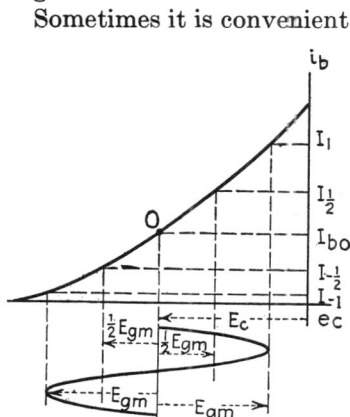

Sometimes it is convenient or necessary to measure the instantaneous alternating currents (with respect to the current corresponding to the time axis I_{bo}), rather than the instantaneous total currents, in making graphical anal-

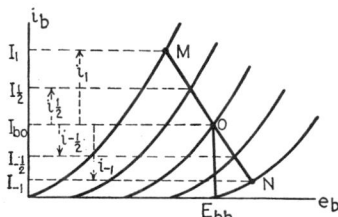

FIG. 4-15.—Use of the dynamic transfer characteristic in the application of Eqs. (4-25).

FIG. 4-16.—Diagram showing the relation between the instantaneous currents measured relative to zero and relative to I_{bo}.

yses.   The following relations are apparent from Fig. 4-16:

$$\left.\begin{array}{ll} I_1 = I_{bo} + i_1 & I_{-\frac{1}{2}} = I_{bo} - i_{-\frac{1}{2}} \\ I_{\frac{1}{2}} = I_{bo} + i_{\frac{1}{2}} & I_{-1} = I_{bo} - i_{-1} \end{array}\right\} \quad (4\text{-}26)$$

in which the lower-case symbols indicate currents measured relative to I_{bo}. By means of Eqs. (4-26), Eqs. (4-25) may be transformed into

$$\left.\begin{array}{l} I_{ba} = \frac{1}{6}(i_1 + 2i_{\frac{1}{2}} + 6I_{bo} - 2i_{-\frac{1}{2}} - i_{-1}) \\ H_1 = \frac{1}{3}(i_1 + i_{\frac{1}{2}} + i_{-\frac{1}{2}} + i_{-1}) \\ H_2 = \frac{1}{4}(i_1 - i_{-1}) \\ H_3 = \frac{1}{6}(i_1 - 2i_{\frac{1}{2}} - 2i_{-\frac{1}{2}} + i_{-1}) \\ H_4 = \frac{1}{12}(i_1 - 4i_{\frac{1}{2}} + 4i_{-\frac{1}{2}} - i_{-1}) \end{array}\right\} \quad (4\text{-}27)$$

If the dynamic transfer characteristic is symmetrical about E_c, then $i_1 = i_{-1}$ and $i_{\frac{1}{2}} = i_{-\frac{1}{2}}$, and Eqs. (4-27) reduce to

$$\left.\begin{array}{ll} I_{ba} = I_{bo} & H_1 = \frac{2}{3}(i_1 + i_{\frac{1}{2}}) \\ H_2 = H_4 = 0 & H_3 = \frac{1}{3}(i_1 - 2i_{\frac{1}{2}}) \end{array}\right\} \quad (4\text{-}28)$$

Equations (4-28) show that, when the dynamic transfer characteristic is symmetrical, the even harmonics are zero and the steady component of plate current does not change when the excitation voltage is applied.   They are useful in the analysis of push-pull amplifiers, which will be defined in Chap. 5.

For equations applicable when the fifth and sixth harmonics are present, the student should refer to other treatments of the subject.[1]

4-10. Field of Application of Equations for Harmonic Analysis. Although the equations of Sec. 4-9 were derived for the special case of excitation applied to the grid circuit, the student may readily show that they may also be used when the excitation is impressed upon the plate circuit.   With suitable changes in symbols, they may be applied to the analysis of currents and voltages of other electrodes than the plate.   Their use may, in fact, be extended to the harmonic analysis of any quantity that varies periodically as the result of the sinusoidal variation of another quantity that is related to the first through a single-valued curve of known form.

4-11. Nonsinusoidal Excitation Voltage.—The formulas for harmonic content developed in this chapter are all based upon the assumption that the alternating grid voltage is sinusoidal. They are not, therefore, of value in analyzing the alternating plate current when the grid voltage is not sinusoidal.   It is possible, however, to construct a wave of plate current by means of the dynamic transfer characteristic and to analyze it by well-known methods of wave analysis.[2]   This neglects the fact that the a-c load resistance and slope of the load line may be different for each input frequency component.   An approximate analysis may be made under the assumption that the components of the wave of plate current are the same as would be obtained if the various components of the grid voltage were applied separately and the corresponding output components added. This would be valid if there were no distortion.   It gives no indication of the intermodulation frequencies and neglects the fact that the dynamic operating point is different for each component than it would be for the resultant grid voltage. Ordinarily, adequate indication of the performance of the tube and circuit may be obtained by graphical methods based upon sinusoidal excitation, with full excitation voltage.

[1] See, for instance, H. J. Reich, "Theory and Applications of Electron Tubes," Sec. 4-9.

[2] MOULLIN, E. B., *Wireless Eng.*, **8**, 118 (1931).

4-12. Significance of Algebraic Signs of Numerical Values.—It should be noted that the algebraic sign of the amplitude of a particular harmonic may turn out to be either positive or negative, the sign indicating the phase relative to the fundamental. If the amplitude is positive, the harmonic adds to the fundamental at the instant when the fundamental has its positive crest value; if the amplitude is negative, the harmonic subtracts from the fundamental at this instant.

Mechanical Aids to Harmonic Measurement.—Scales that make possible the direct reading of percentage second and third harmonic have been described by D. C. Espley and L. I. Farren.[1] These scales, which are based upon a five-point analysis, are particularly useful when a large number of graphical determinations of harmonic content must be made.

4-13. Percentage Harmonic and Distortion Factor.[2]—The percentage of a given harmonic is defined as the ratio of the amplitude of the harmonic to the amplitude of the fundamental multiplied by 100. Thus, if harmonics above the second are negligible, Eqs. (4-24) indicate that the percentage second harmonic is

$$\text{Percentage } H_2 = \frac{I_{\max} + I_{\min} - 2I_{bo}}{2(I_{\max} - I_{\min})} \times 100 \qquad (4\text{-}29)$$

The relative importance of different harmonics in producing audible distortion of speech and music depends to some extent upon the fundamental frequency. A given percentage of harmonic is in general more objectionable the higher the order of the harmonic. High-order harmonics result in unpleasant sharpness of tone or a hissing sound. Actually, however, the intermodulation frequencies, rather than the harmonics, are largely responsible for the disagreeable effects. The principal reason for this is that the intermodulation frequencies are in general inharmonically related to the impressed frequencies. A second reason is that some of the intermodulation frequencies corresponding to impressed frequencies near the upper end of

[1] Espley, D. C., and Farren, L. I., *Wireless Eng.*, **11**, 183 (1934).

[2] Massa, Frank, *Proc. I.R.E.*, **21**, 682 (1933); Federal Radio Commission Rules and Regulations, Secs. 103, 139; Nason, C. H. W., *Radio Eng.*, **13**, 20 (1933); Graffunder, W., Kleen, W., and Wehnert, W., *Electronics* (abst.), November, 1935, p. 48; Bartlett, A. C., *Wireless Eng.*, **12**, 70 (1935).

the audio-frequency band may fall near the center of the band, whereas the harmonics fall outside of the band. The amplification of succeeding amplifiers and the sensitivity of the ear may be greater to these mid-band intermodulation frequencies than to the impressed frequencies.[1]

For a given value of maximum grid swing, the amplitude of a sum- or difference-frequency component associated with any term of the series does not exceed that of the corresponding harmonic produced when a single frequency is applied. The harmonic amplitudes at a given grid swing may, therefore, be used as a measure of distortion. A fairly satisfactory index of audible distortion is the *distortion factor*, which is defined by the equation

$$\delta = \frac{\sqrt{H_2{}^2 + H_3{}^2 + H_4{}^2 + \cdots}}{H_1} \qquad (4\text{-}30)$$

4-14. Graphical Determination of Power Output.—Ordinarily only the fundamental power output is of importance. This is

$$P_o = (0.707H_1)^2 r_b = \tfrac{1}{2}H_1{}^2 r_b \qquad (4\text{-}31)$$

where H_1 is the graphically determined value of fundamental plate-current amplitude. If harmonics higher than the second can be neglected, then the fundamental amplitude given by Eq. (4-24) is a close approximation. The corresponding equation for fundamental power output is

$$P_o = \tfrac{1}{8}(I_{\max} - I_{\min})^2 r_b \qquad (4\text{-}32)$$

But since the slope of the dynamic load line is $1/r_b$ it can be seen from Fig. 4-13 that $(I_{\max} - I_{\min})r_b = E_{\max} - E_{\min}$. Therefore Eq. (4-32) may be transformed into

$$P_o = \tfrac{1}{8}(I_{\max} - I_{\min})(E_{\max} - E_{\min}) \qquad (4\text{-}33)$$

This is equal to one-eighth of the area of the rectangle *KMLN* in Fig. 4-13.

Problems

4-1. *a.* Draw the equivalent plate circuits for the circuits of Fig. 4-17, indicating the polarities of all instantaneous voltages.

b. Write the network equations for the equivalent circuits.

c. Write expressions for e_g in terms of v_g and circuit parameters and currents, which may be used in conjunction with the equations of (*b*) to find the circuit voltages and currents.

[1] Massa, F., *Electronics*, September, 1938, p. 20.

4-2. *a.* Draw the equivalent second-grid circuit for the circuit of Fig. 4-18.

b. Write the expression for e_{g3} in terms of v_{g2}, r_c, and C_c.

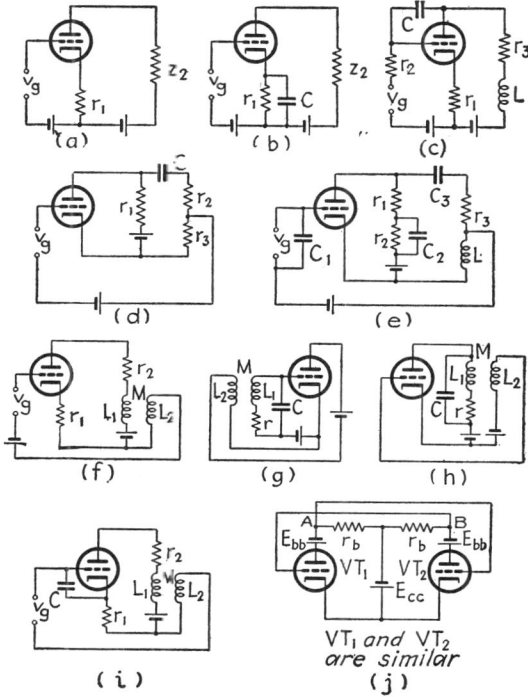

FIG. 4-17.—Diagrams for Prob. 4-1.

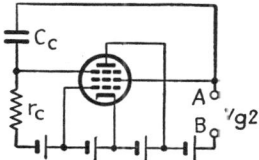

FIG. 4-18.—"Reactance-tube" circuit.   FIG. 4-19.—"Reactance-tube" circuit.

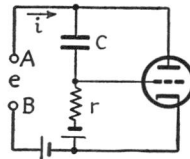

4-3. *a.* Draw the equivalent plate circuit for the circuit of Fig. 4-19.

b. By means of the equivalent circuit derive an expression for i in terms of e and thus show that the circuit acts like an admittance of value

$$y_e = \frac{r(1 + \mu) + r_p - \dfrac{j}{\omega C}}{r_p\left(r - \dfrac{j}{\omega C}\right)} \tag{4-34}$$

c. Show that when r is large in comparison with r_p the circuit acts like a resistance r_e in parallel with a reactance x_e whose values are

$$r_e = \frac{r_p(r^2C^2\omega^2 + 1)}{r^2C^2\omega^2(1 + \mu) + 1} \tag{4-35}$$

$$x_e = -\frac{rC\omega + \dfrac{1}{rC\omega}}{g_m} \tag{4-36}$$

d. Show that when $rC\omega$ is large, Eq. (4-35) reduces to

$$r_e = \frac{r_p}{1 + \mu} \tag{4-37}$$

4-4. *a.* Making use of the similarity between the equivalent circuits of Probs. 4-2 and 4-3, write equations equivalent to Eqs. (4-35) and (4-36) for the circuit of Fig. 4-18.

b. The current to the second grid in Fig. 4-18 is increased by a positive increment of second grid voltage, which is positive, but decreased by a positive increment of third grid voltage, which is negative. Making use of this fact, show that the effective parallel resistance between A and B may be negative, and that the effective parallel reactance may be inductive.

c. Show that the minimum value of negative resistance is equal to $r_{a2}/(1 + \mu_{23})$ and that the negative resistance approaches this value when the resistance r is large in comparison with the reactance of C.

4-5. *a.* By means of the equivalent plate circuit, show that the effective resistance between points A and B of Fig. 4-17*j* is equal to

$$r_e = \frac{2r_pr_b}{r_p + r_b(1 - \mu)} \tag{4-38}$$

b. Determine the condition that makes r_e negative.

4-6. *a.* Construct the simplified plate diagram for a type 45 tube when $E_{bb} = 280$ volts, $E_c = -50$ volts, $R_b = 500$ Ω, and $r_b = 3333$ Ω.

b. Derive a dynamic transfer characteristic from the plate diagram.

4-7. If the static operating voltages of a type 45 tube are $E_{bo} = 240$ volts, $E_c = -50$ volts; the plate supply voltage is 250 volts; and the a-c load resistance is 5000 Ω,

a. Find μ, r_p, and g_m at the static operating point.

b. Find the d-c resistance of the load.

c. Construct the simplified plate diagram.

d. Find the amplitudes of the fundamental and second-harmonic components of plate current at grid swings of 50 volts and 40 volts.

e. Find the fundamental power output at grid swings of 50 volts and 40 volts.

Supplementary Bibliography

A supplementary bibliography on the theory of harmonic generation and on harmonic analysis will be found at the end of Chap. 4 of "Theory and

Applications of Electron Tubes" by H. J. Reich.   The following references cover recent articles on harmonic generation and graphical methods of analysis:

MACFADYEN, K. A.: *Wireless Eng.*, **15,** 310 (1938).
SCOTT, H. J., and BLACK, L. J.: *Proc. I.R.E.*, **26,** 449 (1938).
FAIRWEATHER, A., and WILLIAMS, F. C.: *Wireless Eng.*, **16,** 57 (1939).
WHEELER, H. A.: *Proc. I.R.E.*, **27,** 359, 384 (1939).
THOMSON, W. T.: *Electrical Eng.*, **58,** 488 (1939).
JONKER, J. L. H.: *Wireless Eng.*, **16,** 274, 344 (1939).
VAN DER VEN, A. J. H.: *Wireless Eng.*, **16,** 383, 444 (1939).
BLOCH, A.: *Wireless Eng.*, **16,** 592 (1939).
NIMS, A. A.: *Electronics*, May, 1939, p. 23.
FROMMER, J., and RÉDL, A.: *Wireless Eng.*, **17,** 4 (1940).

CHAPTER 5

AMPLIFIER DEFINITIONS, CLASSIFICATIONS, AND CIRCUITS

The many applications of thermionic electron tubes may be divided into amplification, detection and modulation, generation of alternating voltage, power rectification, current and power control, and measurement. The subject of amplification will be treated in this and the following chapter. The purpose of the present chapter is to define terms that must be used in the discussion of amplifiers, to classify different types of amplifiers, and to show basic circuits of amplifiers. Chapter 6 will deal with the characteristics and the design of amplifiers.

5-1. Signal.—The term *signal* is applied to any alternating voltage or frequency impressed upon the input of an amplifier or other four-terminal network. It is also applied to the resulting fundamental components of output voltage or current, as distinguished from harmonic or intermodulation components.

5-2. Amplifiers.—An *amplifier* may be defined as a device for increasing the amplitude of electric voltage, current, or power, through the control, by the input, of power supplied to the output circuit by a local source. A vacuum-tube amplifier is one that employs vacuum tubes to effect the control of power from the local source.

Amplifiers are but one type of the general four-terminal network. Other types include the transformer and the filter. Wherever possible, the definitions and discussions given in this chapter are worded so as to apply also to other four-terminal networks.

5-3. Amplifier Distortion.—If an amplifier, or other four-terminal network, is distortionless, the application of a periodic wave of any form to the input terminals will result in the production of an output wave that is a replica of the input wave. In general such a periodic wave will consist of a fundamental and

114

one or more harmonics. In order that the output wave form shall be identical with that of the input, three conditions must be satisfied: (1) The output must contain only the frequencies contained in the input. (2) The output must contain all frequencies contained in the input, and the relative amplitudes of the various components must be the same as in the input. (3) If any component of the output is shifted in phase relative to the corresponding component of the input, all components must be shifted by the same number of electrical degrees of the fundamental cycle. Examination of a fundamental wave and its nth harmonic shows that this is equivalent to saying that the phase shift of the nth harmonic, measured in electrical degrees of its own cycle, must be either n times the phase shift of the fundamental or an integer multiple of 180 deg. This can be true only if the phase shift for sinusoidal input is either proportional to the frequency, or zero or 180 deg at all frequencies.[1] Failure to satisfy these three conditions results in three corresponding types of distortion: amplitude distortion (nonlinear distortion), frequency distortion (frequency discrimination), and phase distortion.

Amplitude distortion (nonlinear distortion) is the generation in an amplifier or other four-terminal network of frequencies not present in the impressed signal and is usually associated with a nonlinear relation between output and input amplitudes. In vacuum-tube amplifiers it is the result of curvature of the dynamic tube characteristics. The generation of harmonics and intermodulation frequencies was discussed in Chap. 4. A nonlinear relation between the output and input amplitudes when the dynamic transfer characteristic is curved is predicted by the fact that the third and higher odd-order terms of the series expansion for plate current [Eq. (3-36)] give rise to fundamental components of plate current, the amplitudes of which vary as the cube or higher odd power of the excitation voltage. For this reason, unless the coefficients of all odd-order terms of the series are negligibly small, the voltage, current, and power output are not proportional to the exciting voltage. Amplitude distortion is objectionable in the amplification of speech and music mainly because intermodulation frequencies are in general inharmonically related to the impressed frequencies and there-

[1] FRY, T. C., *Physik. Z.*, **23**, 273 (1922).

fore produce unpleasant discords. Amplitude distortion[1] can be minimized by proper choice of tubes, load impedances, and operating voltages, and by avoiding too high excitation voltage. *Overloading* is the very noticeable amplitude distortion that occurs when the exciting voltage is so large that the normal range of operation on the dynamic transfer characteristic is exceeded. It may be especially pronounced when the input amplitude is so large that plate current in one or more stages ceases to flow during a portion of the cycle.

Frequency distortion in an amplifier or other four-terminal network is the variation of amplification or sensitivity with frequency of the impressed signal. In a vacuum-tube amplifier it results from dependence of circuit and interelectrode impedances upon frequency.[2] It can be minimized by proper design of input, output, and interstage coupling circuits, being least in amplifiers in which the circuits do not contain reactance. The difficulty of preventing frequency distortion increases with the width of the frequency band for which the amplifier is designed and with amplification per stage. Although frequency distortion may not produce disagreeable effects in the amplification of music, it impairs fidelity of tone and may prevent the reproduction of the sounds of some instruments. By eliminating the high frequencies essential to the reproduction of consonants, it may make reproduced speech difficult to understand.

Phase distortion is the shifting of the phase of the output voltage or current of an amplifier or other four-terminal network relative to the input voltage or current by an amount that is not proportional to frequency. Like frequency distortion, it results from the reactance of electrodes and circuit elements and can be made negligible by designing the coupling and other circuit elements so that the reactances have negligible effect throughout the desired frequency range.[2] This causes the phase shift to approximate zero or 180 deg throughout the frequency range. Because frequency distortion usually cannot be detected by ear, it is ordinarily the least objectionable type of distortion in the amplification of sound. It is objectionable, however, in

[1] Bartlett, A. C., *Wireless Eng.*, **12**, 70 (1935); Barrow, W. L., *Phys. Rev.*, **39**, 863 (1932); Espley, D. C., *Proc. I.R.E.*, **22**, 781 (1934).
[2] At ultrahigh frequency electron transit time also causes distortion.

the amplification of television signals and in the use of amplifiers in the oscillographic study of voltage and current wave form.

5-4. Amplifier Classification.—Vacuum-tube amplifiers are commonly classified in four ways: (1) according to use, (2) according to circuits, (3) according to frequency range, and (4) according to the portion of the cycle during which plate current flows.

Voltage, Current, and Power Amplifiers.—When classified as to type of service, amplifiers are termed *voltage amplifiers, current amplifiers,* or *power amplifiers,* depending upon whether they are designed to furnish voltage, current, or power output. The effectiveness with which a voltage amplifier accomplishes its function is indicated by its *voltage amplification. Voltage amplification* is the ratio of the signal voltage available at the output terminals of an amplifier, transformer, or other four-terminal network, to the signal voltage impressed at the input terminals. It will be represented by the symbol μ'.

Current amplification is the ratio of the signal current produced in the output circuit of an amplifier, transformer, or other four-terminal network to the signal current supplied to its input circuit. The effectiveness with which a current amplifier accomplishes its function may sometimes be specified by its current amplification, but usually the input impedance is so high that this term has no useful significance unless the input is shunted by a specified impedance. The performance can be indicated better by the *current sensitivity,* which is defined as the ratio of the signal current produced in the output circuit of an amplifier or other four-terminal network to the signal voltage impressed at the input terminals. Current sensitivity is measured in mhos.

Power amplification is the ratio of the power delivered to the output circuit of an amplifier, or other four-terminal network containing a source of local power, to the power supplied to its input circuit. Because of the high input impedance of many types of power amplifiers, this term may have no useful significance unless the input is shunted by a specified resistance. It is, therefore, usually better to specify the performance of a power amplifier by its *power sensitivity,* which is defined as the square root of the signal-frequency power delivered by the output circuit of an amplifier or other four-terminal network containing a local source of power, to the effective value of the signal voltage impressed at the input terminals.[1]   Power sensitivity is measured in root mhos.

A *frequency-response characteristic* is a graph that relates the amplification or sensitivity of an amplifier or other four-terminal network with the frequency of the impressed signal.   The term is usually applied to a graph of voltage amplification as a function of frequency of the impressed signal.

In amplifiers designed to furnish voltage output, all stages, including the final one, should be voltage amplifiers.   In amplifiers designed to furnish power output, on the other hand, the last stage must be a power amplifier.   All other stages are voltage amplifiers unless the final power tube operates in such a manner that grid current flows during part of the cycle, in which case the next to the last stage must also be a power amplifier. The theory and characteristics of voltage, current, and power amplifiers will be considered in Chap. 6.

5-5. Amplifier Circuits.—The classification of amplifiers according to circuits is based upon the number of stages, upon the type of circuit used to couple successive stages, and upon whether each stage uses a single tube or a symmetrical arrangement of two tubes.   The coupling circuit serves a dual function. It converts the alternating plate current of one tube into alternating voltage to excite the grid of the following tube; and, by preventing application of direct plate voltage of one tube to the grid of the following tube, it allows the proper operating voltages of all electrodes to be maintained.   There are three fundamental types of coupling: *direct coupling, impedance-capacitance coupling,* and *transformer coupling.*

5-6. Direct Coupling.—A direct-coupled amplifier is one in which the plate of a given stage is connected to the grid of the next stage either directly or through a biasing battery.   Basic circuits of two-stage amplifiers with direct coupling are shown in Figs. 5-1 and 5-2.   The biasing battery adjacent to the grid of the second tube in the circuit of Fig. 5-1 is necessitated by the fact that the plate of the first tube is positive relative to its cathode, whereas the grid of the second tube must be negative relative to its cathode.   The need for this battery is avoided

[1] Ballantine, Stuart, *Proc. I.R.E.*, **18**, 452 (1930).

in the circuit of Fig. 5-2 by making the cathode of the second tube positive with respect to the cathode of the first tube.   The voltage of the cathode of the second tube in Fig. 5-2 is adjusted so that the voltage between p and q is less than the drop through z_{b1} by the required grid bias of the second tube.

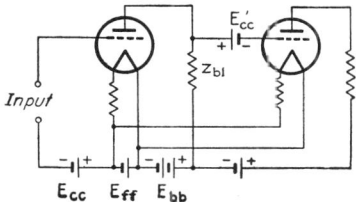

FIG. 5-1.—Direct-coupled amplifier.   FIG. 5-2.—Direct-coupled amplifier.

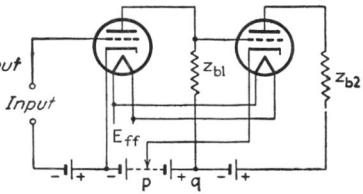

The several voltage sources of Fig. 5-2 may be replaced by a single voltage source and a voltage divider, as in Fig. 5-3a.[1] The function of the condensers, called *by-pass* condensers (see Sec. 6-14), whose reactances are much smaller than the resistances

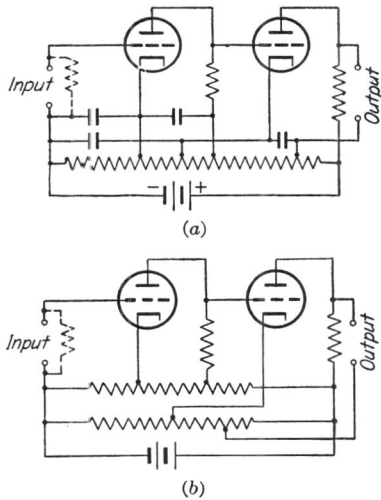

(a)

(b)

FIG. 5-3.—Direct-coupled amplifiers with single source of grid and plate voltages.

that they shunt, is to prevent the application to the grids of signal voltages caused by the flow of alternating plate currents through the voltage divider.   Since the reactance of these con-

[1] LOFTIN, E. H., and WHITE, S. Y., *Proc. I.R.E.*, **16**, 281 (1928); **18**, 669 (1930).

densers increases as the frequency goes down, their use may result in frequency distortion at low frequencies. They need not be used in the circuit of Fig. 5-3b, in which the plate current of the second tube flows through a separate voltage divider and so cannot cause the application of signal voltage to the grid of the first tube. The voltage impressed upon the first grid as the result of the flow of plate current of the first tube through its voltage divider reduces the amplification somewhat, but has no other objectionable effect. This difficulty may be avoided entirely by the use of push-pull circuits,[1] which are discussed in Sec. 5-10.

Direct-coupled amplifiers respond down to zero frequency, *i.e.*, they amplify changes of direct voltage. Although the

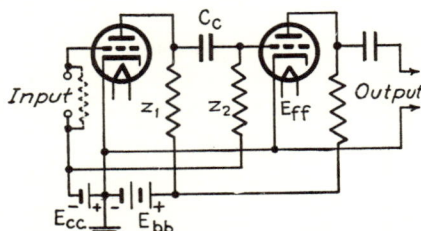

Fig. 5-4.—Impedance-capacitance–coupled amplifier.

small frequency distortion and the response at zero frequency are the advantages of the direct-coupled amplifier, the response to changes of steady voltage makes it difficult to use more than two stages in the circuits of Figs. 5-1, 5-2, and 5-3. Small changes in the operating voltages of the first tube are amplified to such an extent that it is hard to maintain correct grid bias in the final stage of an amplifier having three or more stages. This difficulty may be reduced, however, by the use of inverse feedback[2] (see Sec. 6-31).

5-7. Impedance-capacitance Coupling.—In the impedance-capacitance–coupled amplifier of Fig. 5-4 the plate voltage is kept from the grid of the succeeding tube by the use of a coupling condenser C_c. If the reactance of this condenser is small in comparison to the grid coupling impedance z_2, practically the full

[1] Goldberg, H., *Trans. A.I.E.E.*, **59**, 60 (1940).

[2] Clapp, J. K., *General Radio Experimenter*, **9**, February, 1939, p. 1; Goldberg, *loc. cit.*

voltage developed across z_1 is applied to the grid of the second tube. z_2 is almost always a resistance. The plate coupling impedance z_1 may be a resistance, an inductive reactance, a resonant circuit, or a more complicated type of impedance. When resistance is used, the amplifier is termed a *resistance-capacitance–coupled* amplifier, or simply a *resistance-coupled* amplifier.

5-8. Use of Cathode Resistors to Provide Bias.—It is unnecessary to use a separate voltage source to supply grid-bias voltages. The plate and grid supply voltages of Fig. 5-4 may be replaced by a single voltage source and voltage divider, or the bias voltages may be obtained by the use of cathode resistors, as in Fig. 5-5. The steady components of plate and screen currents

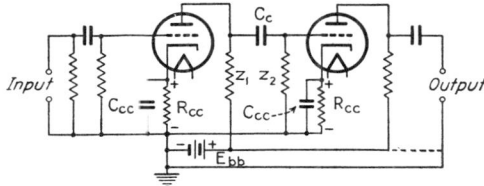

Fig. 5-5.—Impedance-capacitance–coupled amplifier with self-biasing resistors R_{cc}.

through a biasing resistor R_{cc} cause a steady voltage drop that is of such polarity as to make the grid negative with respect to the cathode. The tube is said to be *self-biased*. The correct value of biasing resistance for any stage is equal to the required bias divided by the sum of the static operating plate and screen currents. If the resistance alone is used, the signal voltage produced across this resistance is also applied to the grid, and, being opposite in phase to the input voltage, reduces the amplification. Although the effects of the out-of-phase voltage applied to the grid are not necessarily without benefit (see Sec. 6-31), the loss in amplification may be prevented by shunting the resistance with a by-pass condenser C_{cc}, whose reactance is small at signal frequency. To ensure that the amplification will not fall off at low frequencies, this condenser must have sufficiently high capacitance so that the alternating voltage across R_{cc} is negligible at the lowest frequency to be amplified.

Another method of preventing the application of out-of-phase signal voltage to the grid is by the *decoupling* circuit of Fig. 5-6.

The condenser C_{cc} and resistor R_{cc}' serve as a simple filter by acting as a voltage divider for any alternating voltage appearing across R_{cc}.[1] If the reactance of C_{cc} is small in comparison with the resistance R_{cc}' at the lowest frequency to be amplified, then a negligible portion of the alternating voltage will appear across C_{cc} at this and higher frequencies. The condenser charges up to a voltage equal to the direct voltage across R_{cc} and thus applies this amount of biasing voltage to the grid circuit.

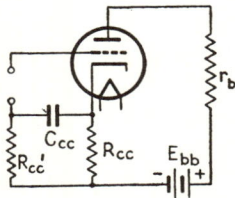

FIG. 5-6.—Single-stage amplifier with self-biasing resistor and decoupling filter.

The by-pass condenser in the circuit of Fig. 5-5 and the condenser-resistance filter in the circuit of Fig. 5-6 also serve to reduce hum by preventing ripple voltage, which appears across R_{cc} as the result of a poorly filtered B supply (see Chap. 11), from being applied to the grid.

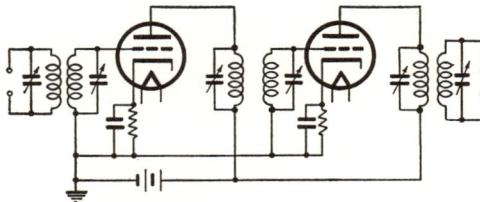

FIG. 5-7.—Doubly tuned transformer-coupled amplifier.

5-9. Transformer Coupling.—Basic circuits of transformer-coupled amplifiers are shown in Figs. 5-7, 5-8, and 5-9. The amplifiers of Figs. 5-7 and 5-8, which incorporate resonant circuits, are used principally at radio frequencies. The transformers may be either air-core or iron-core. The amplifier of Fig. 5-9, which employs untuned iron-core transformers, is used principally at audio frequencies.

5-10. Push-pull Amplifiers.—The circuits illustrated in Figs. 5-1 to 5-9 use a single tube in each stage of amplification. Such amplifiers are said to be *single sided*. It is also possible to use

---

[1] POUND, F. J. A., *Wireless Eng.*, **9**, 445 (1932); KINROSS, R. I., *Wireless Eng.*, **10**, 612 (1932); STEVENS, B. J., *Wireless Eng.*, **11**, 129 (1934); CLARKE, G. F., *Wireless Eng.*, **11**, 370 (1934); WILLIAMS, EMRYS, *Wireless Eng.*, **11**, 600 (1934). See also Sec. 6-14.

two tubes in each stage, connected so that the grid excitation voltages of the two tubes are opposite in phase, as shown in the single-stage transformer-coupled amplifier of Fig. 5-10. An

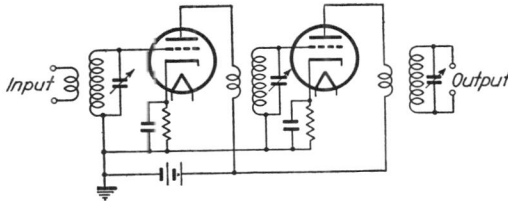

Fig. 5-8.—Singly tuned transformer-coupled amplifier.

amplifier that uses such a symmetrical arrangement of two tubes is called a *push-pull amplifier*. The principal advantage of a push-pull amplifier over a single-sided amplifier is that it does not introduce even harmonics or the accompanying intermodula-

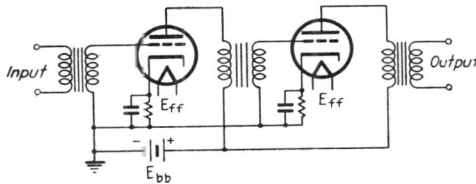

Fig. 5-9.—Untuned transformer-coupled amplifier.

tion frequencies associated with the even-order terms of the series expansion. For this reason push-pull circuits are usually used when low distortion is essential. The low amplitude distortion of push-pull amplifiers also makes possible a great

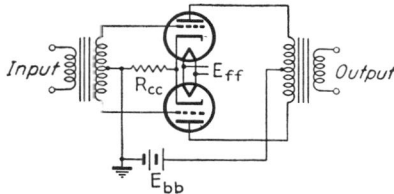

Fig. 5-10.—Single-stage push-pull amplifier.

increase in the power output that can be developed by given tubes without exceeding a specified amount of distortion.

Push-pull amplifiers have a number of other advantages. Fluctuations of supply voltage and hum voltage resulting from insufficient filtering of a B supply are applied to the two tubes of a push-pull amplifier in such a manner that the effects balance out in the output.   In transformer-coupled amplifiers the steady plate currents pass through the primary of the output transformer in opposite directions and, therefore, do not tend to saturate the core if the two tubes are similar.   For this reason a smaller core can be used.   The fundamental components of plate currents of the two tubes, which are opposite in phase, cancel in the biasing resistance R_{cc}, and so there is no loss in amplification when the by-pass condenser is omitted.   Similarly, the fundamental components of plate current of the two tubes cancel in the impedance of the source of plate voltage, preventing loss of amplification in individual stages or danger of oscillation as the result of feedback of signal voltage from any stage to a preceding stage (see Sec. 6-14).

The symmetry of push-pull amplifiers can be made sufficiently close by choice of similar tubes, and by minor circuit adjustments, so that the negative half of the output wave may be considered to have the same form as the positive half.   A periodic wave that has this type of symmetry contains no even harmonics.[1] It follows, therefore, that a properly balanced push-pull amplifier does not generate even harmonics of the applied frequencies. This is also shown by Eqs. (4-28).   That a push-pull amplifier does not generate even harmonics or even-order intermodulation frequencies may be shown rigorously by an analysis based upon the series expansion for plate current.[2]

If the output transformer of Fig. 5-10 is center-tapped, it can be used to excite a following push-pull amplifier stage. Impedance-capacitance coupling may also be used, as shown in Fig. 5-11.   In this circuit there can be no external connection between either side of the input and the cathode circuit, as this would in effect short-circuit the a-c input to one tube.   For this reason the input can be grounded only at the mid-point of the input resistor.   Although push-pull stages may be used throughout a multistage amplifier when it is desired to reduce distortion to a minimum, it is more common to use the push-pull connection only in the final stage, in which the current amplitude, and hence the distortion, is large.

[1] MALTI, M. G., "Electric Circuit Analysis," p. 176, John Wiley & Sons, Inc., New York, 1930.
[2] REICH, H. J., "Theory and Applications of Electron Tubes," p. 164.

The requirement that the exciting voltages of the two tubes of a push-pull amplifier shall be opposite in phase necessitates

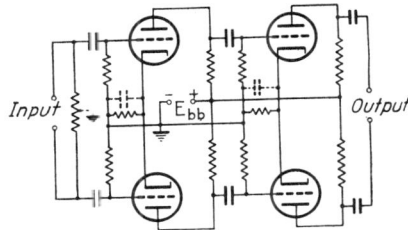

Fig. 5-11.—Resistance-capacitance-coupled push-pull amplifier.

the use of special circuits in coupling a single-sided stage to a push-pull stage by means of resistance-capacitance coupling.[1]

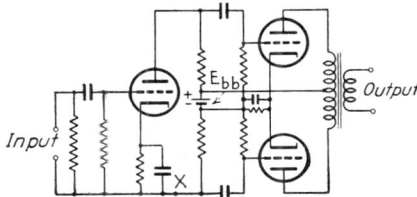

Fig. 5-12.—Amplifier circuit in which resistance-capacitance coupling is used to couple a single-sided stage to a push-pull stage.

One circuit that may be used for this purpose is shown in Fig. 5-12. In this circuit, the 180-deg difference in phase is obtained by splitting the plate resistor of the first stage into two parts and inserting the B-supply voltage between them.[2] (The student can readily show that a B-supply voltage used for the push-pull stage cannot be connected to the first stage at the point X without short-circuiting the input to the lower tube

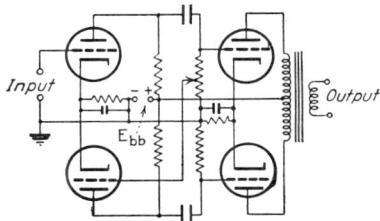

Fig. 5-13.—Use of phase-inverting tube in coupling a single-sided stage to a push-pull stage.

of the push-pull stage.) This circuit has the disadvantage that the input cannot be grounded without tending to unbalance

[1] Aughtie, F., *Wireless Eng.*, **6**, 307 (1929); Davidson, P. G., *Wireless Eng.*, **6**, 437 (1929); Shortt, H. L., *Radio Eng.*, January, 1935, p. 14; McProud, C. G., and Wildermuth, R. T., *Electronics*, October, 1940, p. 50.
[2] Tulauskas, L., *Electronics*, May, 1933, p. 134.

the push-pull stage. This disadvantage is overcome by the circuit of Fig. 5-13, in which the phase reversal is accomplished by means of a "phase-inverting" tube, which may be in the same glass envelope as the main first-stage tube. The input to this tube is obtained from the output of the main first-stage tube, which is opposite in phase to the input. The setting of the potentiometer is adjusted so that equal alternating voltages are applied to the grids of the two push-pull tubes. (A simple method of balancing is to connect a pair of headphones across the biasing resistor of the push-pull stage and to adjust the potentiometer so that only harmonic and other distortion frequencies are heard.)

5-11. Output Circuits.—It is often advantageous or necessary to prevent the steady component of plate current of the output tube from passing through the loud-speaker or other load. This

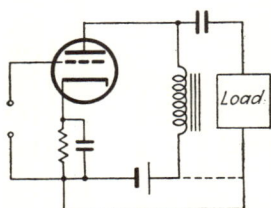

Fig. 5-14.—Choke-condenser-coupled load.

may be done by using an output transformer as in Figs. 5-7 to 5-10, 5-12, and 5-13, a resistance-capacitance network as in Figs. 5-5 and 5-11, a condenser-choke combination as in Fig. 5-14, or a tap on the voltage supply (bridge output), as in Fig. 5-3. The dotted lines in Figs. 5-5 and 5-14 show an alternative connection of the load. The advantage of this connection is that it subjects the coupling condenser to a lower direct voltage; the disadvantage is that the load is at high potential relative to ground if the negative side of the B supply is grounded.

5-12. Use of Center-tapped Filament Transformer with Filamentary Cathodes.—When tubes with filamentary cathodes are operated from an a-c filament supply, the grid and plate circuits are connected to the cathode through a center tap on the filament transformer or through a center-tapped resistor shunted across the filament. The reason for the center connection is to prevent a-c output at supply frequency as the result of a variation of voltage of one end of the filament relative to the grid. The center connection is equivalent to a connection to the mid-point of the filament. When the alternating voltage drop in the filament causes the voltage of the grid relative to one end of the filament to become more negative, it causes the grid voltage relative to the other end to become less negative. If the filament is symmetrical, the decrease of space current from one end of the filament is offset by an equal increase from the other end, and the plate current remains constant. Slight deviation of the filament from symmetry with respect to the mid-point can be compensated by the use of a resistor with an adjustable tap.

5-13. Frequency Range.—According to frequency range, amplifiers are classified as *wide-band* and *narrow-band*. The presence of circuit inductances and capacitances restricts the frequency range over which any amplifier can amplify uniformly. The width of the response band may be reduced to any desired amount by the use of tuned circuits or band-pass filters in the amplifier. For most applications of audio-frequency amplifiers it is desirable to amplify uniformly over as great a frequency range as possible, and so untuned amplifiers are the rule. Tuned amplifiers, which are indispensable in radio-frequency amplification, are seldom of value in audio-frequency work unless it is desired to emphasize or repress certain frequencies. Amplifiers incorporating band-pass filters are of value at both radio and audio frequencies.[1] They may be used in separating and isolating various portions or components of a wide band of frequencies which are simultaneously produced or transmitted.

5-14. Class A, Class AB, Class B, and Class C Amplifiers.— According to the portion of the cycle during which plate current flows, amplifiers are classified as class A, class AB, class B, and class C. A *class A amplifier* is one in which the grid bias and alternating grid voltage are such that plate current in the tube, or in each tube of a push-pull stage, flows at all times. A *class AB amplifier* is one in which the grid bias and alternating grid voltages are such that plate current in the tube, or in each tube of a push-pull stage, flows for appreciably more than half but less than the entire electrical cycle. A *class B amplifier* is an amplifier in which the grid bias is approximately equal to the cutoff value, so that the plate current is approximately zero when no exciting grid voltage is applied and so that plate current in the tube, or in each tube of a push-pull stage, flows for approximately one-half of each cycle when an alternating grid voltage is applied. A *class C amplifier* is an amplifier in which the grid bias is appreciably greater than the cutoff value, so that the plate

[1] BUTTERWORTH, S., *Wireless Eng.*, **7**, 536 (1930).

current in each tube is zero when no alternating grid voltage is applied and so that plate current flows in each tube for appreciably less than one-half of each cycle when an alternating grid voltage is applied.   The suffix 1 may be added to the letter or letters of the class identification to denote that grid current does not flow during any part of the input cycle, and the suffix 2 to denote that grid current flows during some part of the cycle.

Class A1 operation is illustrated in Fig. 5-15.   According to the definition of class A amplification, the lower limit of instantaneous total plate current is zero.   Practically, however, distortion caused by curvature of the dynamic transfer characteristic at low values of plate current limits the minimum plate current in a single-sided amplifier to values that ordinarily are not less

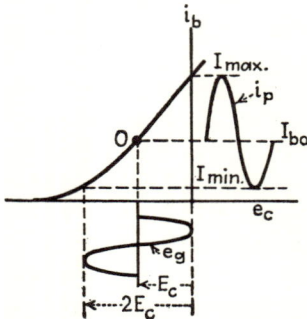

FIG. 5-15.—Single-sided class A1 operation.

than $\frac{1}{15}$ of the maximum plate current and that may be considerably larger.   Since grid current starts flowing when the grid voltage is zero or even slightly negative, the upper limit of plate current is approximately that corresponding to zero grid voltage.   The largest amplitude of alternating plate current is evidently obtained when the grid bias and signal voltage have such values that the grid voltage is equal to or slightly less than zero at the positive crest of exciting voltage and the plate current has the minimum value of I_{min} consistent with allowable amplitude distortion, at the negative crest of exciting voltage.

Although larger amplitude of alternating plate current can be obtained with class A2 operation than with class A1, this advantage is offset by the higher value of static operating current, which increases the power consumption and the loss within the tube (see Sec. 6-20), and by the complications arising from the flow of grid current.   Class A2 operation is, therefore, seldom used.   Class A1 operation is used in voltage amplifiers and in many audio-frequency power amplifiers.   It results in lower distortion than do other types of operation but is less efficient than class AB, B, or C operation.

Class B2 operation is illustrated in Figs. 5-16 and 5-17. If a single tube were used as a class B audio-frequency amplifier, all, or nearly all, of the negative half of the cycle would be cut off, as shown in Fig. 5-16, and amplitude distortion would be excessive. When two tubes are used in push-pull, however, the grid bias can be adjusted so that each tube functions in alternate half cycles during a little more than half the cycle, and the resultant current through the load is very nearly a replica of the exciting grid voltage, as shown in Fig. 5-17. In radio-frequency amplifiers, tuned circuits may be used in the plate circuit to suppress harmonics in the output and thus make possible the use of a single-

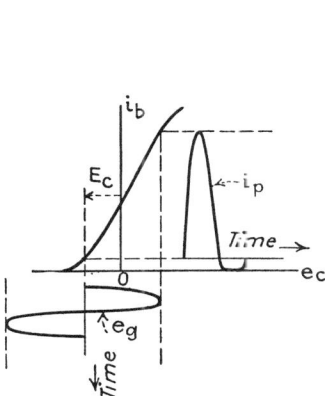

FIG. 5-16.—Single-sided class B2 operation.

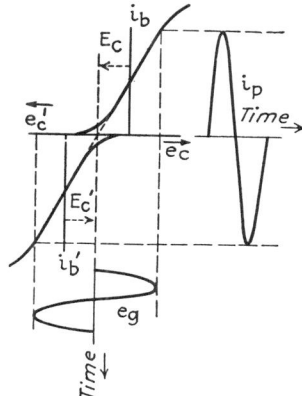

FIG. 5-17.—Push-pull class B2 operation.

sided amplifier. Class B operation is used in audio-frequency amplification only in power amplifiers. Class B amplifiers are capable of delivering large amounts of power at higher efficiency than class A amplifiers, but the harmonic content is greater. Since full advantage of class B amplification is obtained only when the excitation is great enough so that the grids are driven positive during appreciable portions of the cycle, Class B1 amplification is seldom used.

Class AB operation is intermediate between that of class A and class B. Because plate current in a single tube does not flow during the entire cycle, it is necessary to use push-pull circuits to avoid excessive distortion in class AB audio-frequency amplifiers. Usually the grid is not allowed to swing positive, since the flow of grid current results in complications that may offset the advantages.[1] Considerably greater power output and higher efficiency can be attained with class AB1 amplifiers than with class A1 amplifiers.

Because of the fact that plate current flows during less than 180 electrical degrees it is impossible to use class C operation in audio-frequency amplifiers designed for wide frequency bands. In radio-frequency amplifiers, harmonics are suppressed by the use of resonant circuits. The efficiency of class C amplifiers is greater than that of the other classes.

5-15. The Decibel.—Although current, voltage, and power amplification, as well as the magnitude of a given voltage, current, or power, relative to reference values, can be expressed as an ordinary ratio, it has been found to be far more convenient to make use of logarithmic ratios. The unit that has been adopted in this country is the decibel, which is indicated by the symbol db and is defined as follows:

1. The ratio of two amounts of power P_2 and P_1 is said to be n db if

$$n = 10 \log_{10} \frac{P_2}{P_1} \qquad (5\text{-}1)$$

2. The ratio of two voltages E_2 and E_1 or two currents I_2 and I_1 is said to be n db if

$$n = 20 \log_{10} \frac{E_2}{E_1} \qquad \text{or} \qquad n = 20 \log_{10} \frac{I_2}{I_1} \qquad (5\text{-}2)$$

If P_2 exceeds P_1, n is positive, P_2 is said to be "up" n db with respect to P_1, and n is said to indicate a *gain;* if P_1 exceeds P_2, n is negative, P_2 is said to be "down" n db with respect to P_1, and n is said to indicate a *loss.*

By substituting $P = I^2 z \cos \theta$ and $P = E^2 (\cos \theta)/z$ in Eq. (5-1) the student may show that Eqs. (5-1) and (5-2) give the same number of decibels if the impedances in which P_1 and P_2 are developed have the same magnitude and phase angle.

It follows from the definition of a logarithm that if a system is made up of a number of units whose decibel gain or loss is

[1] See, for instance, H. J. Reich, "Theory and Applications of Electron Tubes," Sec. 9-9.

n_1, n_2, n_3, etc., the over-all gain or loss of the system is

$$n = n_1 + n_2 + n_3 + \cdots \tag{5-3}$$

due account being taken of the signs of n_1, n_2, n_3, etc.

It should be noted that the decibel always refers to the ratio of two amounts of power, voltage, or current. A single quantity of power, voltage, or current can be specified in decibels if it is always understood that the value is expressed relative to a fixed reference level, called *zero level*. In telephone engineering, 6 mw has long been accepted as zero power level. The more convenient value of 1 mw, however, is now coming into general use in the communications field. The term *volume unit (vu)* is used in place of "decibel" when 1 mw is used as the reference level.[1]

The small numbers in which it is possible to express the decibel gain corresponding to large amplification ratios and the ease of adding and subtracting, as compared with multiplying and dividing, constitute two advantages of the use of the decibel. Furthermore, the change in gain of an amplifier or attenuator in decibels is a better index of the effect upon the ear of the change in sound output than is the corresponding change in amplification.[2]

A chart for determining decibel gain corresponding to power, voltage, and current ratios is given on page 372.

[1] AFFEL, H. A., CHINN, H. A., and MORRIS, R. M., *Electronics*, February, 1939, p. 28; CHINN, H. A., GANNETT, D. K., and MORRIS, R. M., *Proc. I.R.E.*, **28**, 71 (1940); BRAND, S., *Bell Lab. Record*, **18**, 310 (1940).

[2] PERRY, S. V., *RMA Tech. Bull.* No. 1, Nov. 1, 1940.

CHAPTER 6

ANALYSIS AND DESIGN OF AMPLIFIERS

Voltage amplifiers are usually operated in such a manner that amplitude distortion is small. Much can be learned regarding their performance, therefore, by taking into account only the fundamental components of plate current and making use

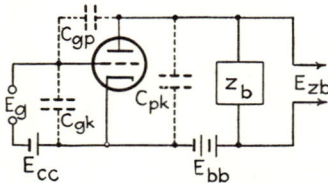

Fig. 6-1.—Single-sided amplifier with impedance load.

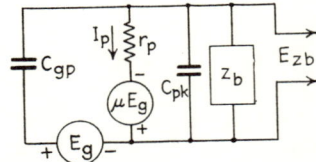

Fig. 6-2.—Equivalent circuit for the amplifier of Fig. 6-1.

of the equivalent-plate-circuit theorem. The results of such an approximate analysis are closely verified by laboratory measurements. When it is necessary to determine the harmonic content or to make more accurate predictions regarding the amplification, the graphical methods explained in Chap. 4 may be employed.

6-1. Voltage Amplification of Tube with Impedance Load.—

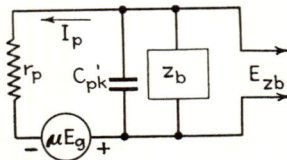

Fig. 6-3.—Simplified equivalent circuit for the amplifier of Fig. 6-1.

The simplest form of vacuum-tube voltage amplifier consists of a single tube with an impedance in the plate circuit, as shown in Fig. 6-1. Figure 6-2 shows the equivalent plate circuit. As far as its shunting effect upon z_b is concerned, C_{gp} may be replaced by an equivalent capacitance $C_{gp}' = C_{gp}(E_g + E_{zb})/E_{zb}$, in parallel with C_{pk}. Since E_{zb} is usually large in comparison with E_g, C_{gp}' is approximately equal to C_{gp}. The equivalent circuit may then be simplified to that of Fig. 6-3, in which $C_{pk}' = C_{pk} + C_{gp}'$. At low frequency the reactance of C_{pk}' is so high that its effect may be neglected. Under this assumption the voltage

132

amplification is

$$\mu' = \frac{E_{zb}}{E_g} = \frac{I_p z_b}{E_g} = \frac{\mu z_b}{r_p + z_b} \tag{6-1}$$

The manner in which μ'/μ varies with the ratio z_b/r_p with pure resistance load and with pure reactance load is shown in Fig. 6-4. The voltage amplification approaches the amplification factor when the load impedance becomes large in comparison with the plate resistance. Inductance load has the advantage that loss of direct voltage resulting from IR drop in the load may be kept to a minimum by making the d-c resistance small. This advantage is more than offset, however, by dependence of load impedance upon frequency, which tends to make

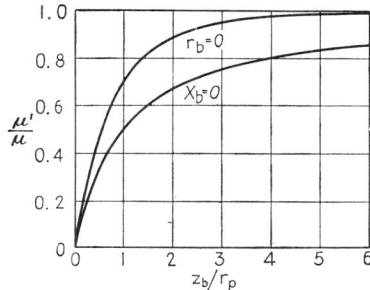

Fig. 6-4.—Curves showing the manner in which the amplification of a single tube with pure resistance and with pure reactance load varies with load impedance.

the amplification fall and to advance the phase of the output voltage with respect to the exciting voltage at low frequency.

At frequencies which are so high that the reactance of C_{pk}' is comparable with the plate resistance, the effective load impedance consists of the parallel combination of z_b and the reactance of C_{pk}'. The voltage amplification, therefore, falls off at high frequency, and the phase of the output voltage is retarded. The upper limit of the range of uniform amplification can be raised at the expense of amplification, by reducing z_b. With resistance load it is not difficult to obtain uniform amplification from zero frequency well into the radio-frequency range. Special methods of improving the high-frequency response may be used.[1]

For triodes with resistance load the manner in which μ' varies with r_b is complicated by the fact that as the resistance is increased the path of operation is lowered and the plate resistance increased. Thus, the plate resistance at the operating point O' of Fig. 6-5 is higher than that at the point O. The amplification does not increase so rapidly, therefore, as would be indicated by Eq. (6-1) if the plate resistance were assumed to be constant. The manner in which the voltage amplification varies with load resistance can

[1] REICH, H. J., "Theory and Applications of Electron Tubes," Sec. 7-7A.

be determined most readily graphically. The voltage amplification is roughly equal to the difference in plate voltage of points of intersection of the load line with two adjacent static plate characteristics, divided by the difference of grid voltage of the two characteristics. This is the ratio E_{zb}/E_g or E_{zb}'/E_g in Fig. 6-5. The accuracy of this method increases, of course, as the interval between the characteristics is decreased. It can be seen from Fig. 6-5 that the rate at which the amplification is increased with load resistance is small at high values of load resistance. For this reason and because of the falling off of amplification at high frequency when r_b is large, the load resistance in practice is usually limited to 500,000 Ω or less, even with triodes having high plate resistance. The voltage amplification that can be realized in practice with triodes approximates 80 per cent of the amplification factor.

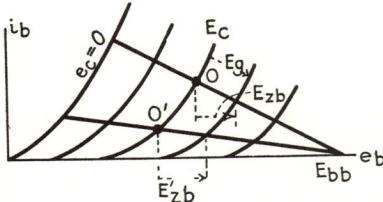

Fig. 6-5.—Plate diagram of a triode with pure resistance load, showing the variation of voltage output with load resistance at constant excitation.

For pentodes with resistance load the action is complicated by the fact that at low values of plate current the spacing of the static characteristics rapidly becomes smaller as the negative grid voltage is increased. The resulting curvature of the dynamic transfer characteristic causes amplitude distortion. The difficulty can be reduced by increasing the plate supply voltage, but the required voltage rapidly becomes prohibitive as the load resistance is increased. Practical values of pentode load resistance are also limited to about 500,000 Ω. Since pentode plate resistances are well in excess of a megohm, the realizable voltage amplification is much smaller than the amplification factor, 350 representing the approximate limit.

Values of voltage amplification approximating the amplification factor of pentodes can be obtained by using the plate resistance of a second pentode as the load resistance,[1] as shown in Fig. 6-6. The a-c resistance of the pentode that is used as load

---

[1] Herd, J. F., *Wireless Eng.*, **8**, 192 (1931); Meissner, E. R., *Electronics*, July, 1933, p. 195; Horton, J. W., *J. Franklin Inst.*, **216**, 749 (1933); Schmitt, O., *Rev. Sci. Instruments*, **4**, 661 (1933).

is high, but its electrode voltages may be adjusted so that the d-c drop through it is small, and so that its plate current is equal to the desired operating plate current of the amplifier pentode. In this manner it is possible to obtain high a-c load resistance without lowering the operating plate voltage and current of the amplifier pentode to values that give excessive distortion. The interelectrode capacitances of the two tubes cause the amplification to fall at the upper end of the audio-frequency range.

6-2. Voltage Amplification of Multistage Amplifiers.—The over-all amplification of a multistage amplifier is equal to the product of the amplifications of the individual stages. (The over-all gain is equal to the sum of the gains of the individual stages.) In forming the equivalent circuit of each stage, the stage must be considered to consist of the tube and all circuit elements coupled to the plate, including the tube capacitances

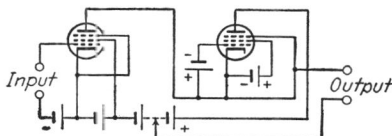

Fig. 6-6.—Single-stage pentode voltage amplifier in which a second pentode is used as the load resistance.

and the input admittance of the following tube.[1] Different types of coupling may, of course, be used in the different stages. The form of the plate load of the final stage depends upon the purpose for which the amplifier is designed.

Voltage Amplification of Direct-coupled Amplifier.—The direct-coupled amplifier illustrated in Figs. 5-1 to 5-3 consists of two stages of the simple amplifier of Fig. 6-1. Because of the effect of the input capacitance of the second tube upon the amplification of the first stage, the amplification begins to fall off at a lower frequency than with a single stage; otherwise the behavior is similar. The over-all amplification is the product of the amplifications of the two stages (the sum of the decibel gains), which may be determined from the equivalent circuit of Fig. 6-3. The direct-coupled amplifier is a special form of an impedance-capacitance—coupled amplifier in which the coupling condenser and grid-leak impedance are infinite. Since the

[1] The student is cautioned against attempting to combine the equivalent circuits of two or more stages into a single equivalent circuit.

impedance-capacitance–coupled amplifier is analyzed in the following sections, the direct-coupled amplifier need not be treated in further detail. If the coupling and output impedances of this type of amplifier are nonreactive, the amplification is independent of frequency from zero frequency up to frequencies at which the effect of interelectrode capacitances becomes apparent. This type of amplifier gives the least frequency and phase distortion and is the only type of multistage amplifier that will amplify at zero frequency, i.e., that will amplify changes in direct voltage or current.

6-3. Impedance-capacitance–coupled Voltage Amplifier.—The basic circuit of a two-stage impedance-capacitance–coupled

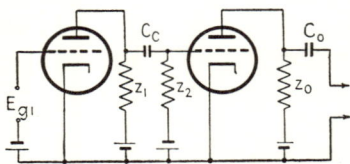

FIG. 6-7.—Two-stage impedance-capacitance–coupled amplifier.

amplifier is shown in Fig. 6-7. The final stage may be considered as a special form of impedance-capacitance–coupled stage in which one or two of the coupling elements are absent. If the amplifier is used to furnish voltage output only, then the load of the final stage may be considered to be merely z_o and the amplification may be found by the use of Eq. (6-1).

The equivalent circuit of an impedance-capacitance–coupled stage is shown in Fig. 6-8. Because the effective plate-to-cathode capacitance C_{pk1} is very much smaller than the capacitance of the coupling condenser C_c, the effect of C_{pk1} upon the behavior of the amplifier is the same as though C_{pk1} were connected in parallel with the input impedance z_{g2} of the following tube.[1] Further simplification results from the assumption that the input conductance of the following tube is negligible. Then the admittance is

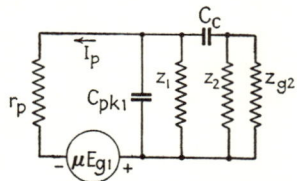

FIG. 6-8.—Equivalent plate circuit for the first stage of the amplifier of Fig. 6-7.

$$Y_{g2} = B_{g2} = j\omega C_{i2} = j\omega[C_{gk2} + (1 + |\mu'_2|)C_{gp2}] \qquad (6-2)^2$$

[1] Strictly, C_{pk1}', as defined on p. 132, rather than C_{pk1}, should be used in this analysis. In tubes suitable for use in voltage amplifiers, however, C_{gp1} is so much smaller than C_{pk1} that little error results from using C_{pk1} instead of C_{pk1}'.

[2] Equation (6-2) would be equivalent to Eq. (4-5) if the load in the plate circuit of the following tube were nonreactive.

in which $|\mu'_2|$ is the magnitude of the voltage amplification of the following stage at high frequency, and C_{gk2} and C_{gp2} are the interelectrode capacitances of the following tube.   The effective input capacitance C_{i2} of the following tube, in parallel with the effective plate-to-cathode capacitance C_{pk1}, may then be replaced by an equivalent capacitance

$$C_2 = C_{pk1} + C_{gk2} + (1 + |\mu'_2|)C_{gp2} \tag{6-3}$$

6-4. Analysis of Resistance-coupled Voltage Amplifier.—The most common type of impedance-capacitance–coupled amplifier is the resistance-coupled amplifier, in which z_1 and z_2 are both resistances.   Figure 6-9 shows the simplified equivalent circuit of

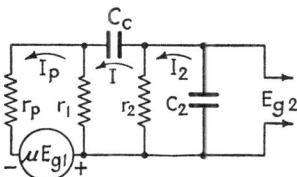

Fig.   6-9.—Approximate equivalent plate circuit for one stage of a resistance-coupled amplifier.

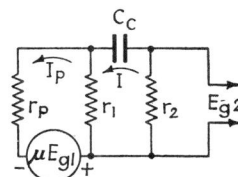

Fig.   6-10.—Simplified equivalent plate circuit for one stage of a resistance–coupled amplifier at low frequencies.

one stage of such an amplifier.   At frequencies below 1000 or 2000 $\sim$ the reactance of C_2 is so high in comparison with r_1 and r_2 that C_2 may be neglected and the circuit simplified to that of Fig. 6-10.   Summation of voltages in the circuit of Fig. 6-10 yields the following equations:

$$I_p(r_p + r_1) - Ir_1 = \mu E_{g1} \tag{6-4}$$

$$I\left(r_1 + r_2 - \frac{j}{\omega C_c}\right) = I_p r_1 \tag{6-5}$$

Examination of Fig. 6-7 shows that the grid of the second tube is made more negative when I_p and I are increased by making the grid of the first tube less negative.   Therefore, $E_{g2} = -Ir_2$ and the voltage amplification is

$$\mu' = \frac{E_{g2}}{E_{g1}} = -\frac{Ir_2}{E_{g1}} \tag{6-6}$$

Solution of the simultaneous Eqs. (6-4), (6-5), and (6-6) gives the following expression for the amplification of a stage of a resistance-capacitance–coupled amplifier at low frequencies:

$$\mu'_l = -\frac{\mu r_1 r_2}{r_1 r_2 + r_1 r_p + r_2 r_p - \frac{j(r_p + r_1)}{\omega C_c}} \tag{6-7}$$

The subscript in μ'_l is used to indicate that this equation holds only at low frequencies.

At frequencies above a few hundred cycles per second the reactance of C_c is ordinarily so low that C_c may be assumed to be short-circuited. The equivalent circuit at high frequencies is, therefore, that of Fig. 6-11. If the impedance of the parallel combination of r_1, r_2, and C_2 is called z_b, then the circuit of Fig. 6-11 is the same as that of Fig. 6-3 when C_{pk}' is neglected in the latter.

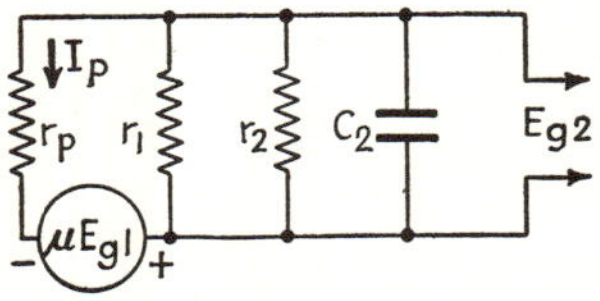

Fig. 6-11.—Simplified equivalent plate circuit for one stage of a resistance-coupled amplifier at high frequencies.

The voltage amplification is given by Eq. (6-1), in which

$$z_b = \frac{1}{\dfrac{1}{r_1} + \dfrac{1}{r_2} + j\omega C_2} \tag{6-8}$$

If the numerator and denominator of the right side of Eq. (6-1) are divided by $z_b r_p$, Eq. (6-1) may be written in the form

$$\mu' = \frac{\dfrac{1}{r_p}}{\dfrac{1}{r_p} + \dfrac{1}{z_b}} = g_m \frac{1}{\dfrac{1}{r_p} + \dfrac{1}{z_b}} \tag{6-9}$$

Substitution of Eq. (6-8) in Eq. (6-9) gives for the high-frequency amplification

$$\mu'_h = \frac{1}{\dfrac{1}{r_p} + \dfrac{1}{r_1} + \dfrac{1}{r_2} + j\omega C_2} \tag{6-10}$$

Examination of Eq. (6-7) shows that as the frequency is increased from a low value, μ'_l increases toward a limiting value, which will be called the *mid-band* amplification and which will be represented by the symbol μ'_m.

$$\mu'_m = \frac{\mu r_1 r_2}{r_1 r_2 + r_1 r_p + r_2 r_p} = g_m \frac{1}{\frac{1}{r_p} + \frac{1}{r_1} + \frac{1}{r_2}} \tag{6-11}$$

By proper choice of circuit constants the amplification may be made to remain constant at the mid-band value over a wide range of frequency.

Examination of Eq. (6-10) shows that, as the frequency is increased at the upper end of the mid-band range, the amplification gradually begins to fall below the mid-band value, and

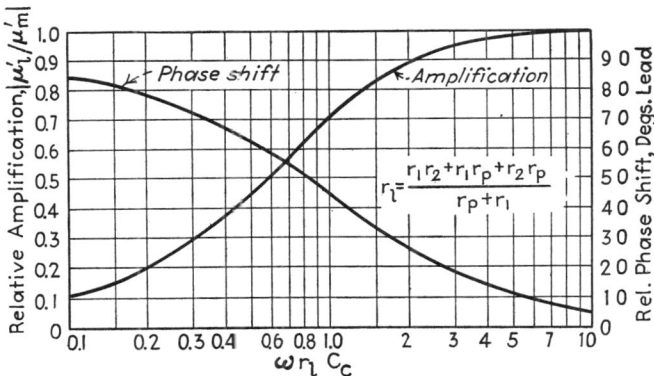

FIG. 6-12.—Generic curves of relative amplification and relative phase shift of a resistance-capacitance–coupled stage at low frequencies.

eventually approaches zero. The loss of amplification at low frequency is explained physically by the voltage-divider action of C_c and r_2. Since the reactance of C_c increases as the frequency is reduced, more voltage appears across the condenser and less is applied to the grid of the following tube. Loss of amplification at high frequency is caused by the action of C_2, which shunts r_1 and r_2 and thus reduces the effective load impedance. The load impedance and, hence, the output voltage go down as the frequency goes up.

Figs 6-12 and 6-13 show generalized curves of the ratio of voltage amplification at any frequency to the mid-band amplification, and of phase shift of the output voltage relative to the mid-band phase of the output voltage at low and at high frequency, respectively. Figure 6-14 shows typical response curves of a single-stage resistance-capacitance–coupled amplifier derived from the curves of Figs. 6-12 and 6-13 for the indicated tube and circuit constants.

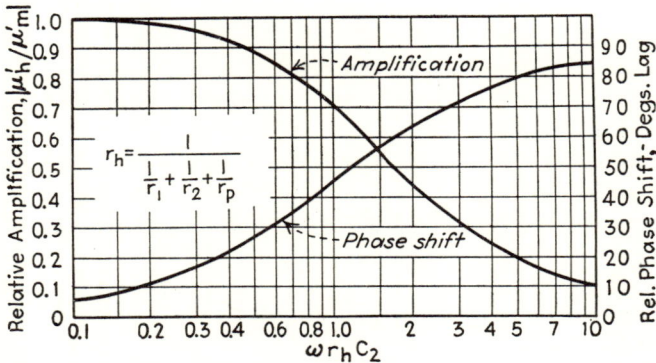

Fig. 6-13.—Generic curves of relative amplification and relative phase shift of a resistance-capacitance–coupled stage at high frequencies.

In practice it is ordinarily desirable to have a wide frequency range over which the amplification remains constant at the mid-band value. This fact justifies the assumption, made in the foregoing treatment, that C_2 may be neglected in the low-frequency analysis and C_c in the high-frequency analysis.

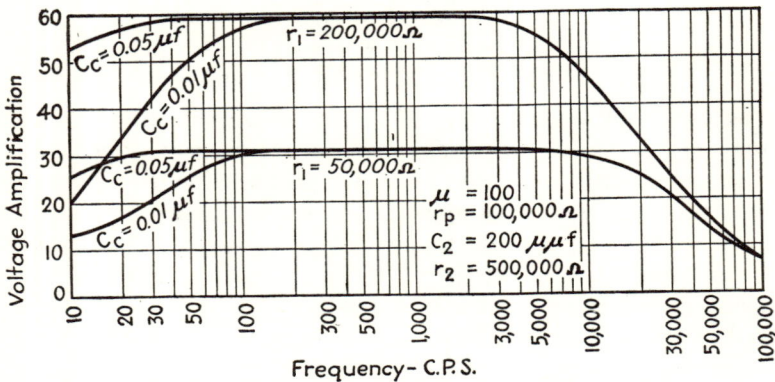

Fig. 6-14.—Frequency-response characteristics for a typical resistance-coupled amplifier.

Analysis of Eq. (6-11) shows that the maximum amplification, the mid-band value, increases with increase of amplification factor μ, coupling resistance r_1, and grid-leak resistance r_2, and decreases with increase of plate resistance r_p. Analysis of Eq. (6-7) shows that the mid-band range, throughout which the amplification is independent of frequency, can be extended at the low-frequency end by increasing r_2 and C_c and, less effectively, by increasing r_1 or r_p. Analysis of Eq. (6-10), on the other hand, shows that the mid-band range is extended in the high-frequency direction by *decreasing* r_1, r_2, r_p, or C_2. For convenient reference, these facts are shown in tabular form in Table 6-I, which lists effects produced by increasing the various tube factors and circuit constants. Improvement of characteristics, consisting of widening of the range of uniform amplification or of increase of maximum amplification, is indicated by a plus sign in this table; a narrowing of the range of constant amplification or a reduction of maximum amplification is indicated by a minus sign; 0 signifies that variation of a given quantity has no effect upon the amplification in a particular portion of the frequency band. The lowering of the upper limit of uniform amplification listed in the bottom row of the table results from the increase of C_2, shown by Eq. (6-3), and so is actually included in the effect tabulated in the preceding row.

TABLE 6-I.—EFFECT OF TUBE FACTORS AND CIRCUIT CONSTANTS UPON RESISTANCE-CAPACITANCE–COUPLED AMPLIFIER RESPONSE

Increase of	Lower frequency limit of mid-band amplification	Mid-band amplification, μ'_m	Upper frequency limit of mid-band amplification
μ	0	+	0
r_p	−	−	−
C_c	−	0	0
r_1	−	+	−
r_2	+	+	−
C_2	0	0	−
μ' of following stage	0	0	−

The improvement of low-frequency response resulting from increase of C_c, and the effect of decrease of r_1 upon the upper limit of uniform amplification and upon amplification throughout the whole frequency range, are clearly shown by Fig. 6-14.

6-5. Design of Resistance-coupled Amplifiers.—Since circuit constants suitable for use with different types of tubes in resistance-coupled amplifiers are specified by tube manufacturers, it is seldom necessary to design a special circuit. When this is done, however, the first step is to choose tubes whose amplification factor exceeds the desired amplification per stage. The grid coupling resistance r_2 of each stage should then be chosen so that it does not exceed the maximum value specified for the following tube.[1] The plate coupling resistances r_1 should be chosen next. These should not as a rule exceed in value either the grid coupling resistances, five times the plate resistances, or 500,000 Ω. The amplification of each stage in the mid-band range can be determined from Eq. (6-11). For tubes with high plate resistance, this approximates the product of g_m and the resistance of r_1 and r_2 in parallel, as the student may readily show. If the mid-band amplification is high enough to meet requirements, the approximate amplification of the following stage should be used in Eq. (6-3) to find C_2 for each stage. Then, by means of Eq. (6-10) or the curve of Fig. 6-13, the amplification may be determined at high frequency. If the upper frequency limit of uniform response is too low, the plate (and grid) coupling resistances should be lowered in value and the amplifier rechecked for mid-band and high-frequency amplification. Finally, a value of C_c should be chosen that will give adequate response at low frequency, as determined from Eq. (6-7) or Fig. 6-12.

It should be noted that the values of r_p and μ that are used in computing the amplification are those at the operating point. They can be determined most readily graphically. The operating point is found from the intersection of the static operating line with the static plate characteristic corresponding to the grid bias. The static load line must, of course, correspond with a resistance equal to the sum of all d-c resistances in the plate circuit.

When grid current is allowed to flow in a resistance-coupled amplifier, a part of the current that would otherwise flow through the grid-coupling resistor flows through the tube during the portion of the cycle in which the grid current flows. The resulting reduction in IR drop across the grid resistor tends to flatten

---

[1] If the grid coupling resistance is made too large, there is danger of cumulative rise of grid voltage and, therefore, plate current, as the result of secondary emission from the grid and ionization of residual gas. See H. J. Reich, "Theory and Applications of Electron Tubes," pp. 184–185.

the positive crests of excitation voltage and thus causes amplitude distortion. Suitable bias for class A1 operation can usually be determined from the plate diagram by inspection. Ordinarily the grid swing of a voltage amplifier is so small that the amplitude distortion is well within the allowable value. When the grid swing is large, however, it may be advisable to check the final stage for harmonic content. By application of the graphical methods outlined in Chap. 4, it is possible to determine the grid bias that will give the greatest allowable grid swing without exceeding the allowable distortion. In making such a determination and in finding the maximum crest output voltage graphically, it must be borne in mind that grid current may start flowing when the grid is $\frac{1}{2}$ to $\frac{3}{4}$ volt negative. Grid current therefore limits the allowable grid swing to values that

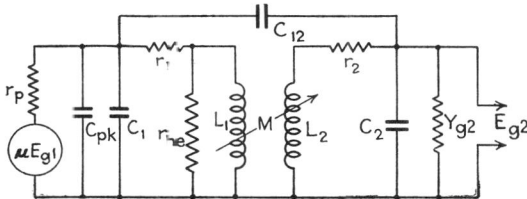

Fig. 6-15.—Complete equivalent plate circuit for a stage of a transformer-coupled audio-frequency amplifier.

are smaller than the grid bias. This is of particular importance in amplifiers using high-mu tubes, for which the grid bias is small. The crest output voltage may be appreciably less than $\mu' E_c$ (see Probs. 6-5 and 6-6).

6-6. Transformer-coupled Audio-frequency Voltage Amplifier. The analysis and design of the transformer-coupled audio-frequency voltage amplifier are complicated by the action of distributed winding capacitances. Because the performance of such an amplifier is determined largely by the characteristics of the coupling transformer, a complete rigorous analysis is of interest chiefly to the transformer manufacturer. A qualitative understanding of the effect of the tube factors and circuit parameters is helpful, however, in making an intelligent selection of tubes and transformers and in choosing between transformer- and resistance-coupled amplifiers.

An equivalent circuit that closely represents one stage of a transformer-coupled amplifier is shown in Fig. 6-15. C_1, C_2, and C_{12} are lumped capacitances that replace the distributed winding capacitances, r_{he} is an equivalent resistance that accounts for the hysteresis and eddy-current core losses, and r_1, r_2, L_1, L_2, and M are the resistances, self-inductances, and mutual inductance of the windings. In a well-designed transformer the core losses are so small that r_{he} may be neglected. A complete rigorous analysis based upon the circuit of Fig. 6-15 is somewhat involved.[1] For the purpose of this book an analysis based upon two simplified diagrams is more suitable.

1. *Amplification at Low and Intermediate Frequencies.*—Below a few hundred cycles the reactance of the distributed capacitance of the windings is so high (approximately 10^6 Ω) that its effect may be neglected. In class A1 amplification the admittance of the following tube is also negligible. The secondary of the

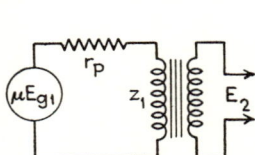

Fig. 6-16.—Simplified equivalent plate circuit of a transformer-coupled audio-frequency stage at low and mid-band frequencies.

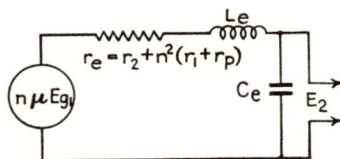

Fig. 6-17.—Simplified equivalent plate circuit of a transformer-coupled audio-frequency stage at high frequencies.

transformer may therefore be considered to be unloaded. If the small core losses are neglected, the equivalent circuit reduces to that of Fig. 6-16. z_1, the primary impedance, is equal to $r_1 + j\omega L_1$, where L_1 is the total primary inductance. The voltage induced across the primary is

$$E_1 = \frac{\mu E_{g1} z_1}{r_p + z_1} = \mu E_{g1} \frac{\sqrt{r_1^2 + \omega^2 L_1^2}}{\sqrt{(r_1 + r_p)^2 + \omega^2 L_1^2}} \qquad (6\text{-}12)$$

The primary resistance is so much smaller than the reactance even at low frequency that it may be neglected in the numerator of Eq. (6-12). With this approximation the secondary voltage is

$$E_2 = nE_1 = \frac{n\mu E_{g1}}{\sqrt{1 + \left(\dfrac{r_1 + r_p}{\omega L_1}\right)^2}} \qquad (6\text{-}13)$$

[1] KOEHLER, GLENN, *Proc. I.R.E.*, **16**, 1742 (1928). See also H. J. Reich, "Theory and Applications of Electron Tubes," Sec. 7-9.

where n is the ratio of secondary to primary turns. The voltage amplification of the stage is

$$\mu'_l = \frac{E_2}{E_{g1}} = \frac{n\mu}{\sqrt{1 + \left(\frac{r_1 + r_p}{\omega L_1}\right)^2}} \tag{6-14}$$

As ω is increased μ'_l increases, approaching the limiting value $n\mu$. The curve relating low-frequency amplification with frequency is of the same form as the upper curve of Fig. 6-4 (the scale of ordinates being multiplied by n). The frequency at which μ'_l approaches the value $n\mu$ goes down as the ratio $L_1/(r_p + r_1)$ is increased and may be below 100 cycles in a well-designed amplifier. Equation (6-14) shows that the loss of amplification at low frequency is the result of falling of the primary reactance with frequency.

2. *Amplification at High Frequency.*—When the frequency becomes so high that the distributed capacitance cannot be neglected, the circuit approximates that of Fig. 6-17, in which C_e represents an equivalent capacitance replacing the primary, secondary, and interwinding capacitances of the transformer and the input capacitance of the following tube; L_e is the total equivalent leakage inductance; and r_e is the total equivalent winding and plate resistance, all quantities being referred to the secondary. The voltage applied to the grid of the following tube is that across the condenser. The voltage amplification is

$$\mu'_h = \frac{E_2}{E_{g1}} = \frac{n\mu}{\omega C_e \sqrt{r_e^2 + \left(\omega L_e - \frac{1}{\omega C_e}\right)^2}} \tag{6-15}$$

This has a maximum value approximately at the frequency that makes the reactive term under the radical zero. The voltage amplification at resonance is, therefore, approximately

$$\mu'_r = \sqrt{\frac{L_e}{C_e}} \cdot \frac{\mu n}{r_e} \tag{6-16}$$

By proper design it is possible to make the factor $\frac{1}{r_e} \sqrt{\frac{L_e}{C_e}}$ approximately equal to unity, so that there is little rise in amplification because of resonance, and the amplification is substantially constant and equal to $n\mu$ up to 8000 or 10,000 cycles.

Equation (6-15) shows that μ' falls above resonance frequency. Both the factor ωC_e, outside of the radical, and the factor ωL_e, under the radical, increase with frequency, so that the gain eventually falls to zero. Physically, the increase of ωC_e is associated with the shunting effect of the distributed capacitance, and the increase of ωL_e with the loss in voltage in leakage reactance. Figure 6-18 shows the frequency-response curve of a transformer-coupled amplifier.

It should be noted that in a well-designed transformer-coupled audio-frequency voltage amplifier the voltage amplification is equal to $n\mu$ throughout most of the frequency range for which the transformer is designed.

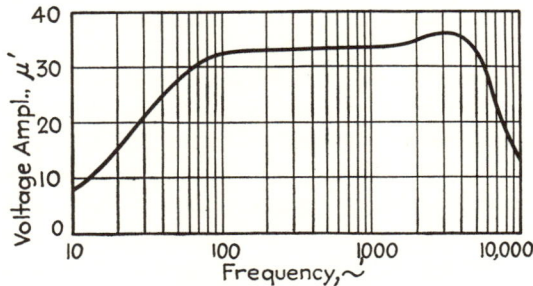

Fig. 6-18.—Frequency-response curve of a transformer-coupled audio-frequency amplifier.

6-7. Transformer Design.—The correct designing of an audio-frequency coupling transformer is not a simple matter, as a compromise must be made between conflicting requirements. Equation (6-14) shows that for satisfactory response at low audio frequencies the primary inductance must be high. Even with high permeability cores this requires the use of a large number of turns. A high resonance frequency, beyond which the gain falls rapidly, calls for low leakage inductance and small distributed capacitance. The leakage inductance and distributed capacitance can be minimized by proper methods of winding and careful choice of shape and arrangement of coils,[1] but with any type of winding the increase of distributed capacitance with number of turns affects the high-frequency response adversely. Since a high transformation ratio requires either

[1] Koehler, *loc. cit.*

a small number of primary turns or a large number of secondary turns, or both, it follows that the increase in voltage amplification which results from the use of a high transformation ratio can be obtained only at the expense of poor response at low or high frequency or both. In early receivers for broadcast reception, high amplification was obtained by the use of audio transformers with small primaries. As a result these receivers were noted for their lack of bass tones. Well-designed modern transformers for class A voltage amplifiers do not ordinarily use transformation ratios higher than 3 to 1. It can be seen from a study of Eqs. (6-14) and (6-15) that high plate resistance is unfavorable to good response at both low and high frequencies. It is important to note that, because of dependence of amplification upon plate resistance at low and high frequencies, the published response curves of an audio-frequency transformer apply only to the tube for which the transformer was designed.

6-8. Comparison of Resistance-capacitance– and Transformer-coupled Audio Amplifiers.—The fact that uniform amplification in excess of the amplification factor of the tube can be obtained with transformer coupling if the plate resistance is not too high made the use of transformer coupling decidedly advantageous before the development of tubes with high amplification factors. Unfortunately, however, high amplification factor is accompanied by high plate resistance, and so high-mu tubes like the type 6SJ7 pentode cannot be satisfactorily used with transformer coupling. The response is poor at low frequency, because of the low ratio of primary reactance to plate resistance; and at high frequency because of the low value of $\frac{1}{r_e}\sqrt{\frac{L_e}{C_e}}$. A voltage amplification of 50 represents about the highest that can be obtained with transformer coupling without sacrifice of response at low or high frequency. With resistance-capacitance coupling, even though the stage amplification is much lower than the amplification factor of the tube, the high amplification factors of tubes like the 6SJ7 make it possible to obtain an amplification of 100 or more per stage. Because likelihood of oscillation makes it difficult to use more than two transformer-coupled stages on a common voltage supply, higher amplification at audio frequencies can as a rule be obtained with resistance-capacitance coupling than with transformer coupling. Resistance-capacitance coupling is considerably cheaper than transformer coupling, weighs less, and requires less space. Because of the lower direct voltage drop in the plate circuit, and because of induced voltage in the transformer, higher voltage output may be obtained with a given plate supply voltage with transformer output than with resistance output.

6-9. Inductance-capacitance   Coupling.—Inductance-capacitance coupling has the advantage over resistance-capacitance coupling of lower direct voltage drop in the plate load. Because there is only one winding, it is possible to obtain somewhat higher inductance than in the primary of a transformer. Although this higher inductance improves the low-frequency response over that of a transformer-coupled amplifier, it is still too low to prevent the amplification from falling off at low frequency with high–amplification-factor tubes. The high-frequency response is also somewhat better than in transformer-coupled amplifiers because of the lower distributed capacitance of the single winding. These advantages are offset by the fact that the voltage is not stepped up as it may be by a transformer. Inductance-capacitance coupling is now seldom used. It may be analyzed by the methods that have been used in this chapter.

6-10. Choice of Tubes for Audio-frequency Voltage Amplifiers. Equations (6-1), (6-11), and (6-14) to (6-16) show that the maximum amplification obtainable with a voltage amplifier is proportional to the amplification factor of the tube. For this reason the amplification factor may be considered to be the "figure of merit" of a tube used in an audio-frequency voltage amplifier. Other factors such as plate resistance and plate current are also of importance in choosing the tubes for a voltage amplifier. High plate resistance reduces the attainable gain of direct- or resistance-capacitance–coupled amplifiers and causes frequency distortion in transformer-coupled amplifiers. High plate current causes high direct voltage drop in the coupling resistor of direct- or resistance-capacitance–coupled amplifiers and tends to cause amplitude and frequency distortion in transformer-coupled amplifiers because of core saturation. It also increases the power consumption in the plate circuit.

Higher voltage amplification is in general attainable with pentodes than with triodes in resistance-coupled amplifiers, but amplitude distortion may be greater and, because of higher plate resistance, it is more difficult to design for uniform response over a wide band. Since the amplification attainable with pentodes approximates $\dfrac{r_1 r_2}{r_1 + r_2} g_m$, the transconductance may be considered to be the figure of merit of pentodes in resistance-coupled voltage amplifiers. The high plate resistance of pentodes makes them unsuitable for use in transformer-coupled audio-frequency amplifiers.

6-11. Control of Amplification of Audio-frequency Amplifiers. The most common method of controlling the amplification of audio-frequency voltage amplifiers is by means of a voltage divider that varies the excitation voltage of one of the tubes, usually the first. In transformer-coupled amplifiers the voltage divider is shunted across the secondary of the input transformer, as in Fig. 6-19a; in resistance-coupled amplifiers it may serve

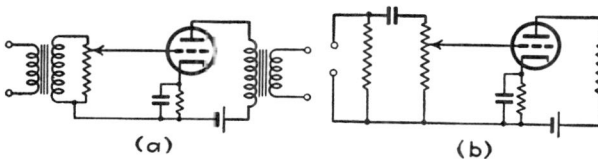

(a)   (b)

Fig. 6-19.—Methods of controlling amplification of transformer- and resistance-coupled audio-frequency amplifiers.

as the grid coupling resistance, as in Fig. 6-19b. In the transformer-coupled circuit, the resistance of the voltage divider should be high in order to prevent appreciable loading of the transformer. Potentiometers of 500,000-Ω resistance or higher are commonly used.

Because the voltage amplification of resistance-coupled amplifiers using pentodes or other high-plate-resistance tubes is nearly proportional to g_m, the amplification of such amplifiers can be readily controlled by varying the transconductance by means of grid bias. In order to make it possible to reduce the transconductance to a low value without danger of having the grid swing beyond cutoff, the signal is applied to a remote-cutoff grid (see Fig. 3-7). Although the gain-control voltage may be applied to the same grid as the signal, less control voltage is required if it is applied to an additional sharp cutoff grid. It may be applied simultaneously to both grids. The 6L7 type of tube is suitable for this purpose. This type of control has the advantage that it may be accomplished by means of a rheostat or potentiometer that is located at a distance from the amplifier and is by-passed by a condenser at the amplifier. If two tubes controlled in this manner and excited by separate signal voltages use a common plate load resistance, then a gradual transition may be made from one signal to the other by raising one control voltage and lowering the other.

6-12. Tone Control.[1]—Difference in the acoustical properties of different rooms, nonuniform response of loud-speakers, individual preferences, and the fact that the sensitivity of the ear falls off at low and high frequencies often make it desirable or necessary to change the frequency characteristics of audio-frequency amplifiers. Minor changes in the characteristic of an amplifier can be obtained by the use of simple filters. One commonly used filter consists of a condenser in series with a variable resistance, shunted across some point of the amplifier, usually between grid and cathode of one of the tubes. Decrease of resistance cuts down the response at the higher frequencies. Sometimes tone control is combined with the manual gain control in such a manner that the amplification is reduced more at the middle of the audio range than at the upper and lower ends. This tends to correct for the apparent loss of low and high tones at low sound level caused by the nonuniform response of the ear.

6-13. Tuned Radio-frequency Amplifiers.—Radio-frequency amplifiers of the type used in radio receivers are coupled by means of singly or doubly tuned transformers. Typical circuits are those of Figs. 5-7 and 5-8. Like the audio-frequency amplifiers treated in the foregoing sections, they may be analyzed by the use of equivalent circuits.[2] Such analyses show that the maximum amplification is proportional to $\sqrt{\mu g_m}$ in singly

---

[1] SCROGGIE, M. G., *Wireless Eng.*, **9**, 3 (1932); Hazeltine Service Corp., *Radio Eng.*, June, 1935, p. 7; COLEBROOK, F. M., *Wireless Eng.*, **10**, 4 (1933) (with bibliography of seven items); CALLENDER, M. V., *Proc. I.R.E.*, **20**, 1427 (1932).

[2] EVERITT, W. L., "Communication Engineering," McGraw-Hill Book Company, Inc., New York, 1937; TERMAN, F. E., "Radio Engineering," McGraw-Hill Book Company, Inc., New York, 1937; GLASGOW, R. S., "Principles of Radio Engineering," McGraw-Hill Book Company, Inc., New York, 1936; HUND, AUGUST, "Phenomena in High-frequency Systems," McGraw-Hill Book Company, Inc., New York, 1936. See also H. J. Reich, "Theory and Applications of Electron Tubes," Secs. 7-17 to 7-22.

tuned amplifiers and to g_m in doubly tuned amplifiers. The response curve of a singly tuned amplifier is of the same form as the curve of admittance *vs.* frequency of a simple series circuit containing inductance, capacitance, and resistance. The sharpness of the resonance peak increases with decrease of coupling between primary and secondary, with decrease of resonant frequency of the secondary, with increase of ratio of secondary inductance to secondary resistance, and with increase of plate resistance. The response curve of a doubly tuned amplifier has two peaks which approach each other and finally merge into a single peak as the coupling is reduced. By combining a closely coupled doubly tuned stage with a singly tuned stage or a loosely coupled doubly tuned stage, it is possible to obtain an over-all response curve that approximates rectangular form.

Dependence of amplification of tuned radio-frequency amplifiers upon transconductance makes possible the control of amplification by variation of operating voltages. In order to maintain constant output voltage, the negative bias of one or more grids is increased with excitation voltage. This means that the operating point is nearest to cutoff when the grid swing is high. To minimize distortion resulting from curvature of the transfer characteristic in the vicinity of cutoff and from the actual cutting off of plate current during the negative peaks of exciting voltage, the signal voltage is applied to a remote-cutoff grid. The gain-control voltage may be impressed upon the same grid, upon an additional sharp-cutoff grid, or upon both.

To prevent oscillation in tuned radio-frequency amplifiers as the result of feeding back of output voltage to the grid through the grid-plate tube capacitance, low grid-plate capacitance is essential. For this reason, and because of their high values of transconductance and amplification factor, pentodes or tetrodes are used in tuned radio-frequency amplifiers.

6-14. Use of By-pass Condensers.—The presence of impedance in the voltage supply of a multistage amplifier or in a common lead between the voltage supply and the plates or other electrodes may result in objectionable feeding back of output voltage to the input and may thus cause oscillation.[1] An example of a circuit in which a resistance common to several

[1] ANDERSON, J. E., *Proc. I R.E.*, **15**, 195 (1927); TAMM, R., *E.T.Z.*, **57**, 631 (1930).

stages may lead to oscillation is given by Fig. 6-20. The resistance r may be that of a worn battery, a poorly designed power supply, or a voltage-dropping resistor. The arrows indicate the directions of the instantaneous alternating plate currents of the three tubes resulting from an instantaneous applied voltage that swings the grid voltage of the first tube in the positive direction. Because of amplification, $i_{p1} + i_{p3}$ exceeds i_{p2}, and so the drop through r is in the direction shown. This voltage drop is added to that caused by the flow of i_{p1} through the plate resistor of the first stage, and so the alternating voltage applied to the grid of the second tube is greater than it would be if r were zero. A number of other similar feedback effects

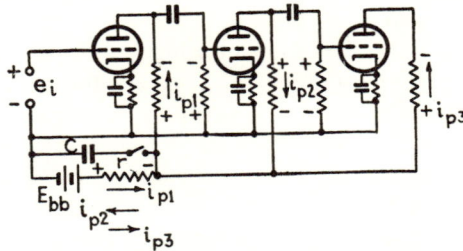

Fig. 6-20.—Circuit diagram showing the manner in which common plate-supply impedance may cause oscillation in a multistage resistance-coupled amplifier having an odd number of stages.

take place between stages because of r, but these are of smaller magnitude. If r is large, and the gain of the amplifier high, the feedback may be sufficiently great to cause oscillation (see Sec. 8-3). This may be prevented by shunting r with a condenser C, whose reactance is small throughout the amplification range.

A common source of feedback in audio-frequency amplifiers is B-supply regulation. Because of variation of voltage drop through the rectifier tubes and filter, the terminal voltage of a B supply varies with the current drain. This type of feedback causes low-frequency oscillation, aptly termed *motorboating*. Feedback resulting from B-supply regulation can be reduced by using in each stage a *decoupling filter* consisting of a resistance and condenser, as shown by the heavy lines of Fig. 6-21a.[1]

[1] Baggally, W., *Wireless Eng.*, **11**, 179 (1934); Cocking, W. T., *Wireless World*, **29**, 322, (1931). See also Sec. 5-8.

Better filtering may be obtained, particularly in radio-frequency amplifiers, by the use of chokes instead of resistors, as illustrated by the heavy lines of Fig. 6-21b. Chokes have the additional advantage of not reducing the operating plate voltage greatly. Better methods of preventing motorboating are to make the gain of the amplifier small enough at very low frequency so that this low-frequency oscillation cannot occur,[1] or to use push-pull circuits. When voltage-dropping resistors must be used to reduce the electrode voltages of the tubes of a number of stages, it is in general advisable to use individual resistors and by-pass condensers for the different tubes.

6-15. Shielding.—The high amplification obtained in radio-frequency amplifiers and in audio-frequency amplifiers using

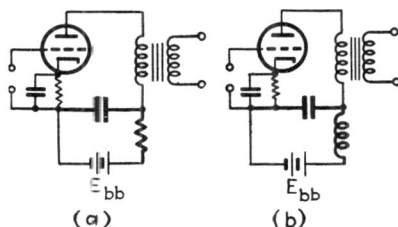

FIG. 6-21.—Plate decoupling filters.

tetrodes or pentodes usually necessitates the complete shielding of the individual stages in multistage amplifiers to prevent oscillation. It may also be necessary to shield input leads to the amplifier to prevent the picking up of stray fields and to prevent feedback from the output to the input.

Limit of Amplification.—Amplification is usually limited by a tendency of the amplifier to oscillate as the result of the feeding back of some of the output voltage to the input. This can be minimized by shielding, by careful placing of apparatus, and by the use of chokes and by-pass condensers and of more than one power supply. By means of successive amplifiers operated from separate power supplies, very high gain or power output can be obtained. Because of inherent fluctuations of currents in amplifiers, however, there is a lower limit to the input voltage or current that can be amplified to a given output level. Current and voltage fluctuations in an amplifier are called *noise*. Noise

[1] RCA Application Note 67.

results from a number of causes, among which are the shot effect, ionization, secondary emission, vibration of tube elements, imperfect contacts, fluctuations of resistance of old or damaged batteries, incomplete filtering of power supplies, variation of resistance of circuit elements, and random motion of electrons through high resistances.[1] The shot effect (see Sec. 2-14) can be kept to a minimum by operating tubes well above temperature saturation. Ionization and secondary emission, which have been greatly reduced in modern tubes, can be eliminated when necessary by the use of very low voltages. "Microphonic" effects resulting from the vibration of tube elements have been largely eliminated in modern tubes by improving the methods of mounting and supporting the elements. Current fluctuations produced by the random motion of electrons in resistances are in some respects similar to those produced by the shot effect. The disturbance caused by this thermal agitation is a function of the temperature and increases with the width of the frequency band over which the amplifier amplifies. In order to minimize noise, it is advisable not to make the frequency range of the amplifier wider than necessary.

6-16. Measurement of Voltage Amplification.—Figure 6-22 shows the circuit that is commonly used for the measurement of

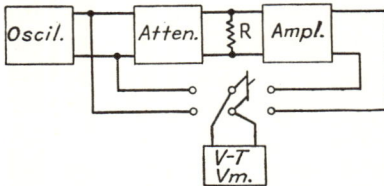

Fig. 6-22.—Circuit for the measurement of voltage amplification.

voltage amplification of an amplifier. When the attenuation of the attenuator is equal to the gain of the amplifier, the deflection of the vacuum-tube voltmeter does not change when the position of the switch is changed. If the attenuator is calibrated in decibels, it gives a direct reading of the amplifier gain in decibels. The purpose of the resistor R is to provide the proper terminating resistance for the attenuator. If a calibrated attenuator is not available, it may be replaced by a voltage divider, as in Fig. 6-23. The voltage amplification μ' is equal to the ratio r_2/r_1 when the same voltmeter reading is obtained with the switch in the two positions. When high accuracy is not essential, a

[1] See bibliography at the end of this chapter and at the end of Chap. 7 of H. J. Reich, "Theory and Applications of Electron Tubes."

cathode-ray oscilloscope may be used in place of the vacuum-tube voltmeter in the circuits of Figs. 6-22 and 6-23 (see Sec. 12-5).

Frequency response curves are usually obtained by making a series of measurements of voltage amplification at various frequencies throughout the range of the amplifier. Oscillographic methods have been developed in which the response curve is observed directly on the screen of an oscillograph.[1] Much useful information concerning the frequency and phase distortion of an amplifier can also be obtained by determining the manner in which it distorts periodic triangular or square waves of voltage.[2]

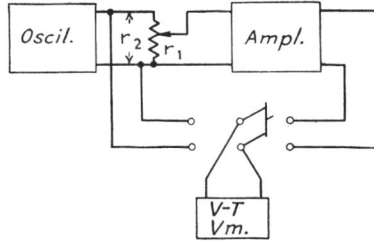

FIG. 6-23.—Circuit for the measurement of voltage amplification.

6-17. Current Amplification.—Figure 6-24 shows a single-stage current amplifier. The current amplification is

$$\frac{I_p}{I_i} = \frac{\mu E_g}{r_p + z_b} \cdot \frac{1}{I_i} = \frac{\mu z_c}{r_p + z_b} \qquad (6\text{-}17)$$

The current amplification increases as z_b is decreased, approaching the limiting value $g_m z_c$. The current sensitivity is $\mu/(r_p + z_b)$, which approaches the value g_m as z_b is decreased. This indicates the importance of transconductance in tubes used for current amplification. In a multistage current amplifier, all except the last stage are voltage amplifiers and require tubes with high amplification factor to give high over-all current sensitivity.

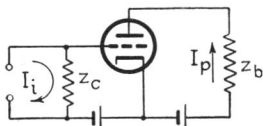

FIG. 6-24.—Single-stage current amplifier.

Current amplifiers are useful in the operation of relays[3] and electromagnetic oscillographs.[4] One common application is

[1] DIAMOND, H., and WEBB, J. S., *Proc. I.R.E.*, **15**, 767 (1927).

[2] REICH, H. J., *Proc. I.R.E.*, **19**, 401 (1931); STOCKER, A. C., *Proc. I.R.E.*, **25**, 1012 (1937); SWIFT, G., *Communications*, February, 1939, p. 22; BEDFORD, A. V., and FREDENDAHLE, G. L., *Proc. I.R.E.*, **27**, 277 (1939); ARGUIMBAU, L. B., *General Radio Experimenter*, **14**, December, 1939, p. 1.

[3] GEORGE, E. E., *Electronics*, August, 1937, p. 19; DUDLEY, B., *Electronics*, May, 1938, p. 18; MUEHTER, M. W., *Electronics*, December, 1933, p. 336.

[4] JACKSON, W., *Wireless Eng.*, **11**, 64 (1934); REICH, H. J., and MARVIN,

in the amplification of the current of phototubes used to control relays.   Circuits for this purpose are analyzed in Chap. 10. Another application of current amplifiers is in the regulation of generator voltage.[1]   A typical circuit is shown in basic form in Fig. 6-25, in which VT_1 is a voltage amplifier, VT_2 is a current amplifier, and VT_3 is a glow tube that reduces the voltage applied to the grid of VT_1 from the positive terminal of the generator and thus lowers the required biasing battery voltage (see Sec. 9-4). The action is as follows: Reduction of terminal voltage makes the grid of VT_1 more negative and so makes that of VT_2 less negative. The resulting increase of plate current of VT_2 raises the field current of the exciter, which in turn raises the excitation of the

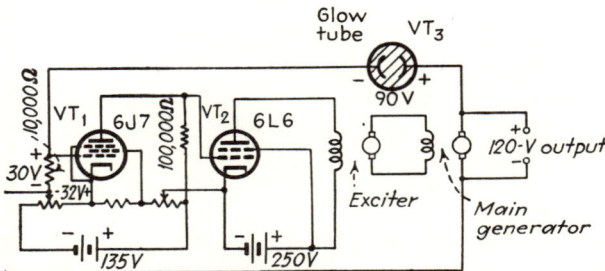

Fig. 6-25.—Vacuum-tube voltage regulator for a d-c generator.

main generator and restores the terminal voltage nearly to its original value.   Obviously the exciter may be eliminated if the current of VT_2 is sufficient to excite the generator directly. VT_1 may also be eliminated if very high constancy of voltage is not required.   By the addition of a rectifier, the circuit may be adapted to alternator regulation.

6-18. Trigger Circuits.—In the circuit of Fig. 6-26, the flow of plate current of one tube through its load resistance r_b makes the grid of the other tube negative.   If the value of r_b is large enough, the other tube is biased to cutoff.   As a result, current

G. S., *Rev. Sci. Instruments*, **2**, 814 (1931); Waldorf, S. K., *J. Franklin Inst.*, **213**, 605 (1932).

[1] Van der Bijl, H. J., "The Thermionic Vacuum Tube and Its Applications," p. 371, McGraw-Hill Book Company, Inc., New York, 1920; Verman, L. C., and Reich, H. J., *Proc. I.R.E.*, **17**, 2075 (1929); Verman, L. C., and Richards, L. A., *Rev. Sci. Instruments*, **1**, 581 (1930).

flows in only one tube at a time.[1]   The current may be caused to transfer abruptly from one tube to the other at critical values of electrode voltages by changing the voltage of either electrode of either tube in the direction to decrease the plate current of the conducting tube or to cause current to flow in the other

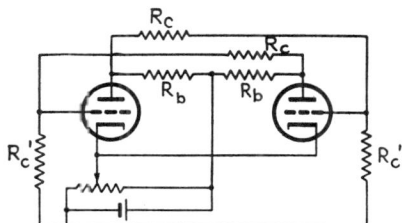

FIG. 6-26.—Eccles-Jordan trigger circuit.

tube.   Transfer can be initiated by a voltage pulse of short duration, and even by touching the grid terminal of one tube. Figure 6-27 shows a circuit that has two stable values of screen current and corresponding values of plate current.   An abrupt change from one value to the other takes place at critical values of electrode voltages, and may be caused by voltage pulses.[2]   Circuits such as these, which are called *trigger circuits*, are the basis of oscillators and of electronic switches, measuring instruments, and controls.

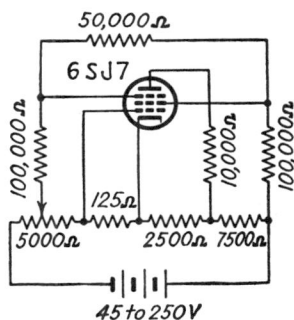

FIG. 6-27.—Pentode trigger circuit.

6-19. Methods of Analysis of Power Amplifiers.—The amplitude of the alternating plate current of power-amplifier tubes under rated conditions of operation is so great that amplitude distortion is not negligible.   A rigorous analysis based upon the series expansion for plate current should, therefore, take into account the second- and higher-order terms.   By considering only the first term of the series, however, it is possible to derive a number of approximate relations, which, although they do not

[1] ECCLES, W. H., and JORDAN, F. W., *Radio Rev.*, **1**, 143 (1919).   Other references are given at the end of this chapter.   See also H. J. Reich, "Theory and Applications of Electron Tubes," Sec. 7-16.

[2] REICH, H. J., *Rev. Sci. Instruments*, **9**, 222 (1938).

yield accurate numerical results, are useful in making a qualitative study of the effects of various circuit and tube factors upon the performance of class A power amplifiers. Considerable error may result from the application of these formulas to numerical problems. For this reason graphical analyses or, preferably, laboratory measurements must be made when accurate results are essential or when it is necessary to determine amplitude distortion.

As explained in Chap. 4, graphical analyses become very complicated when load reactance is taken into consideration. Although loud-speakers and other ordinary loads are not non-reactive, the assumption is usually made that the reactive component of load impedance may be neglected and the path of operation drawn as a straight line of negative slope equal to the reciprocal of the effective a-c load resistance. This assumption is justified because it leads to results that, although not accurate, are of great value in the analysis and design of amplifiers and that could otherwise be obtained only with great difficulty. For methods that take reactance into consideration, the student may refer to papers that have been written on the subject.[1]

6-20. Power Relations in Vacuum-tube Plate Circuits.— Although the vacuum tube is replaced by an equivalent generator in series with the plate resistance in analyses based upon the equivalent plate circuit, power in an actual plate circuit can come from only one source, the B supply. The power supplied to the plate circuit by the source of direct plate voltage is

$$P_i = \frac{1}{T} \int_0^T E_{bb} i_b \, dt = E_{bb} \frac{1}{T} \int_0^T i_b \, dt = E_{bb} I_{ba} \qquad (6\text{-}18)$$

Where T is the period of the fundamental component of plate current. This input power is converted into a-c and d-c power developed in the load and into plate dissipation (heat) in the tube. This fact may be stated in the form of the equation

$$P_i = P_p + P_o + I_{ba}{}^2 R_b \qquad (6\text{-}19)$$

[1] GREEN, E., *Wireless Eng.*, **3**, 402, 469 (1926); ARDENNE, M. VON, *Proc. I.R.E.*, **16**, 193 (1928); BARCLAY, W. A., *Wireless Eng.*, **5**, 660 (1928); WHITEHEAD, C. C., *Wireless Eng.*, **10**, 78 (1933); SÖCHTING, F., *Wireless Eng.* (abstr.), **10**, 165 (1933); PREISMAN, A., *RCA Rev.*, **2**, 124, 240 (1937) (with bibliography); JONKER, J. L. H., *Wireless Eng.*, **16**, 274, 344, (1939); FAIRWEATHER, A., and WILLIAMS, F. C., *Wireless Eng.*, **16**, 57 (1939).

in which P_p is the plate dissipation, P_o is the a-c output power developed in the load, and $I_{ba}{}^2R_b$ is the d-c power developed in the load.

Equation (6-19) may be rewritten in the form

$$P_p = P_i - P_o - I_{ba}{}^2R_b \qquad (6\text{-}20)$$

which states that the plate is not called upon to dissipate the portion of the input power that appears as output. If the input power remains essentially constant, the plate dissipation must rise as the output power is decreased by decreasing the excitation voltage. This is true in class A amplifiers, in which the average plate current I_{ba} under excitation does not differ greatly from the quiescent plate current I_{bo}. Plate dissipation in class A operation is thus a maximum when the excitation voltage is zero. At zero excitation, I_{ba} becomes I_{bo} and P_i, as given by Eq. (6-18), becomes $E_{bb}I_{bo}$. Equation (6-20) then becomes

$$\text{Max. class A}\quad P_p = I_{bo}E_{bb} - I_{bo}{}^2R_b = I_{bo}(E_{bb} - I_{bo}R_b) \quad (6\text{-}21)$$

By means of Eq. (3-28), Eq. (6-21) may be transformed into

$$\text{Max. class A}\quad P_p = I_{bo}E_{bo} \qquad (6\text{-}22)$$

In class A amplification, therefore, the plate dissipation will always be within the allowable value if the *zero-excitation* plate dissipation $I_{bo}E_{bo}$ does not exceed the rated maximum plate dissipation. In class B and class C operation, on the other hand, the power input falls more rapidly than the power output as the excitation is reduced, becoming zero at zero excitation, and so the *full-excitation* plate dissipation must not exceed the allowable plate dissipation. As explained in Chap. 2, the energy lost in plate dissipation first appears as kinetic energy of the electrons, which is in turn converted into heat when the electrons strike the plate. The allowable dissipation depends upon the maximum temperature that the plate can acquire without giving off absorbed gas or emitting electrons. When not definitely specified, the maximum allowable plate dissipation may be assumed to equal the product of the maximum values of rated operating plate current and plate voltage.

6-21. Plate-circuit Efficiency.—*Plate-circuit efficiency* is defined as the ratio of the fundamental a-c power output to the power input of the plate circuit

$$\eta_p = \frac{P_o}{P_i} \qquad (6\text{-}23)$$

Plate-circuit efficiency is important for two reasons. First, increase of plate-circuit efficiency may result in reduction of first cost of an amplifier and associated power supply. Since the allowable plate dissipation is related to tube size, the required size of tube tends to decrease with increased plate efficiency. Increased efficiency reduces the required capacity of the B supply. Secondly, economy of operation increases with plate-circuit efficiency, both because of reduction of power input to the plate circuit, and because of possible reduction of cathode heating power as the result of reduced tube size. Economy of operation is of particular importance in battery-operated amplifiers and in very large a-c–operated amplifiers.

It was pointed out in Sec. 5-11 that the load is usually coupled to the plate by means of an output transformer or a choke-condenser filter. Since the primary resistance of a well-designed output transformer or the resistance of an output choke is only a few hundred ohms, the d-c power $I_{ba}{}^2 R_b$ developed in the load, which serves no useful purpose, is ordinarily negligible. The output transformer or filter, therefore, not only prevents any objectionable effects that might result from the flow of direct current through the load, but also increases the plate-circuit efficiency.

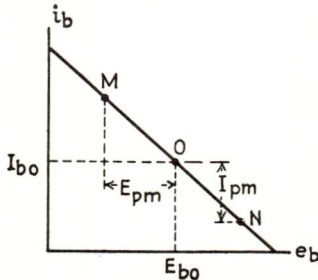

Fig. 6-28.—Generalized class A path of operation.

It is readily proved that the maximum theoretical efficiency of class A amplifiers with transformer-coupled load is 50 per cent when the distortion is negligible. In Fig. 6-28 is shown the path of operation of a class A amplifier. Since the discussion is not limited to any special type of tube, no static characteristics are shown. If the distortion is negligible, the waves of plate current and voltage are sinusoidal, and the power output is $\frac{1}{2}I_{pm}E_{pm}$. Since distortion is assumed to be zero, I_{ba} is equal to I_{bo}. If the d-c resistance of the plate circuit is negligible, E_{bb}

is equal to E_{bo}. The power input, as given by Eq. (6-18), is $I_{bo}E_{bo}$. Equation (6-23) gives the plate-circuit efficiency as $\dfrac{I_{pm}E_{pm}}{2I_{bo}E_{bo}}$. As the path of operation is extended, I_{pm} and E_{pm} increase. Their maximum values are obtained when the path extends to the current axis in one direction and the voltage axis in the other. Then the plate current is just reduced to zero at the negative peak of excitation voltage, and the plate voltage is reduced to zero at the positive peak of excitation voltage. Under this condition of operation $I_{pm} = I_{bo}$ and $E_{pm} = E_{bo}$. The plate-circuit efficiency is then $\frac{1}{2}$, or 50 per cent. Actual class A efficiencies are less than 50 per cent (see Secs. 6-24 and 6-25). Class B and C efficiencies may exceed 50 per cent.

6-22. Power Output.—If only the first term of the series expansion for plate current is considered and v_p is zero the r-m-s plate current is

$$I_p = \frac{\mu E_g}{r_p + z_b} \tag{6-24}$$

The approximate power output is

$$P_o = I_p{}^2 r_b = \frac{\mu^2 E_g{}^2 r_b}{(r_p + z_b)^2} \tag{6-25}$$

Equation (6-25) may be written in the form

$$P_o = g_m \mu E_g{}^2 \frac{m \cos \theta}{[1 + m(\cos \theta + j \sin \theta)]^2} \tag{6-26}$$

where $\theta = \tan^{-1} \dfrac{x_b}{r_b}$ and $m = \dfrac{|z_b|}{r_p}$. Equation (6-26) indicates that tubes used to deliver power should have a high product of amplification factor by transconductance. It also shows that the power output depends upon the load power factor and upon the ratio of the load impedance to the plate resistance and is proportional to the square of the excitation voltage. As would be expected, the power output at a load impedance of given magnitude is greatest for nonreactive load, for which $\theta = 0$.

6-23. Optimum Power Output.—*Optimum power output* is defined broadly as the greatest power output that can be obtained at a given operating plate voltage subject to limiting restrictions on operation.   The load resistance that gives optimum power is called *optimum load resistance*.   Restrictions on operation that must be taken into consideration in the determination of optimum power and optimum load resistance include allowable amplitude distortion, allowable grid current, available grid-circuit input power, and grid and plate dissipation.

6-24. Class A1 Triode Power Amplifiers.—In class A amplifiers the objectionable effects of the flow of grid current more than offset the advantages resulting from the increase in excitation voltage that may be obtained by allowing the grid to swing positive.   For this reason class A2 operation is seldom used, and it will not be discussed further.   In class A1 amplifiers the operating restrictions that must be considered in determining optimum power output are that amplitude distortion and plate dissipation must not exceed the allowable values and that grid current must not flow.   The allowable harmonic distortion is commonly taken as 5 per cent, although smaller values are often desirable, and larger values may be tolerated when high power output and high efficiency are of primary importance.[1]   With triodes, the distortion is associated almost entirely with the second-order term of the series expansion for plate current and so, when the excitation is sinusoidal, the only harmonic of appreciable amplitude is the second.

Experimental curves such as those of Fig. 6-29 show that optimum power output in single-sided class A1 operation of triodes with transformer-coupled load is obtained when the load resistance is approximately twice the plate resistance corresponding to the operating voltages, *i.e.*,

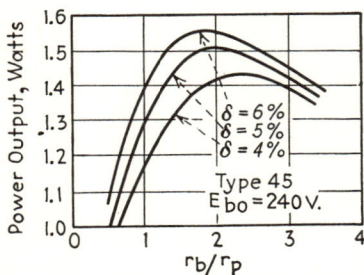

Fig. 6-29.—Experimentally determined curves of full power output of a type 45 triode in class A1 operation.

$$\text{Opt. } r_b \cong 2r_p \qquad (6\text{-}27)^2$$

---

[1] MASSA, FRANK, *Proc. I.R.E.*, **21**, 682 (1933); *Electronics*, September, 1938, p. 20.

[2] Seemingly, Eq. (6-27) is in disagreement with Maxwell's rule that maximum power is transferred from a generator to a load when the load impedance is equal to the generator impedance.   The student may show,

Equation (6-27) may also be derived by an analysis based upon the assumption that the plate characteristics are straight, linear, and parallel above I_{min} (see Fig. 4-13), which is assumed to remain constant as r_b is varied.[1] Under the same assumptions the optimum bias and optimum power output are given by the relations[1]

$$\text{Opt. } E_c = \frac{0.7E_{bo}}{\mu} \tag{6-28}$$

$$\text{Opt. } P_o = \tfrac{1}{9}\mu g_m E_c{}^2 \tag{6-29}$$

The theoretical plate circuit efficiency is 25 per cent when the load resistance is twice the plate resistance.   The corresponding power sensitivity is[1]

$$\text{P. S. at opt. load } = \sqrt{\tfrac{2}{9}\mu g_m} \tag{6-30}$$

Since actual characteristics depart materially from the ideal form assumed in the derivation of Eqs. (6-27) to (6-30), much better determinations of optimum operating conditions can be made by graphical or experimental methods.   A small increase or decrease of bias from the value indicated by Eq. (6-28) may produce an appreciable increase in power output without increase of distortion (see Prob. 6-13).   Choice of bias is also affected by the allowable plate dissipation.   At high plate voltage, limitation of zero-signal plate dissipation to the allowable value may necessitate the use of higher bias than $0.7E_{bo}/\mu$, and the optimum load resistance may be considerably higher than twice the plate resistance.   Practical values of triode plate circuit efficiency at optimum load in single-sided class A1 operation approximate 22 or 23 per cent.

6-25. Class A1 Pentode Power Amplifiers.—Pentodes have two advantages over triodes in class A1 power amplifiers: they have higher plate-circuit efficiency and they have higher power

---

however, that, for a given value of E_{bo} and constant I_{min} (see Fig. 4-13), the grid bias must be increased with load resistance. Since the greatest grid swing that can be used without the flow of grid current is approximately equal to the bias, the excitation for optimum power output must also be increased with load resistance. Maxwell's rule, on the other hand, holds only for constant generator voltage.

[1] For derivations of these relations see H. J. Reich, "Theory and Applications of Electron Tubes," Secs. 8-6 to 8-8.

sensitivity.   Practical plate-circuit efficiencies usually approximate 33 to 35 per cent with suppressor pentodes and 48 or 49 per cent with beam pentodes.   The higher plate-circuit efficiency of pentodes is associated with the shape of the plate characteristics, which is such as to allow the path of operation to extend more nearly to zero plate voltage, as required for the ideal maximum efficiency of 50 per cent.   Physically, the higher efficiency of pentodes is explained by the effect of the positive screen voltage, which reduces the plate voltage necessary to produce a given plate current and thus allows a greater percentage of the plate supply voltage to appear across the load.   The importance of high plate-circuit efficiency has been discussed in Sec. 6-21.

The higher power sensitivity of pentodes is possible because, with a given transconductance, pentodes can be designed with much higher amplification factors than triodes (see pages 64 and 69).   The advantages of power pentodes over triodes are partly offset by their much greater amplitude distortion and by a number of other less important disadvantages.   With pentodes, the amplitude distortion is associated not only with the second-order term of the series, but also with the third and fourth.   The third and fourth harmonics and corresponding cross-modulation frequencies, therefore, have appreciable amplitudes.   Because of the high amplitude distortion, pentodes must often be used in push-pull in order to bring the distortion within the allowable value.   Amplitude distortion is less with beam pentodes than with suppressor pentodes.

The shape of the characteristics of pentodes is such that it is not possible to derive simple theoretical equations for optimum load resistance, optimum power, and optimum bias, as has been done for triodes.   For this reason the correct operating conditions must be determined entirely by graphical methods or by laboratory measurement.

Figure 6-30 illustrates typical curves of power output and harmonic content of a pentode in single-sided class A1 operation as a function of load resistance.   The exact shapes of these curves and the relative positions of their maxima or minima are dependent upon the type of tube and upon operating voltages. The large percentage of second harmonic at low load impedance is associated with the unequal spacing of the plate characteristics at low plate current, which flattens the negative peak of alternating plate current. At high load impedance, on the other hand, the large percentage of second harmonic results from the crowding together of the characteristics at low plate voltage, which flattens the positive peak of alternating plate current. The second harmonic is zero at approximately the load resistance for which the positive and negative swings of plate current are equal. It is possible to design and operate a pentode so that the load for maximum power also gives minimum second harmonic, but in general this is not true. The form of the static plate characteristics is such that the minimum value of total harmonic content usually ranges from 6 to 10 per cent at full class A1 power output.

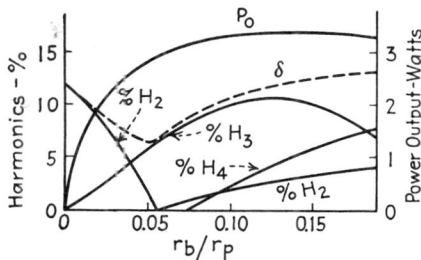

Fig. 6-30.—Typical curves of power output and harmonic distortion of a power pentode.

Since the load for maximum power output is, in general, different from that for minimum distortion, choice of the load must involve a compromise between large power output and small distortion. Because of the relatively high minimum distortion, distortion is ordinarily the determining factor, and the most suitable load does not differ greatly from that corresponding to zero second harmonic. It should be noted that the triode optimum-load relation $r_b = 2r_p$ *does not hold for pentodes*, optimum power output being obtained for load resistances ranging from about $r_p/4$ to $r_p/8$.

If the plate voltage is removed from a pentode without also removing the screen voltage, the current that normally flows to the plate is added to the screen current. The resulting increase of screen dissipation may cause the screen temperature of power pentodes to rise to a damaging value. For this reason great care should be taken not to open the plate circuit accidentally during operation of the tube.

6-26. Graphical Determination of Operating Conditions and Performance of Class A Power Amplifiers.—Since the operating conditions specified in manufacturers' tube manuals are satisfactory for ordinary applications, it is not often necessary to make determinations of operating voltages and currents or of optimum load resistance, power output, efficiency, and distortion. When other operating conditions are to be used, graphical methods of analysis may usually be applied.

For triodes in single-sided class A1 operation, the operating point may be located tentatively by using the optimum grid bias determined by means of Eq. (6-28). If the operating plate current corresponding to this bias exceeds the maximum allowable plate dissipation divided by the operating plate voltage, the plate current should be decreased to this value by increasing the grid bias. The dynamic load line should then be drawn so that harmonic distortion, determined by graphical methods, does not exceed the allowable value, usually 5 per cent. For 5 per cent second harmonic the ratio of the length of the portion of the load line above the operating point to the length of the portion below the operating point (the ratio of the length MO to the length ON in Fig. 4-13) should be approximately 1.22.[1] The required load resistance is equal to the reciprocal of the slope of the load line. The power output corresponding to a grid swing equal to the grid bias should be determined graphically from the plate diagram by the method explained in Sec. 4-14 and may be checked roughly by means of Eq. (6-29). Since the optimum bias indicated by Eq. (6-28) is only an approximation, it is advisable to draw the load line and determine the power output also for values of bias somewhat larger than $0.7E_{bo}/\mu$ and, if the bias can be decreased without causing the plate dissipation to exceed the allowable value, for values somewhat smaller than $0.7E_{bo}/\mu$. The value that gives the greatest power output should be chosen. The plate-circuit efficiency is found by dividing the graphically determined optimum power output by the input power computed by Eq. (6-18).

---

[1] This may be shown by simultanevus solution of Eq. (4-29) with the equation $I_{max} - I_{bo} = 1.22(I_{bo} - I_{min})$. It should be noted that since this rule for the determination of the load line corresponding to 5 per cent second harmonic is based upon the assumption that higher harmonics are negligible, it cannot be applied to pentodes.

Inasmuch as no formula for optimum grid bias can be derived for pentodes, the optimum operating conditions must be found by determining graphically or experimentally the power output and amplitude distortion for various values of grid bias and load resistance. Because of the large amplitudes of third and fourth harmonics, Eqs. (4-25), rather than Eqs. (4-24), must be used in the graphical determination of amplitude distortion.

6-27. Laboratory Determination of Optimum Power Output and Optimum Load.[1]—The power output of an amplifier with known load resistance may be determined by measuring the r-m-s voltage across the load or the current through the load. A thermal meter or a copper oxide rectifier meter is usually

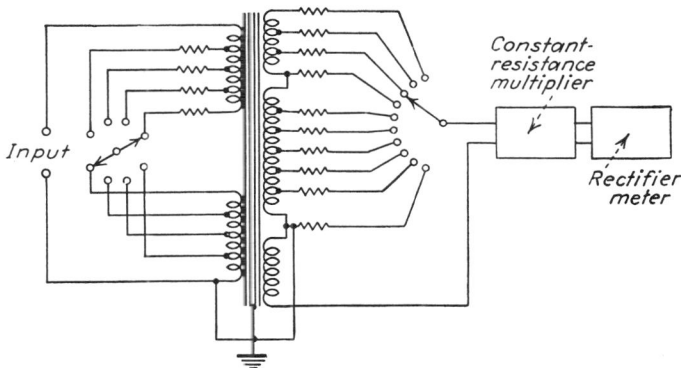

Fig. 6-31.—Circuit diagram of General Radio power-output meter.

used for the purpose. Figure 6-31 shows the circuit diagram of the General Radio output meter, by means of which power may be quickly measured at various values of effective load resistance. The meter embodies a variable-ratio transformer, compensated by means of resistances so that a constant percentage of the power is expended in the secondary load. The load is a constant-resistance network which also serves the function of a four-range multiplier for the voltmeter. The indicating instrument is a copper oxide rectifier voltmeter. The effective load may be varied in 40 steps from 2.5 Ω to 20,000 Ω. The multiplier provides 5-, 50-, 500-, and 5000-mw ranges of power.

[1] KELLOGG, E. W., *J. Am. Inst. Elec. Eng.*, **40**, 490 (1925); WARNER, J. C., and LOUGHREN, A. V., *Proc. I.R.E.*, **14**, 735 (1928); HANNA, C. R., SUTHERLIN, L., and UPP, C. B., *Proc. I.R.E.*, **16**, 462 (1928).

The scale is also calibrated to read power in volume units (see Sec. 5-15).

Harmonic content can be measured most readily with an electronic harmonic analyzer, of which there are a number of types on the market.[1]

The determination of optimum power output and optimum load requires a series of measurements. A suitable circuit is shown in Fig. 6-32. For each load impedance there is a limiting value of bias and signal amplitude beyond which the harmonic content exceeds the allowable value. Curves of power output and harmonic content as a function of load impedance must be constructed for various values of bias. The simplest laboratory procedure is to set the bias at fixed values and to take readings of power output and harmonic content at five or six values of load

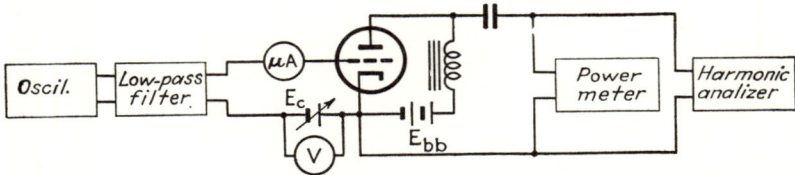

Fig. 6-32.—Circuit for the determination of optimum power output and optimum load resistance.

impedance. If operation is to be restricted to the region in which no grid current flows, the signal must be adjusted for each value of bias and load so that grid current does not quite flow. The signal amplitude at which grid current commences can be determined by a galvanometer or by headphones in series with the grid.

Figure 6-33 shows curves of power and harmonic content for a type 45 tube. The load impedance at which the harmonic content is just equal to the maximum allowable value at each value of bias may be determined from the curves of harmonic content. These values of impedance and bias then determine points on the power curves corresponding to the given harmonic content. The dashed curves of Fig. 6-33 show the power output at 4, 5, and 6 per cent second harmonic as a function of load resistance. From these the optimum load and power output

[1] For a discussion of harmonic analyzers, see H. J. Reich, "Theory and Applications of Electron Tubes," Secs. 15-33 to 15-38.

at the given value of distortion may be read.   (Readings of third harmonic taken simultaneously with second harmonic showed the former to be negligible in comparison with the latter.)

6-28. Push-pull Power Amplifiers.—The advantages of push-pull amplifier circuits were discussed in Sec. 5-10.   The most

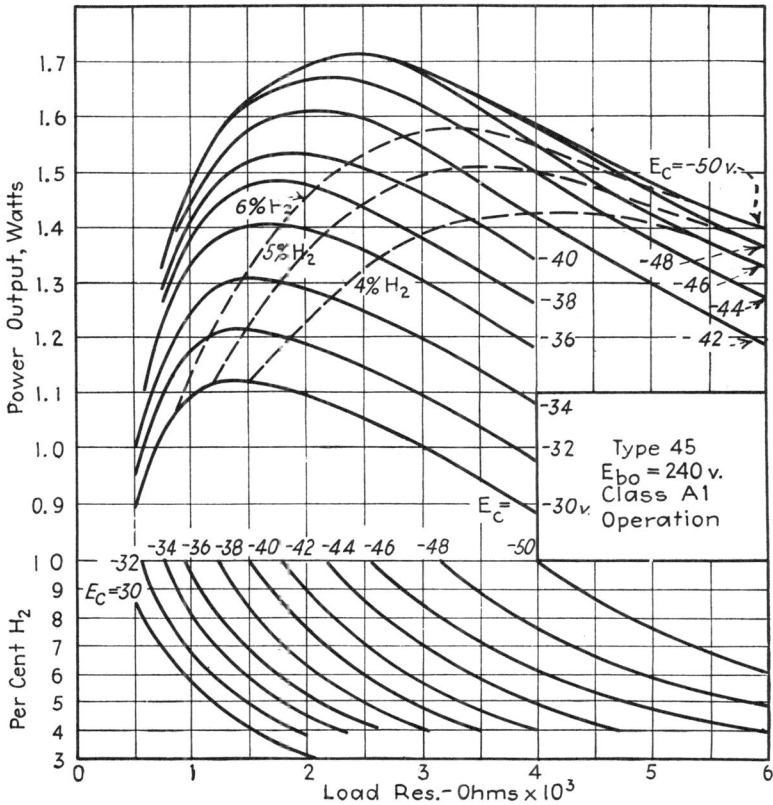

Fig. 6-33.—Experimentally determined curves of power output and harmonic distortion of a type 45 tube.   The dashed curves show power output at constant percentage second harmonic.

important of these is the greatly reduced amplitude distortion at given power output or greatly increased power output at given distortion.   Although Eq. (6-28) will usually give a satisfactory value of bias for push-pull class A1 operation of triodes, Eqs. (6-27), (6-29), and (6-30) are not applicable.   The performance of push-pull amplifiers is best determined experimentally, or graphically. Graphical methods of analysis of push-pull amplifiers are too involved to be included in this text.[1]

Push-pull operation is particularly advantageous with pentodes. Since even harmonics and intermodulation frequencies are not generated in push-pull circuits, the amplitude distortion may be made small by choosing a load resistance that gives low third-harmonic amplitude. Push-pull circuits are essential in class AB and class B amplifiers.

6-29. Class AB Power Amplifiers.—The distinguishing feature of class B, class AB, and class C amplifiers as a group is that plate current in individual tubes does not flow during the whole cycle. Class B and class C operation were originally used in radio-frequency amplifiers. Later it was shown that the high power output and efficiency of class B operation could also be attained without excessive distortion in audio-frequency amplifiers.[2] More recently class B audio power amplifiers have to a great extent been displaced by class AB amplifiers using beam power tubes, which give much lower amplitude distortion and operate at only slightly lower efficiency. Class B operation now finds its principal application in radio-frequency amplifiers; in battery-operated audio-frequency power amplifiers, where low power consumption is essential; and in high-power audio-frequency power amplifiers used to supply signal excitation in linear plate modulation (see Sec. 7-5). Class C operation, as explained in Chap. 5, can be used only in radio-frequency amplifiers.

Because of reduction of operating plate current, use of class AB bias in place of class A bias decreases plate dissipation and increases plate-circuit efficiency. At a given plate dissipation, therefore, it allows the use of a higher plate voltage and, consequently, the development of greater power output. Amplitude distortion is kept within allowable limits by the use of push-pull circuits. There is no abrupt increase of amplitude distortion in push-pull amplifiers as the bias is increased beyond the class A range. Therefore, class AB operation is usually used in push-pull amplifiers, in preference to class A1 operation. If the preceding

[1] Thompson, B. J., *Proc. I.R.E.*, **21**, 591 (1933). See also H. J. Reich, "Theory and Applications of Electron Tubes," Secs. 8-21 to 8-31.

[2] Barton, L. E., *Proc. I.R.E.*, **19**, 1131 (1931); **20**, 1035 (1932).

stage is designed to supply the power required in the grid circuit as the result of grid current flow, very large values of power output may be obtained by the use of sufficiently high excitation to result in class AB2 operation.

An example of the large output that can be obtained with small tubes and moderate plate voltage in class AB2 operation is given by the 6L6 beam power pentode, which will deliver an output of 60 watts (2 tubes) at 65 per cent plate-circuit efficiency (61 per cent including screen-circuit losses), and 2 per cent total harmonic, at a plate voltage of 400 and 0.35-watt average grid-driving power. In class AB1 operation the output is 32 watts at approximately 63 per cent efficiency (58 per cent including screen power, 54 per cent including screen and biasing power, and 45 per cent including also cathode heating power).

6-30. Turn Ratio of Output Transformer.—Usually the load to be used in the plate circuit of a power amplifier differs from the required optimum value. It is then necessary to choose the turn ratio of the output transformer so that the driving-point (input) impedance of the loaded transformer is equal to the required load resistance. The ratio of primary to secondary turns is equal to the square root of the ratio of the required load to the actual secondary load.[1]

In specifying the optimum load resistance for push-pull operation, the plate-to-plate value is often listed. This is the load resistance that would give optimum power output if connected across the primary of the output transformer from plate to plate. The value to be used across the secondary is equal to the plate-to-plate load resistance divided by the square of the ratio of total primary turns to secondary turns. Conversely, for a specified secondary load, the ratio of total primary turns to secondary turns is the square root of the ratio of plate-to-plate load to actual secondary load.

6-31. Inverse Feedback Amplifiers.[2]—Much improvement in the operating characteristics of an amplifier may be obtained by

[1] Reich, H. J., "Theory and Applications of Electron Tubes," Sec. 8-20.

[2] Nyquist, H., *Bell System Tech. J.*, **11**, 126 (1932); Baggally, W., *Wireless Eng.*, **10**, 413 (1933); Black, H. S., *Elec. Eng.*, **53**, 114 (1934); *Bell Laboratories Record*, **12**, 290 (1934). See also H. J. Reich, "Theory and Applications of Electron Tubes," p. 220. For additional references see the supplementary bibliography at the end of this chapter.

feeding a portion of the output voltage back to the input. The output of the amplifier may be considered to be made up of the amplified signal plus a smaller amount of distortion and noise. If part of the output is returned to the input in proper phase

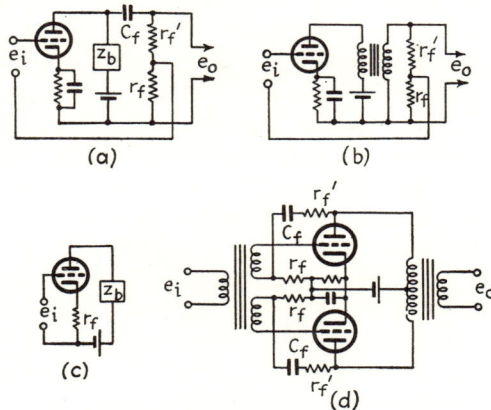

Fig. 6-34.—Inverse-feedback amplifier circuits.

relative to the impressed signal, the amplified feedback voltage will tend to cancel the output noise and distortion. This advantage is obtained at the expense of reduced signal output and so the feedback is said to be *inverse*. Other equally impor-

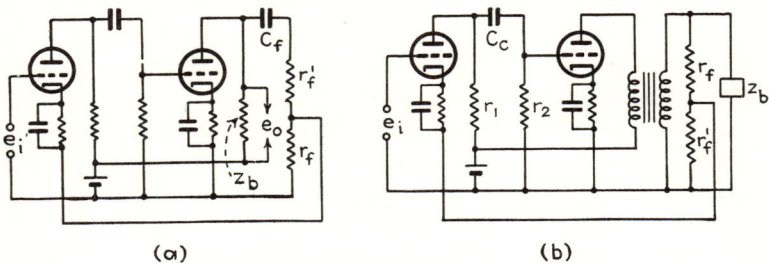

Fig. 6-35.—Inverse-feedback amplifier circuits.

tant improvements result from the use of inverse feedback. The benefits may be summarized as follows:

1. Reduction of amplitude distortion.
2. Reduction of noise.
3. Reduction of frequency and phase distortion.
4. Increase of stability (reduction of variation of amplification or of current or power sensitivity with operating voltages and tube age).

5. Reduction of variation of amplification or sensitivity with input voltage.

6. Reduction of variation of amplification or sensitivity with load impedance.

7. Increased damping of loud-speaker transients.

8. Reduction of loud-speaker resonance.

Circuits of single-stage and two-stage inverse-feedback amplifiers are shown in Figs. 6-34 and 6-35.

Problems

6-1. Show that the voltage amplification of a single-stage amplifier with nonreactive load r_b and self-biasing resistor R_{cc} without a by-pass condenser (see Fig. 4-17a) is

$$\mu' = \frac{\mu r_b}{r_p + r_b + (\mu + 1)P_{cc}} \quad (6\text{-}31)$$

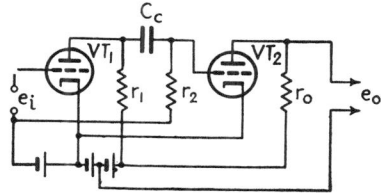

FIG. 6-36.—Circuit for Prob. 6-2.

6-2. *a.* Draw the equivalent circuits for the amplifier of Fig. 6-36.

b. Neglecting interelectrode capacitances, derive a general expression for the voltage amplication of each stage.

c. VT_1 and VT_2 are type 6J5 tubes, operated at a plate supply voltage of 250 volts and a bias of -8 volts, and the circuit elements have the following values:

$$r_1 = 50,000\ \Omega \qquad C_c = 0.005\ \mu f$$
$$r_2 = 250,000\ \Omega \qquad r_o = 50,000\ \Omega$$

Find the gain in decibels of each stage and of the amplifier at 60, 100, and 1000 cycles.   Check by means of Fig. 6-12.

d. Repeat (*c*), substituting type 6SJ7 tubes for type 6J5.   Use the values $\mu = 1500$ and $r_p = 1.5$ megohms.

e. Discuss the suitability of these amplifiers for use at frequencies between 50 and 3000 $\sim$.

f. Determine the size of the cathode resistors necessary to provide the required bias when type 6J5 tubes are used.

6-3. Design a two-stage resistance-capacitance–coupled voltage amplifier using 6SF5 tubes, which will give the highest voltage amplification consistent with uniform response in the range from 100 to 10,000 $\sim$.   The output of the amplifier is to be applied to the deflecting plates of a cathode-ray oscillograph.   The capacitance of these plates and their leads is 5 μf.

6-4. *a.* Plot a frequency-response curve for the amplifier of Prob. 6-2, using type 6J5 tubes and the circuit constants listed in part (*c*) and taking interelectrode capacitances into account.   The output of the second stage is shunted by a 4 μf capacitance. $C_{gk} = C_{gp} = 3.4\ \mu f$; $C_{pk} = 3.6\ \mu f$, *b.* What should be done to reduce frequency distortion in this amplifier?

6-5. By graphical methods determine the maximum crest fundamental voltage output and the voltage amplification of a type 6J5 triode in class A1 operation under the following operating conditions:

$$E_{bb} = 250 \text{ volts}$$
$$E_c = -6 \text{ volts}$$
$$r_b = R_b = 100,000 \ \Omega$$

The harmonic content must not exceed 5 per cent. Grid current starts flowing at $e_c = -0.5$ volt.

6-6. *a.* By graphical methods determine the maximum crest fundamental voltage output and the voltage amplification of a type 6SF5 triode in class A1 operation under the following operating conditions:

$$E_{bb} = 300 \text{ volts}$$
$$E_c = -1.5 \text{ volts}$$
$$r_b = R_b = 500,000 \ \Omega$$

The harmonic content must not exceed 5 per cent. Grid current starts flowing at $e_c = -0.75$ volt.

b. Repeat (*a*) for a 6SF5 tube in the first stage of the circuit of Fig. 6-36.

$$E_{bb} = 300 \text{ volts} \qquad r_1 = 500,000 \ \Omega$$
$$E_c = -1.5 \text{ volts} \qquad r_2 = 1,000,000 \ \Omega$$
$$f = 1000 \sim \qquad C_c = 0.01 \ \mu\text{f}$$

6-7. *a.* By graphical methods find the voltage amplification of a type 6SF5 triode for the following operating conditions:

$$E_{bb} = \quad 250 \text{ volts} \qquad r_b = R_b = 1 \text{ megohm}$$
$$E_c = -1.5 \text{ volts} \qquad E_{gm} = 1 \text{ volt}$$

b. Find r_p and μ at the operating point and find μ' by the use of Eq. (6-1).

c. Find the required resistance of the self-biasing resistor.

d. By means of Eq. (6-31) of Prob. 6-1 find the voltage amplification when the self-biasing resistor is used.

6-8. An audio-frequency interstage coupling transformer has the following constants:

Primary inductance L_1.....................	25 henrys
Equivalent leakage inductance, referred to the secondary, L_e............................	2 henrys
Equivalent distributed capacitance, referred to the secondary, C_e........................	80 $\mu\mu$f
Primary resistance r_1.......................	850 Ω
Secondary resistance r_2.....................	10,000 Ω
Turn ratio n.............................	3

a. This transformer is used to couple a type 6J5 tube to a type 2A3 tube. The operating voltages of the 6J5 are $E_{bo} = 250$ volts and $E_c = -8$ volts. Construct a frequency-response curve for the first tube and transformer.

b. Show that the type 6J5 tube could not be satisfactorily replaced by a type 6SJ7 tube.

6-9. Design a two-stage amplifier for use with an electromagnetic oscillograph that requires a crest alternating current of 50 ma for full deflection. Resistance of the element is 5 Ω. In order to make possible the study of transients at very low frequency, the response should be uniform down to zero frequency. Full deflection must be obtained with an input voltage that does not exceed 1 volt, and amplitude distortion must not exceed 5 per cent. Specify all circuit constants and voltages.

6-10. The amplifier shown in Fig. 6-37 "motorboats" (oscillates at a frequency of 2 or 3 ∼) when used with a B supply of poor regulation. The motorboating stops when the switch *S* is opened but not when the first tube is removed. Explain.

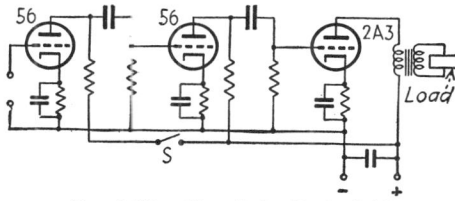

Fig. 6-37.—Circuit for Prob. 6-10.

6-11. The terminal voltage of a d-c generator is regulated by applying the voltage to the input of a two-stage amplifier in such a manner that decrease of terminal voltage increases the field excitation and thus raises the voltage. The action is as follows: If the terminal voltage tends to fall by 1.05 volts with increase of load, the amplifier increases the field current sufficiently to raise the induced voltage by 1 volt, so that the net change in terminal voltage is only 0.05 volt. The average field current is 50 ma. In the normal range of field current a 1-ma change results in a 0.1-volt change of induced voltage.

a. Choose a suitable tube to control the 50-ma field current. Field resistance = 2000 Ω.

b. Determine the change of grid voltage of this tube that is necessary in order to raise the induced voltage by 1 volt.

c. Choose a first-stage amplifier circuit and tube such that the 0.05-volt drop in terminal voltage will give the necessary change in the grid voltage of the second tube.

d. Draw a circuit diagram, specifying all circuit constants, tube operating voltages, and supply voltages.

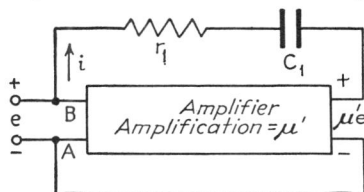

Fig. 6-38.—Reactance-transformation circuit.

6-12. By the use of low load resistance in the final stage and by the use of inverse feedback, the voltage amplification μ' of the amplifier in Fig. 6-38 is made independent of r_1 and C_1 throughout the mid-band frequency range. If the input impedance of the amplifier is infinite, show that between the input terminals the entire circuit acts like a parallel combination of negative resistance and inductive reactance whose values are

$$r_e = \frac{r_1 + \dfrac{1}{\omega r_1 C_1{}^2}}{1 - \mu'} \tag{6-32}$$

$$x_e = -\frac{\omega r_1{}^2 C_1 + \dfrac{1}{\omega C_1}}{1 - \mu'} \tag{6-33}$$

6-13. *a.* Locate the optimum operating point for a type 45 triode operated at a plate voltage of 200 volts. The load is nonreactive and is coupled to the tube through a transformer of small primary resistance. The allowable plate dissipation is 10 watts, and the allowable second-harmonic content is 5 per cent.

b. Draw the optimum load line.

c. Determine the optimum power output graphically.

d. From the load line, find the optimum load resistance.

e. Determine the plate resistance at the operating point.

f. Using the values of r_b and r_p found in (*d*) and (*e*), find the optimum power output by means of the equivalent plate circuit.

g. Check the optimum power output by means of Eq. (6-29).

h. Find the power input to the plate circuit.

i. Using the graphically determined value of optimum power output, find the plate-circuit efficiency.

j. Using the graphically determined value of optimum power output, find the power sensitivity.

k. If the resistance of the load across the secondary of the output transformer is 40 Ω, find the required turn ratio.

Supplementary Bibliography

Extensive supplementary bibliographies will be found throughout and at the ends of Chaps. 7, 8, and 9 of "Theory and Applications of Electron Tubes," by H. J. Reich. The following references cover recent work. A bibliography covering the year 1940 is given in *Proc. I.R.E.*, **29**, 90 (1941).

Direct-coupled Amplifiers

Engineering Staff, Aerovox Corp.: *Electronics*, March, 1938, p. 42.
TATEL, H., MONCTON, H. S., and LUHR, O.: *Rev. Sci. Instruments*, **9**, 229 (1938).
KORFF, S. A.: *Rev. Sci. Instruments*, **9**, 256 (1938).
TREVIÑO, S. N., and OFFNER, F.: *Rev. Sci. Instruments*, **11**, 412 (1940).

Resistance-capacitance–coupled Amplifiers

EVEREST, F. A.: *Electronics*, January, 1938, p. 16; May, 1938, p. 24.
RHOAD, E. J.: *Communications*, January, 1938, p. 11.
JOHNSTONE, D. M.: *Wireless Eng.*, **15**, 208 (1938).
PREISMAN, A.: *RCA Rev.* **2**, 421 (1938).

HEROLD, E. W.: *Communizations*, August, 1938, p. 11.
SHEAFFER, C. F.: *Electronics*, September, 1938, p. 14.
SEELEY, S. W., and KIMBALL, C. N.: *RCA Rev.*, **3**, 290 (1939).
BEDFORD, A. V., and FREDENDALL, G. L.: *Proc. I.R.E.*, **27**, 277 (1939).
POLLACK, D.: *Electronics*, April, 1939, p. 38.
PREISMAN, A.: *RCA Rev.*, **3**, 473 (1939).
NIMS, A. A.: *Electronics*, May, 1939, p. 23.
RAMO, S.: *Communications* May, 1939, p. 16.
EPHRAIM, B.: *Communications*, June, 1939, p. 12.
WHEELER, H. A.: *Proc. I.R.E.*: **27**, 429 (1939).
LIU, Y. J., and TRIMMER, J. D.: *Electronics*, September, 1939, p. 35.
FARRINGTON, J. F.: *R.M.A. Eng.*, **4**, 13, (1939).
FREEMAN, W. H.: *Electronics*, January, 1940, p. 35.
EVEREST, F. A., and JOHNSTON, H. R.: *Proc. I.R.E.*, **28**, 71 (1940).
HAEFF, A. V.: *Proc. I.R.E.*, **28**, 126 (1940).
BARCUS, L. M.: *Electronics*, June, 1940, p. 44.
STRONG, C. E.: *Electronics*, July, 1940, p. 14.
TRIMMER, J. D., and LIU, Y. J.: *Electronics*, July, 1940, p. 22.
FARRINGTON, J. F.: *Communications*, September, 1940, p. 3.

Class A Power Amplifiers

LEVY, M. L.: *Electronics*, March,1938, p. 26.
EVERITT, W. L., and SPANGENBERG, K.: *Proc. I.R.E.*, **26**, 612 (1938).
CHAFFEE, E. L.: *J. Applied Physics*, **9**, 471 (1938).
DAVIS, F. M.: *Electronics*, December, 1938, p. 56.
FAIRWEATHER, A., and WILLIAMS, F. C.: *Wireless Eng.*, **16**, 57 (1939).
COOK, E. G.: *Electronics*, June, 1939, p. 38.
JONKER, J. L. H.: *Wireless Eng.*, **16**, 274, 344 (1939).
VAN DER VEN, A. J. H.: *Wireless Eng.*: **16**, 383, 444 (1939).
BLOCK, A.: *Wireless Eng.*, **16**, 592 (1939).
PREISMAN, A.: *Communications*, December, 1939, p. 5.
TREVIÑO, S. N., and OFFNER, F.: *Rev. Sci. Instruments*, **11**, 412 (1940).

Class B and Class C Amplifiers

LAMBERT, R.: *Proc. I.R.E.*, **26**, 372 (1938).
GORDON, M.: *Wireless Eng.*, **16**, 457 (1939).
SCHULZ, E. H.: *Electronics*, December, 1939, p. 32.

Feedback Amplifiers

REID, D. G.: *Wireless Eng.*, **14**, 588 (1937).
BRAYSHAW, G. S.: *Wireless Eng.*, **14**, 597 (1937).
FISHER, C. B.: *R.M.A. Eng.*, November, 1937, p. 19 (with extensive bibliography).
FARREN, L. I.: *Wireless Eng.*, **15**, 23 (1938).
FROMMER, J.: *Wireless Eng.*, **15**, 20, 90 (1938).
MARINESCO, M.: *Wireless Eng.*, **15**, 21 (1938).
BARTLETT, A. C.: *Wireless Eng.*, **15**, 90 (1938).

STEVENS, B. J.: *Wireless Eng.*, **15**, 143 (1938).
FRITZINGER, G. H.: *Proc. I.R.E.*, **26**, 207 (1938).
GINZTON, E. L.: *Proc. I.R.E.:* **26**, 1367 (1938).
MAYER, H. F.: *Proc. I.R.E.*, **27**, 213 (1939).
YOUNG, L. G.: *Electronics*, August, 1939, p. 20.
TERMAN, F. E., BUSS, R. R., HEWLETT, W. R., and CAHILL, F. C.: *Proc. I.R.E.*, **27**, 649 (1939).
BARTELS, H.: *Electronics*, January, 1940, p. 74 (abstr.).
PEDERSON, P. O.: *Proc. I.R.E.*, **28**, 59 (1940).
STEWART, H. H., and POLLOCK, H. S.: *Electronics*, February, 1940, p. 19.
RIVLIN, R. S.: *Wireless Eng.*, **17**, 298 (1940).
BODE, H. W.: *Bell System Tech. J.*, **19**, 421 (1940).
SANDEMAN, E. K.: *Wireless Eng.*, **17**, 342 (1940).

Trigger Circuits

TOOMIM, H.: *Rev. Sci. Instruments*, **10**, 191 (1939).
REICH, H. J.: *Electronics*, August, 1939, p. 14.
NOTTINGHAM, W. B.: *Rev. Sci. Instruments*, **11**, 2 (1940).
KALLMANN, H. E.: *Proc. I.R.E.*, **28**, 351 (1940).

Low-frequency Amplifier Using High-frequency Carrier

BLACK, L. J., and SCOTT, H. J.: *Proc. I.R.E.*, **28**, 269 (1940).

Current Fluctuations in Tubes

PERCIVAL, W. S., and HORWOOD, W. L.: *Wireless Eng.*, **15**, 128, 202, 213, 268, 322, 440 (1938).
RACK, A. J.: *Bell System Tech. J.*, **17**, 592 (1938).
SILVERMAN, D.: *Electronics*, February, 1939, p. 34 (an extensive bibliography covering noise and noise measurement).
JANSKY, K. G.: *Proc. I.R.E.*, **27**, 763 (1939).
THOMPSON, B. J.: *RCA Rev.*, **4**, 269 (1940).
NORTH, D. O.: *RCA Rev.*, **4**, 441 (1940); **5**, 106 (1940); **5**, 244 (1940).

Amplifier Distortion

MACFADYEN, K. A.: *Wireless Eng.*, **15**, 310 (1938).
SCOTT, H. J., and BLACK, L. J.: *Proc. I.R.E.*, **26**, 449 (1938).
TITTLE, H. C.: *R.M.A. Eng.*, May, 1938, p. 9.
WHEELER, H. A.: *Proc. I.R.E.*, **27**, 359, 384 (1939).

CHAPTER 7

MODULATION AND DETECTION

Transmission of intelligence through space by means of electromagnetic radiation cannot be accomplished satisfactorily at audio frequencies. There are several reasons for this: (1) The radiation efficiency of antennas is very low at audio frequencies, and so the range is small. (2) Efficient radiation and reception of electromagnetic waves require the use of antennas and circuits tuned to the frequencies of the waves. The antennas required at audio frequencies would be impractical because of their great lengths, and they would not respond equally well to all frequencies in the audio range. (3) If transmission were effected at audio frequencies, all transmitters would operate over the same frequency range and so the programs of various transmitters would be heard simultaneously at the receiver. These difficulties are avoided by radiating a radio-frequency wave, the amplitude, frequency, or phase of which is varied in accordance with the audio-frequency signals that it is desired to transmit. At the receiver, the variations of amplitude, frequency, or phase of the received wave are reconverted into audio-frequency voltages.

7-1. Modulation.—The process whereby some characteristic, usually amplitude, frequency, or phase, of a sinusoidally changing voltage, current, or other quantity is varied in accordance with the time variations of another voltage, current, or other quantity, is called *modulation*. The term *carrier* is applied to the quantity the characteristic of which is varied, and the term *modulation* (*signal*) to the quantity in accordance with which the variation is performed. The *carrier frequency* is the frequency of the unmodulated carrier. Usually the modulation frequency is considerably lower than the carrier frequency.

Since the sounds of the human voice and of musical instruments involve a large number of frequencies produced simultaneously, the form of the modulating wave is rarely sinusoidal.

179

To simplify theoretical analyses, however, the assumption is generally made that the modulation is sinusoidal. It is then necessary to investigate also the effects of the interaction of two or more components of a complex modulating wave in the modulation process and in the process of reproducing these components from the modulated wave.

It will be shown that both the process of modulation and that of recovering the original modulation frequencies, which is one form of a more general process called *detection* (Sec. 7-6), involve the generation of frequencies not present in the impressed excitation. The similarity of the processes of modulation and detection by vacuum tubes is particularly marked in the case of amplitude modulation. They differ mainly as to the frequencies impressed upon the circuit and the frequencies selected from the output by some form of filter.

7-2. Amplitude Modulation.—A quantity y varying sinusoidally with an amplitude A, an angular frequency ω_k, and a phase angle ϕ may be represented by the equation

$$y = A \sin (\omega_k t + \phi) \tag{7-1}$$

Since the phase angle ϕ is constant in amplitude modulation and is determined by the instant in the carrier cycle at which it is decided to start observing time, there is no important loss of generality in setting ϕ equal to zero.

Let the phase angle be zero and the amplitude be varied sinusoidally at modulation frequency ω_m between the limits $1 + M$ and $1 - M$, as indicated by the equation

$$A = K(1 + M \sin \omega_m t) \tag{7-2}$$

in which K and M are constants and ω_m is less than ω_k. Equation (7-1) then becomes

$$y = K(1 + M \sin \omega_k t) \sin \omega_k t \tag{7-3}$$

Equation (7-3) represents a wave the frequency of which is constant and the amplitude of which is varied at modulation frequency between the limits $1 + M$ and $1 - M$, as shown in Fig. 7-1 for several values of M. The coefficient M, which is called the *modulation factor* or *degree of modulation*, determines the extent to which the carrier is modulated. When M is zero, the carrier is unmodulated and its amplitude remains constant, as shown by curve *a* of Fig. 7-1. When *M* lies between zero and unity, the modulated wave is of the form of curve *c* of Fig. 7-1. When *M* is unity, the amplitude varies between zero and twice the unmodulated value, as shown by curve *d* of Fig. 7-1, and modulation is said to be *complete*.

It should be noted that there is no direct relation between the amplitude of the envelope of the modulated wave *c* or *d* and the modulation-frequency wave *b* in accordance with which

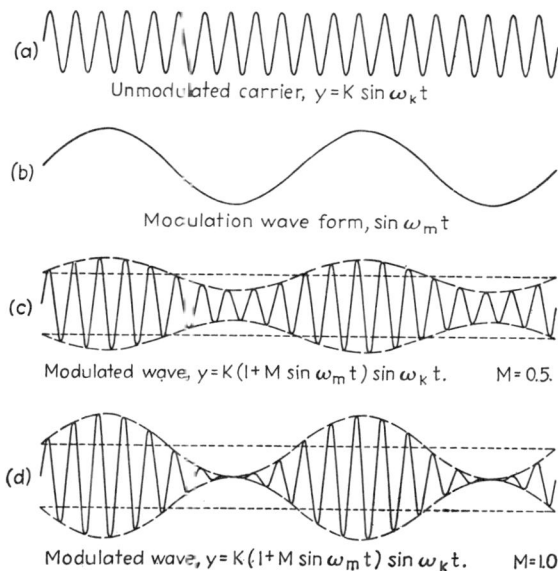

(a) Unmodulated carrier, $y = K \sin \omega_k t$

(b) Modulation wave form, $\sin \omega_m t$

(c) Modulated wave, $y = K(1 + M \sin \omega_m t) \sin \omega_k t$.   M = 0.5.

(d) Modulated wave, $y = K(1 + M \sin \omega_m t) \sin \omega_k t$.   M = 1.0

FIG. 7-1.—Amplitude modulation.

the modulation is performed. The degree of modulation associated with modulation excitation of given amplitude depends not only upon the amplitudes of the carrier and modulation excitations, but also upon the characteristics of the circuit by means of which the carrier is modulated. In particular, the modulation factor is not necessarily unity when the carrier and modulation-excitation voltages impressed upon a modulator are equal in amplitude. The wave form and frequency of the envelope are, however, the same as those of the modulation excitation applied to the modulator unless the modulator introduces distortion in the form of undesired frequency components.

In the simple case that has been discussed, in which the form of the modulating wave is assumed to be sinusoidal, the modulation factor is equal to the ratio of the difference between the maximum or minimum amplitude of the modulated wave and the amplitude of the unmodulated carrier wave to the amplitude of the unmodulated carrier wave.   When the modulating wave is not sinusoidal, however, the maximum increase and decrease of amplitude from the unmodulated value may not be equal, and a more general definition of modulation factor is necessary. The modulation factor is defined as the maximum departure (positive or negative) of the envelope of the modulated wave from its unmodulated value, divided by its unmodulated value. The modulation factor times 100 per cent is called the *percentage modulation*.   Sometimes in the discussion of an asymmetrically modulated wave it is necessary to distinguish between the modulation factors corresponding to the minimum and the maximum amplitudes of the modulated waves. These are called the *inward* and *outward* modulation factors, respectively.

7-3. Side Frequencies in Amplitude Modulation.—By trigonometrical expansion, Eq. (7-3) may be changed into the form

$$y = K \sin \omega_k t - \tfrac{1}{2} KM[\cos (\omega_k + \omega_m)t - \cos (\omega_k - \omega_m)t] \quad (7\text{-}4)$$

Equation (7-4) shows that an amplitude-modulated wave is made up of three components having frequencies equal to the carrier frequency, the carrier frequency plus the modulation frequency, and the carrier frequency minus the modulation frequency.   The process of amplitude modulation, therefore, involves the generation of sum and difference frequencies, called the *upper side frequency* and *lower side frequency*, respectively. When the carrier is modulated by a band of modulation frequencies, applied individually or simultaneously, the side frequencies lie in bands, called the *upper side band* and *lower side band*.   The frequency width of the side bands is the same as that of the modulation-frequency band.   It is important to note that the modulation frequency is not in itself present in the modulated wave.

For reasons stated in the introduction to this chapter, carrier frequencies used in transmission by means of electromagnetic radiation lie in the radio-frequency range.   It is entirely possible, however, to modulate an audio-frequency carrier by means of

signals of lower audio frequency.   This is done in carrier telephony over wires.[1]   If telephone signals were transmitted only at
their original audio frequencies, only one conversation could be
transmitted at one time over a pair of wires.   By modulating
carrier frequencies with the voice frequencies, however, a large
number of conversations can be transmitted simultaneously.
Suppose, for instance, that the range from 100 to 2500 cycles is
adequate for the transmission of intelligible speech.   Then the
modulation of carriers of 3000, 6000, 9000, 12,000 cycles, etc.,
will result in the production of upper side bands in the ranges
3100 to 5500, 6100 to 8500, 9100 to 11,500, 12,100 to 14,500 cycles,
etc.   The carrier and lower-side-band components of the modulated waves can be removed by means of filters.   The upper
side bands, together with the original voice band, can then be
transmitted simultaneously without interference.   This is known
as single-side-band transmission.   At the receiving end the
frequencies in the various channels are separated by band-pass
filters and reconverted to the original 100- to 2500-cycle range
by a similar process.   In modern carrier telephony systems
carrier frequencies of 20 kc or higher are used.

**7-4. Amplitude Modulation by Curvature of Tube Character-
istics.**—By substituting $e = E_1 \sin \omega_m t + E_2 \sin \omega_k t$ in the first
two terms of the series expansion for plate current, the reader
may readily show that, when a vacuum tube is excited simultaneously with carrier and modulation-frequency voltages, the
plate current contains carrier and side-frequency components, as
well as components whose frequencies are equal to the modulation
frequency, twice the carrier frequency and twice the modulation
frequency.   If the plate circuit load is a parallel resonant circuit
tuned to the carrier frequency, then the impedance of the load
is high at the carrier frequency and at the side frequencies, which
do not differ greatly from the carrier frequency, but negligible
at the modulation and harmonic frequencies.   Consequently
the voltage developed across the tuned circuit contains only the
carrier and side frequencies.   If the circuit is properly tuned, the
amplitudes of the side-frequency components are equal, and hence
an undistorted amplitude-modulated voltage appears across the

[1] COLPITTS, E. H., and BLACKWELL, O. B., *J. Am. Inst. Elec. Eng.*, **40**,
205 (1921); AFFEL, H. A., DEMAREST, C. S., and GREEN, C. W., *Bell System
Tech. J.*, **7**, 564 (1928).

tuned circuit. Thus the tube generates a number of new frequencies, including those required in the production of a modulated wave. The tuned circuit suppresses those not desired, leaving in the output only the essential carrier and side frequencies.

Since the excitation voltage e is equal to $e_g + v_p/\mu$, the modulation and carrier excitation voltages may be applied in either the grid circuit or the plate circuit of a triode, one may be applied in each, or they may be applied to a diode circuit. They may also be applied to any two electrodes of a multigrid tube. Because the production of side frequencies with this type of modulator is associated with the second-order term of the series expansion for alternating plate current, the modulation is referred to as *square-law*, or *parabolic, modulation*. A square-law modulator

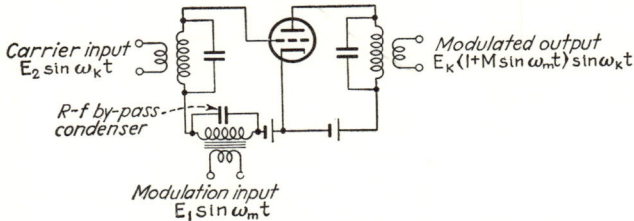

Fig. 7-2.—Van der Bijl modulator.

in which the excitation voltages are applied to the grid circuit of a triode, as shown in Fig. 7-2, is called a van der Bijl modulator. For reasons that will be explained, square-law modulation is now seldom used.

The mechanism of modulation by the van der Bijl modulator can be shown by means of a transfer diagram. Fig. 7-3 shows that when the carrier excitation alone is impressed, the amplitude of the carrier-frequency plate current is much greater for the smaller grid bias E_c' than for the larger bias E_c''. If the bias is varied between these values, the amplitude of the carrier component of the plate current also varies. This is accomplished in effect by choosing an intermediate value of bias E_c and applying also the modulation excitation, as shown in Fig. 7-4. The wave a of plate current may be separated into the components shown by curves b and c of Fig. 7-4. Curve b may be further resolved into a steady component, a modulation-frequency component, and modulation-harmonic components; curve c

into a varying-amplitude carrier-frequency component (carrier plus side-frequency components) and carrier-harmonic components. Since the impedance of the tuned plate load is high

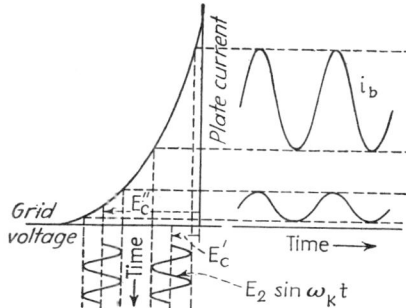

FIG. 7-3.—Variation of amplitude of carrier-frequency plate current with grid bias.

only at and near carrier frequency, the voltage appearing across the load is of the form of the varying-amplitude carrier component of Fig. 7-4c, *i.e.*, the modulated carrier.

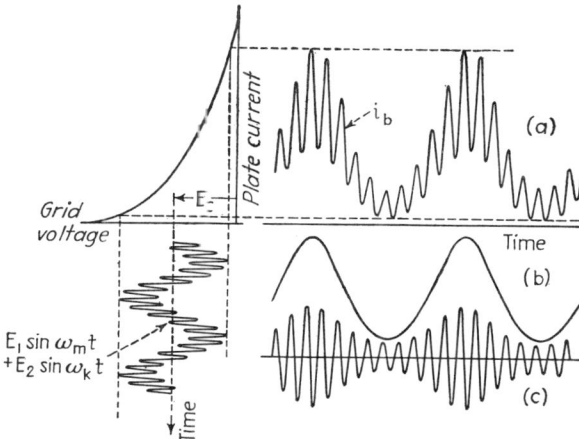

FIG. 7-4.—Amplitude modulation by curvature of transfer characteristic. Waves (b) and (c) are two components into which the wave (a) of plate current may be resolved.

A more rigorous analysis, based upon the series expansion, shows that the presence of higher order terms than the second in the series results in side-frequency components equal to the carrier frequency plus and minus integral multiples of the modulation frequency. These show up in the modulated wave as distortion of the envelope from sinusoidal form. When the carrier is modulated simultaneously with two or more modulation frequencies, various other intermodulation frequencies, including the carrier frequency plus and minus the sums and differences of the various modulation frequencies, are present in the output.

7-5. Amplitude Modulation by Complete Rectification.— Because the degree of modulation attainable in square-law modulation without excessive distortion is small and because the power efficiency is low, modulation by means of vacuum tubes is now accomplished almost entirely by making use of the unilateral conductivity of electron tubes at cutoff, rather than of curvature of tube characteristics. Figure 7-5 shows a simple diode circuit that can be used to produce a modulated voltage. The action of this circuit can be explained readily by use of a tube characteristic. The parallel resonant circuit is tuned to carrier frequency and therefore acts as a resistance at carrier frequency. Since the tube is a perfect rectifier, *i.e.*, since current flows in one direction only, plate current flows only during portions of the cycle in which the plate is positive, and so the plate current consists, in general, of pulses. The manner in which the plate current varies with time when a carrier-frequency excitation voltage is applied to the circuit is shown in Fig. 7-6 for several values of fixed plate biasing voltage E_b. Because the current pulses occur at carrier-frequency intervals, the plate current contains a carrier-frequency component, the amplitude of which increases as the bias is changed in a positive direction between values equal to minus and plus the crest excitation voltage. If the bias E_b is replaced or supplemented by a modulation-frequency alternating voltage, the amplitude of the carrier component of plate current varies at modulation frequency. This is accomplished by impressing the modulation excitation in series with the carrier excitation and optional bias, as in Fig. 7-5. The form of the total excitation voltage and the resulting plate current when the fixed bias is zero are

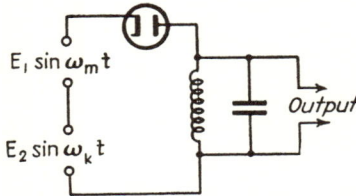

$E_1 \sin \omega_m t$

$E_2 \sin \omega_k t$

Output

Fig. 7-5.—Diode modulator circuit.

shown in Fig. 7-7.   The wave a of plate current may be separated
into the components shown by curves b and c of Fig. 7-7.   Curve

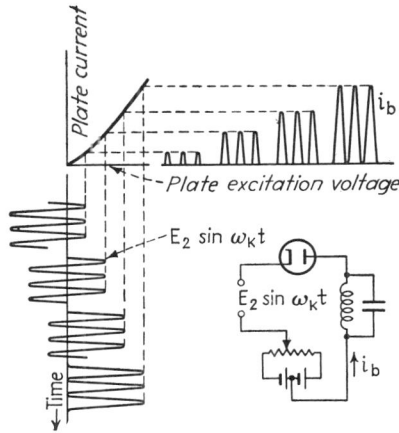

FIG. 7-6.—Variation of amplitude of alternating plate current with bias in diode
modulator having carrier excitation only.

b may be further resolved into a steady component and components whose frequencies are the modulation frequency and
its harmonics.   Curve c may be resolved into a varying-ampli-

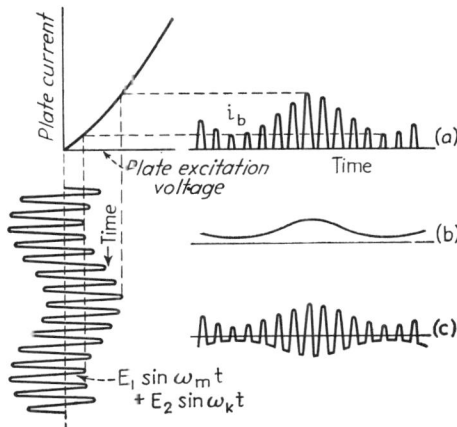

FIG. 7-7.—Amplitude modulation by complete rectification.   Waves (b) and
(c) are two components into which the wave (a) of plate current may be resolved.

tude carrier-frequency component and carrier-harmonic components.   Since the resonant circuit is tuned to the carrier

frequency, its impedance is high only at and near the carrier frequency, and so only the modulated-carrier component of plate current produces appreciable output voltage.

A theoretical analysis indicates that if the tube characteristic were linear down to zero current and the load a pure resistance, the fundamental component of plate current H_1 resulting from carrier excitation of fixed amplitude E_k would vary with bias E_b in the manner shown by the *modulation characteristic* of Fig. 7-8.[1] Experimental curves for the circuit of Fig. 7-6 differ from the curve of Fig. 7-8 because of curvature of the diode characteristic and because the load is not a pure resistance. When the L/C ratio of the tuned circuit is high, the curve flattens off at a positive value of E_b that is considerably less than E_k, and the portion of the modulation characteristic which is essentially linear is smaller than that of the theoretical characteristic of Fig. 7-8. If the modulation-frequency variation of E_b, *i.e.*, the modulation-frequency excitation, takes place over a range throughout which the characteristic is essentially linear, the amplitude of the carrier-frequency component of plate current and of output voltage vary nearly linearly with instantaneous modulation excitation voltage. For this reason modulation by complete rectification is called *linear modulation*. When the modulation is truly linear, the output voltage across the tuned circuit contains only the three desired frequency components and the wave form of the envelope of the modulated wave is undistorted. If the range of operation extends beyond the linear portion of the modulation characteristic, the output contains additional components whose frequencies are equal to the carrier frequency plus and minus integral multiples of the signal frequency.

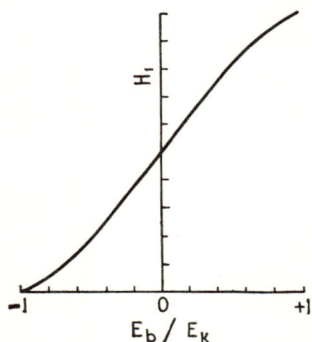

Fig. 7-8.—Ideal linear diode modulation characteristic.

The simple diode modulator circuit of Fig. 7-5 is not used in practice. Generally the carrier excitation is applied to the control grid of a triode or tetrode and the modulation excitation to the plate. Complete rectification takes place because of

[1] Reich, H. J., "Theory and Applications of Electron Tubes," p. 122.

cutoff of the plate characteristic.   Less power need be furnished
by the source of carrier excitation than in a diode circuit, and
amplification produced by the tube reduces the required carrier
excitation amplitude below that required with a diode.   This
type of modulation is called *linear plate modulation (plate voltage
modulation)*.   The circuit of the linear plate modulator is similar
to that of Fig. 7-2 except that the modulation input transformer
is in the plate circuit, instead of in the grid circuit.   As in a
diode modulator, all but the modulated carrier-frequency

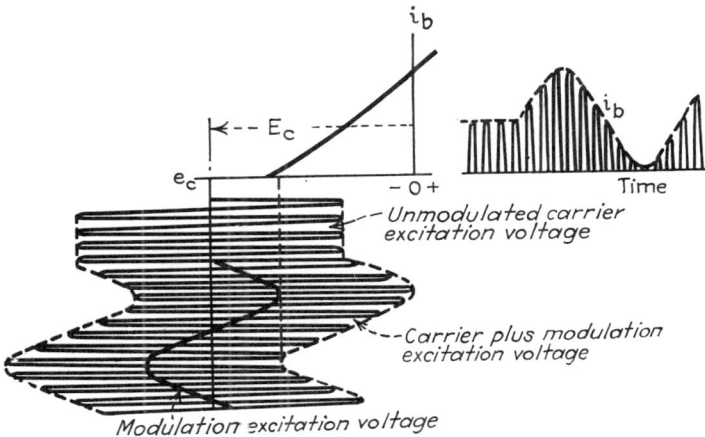

FIG. 7-9.—Linear grid modulation.   A parallel resonant circuit converts the
carrier and side-frequency components of plate current into output voltage.

(carrier and side-frequency) components are removed nearly
completely from the output by means of the tuned plate load.

   In linear plate modulation the source of modulation voltage
must furnish a large part of the power supplied to the plate
circuit.   The power that must be supplied by the source of
modulation voltage is less in *linear grid modulation (grid-bias
modulation)* in which the modulation voltage, as well as the
carrier voltage, is applied to the grid circuit.[1]   Linear grid
modulation has the additional advantage of requiring much
lower modulation excitation voltage, but gives somewhat higher
distortion and is less efficient.   Linear grid modulation is illustrated graphically in Fig. 7-9.   As in other modulation circuits,

[1] KISHPAUGH, A. W., and CORAM, R. E., *Proc. I.R.E.*, **21**, 212 (1933).

the tuned plate load converts the carrier and side-frequency components of plate current into output voltage.

Several modifications of the basic linear modulation circuits have been developed in order to increase the efficiency or to reduce the required modulation-frequency exciting voltage. The modulation excitation may, for instance, be applied in series with the cathode of a triode, it may be applied simultaneously to the plate and screen of a tetrode or a beam pentode, or it may be applied to the suppressor of a pentode.[1]

Equation (7-4) shows that the carrier-frequency component of an amplitude-modulated wave is independent of the degree of modulation. The continuous radiation of energy associated with the carrier component of the wave limits the efficiency that may be attained in a transmitter. Several systems of amplitude modulation that give higher efficiency have been proposed.[2] As will be shown in a later section, higher efficiency is also attained in frequency modulation.

7-6. Detection of Amplitude-modulated Waves.—The process whereby the modulation frequency is derived from a modulated wave is a special case of a more general process called *detection*. Detection may be defined as the process whereby the application of a voltage of a given frequency or frequencies to a circuit containing an asymmetrically conducting device produces currents of certain desired frequencies or desired changes in average current. The detection of a modulated wave to produce the modulation frequency is often termed *demodulation* in this country.[3] Other examples of detection are the production of a difference or *beat* frequency by the simultaneous application of two frequencies to a detector, and the production of a steady voltage or current by the application of an alternating voltage. According to the broad definition just given, modulation may, in fact, be considered a special form of detection. As already pointed out, the processes involved in amplitude modulation

[1] GREEN, C. B., *Bell Lab. Record*, **17**, 41 (1938).

[2] CHIREIX, H., *Proc. I.R.E.*, **23**, 1370 (1935); DOHERTY, W. H., *Proc. I.R.E.*, **24**, 1163 (1936); DOME, R. B., *Proc. I.R.E.*, **26**, 963 (1938); GAUDERNACK, L. F., *Proc. I.R.E.*, **26**, 983 (1938); RODER, H., *Proc. I.R.E.*, **27**, 386 (1939); VANCE, A. W., *Proc. I.R.E.*, **27**, 506 (1939).

[3] "Standards on Radio Receivers," p. 5, Institute of Radio Engineers, New York, 1938.

are similar to those involved in detection of amplitude-modulated waves. Detection of amplitude-modulated voltages, like their production, may be accomplished either as the result of curvature of vacuum-tube characteristics or of complete rectification at cutoff.

7-7. Detection by Curvature of Current-voltage Characteristic.—If a wave of alternating voltage is applied to the grid or plate circuit of a diode or triode, together with proper operating voltages to bring the operating point to a point of the characteristic where the curvature is high, the wave of plate current is asymmetrical, as shown by the transfer diagrams of Figs. 3-19, 3-21, and 7-10. If the input wave is sinusoidal, the plate current contains a steady component, the applied frequency, and its harmonics. If the excitation voltage contains two or more frequencies, the plate current contains components having these frequencies, their harmonics, and the sums and differences of the impressed frequencies and their integral multiples, and a steady component. This process of frequency generation, which is identical with that of the production of a modulated wave by curvature of the characteristic, has already been discussed in Secs. 3-22 and 7-4. The production of a difference-frequency voltage by the simultaneous application of two voltages of different frequencies to a detector is of value in heterodyne radio receivers (see Sec. 7-11) and heterodyne (beat-frequency) oscillators (see Sec. 8-8).

Figure 7-10 shows the form of the asymmetrical wave of plate current for unmodulated carrier excitation and for excitation consisting of an amplitude-modulated voltage. The wave may be analyzed into a number of components, including that indicated by the dotted line, which shows the average current in each carrier-frequency cycle. For modulated excitation the dotted curve is seen to contain a steady component and an alternating component having the same frequency as the envelope of the impressed modulated voltage, *i.e.*, modulation frequency. That steady and modulation-frequency components of plate current are generated may be proved rigorously by substituting an excitation voltage of the form of Eq. (7-4) in the first two terms of the series expansion for plate current (see Prob. 7-3). Such an analysis also predicts the generation of a component whose frequency is twice the modulation frequency, and whose amplitude is equal to that of the modulation-frequency component multiplied by $M/4$. As in modulation, therefore, the vacuum tube of the detector generates a number of frequencies that differ from those impressed. The plate load impedance serves to convert the component of plate current of desired frequency, the modulation frequency, into output voltage and to suppress the carrier-frequency components. This is accomplished by using for the load the parallel combination

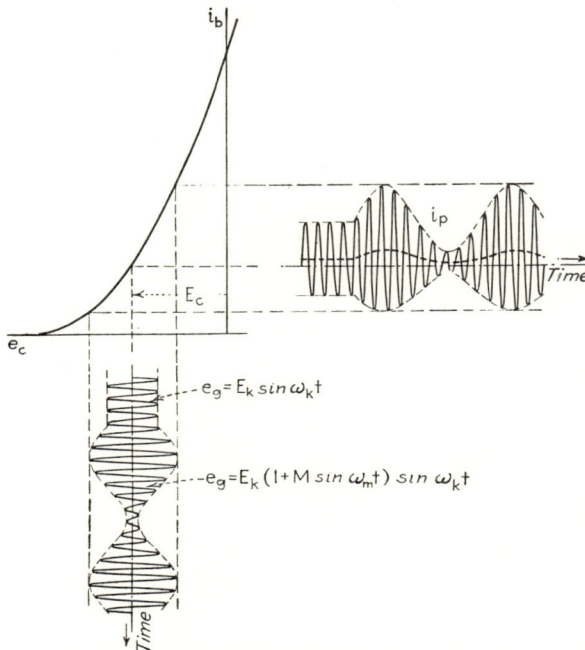

FIG. 7-10.—Detection of amplitude-modulated wave by curvature of triode transfer characteristic.

of a high resistance and a condenser whose reactance is negligible at carrier frequency but high at modulation frequency. Because it is associated with the second-order term of the series expansion, this type of detection is called *square-law detection*.

Figure 7-11 shows the circuit of a single-tube square-law detector. The function of the condenser C' is to prevent the direct voltage and changes of direct voltage resulting from detection from appearing in the output. R_{cc} provides grid bias. A more nearly parabolic transfer characteristic may be attained by the use of a balanced push-pull circuit.   Such a circuit, shown in Fig. 12-2, is occasionally of value when a true square-law detector is required for measuring purposes (see Sec. 12-2). Because of its relatively low output and its high second-harmonic distortion (10 per cent when $M = 40$ per cent, and 25 per cent

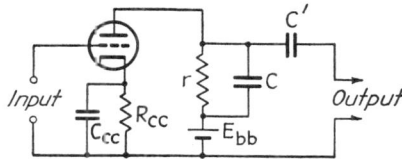

Fig. 7-11.—Square-law plate detector.

when $M = 100$ per cent), the square-law detector has been largely replaced by types making use of complete rectification.

7-8. Detection by Complete Rectification.—When a wave of modulated voltage is applied to a diode in series with a pure resistance, plate current flows only during the positive half cycles of impressed voltage.   The current wave consists of pulses and is very nearly a replica of the positive portions of the applied

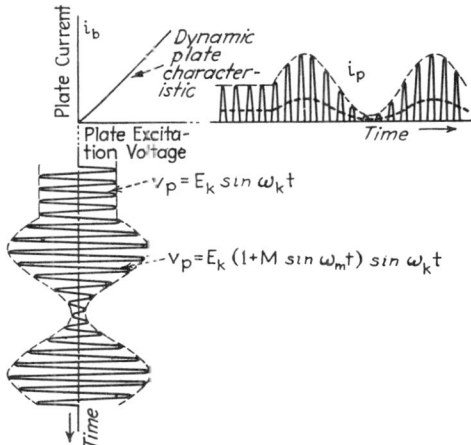

Fig. 7-12.—Detection of modulated wave by ideal linear diode.

voltage wave, as shown in Fig. 7-12.   It may be analyzed into components that include a carrier component and carrier-frequency harmonic components, in addition to a component indicated by the dotted curve, which shows the average current in each carrier-frequency cycle.   Since each pulse is very nearly a half sine wave, the average current indicated by the dotted curve varies at the same frequency as the envelope of the impressed voltage, *i.e.*, modulation frequency. It also contains a steady component. The voltage across the resistance, therefore, contains the desired modulation frequency in addition to steady, carrier-frequency, and harmonic components. The components having frequencies equal to the carrier and its harmonics may be suppressed by shunting the resistance with a condenser whose reactance is negligible at carrier frequency. This also prevents carrier-frequency voltage drop in the resistance and thus increases the modulation-frequency output voltage.

Addition of the condenser C in parallel with the resistance r, as shown in Fig. 7-13, alters the physical action of the circuit, since current no longer flows during the entire positive half cycles, but only during small portions of the cycles following

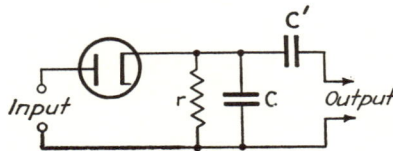

FIG. 7-13.—Diode detector circuit.

positive crest impressed voltage. If the resistance were omitted and the excitation consisted of an unmodulated carrier voltage, the condenser would be charged to a voltage equal to the crest impressed voltage, the carrier amplitude. An increase of amplitude of impressed voltage would cause an equal increase of condenser voltage but, because the tube is a perfect rectifier, the condenser could not discharge following a decrease of impressed voltage, and so the condenser voltage would not fall. The function of the resistance is to allow the condenser to discharge when the amplitude of the impressed voltage is lowered. If the ratio of the resistance to the capacitance is made low enough, the condenser voltage can follow rapid reductions of amplitude. Then, when a modulated voltage is impressed upon the circuit, the condenser voltage is very nearly equal to the amplitude of the impressed voltage at all times, and so the condenser voltage is practically identical in wave form with the envelope of the impressed voltage. It therefore contains a steady component plus a modulation-frequency component.

The charging current that can flow into the condenser for a given value of instantaneous impressed voltage is limited by the tube, by the impedance of the source, and by leakage through the load resistance. If the condenser is too large, several carrier-frequency cycles may be required for the condenser voltage to reach equilibrium after an increase or a decrease of amplitude of impressed alternating voltage. Then, if the impressed amplitude fluctuates rapidly, the changes in condenser voltage are less than the changes in amplitude. The change in condenser voltage for a given change of impressed amplitude decreases as the frequency of the amplitude variation is increased. Since the envelope of a modulated wave varies at modulation frequency, it follows that the use of too large a condenser causes frequency distortion of the detector output. With a large condenser and load resistance and low tube resistance and source resistance, the condenser voltage may be able to respond fully to an increase of amplitude of impressed voltage, but not to a decrease of amplitude. Frequency distortion will then be accompanied by amplitude distortion in the detection of a modulated wave. Both may be made negligible by satisfying the relation $2\pi f_m rC \leqq \sqrt{(1/M)^2 - 1}$, in which f_m is the highest modulation frequency with which the carrier is modulated.[1]

When the detector is resistance-capacitance coupled to the grid of an amplifier tube, the detector load resistance at modulation frequency is that of r in parallel with the amplifier grid leak (the coupling capacitance being assumed negligible at modulation frequency), whereas the d-c resistance is that of r alone. To prevent the amplitude distortion discussed above, it is then necessary to satisfy the relation $2\pi f_m r_m C \leqq \sqrt{(r_m/rM)^2 - 1}$ where f_m is the highest modulation frequency and r_m is the effective load resistance at modulation frequency.[2] The difference between the modulation-frequency and d-c resistances of the load with resistance-capacitance coupling causes another type of amplitude distortion because of complete cutting off of diode

[1] TERMAN, F. E., and MORGAN, N. R., *Proc. I.R.E.*, **18**, 2160 (1930); NELSON, J. R., *Proc. I.R.E.*, **19**, 489 (1931); NELSON, J. R., *Proc. I.R.E.*, **20**, 989 (1932); TERMAN, F. E., and NELSON, J. R., *Proc. I.R.E.*, **20**, 1971 (1932).

[2] ROBERTS, F., and WILLIAMS, F. C., *J. Inst. Elec. Eng. (London)*, **75**, 379 (1934); BENNON, S., *Proc. I.R.E.*, **25**, 1565 (1937).

current during the inward modulation crests when the degree
of modulation is high. This type of distortion, which results in
"clipping" of the negative peaks of modulation output voltage, may be prevented by keeping the degree of modulation
less than a limiting value given approximately by the relation
$M = (r_m + 2r_s)/(r + 2r_s)$, where r_s is the effective resistance of
the source at carrier frequency.[1]

The load resistance not only allows the condenser to discharge
in response to the envelope of the impressed voltage, but also
allows it to discharge during the portions of the carrier-frequency
cycle in which the instantaneous impressed voltage is less than
the condenser voltage. This causes the condenser voltage to
vary by a small amount at carrier frequency. The presence of
carrier-frequency voltage in the output is the limiting factor in
determining the minimum condenser capacitance that can be
used. The ratio of the amplitude of the carrier-frequency voltage in the output to the amplitude of the signal-frequency
voltage is approximately $1/\pi_k f r_m C$, where f_k is the carrier frequency. Since the carrier frequency is usually at least ten
times the highest signal frequency, there is no difficulty in
making C large enough to meet this requirement without making
it too large to avoid modulation-frequency distortion. To
minimize loading of the source of modulated voltage, the load
resistance should be high. Values ranging from 100,000 Ω to
1 megohm are normally used. A capacitance of approximately
150 $\mu\mu$f is suitable for C in the broadcast band.

Figure 7-14 shows a variant of the circuit of Fig. 7-13. The
former differs from the latter mainly in that the condenser
discharges through the resistance and source in series, rather
than through the resistance only. Since the impedance of the
source is low at modulation frequency, this does not affect
the behavior of the circuit. Because of the low impedance of the
source at modulation frequency, the modulation voltage across
the tube in the circuits of both Fig. 7-13 and Fig. 7-14 equals
that across the condenser C, and so the output may be taken
from across the tube instead of the condenser. Carrier-frequency
voltage will, however, then be present in the output.

[1] WHEELER, H. A., *Proc. I.R.E.*, **26**, 745 (1938); COURT, W. P. N., *Wireless Eng.*, **16**, 548 (1939); STURLEY, K. R., *Wireless Eng.*, **17**, 19 (1940);
PREISMAN, A., *Communications*, August, 1940, p. 18; September, 1940, p. 8.

The instantaneous value of modulation output voltage of a properly designed detector that functions by virtue of complete rectification of a diode is proportional to the instantaneous amplitude of the envelope of the impressed modulated voltage. Such a detector is, therefore, said to be *linear*.

7-9. Linear Plate Detection (Linear Transrectification).— Because the plate current of a vacuum tube can be cut off by application of negative voltage to a grid, action similar to that

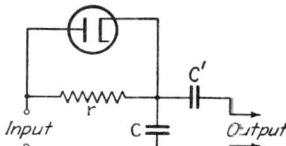

FIG. 7-14.—Diode detector circuit.

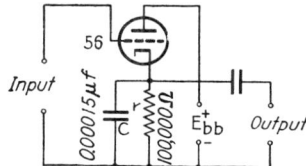

FIG. 7-15.—Linear plate detector.

of a linear diode detector is obtained when an amplitude-modulated voltage is impressed upon a grid circuit of a triode or multigrid tube biased to cutoff. The modulation-frequency output is developed across a condenser-resistance load in the plate circuit, as shown in the circuit of Fig. 7-15. Such a detector is called a *linear plate detector*. In the circuit of Fig. 7-15 the bias is obtained from the steady component of voltage across the load resistance. Since the bias depends upon the flow of plate current, it must of necessity be somewhat smaller than the cutoff value and so detection at low excitation is by curvature of the transfer characteristic. At high excitation the action approximates that of a linear diode. The distortion of a linear plate detector is general y greater than that of a linear

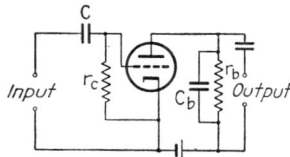

FIG. 7-16.—Linear grid detector.

diode detector, but it has the advantages of greater sensitivity and high input impedance.

7-10. Linear Grid Detection.—Figure 7-16 shows the circuit of a linear gr d detector. Comparison with Fig. 7-14 shows that, as far as the grid circuit is concerned, the action is the same as that of the linear diode detector of Fig. 7-14 when the output in the latter is taken from across the tube. The modulation-frequency voltage appearing between the grid and cathode produces an amplified modulation-frequency voltage across the plate resistor. Because carrier-frequency voltage is also impressed between grid and cathode, the condenser C_b must be used across the plate load resistance r_b in order to suppress carrier voltage from the output. The grid resistor r_c may be connected across the condenser, instead of between the grid and the cathode. The grid circuit is then of the form of the diode detector of Fig. 7-13.

In the linear grid detector, rectification in the grid circuit produces the biasing voltage necessary in using the triode to amplify the modulation-frequency voltage. Unfortunately, this bias cannot be readily adjusted for least distortion in amplification. This difficulty constitutes one disadvantage of the linear grid detector. A second disadvantage is that detection caused by transfer-characteristic curvature is superimposed upon that produced by grid rectification and thus reduces the output voltage. The advantage of the linear grid detector over the linear diode detector is its higher sensitivity, which results from amplification of the modulation-frequency voltage generated in the grid circuit. This advantage can be attained without the attending disadvantages by the use of a diode detector and a separate stage of audio-frequency amplification. Increase in the number of tubes is avoided by using a tube that combines a diode and a triode or pentode in one envelope.

If sufficient additional fixed positive bias is used in the circuit of Fig. 7-16, grid current flows continuously and detection is the result of curvature of the grid characteristic, rather than of complete rectification. Although used in early radio receivers, this type of detector has been entirely superseded by linear diode detection in communication work.

7-11. Radio Communication by Means of Amplitude-modulated Waves.—The block diagram of Fig. 7-17a shows the essential steps in communication by means of amplitude-modulated waves. The reader should note the frequencies present at various points in the system. In the *superheterodyne* type of receiver now used almost exclusively in broadcast reception, the carrier frequency is transformed to a value of 450 kc before the modulated signal is amplified to the level required for detection. This is accomplished by impressing the modulated signal and the output of a local oscillator, whose frequency is 450 kc higher than that of the incoming carrier, upon a frequency **converter** or *first detector*, as shown in Fig. 7-17b. The 450-kc *intermediate-frequency amplifier* selects the desired difference-frequency components from the output of the first detector. Because most of the amplification is accomplished at the fixed intermediate frequency, the superheterodyne circuit makes possible the high amplification and selectivity that can be attained with a large number of tuned amplifier stages without requiring the simultaneous variation of more than three condensers (first amplifier, oscillator, and first detector) in the operation of the receiver.

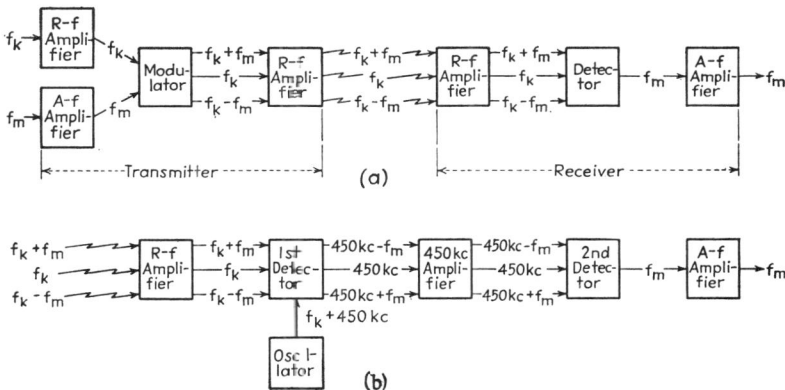

FIG. 7-17.—(a) Essential steps in communication by means of amplitude-modulated waves. (b) Block diagram of superheterodyne receiver.

7-12. Frequency Modulation.[1]—Frequency modulation is the process whereby the frequency of one wave or oscillation is varied with time in accordance with the time variations of another wave or oscillation. Figure 7-18 shows a wave of a quantity y, the value of which varies periodically with time at a frequency that is a function of time. The amplitude has a constant value K. If the variation of frequency is sufficiently slow so that each cycle can be assumed to be essentially sinusoidal, then the value of y at any instant t_1 is equal to $\sin \theta$,

[1] CARSON, J. R., *Proc. I.R.E.*, **10**, 57 (1922); **17**, 187 (1929). VAN DER POL, B., *Proc. I.R.E.*, **18**, 1194 (1930). SMITH, C. H., *Wireless Eng.*, **7**, 609 (1930). RODER, H., *Proc. I.R.E.*, **19**, 2145 (1931) (with bibliography of 21 items). LUCK, D. G. C., and RODER, H., *Proc. I.R.E.*, **20**, 884 (1932). ARMSTRONG, E. H., *Proc. I.R.E.*, **24**, 689 (1936). See also supplementary bibliography at the end of this chapter.

where θ is the number of degrees elapsed in the cycle in progress at the instant t_1. It can be seen from Fig. 7-18 that the value of θ, and hence of y, at that instant depends not only upon the frequency at that instant, but also upon the manner in which the frequency varied previously. If n is the number of cycles that have elapsed between the instants $t = 0$ and $t = t_1$, then the value of y at the instant t_1 may be expressed by the relation

$$y_1 = K \sin n(2\pi) \qquad (7\text{-}5)$$

Thus, in Fig. 7-18, $n = 5 + \theta/2\pi$ and $y_1 = K \sin (10\pi + \theta) = \sin \theta$. t_1 is equal to the number of cycles between zero and t_1 multiplied by the period of each cycle. The portion Δn of a cycle that elapses during any small interval between t and

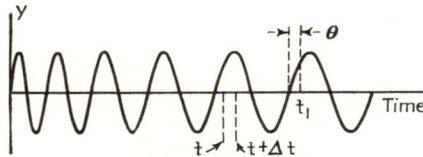

Fig. 7-18.—Frequency-modulated wave.

$t + \Delta t$ is equal to the ratio of the interval Δt to the period T for that cycle. Thus

$$\Delta n = \frac{\Delta t}{T} = f \, \Delta t \qquad (7\text{-}6)$$

where f is the value of the frequency at the instant t. Therefore the number of cycles in the interval 0 to t_1 is

$$n = \int_0^{t_1} f \, dt \qquad (7\text{-}7)$$

If the instantaneous frequency f is varied sinusoidally at modulation frequency f_m about an unmodulated carrier value f_k in accordance with the relation

$$f = f_k(1 + B \cos 2\pi f_m t) \qquad (7\text{-}8)$$

then

$$n = \int_0^{t_1} f_k(1 + B \cos 2\pi f_m t) \, dt \qquad (7\text{-}9)$$

$$n = f_k \left(t_1 + \frac{B}{2\pi f_m} \sin 2\pi f_m t_1 \right) \qquad (7\text{-}10)$$

and

$$y_1 = K \sin \left(2\pi f_k t_1 + \frac{B f_k}{f_m} \sin 2\pi f_m t_1 \right) \qquad (7\text{-}11)$$

Since t_1 may have any value, the subscript $_1$ may be omitted and Eq. (7-11) written in the form

$$y = K \sin (\omega_k t + M_f \sin \omega_m t) \qquad (7\text{-}12)$$

in which $M_f = B\omega_k/\omega_m = Bf_k/f_m$. Equation (7-12) is that of a constant-amplitude wave, the frequency of which is varied in accordance with Eq. (7-8). Bf_k, which is shown by Eq. (7-8) to be the maximum change in frequency from the unmodulated carrier value, is called the *frequency deviation* and will be represented by the symbol f_d. M_f, which is equal to f_d/f_m, the ratio of the frequency deviation to the modulation frequency, is called the *deviation ratio* or *frequency modulation index*.

Equation (7-12) may be expanded in the form[1]

$$\begin{aligned}
y = K\{ & J_0(M_f) \sin \omega_k t + J_1(M_f)[\sin (\omega_k + \omega_m)t - \sin (\omega_k - \omega_m)t] \\
& + J_2(M_f)[- \sin (\omega_k + 2\omega_m)t + \sin (\omega_k - 2\omega_m)t] \\
& + J_3(M_f)[\sin (\omega_k + 3\omega_m)t - \sin (\omega_k - 3\omega_m)t] \\
& + J_4(M_f)[- \sin (\omega_k + 4\omega_m)t + \sin (\omega_k - 4\omega_m)t] \\
& + \cdots \}
\end{aligned} \qquad (7\text{-}13)$$

in which the coefficients $J_n(M_f)$ are Bessel functions of the first kind. The coefficients for any given value of M_f may be evaluated by the use of published tables that list numerical values of $J_0(x)$, $J_1(x)$, $J_2(x)$, etc., for various values of x.[2]

Equation (7-13) shows that a frequency-modulated wave theoretically contains an infinite number of side frequencies, separated in frequency value by the modulation frequency. The values of $J_n(M_f)$ decrease very rapidly, however, beyond a value of n that is slightly greater than M_f. This can be seen from Fig. 7-19, which shows as a function of M_f the highest order of the side frequencies whose amplitudes are greater

[1] VAN DER POL, *loc. cit.;* RODER, *loc. cit.*

[2] JAHNKE, E., and EMDE, F., "Tables of Functions with Formulae and Curves," 3d ed., B. G. Teubner, Leipzig and Berlin (1938); GRAY, A., and MATHEWS, G. B., "A Treatise on Bessel Functions," Macmillan & Company, Ltd., London (1922). See also Roder, *op. cit.*, p. 2175.

than 5 per cent or than 10 per cent of that of the unmodulated carrier.[1]

Because M_f is inversely proportional to f_m, the number of side frequencies of appreciable amplitude decreases with increase of modulation frequency and, when the deviation is large in comparison with the highest modulation frequency, the over-all

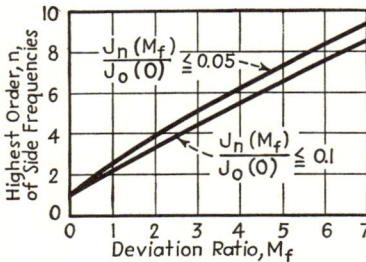

FIG. 7-19.—Highest order of side frequencies whose amplitudes are greater than 5 per cent or than 10 per cent of the unmodulated carrier, plotted as a function of deviation ratio.

band width does not vary greatly as the modulation frequency changes throughout the audio-frequency range. This fact can be shown with the aid of Fig. 7-19 by noting that the total band width of the upper and of the lower frequency bands in which the side frequencies lie is equal to nf_m, where n is the order of the highest-order side frequency component of appreciable amplitude. Inspection shows that for the 10 per cent curve n is approximately equal to $1.0 + 1.1M_f$. Hence the width of the upper and of the lower band is approximately

$$\left[1.0 + 1.1\left(\frac{Bf_k}{f_m} \right) \right] f_m = f_m + 1.1 f_d$$

where f_d is Bf_k, the deviation in cycles per second. The total band width is approximately $2f_m + 2.2f_d$, which does not vary greatly with f_m when f_d/f_m, i.e., M_f, is large. A similar expression may be derived for the 5 per cent curve of Fig. 7-19 but, because of greater curvature of this curve, the expression is not quite so simple. More complete analyses have been made.[2] In present frequency-modulation broadcasting systems the maximum deviation is 75,000 $\sim$ and the highest modulation frequency is 15,000 $\sim$. M_f is, therefore, 5 and the band width at full deviation varies from about 165,000 $\sim$ to 200,000 $\sim$ as the modulation frequency varies in the audio-frequency range. Fig. 7-20 shows the manner in which the number, distribution,

[1] RODER, *loc. cit.* In using Fig. 7-19, n is read as the next lower integer to the value indicated by the curve. Thus, for $M_f = 1$, $n = 2$.

[2] BLACK, L. J., and SCOTT, H. J., *Electronics*, September, 1940, p. 30.

and amplitude of the carrier and side-frequency components change with modulation frequency for a frequency deviation of 60,000 ∼.[1]

It should be noted that the amplitudes of the side-frequency components of a frequency-modulated wave depend both upon the amplitude of the original modulation-frequency excitation [through variation of B in Eq. (7-8)] and upon the modulation frequency, as has just been shown.

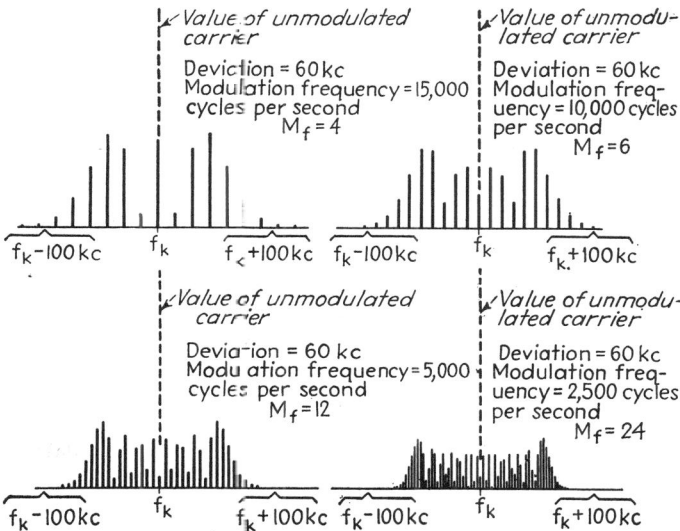

FIG. 7-20.—Amplitudes and distribution of side-frequency components of frequency-modulated wave for 60-kc deviation and four values of modulation frequency.

A more complete analysis than that which has just been presented shows that the side frequencies produced when the carrier is modulated simultaneously at two or more frequencies are not in general equal to the side frequencies produced when the carrier is modulated individually at these same frequencies. When the total deviation is the same, however, the side frequencies remain within a band of the same approximate width.[2]

7-13. Phase Modulation.—An analysis similar to that made in the preceding section for frequency modulation shows that when

[1] EVERITT, W. L., *Trans. A.I.E.E.*, **59**, 613 (1940).
[2] CROSBY, M. G., *RCA Rev.*, **3**, 103 (1938).

the phase angle of the carrier is varied in accordance with the relation $\phi = \phi_0(1 + B \sin \omega_m t)$ the resulting phase-modulated wave is of the form[1]

$$y = K \sin (\omega_k t + M_p \sin \omega_m t) \qquad (7\text{-}14)$$

in which M_p, the *phase modulation index*, is equal to $\phi_0 B$.   Equal tion (7-14) differs from Eq. (7-12) only in that M_p replaces M_f. It may, therefore, be expanded into an equation of the same form as Eq. (7-13).   Since M_p is not inversely proportional to f_m as in frequency modulation, however, the number of side frequencies of appreciable amplitude is independent of f_m and so the required band width is proportional to the modulation frequency.   Because of the much larger band width required at high modulation frequency, because of the more complicated circuits required for detection, and because of sensitivity of the receiver to microphonic tube vibrations,[2] phase modulation is less satisfactory than frequency modulation in radio broadcasting and has thus far been used only experimentally.

7-14. Frequency-modulation Circuits.—The most direct method of producing frequency modulation is by variation of oscillator frequency in response to the time variation of the modulation-frequency signal.   Since the frequency of most oscillators is controlled by the reactance of a parallel resonant circuit (see Chap. 8), the frequency may be varied by use of a circuit in which the effective capacitive or inductive reactance is varied by means of the grid voltage of a vacuum tube.   Two such circuits are shown in Figs. 7-21 and

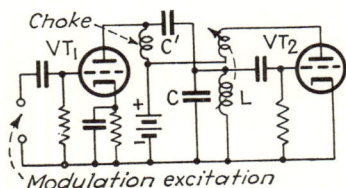

Fig. 7-21.—Frequency modulator.

7-22.[3]   In the circuit of Fig. 7-21 the main tuning capacitance C of the oscillator is shunted by the auxiliary capacitance C' in series with the plate resistance of the tube VT_1. Variation of the control-grid voltage of VT_1 changes the plate resistance and, hence, the effective capacitance of the series combination of r_p and C'.

[1] Roder, *loc. cit.*
[2] Crosby, M. G., *Proc. I.R.E.*, **27**, 126 (1939).
[3] Travis, C., *Proc. I.R.E.*, **23**, 1125 (1935).

In the circuit of Fig. 7-22, the alternating plate voltage of VT_2 is the voltage across C' and r, whereas the voltage of the first grid is that across r. Since the voltage across r leads that across r and C', and the grid voltage has more effect upon the plate current than does the plate voltage, the plate current leads the plate voltage. The tube, therefore, acts as an impedance having a capacitive component. By means of the equivalent plate circuit of VT_2, the student may show that the effective reactance of the tube is $-j\dfrac{r^2\omega^2C'^2 + 1}{g_m r\omega C'}$ (see Prob. 4-3). Because of dependence of g_m upon electrode voltages, the effective reactance may be varied by the voltage of one or

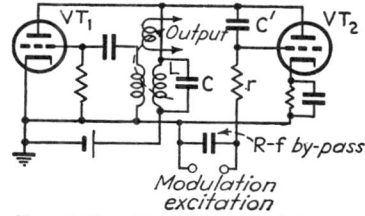

Fig. 7-22.—Frequency modulator.

more grids of VT_2. By proper choice of tube, operating voltages, and circuit constants, the frequency can be made to vary linearly with grid voltage. The frequency variation is then proportional to the instantaneous value of modulating voltage impressed upon the grid or grids. A number of modifications of these basic circuits may be made to meet specific requirements.[1]

An entirely different principle is used in the Armstrong system of modulation.[2] If M_f is less than about 0.5, all but the first two terms of Eq. (7-13) are very small.[3] Equation (7-13) then differs in form from Eq. (7-4) for an amplitude-modulated wave only in a 90-deg difference in phase of the side-frequency terms and in the fact that the side-frequency coefficients of Eq. (7-13) decrease with increase of modulation frequency whereas those of Eq. (7-4) are independent of frequency. $J_1(M_f)$ varies very nearly linearly with M_f for values of M_f ranging from zero to 0.5. Hence if a 90-deg phase shift is made in the second term of Eq. (7-4), if the degree of amplitude modulation M is made inversely proportional to modulation frequency, and if K is of

[1] FREEMAN, R. L., *Electronics*, November, 1936, p. 20; FOSTER, D. E., and SEELEY, S. W., *Proc. I.R.E.*, **25**, 289 (1937); SHEAFFER, C. F., *Proc. I.R.E.*, **28**, 66 (1940); CROSBY, M. G., QST, June, 1940, p. 46; CROSBY, M. G., *RCA Rev.*, **5**, 89 (1940).

[2] ARMSTRONG, *loc. cit.*

[3] JAFFE, D. L., *Proc. I.R.E.*, **26**, 475 (1938).

the proper value, the wave represented by Eq. (7-4) will be identical with that represented by Eq. (7-13) at all values of modulation frequency. This is accomplished in the Armstrong system by amplitude-modulating the carrier by means of a circuit in which the carrier is suppressed in the output, shifting the resulting side-frequency output 90 deg in phase, and then recombining it with the unmodulated carrier. M is made inversely proportional to modulation frequency by passing the modulation-frequency excitation through an "equalizer" that makes its amplitude inversely proportional to the modulation frequency before impressing it upon the modulator. The equalizer usually consists of a resistance-capacitance network.

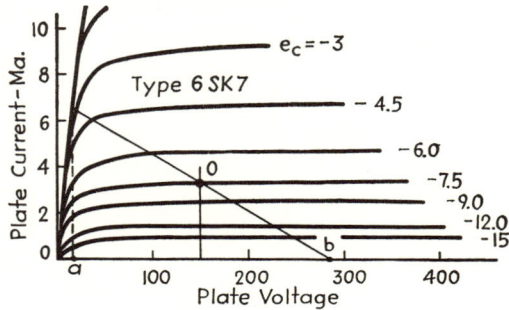

Fig. 7-23.—Plate diagram for limiter.

The maximum value of approximately 0.5 that can be used for M_f directly in the Armstrong system is too small to give the benefits that can be attained by the use of frequency modulation in radio communication (see Sec. 7-16). This difficulty is avoided by performing the modulation at a much lower carrier frequency than that desired for transmission. By means of a series of frequency-multiplying circuits the frequency of the modulated voltage is then multiplied to the desired value. This process also raises the deviation ratio to the desired value.

7-15. Detection of Frequency-modulated Voltage.—Prior to detecting a frequency-modulated voltage it is necessary to eliminate any amplitude variation that may have been introduced subsequent to modulation. This is accomplished by impressing the voltage upon the input of a *limiter*, which is merely a tuned radio-frequency amplifier operated at low plate voltage. The action of such a circuit may be understood by reference to the plate diagram of Fig. 7-23. Since the d-c resistance of the tuned plate circuit is small, the operating plate voltage is practically equal to the supply voltage. At resonance, however, the a-c load resistance is high. It can be seen from Fig. 7-23 that, no matter how large the grid excitation is made, the plate voltage cannot swing beyond the limits indicated by points a and b. Hence, beyond the excitation that causes the voltage to swing to these limits, increase of grid excitation has no effect upon the amplitude of the fundamental output voltage. Harmonics are suppressed by the tuned circuit. In practice, excitation is made large enough and the operating voltage sufficiently low so that the output amplitude remains constant in spite of fluctuations of impressed voltage.

The detection of frequency-modulated voltages is accomplished by first causing the changes of frequency to vary the amplitude of the voltage and then detecting the resulting amplitude-modulated wave by means of a diode detector in a manner discussed in Sec. 7-8. The circuit used to produce amplitude modulation as the result of frequency modulation is called a *discriminator*. This term is commonly applied to the complete detector, including the diode portion.

The simplest type of discriminator is a series resonant circuit tuned slightly off resonance with the carrier.[1] The voltage produced across either the condenser or the inductance varies approximately linearly with frequency over a limited range of frequency, and so variations of frequency produce proportional variations of amplitude. A similar action takes place in tuned-radio-frequency amplifiers tuned slightly off resonance with the carrier frequency. For this reason careful tuning is desirable in amplifiers used for frequency-modulated voltages. (Note, however, that the limiter removes amplitude variations resulting from this cause.)

A more common discriminator circuit is shown in Fig. 7-24. This circuit was originally designed for use in automatically tuned radio receivers to produce a direct voltage as the result of a change of frequency.[2] The action of the circuit is as follows:

[1] ANDREW, V. J., *Proc. I.R.E.*, **20**, 835 (1932); CHAFFEE, J. G., *Proc. I.R.E.*, **23**, 517 (1935); RODER, H., *Proc. I.R.E.*, **25**, 1617 (1937).

[2] TRAVIS, *loc. cit.;* ARMSTRONG, *op. cit.*, p. 699; CROSBY, M. G., *Proc. I.R.E.*, **24**, 898 (1936); FOSTER and SEELEY, *loc. cit.;* RODER, H., *Proc. I.R.E.*, **26**, 590 (1938).

The voltage E_1 impressed upon the circuit of the diode VT_1 is the vector sum of E' and E'', whereas the voltage E_2 impressed upon the circuit of VT_2 is the vector sum of E' and E'''. As explained in Sec. 7-8, if the reactance of C_4 and C_5 at carrier frequency is low in comparison with the shunting resistances, then C_4 and C_5 charge in the indicated polarities to voltages nearly equal to the crest voltages E_1 and E_2 impressed in the respective circuits. The output voltage E_o is the sum of the condenser voltages.

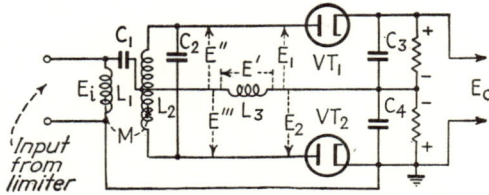

Fig. 7-24.—Discriminator circuit.

Since the reactance of C_4 is negligible, the series combination of C_1 and L_3 is in parallel with L_1 and the voltage E' across L_3 is either in phase with or 180 deg out of phase with the primary voltage E_i. It will be assumed that the reactance of L_3 exceeds that of C_1, so that E' is in phase with E_i. By virtue of circuit symmetry, the voltages E'' and E''' are each equal in magnitude to half the voltage E_c across C_2. E'' is of the same sign as E_c; E''' is opposite in sign. The voltage across C_2 can be deter-

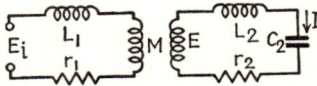

Fig. 7-25.—Equivalent circuit for the transformer of the discriminator of Fig. 7-24.

mined with the aid of the equivalent circuit of Fig. 7-25, in which L_2 and r_2 are the self-inductance and resistance of the transformer secondary and M is the mutual inductance. The induced voltage E is 90 deg out of phase with the primary current. As the primary resistance r_1 is small, E_i is also practically 90 deg out of phase with the primary current, and so E is in phase with or 180 deg out of phase with E_i. It will be assumed to be opposite in phase to E_i. Figure 7-26a shows the vector diagram of the secondary of the equivalent circuit at resonance.[1] E_c lags E by 90 deg. The vector diagrams of Fig. 7-27a, showing the vector

[1] The voltage E_r is actually very small in comparison with E_c. It is exaggerated in Fig. 7-26 for the sake of clarity.

sum of E' and E'' and of E' and E''' indicate that the voltages E_1 and E_2 impressed in the two diode circuits are equal. The voltages across C_3 and C_4 are, therefore, also equal in magnitude. Because they are of opposite polarity, the output voltage E_o is zero.

Figure 7-26b shows the vector diagram for the equivalent secondary circuit at a frequency slightly above resonance.[1] I, E_c, and E_L are all smaller than at resonance, but the reduction of E_c is greater than that of E_L, and so E_c lags E by more than 90 deg. Figure 7-27b shows that the magnitude of E_1

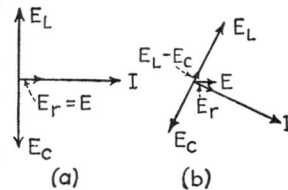

FIG. 7-26.—Vector diagrams for the secondary of the equivalent circuit of FIG. 7-25.

now exceeds that of E_2. Therefore, the voltage across C_3 exceeds that across C_4, and E_o has a positive value. Below resonance,

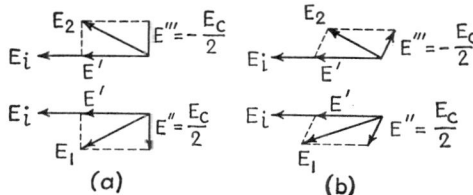

FIG. 7-27.—Vector diagrams for the circuit of Fig. 7-24.

on the other hand, E_2 exceeds E_1 in magnitude and E_o is negative. A typical curve of E_o as a function of frequency change from the resonance value f_0 is shown in Fig. 7-28. The linearity of this curve in the vicinity of resonance makes possible the conversion of the frequency-modulated input voltage into the modulation-frequency output voltage without distortion. If the circuit is tuned to the carrier frequency, then the instantaneous output voltage is proportional to

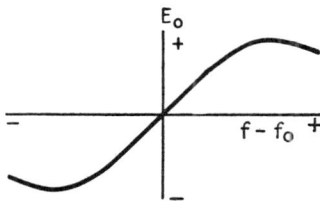

FIG. 7-28.—Detection characteristic for the discriminator of Fig. 7-24.

the instantaneous value of modulation-frequency voltage used to modulate the carrier. The output voltage is therefore of the same wave form as the original modulation voltage.

[1] In the vicinity of resonance, the vector $E_L - E_c$ is actually much smaller than shown.

7-16. Advantages of Frequency Modulation in Radio Communication.—Frequency modulation has a number of advantages over amplitude modulation in radio communication. These are[1]

1. Greatly reduced interference from static and other noise. Except at low values of carrier-noise ratio, the ratio of the audio-frequency signal output to the noise output is greater in a frequency-modulation system, and increases in proportion to the deviation ratio.[2] This fact explains the desirability of using large deviation ratio.

2. Greatly reduced interference from stations operating in the same channel.[2] If the amplitude of one modulated signal is greater than twice that of another of the same carrier frequency, the interference of the weaker signal is negligible. For a 3 to 1 ratio of signal strengths and a maximum deviation of 75 kc, the level of the interference is 40 db below that of the desired modulation output.

3. Because of reduced noise interference, a wider audio-frequency band can be used without excessive noise. Thus greater tone fidelity is obtained.

4. Increased transmitter efficiency. In frequency modulation, increase of side-frequency amplitudes with modulation is accompanied by reduction of amplitude of the carrier component and the total power furnished by the transmitter remains constant. The transmitter may therefore be operated in such a manner that its efficiency is high at all times.[3] This is in contrast with amplitude modulation, in which the amplitude of the carrier-frequency component of the modulated wave is independent of modulation factor and the total power furnished by the transmitter increases with modulation.

A difficulty encountered in the use of frequency modulation in broadcasting is that of maintaining the average carrier frequency constant without preventing the desired modulation. This is accomplished in the Armstrong system by the use of crystal control (see page 225). In the reactance-tube system the

[1] Proof of these facts is beyond the scope of this book. For further details the reader should refer to the articles listed in the next footnote.

[2] ARMSTRONG, *loc. cit.;* CROSBY, M. G., *Proc. I.R.E.,* **25,** 472 (1937); RODER, H., *Electronics,* May, 1936, p. 22; WEIR, I. R., *Gen. Elec. Rev.,* **42,** 188 and 270 (1939); LEVY, M. L., *Electronics,* June, 1940, p. 26; GUY, R. F., and MORRIS, R. M., *RCA Rev.,* **5,** 190 (1940).

[3] RODER, H., *Proc. I.R.E.,* **19,** 2145 (1931); CHAFFEE, J. G., *Proc. I.R.E.,* **23,** 517 (1935); EVERITT, *loc. cit.*

frequency is kept constant by the use of automatic frequency control and by more complicated methods.[1]

In order to obtain the advantage of freedom from interference the deviation, and hence the band width, must be large. The great demand for broadcasting and other communication channels makes it infeasible to use wide bands except at ultrahigh frequencies. The range from 42 to 50 Mc has been set aside for frequency-modulated waves and 200 kc has been designated as the channel width. This allows a maximum deviation of approximately 75 kc for an audio-frequency modulation range up to 15 kc. Although low level of natural static constitutes an advantage of ultrahigh-frequency transmission, it also has a number of disadvantages. These are

1. The transmission range is small. Because ultrahigh-frequency waves are not reflected by the ionized layer of the earth's upper atmosphere, they move in straight paths and their range is theoretically limited to the distance of the horizon. It has been found in practice that consistent reception may be achieved over about three times this range. By locating the transmitting antennas on the tops of mountains and tall buildings, ranges of about 150 miles are now attained.

2. Buildings, hills, and other objects cast shadows and thus prevent satisfactory reception in some areas.

3. Automobile ignition systems and other electrical equipment set up serious local interference.

The Yankee network of the New England region overcomes the difficulty of limited range by the use of sufficiently close transmitter spacing to give complete coverage. The programs that originate at one transmitter are rebroadcast at the same frequency by other transmitters of the chain without being changed to audio frequency in the process. In this manner excellent quality is maintained.[2]

Problems

7-1. Transform Eq. (7-3) into Eq. (7-4).

7-2. Find the power supplied to a resistance r by a generator whose terminal voltage is of the form of Eq. (7-4), and determine what portion of the power is associated with the carrier component and with each side-frequency component.

[1] MORRISON, J. F., *Communications*, August, 1940, p. 12; *Proc. I.R.E.*, **28**, 444 (1940).

[2] ARMSTRONG, E. H., *Elec. Eng.*, **59**, 485 (1940).

7-3. By substituting Eq. (7-4) in the first two terms of Eq. (3-32), prove that the output of a square-law detector excited by an amplitude-modulated voltage contains a steady component, a modulation-frequency component, and a component whose frequency is twice the modulation frequency.

Supplementary Bibliography

Frequency Modulation

Roder, H.: *Telefunken Z.*, **53,** 48 (1929).
Eckersley, T. L.: *Wireless Eng.*, **7,** 482 (1930).
Eastman, A. V., and Scott, E. D.: *Proc. I.R.E.*, **22,** 878 (1934).
Scott, E. D., and Woodyard, J. R.: *Univ. Wash. Eng. Expt. Sta. Bull.* 68.
Carson, J. R., and Fry, T. C.: *Bell System Tech. J.*, **16,** 513 (1937).
Fisher, C. B.: *R.M.A. Eng.*, November, 1938, p. 11.
Editorials, *Wireless Eng.*: **16,** 547 and 597 (1939); **17,** 197 and 339 (1940).
Noble, D. E.: *QST*, August, 1939, p. 11.
Editorial, *Electronics*, November, 1939, p. 20.
Metschl, E. C.: *E.T.Z.*, November, 1939, p. 1357.
Yocum, C. H.: *Communications*, November, 1939, p. 5; December, 1939, p. 14.
Tyler, G. W.: *R.M.A. Eng.*, **4,** 16 (1939).
Shelby, R. E.: *Electronics*, February, 1940, p. 14.
Chaffee, J. G.: *Bell Lab. Record*, **18,** 177 (1940).
Hughes, L. E. C.: *Electrician*, March 8, 1940, p. 188.
Crosby, M. G.: *RCA Rev.*, **4,** 473 (1940).
Carson, J. R.: *Wireless Eng.*, **17,** 477 (1940).
Gunther, F. A.: *Communications*, April, 1940, p. 11.
Shea, R. F.: *Communications*, June, 1940, p. 17.
Scott, H. J.: *Communications*, August, 1940, p. 10.
Pieracci, R. J.: *Proc. I.R.E.*, **28,** 374 (1940).
Browning, G. H.: *QST*, September, 1940, p. 19.
Lawson, D. I.: *Wireless Eng.*, **17,** 388 (1940).
David, W. R.: *Communications*, October, 1940, p. 8.
Sabaroff, S.: *Communications*, October, 1940, p. 11.
Worcester, J. A., Jr.: *R.M.A. Tech. Bull.* **2,** Nov. 12, **1940.**
Wheeler, H. A.: *Proc. I.R.E.*, **28,** 537 (1940).
Landon, V. D.: *Electronics*, February, 1941, p. 26.
Wiess, W.: *Communications*, March, 1941, p. 16.

Additional references on the subjects of modulation and detection will be found throughout and at the end of Chap. 5 of "Theory and Applications of Electron Tubes," by H. J. Reich. The following bibliography covers recent work. For a bibliography covering the year 1940, see *Proc. I.R.E.*, **29,** 90 (1941).

Amplitude Modulation

Friend, A. W.: *Proc. I.R.E.*, **26,** 786 (1938).
Moullin, E. B.: *Wireless Eng.*, **15,** 371 (1938).
Terman, F. E., and Woodyard, J. R.: *Proc. I.R.E.*, **26,** 926 (1938).

ECKERSLEY, P. P.: *Proc. I.R.E.*, **26,** 1041 (1938).
HATHAWAY, J. L.: *Electronics*, October, 1939, p. 28.
BRAINERD, J. G.: *Proc. I.R.E.*, **28,** 136 (1940).
GRAMMER, G.: *QST*, February, 1940, p. 14.
TERMAN, F. E., and BUSS, R. R.: *Proc. I.R.E.*, **29,** 104 (1941).

Linear Detection

RODER, H.: *Communications*, February, 1938, p. 15 (with bibliography of
    22 items on suppression of weak by strong signal).
MOULLIN, E. B.: *Proc. of the Wireless Section, I.E.E.* (*London*), March, 1938.
LAPORT, E. A.: *RCA Rev.*, **3,** 121 (1938).
WILLIAMS, F. C., and FAIRWEATHER, A.: *Wireless Eng.*, **16,** 330 (1939).

CHAPTER 8

VACUUM-TUBE OSCILLATORS

A very important application of electron tubes is in the generation of alternating voltage and current. Advantages of electron-tube oscillators over alternators include their wide frequency range, excellent wave form, constancy of frequency, and portability. The fact that the amplitude and frequency of the output of electron-tube oscillators may be rapidly varied by means of voltage is one of the factors that have made possible the development of radio communication and broadcasting to their present state of advancement. Electron-tube oscillators have also become an indispensable part of the equipment of scientific, educational, and commercial laboratories.

8-1. Types of Oscillators.—The following classification, although it is not complete as to modifications of fundamental types, indicates the principal kinds of vacuum-tube oscillators:

1. Negative-resistance:
    a. Dynatron.
    b. Negative-transconductance.
    c. Push-pull.
    d. Negative-grid-resistance.
2. Feedback:
    a. Tuned-plate.
    b. Tuned-grid with inductive feedback.
    c. Tuned-grid with capacitive feedback (same as 1d).
    d. Hartley.
    e. Colpitts.
    f. Tuned-grid–tuned-plate and other complex types using more than one tuned circuit.
3. Magnetostriction and piezoelectric.
4. Heterodyne.
5. Resistance-tuned.
6. Relaxation:
    a. Glow-discharge and arc-discharge.
    b. Multivibrator.

    c. van der Pol (negative-transconductance).

    d. Saw-tooth-wave, using high-vacuum tubes.

  7. Magnetron.

  8. Barkhausen-Kurtz.

  9. Ionic.

 10. Mechanical-electronic.

8-2. Negative-resistance Oscillators.[1]—A two-terminal circuit element is said to have *negative a-c resistance* if a positive increment of current through the element results in a negative increment of terminal voltage. It follows that the current-voltage characteristic of a circuit element has a negative slope throughout the range of current in which the resistance is negative. Quantitatively, negative a-c resistance, like positive a-c resistance, may be defined as the reciprocal of the slope of the current-voltage characteristic, or as the partial derivative of the voltage with respect to the current. In certain elements the d-c resistance may also be negative. In such elements the flow of direct current is opposite in direction to the applied direct voltage. A negative-resistance element always involves a source of power.

The distinction between negative-resistance oscillators and feedback oscillators is in a sense artificial. A mathematical analysis of feedback oscillators yields as the criterion for sustained oscillations that the sum of certain parameters shall be equal to or less than zero. This criterion may always be written in such a form that one term is the positive circuit resistance. The other terms must, therefore, also have the dimensions of resistance, and at least one of them must be numerically negative in order that their sum shall be equal to or less than zero. One may say, therefore, that sustained oscillations can result if the tube in conjunction with the circuit can produce an equivalent negative resistance. Certain devices exhibit a negative a-c resistance without the action of an additional circuit, whereas the equivalent negative resistance in most feedback oscillators is dependent upon the action of the circuit. Under the first classification of the list of Sec. 8-1 will be considered only those oscillators in which the negative resistance is inherent in the tube,

---

[1] For a bibliography of 55 items on this subject, see E. W. Herold, *Proc. I.R.E.*, **23**, 1201 (1935).

or in the tube and associated resistors and capacitors, and does not require the presence of the tuned circuit.

Mathematical analysis shows that sustained oscillations may be set up if either a parallel or a series combination of inductance and capacitance is connected across a device that exhibits negative a-c resistance. The dotted resistance of the circuit of Fig. 8-1 represents any device that has a negative a-c resistance.

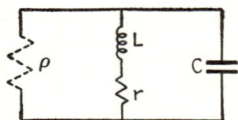

Fig. 8-1.—Basic negative-resistance oscillator circuit.

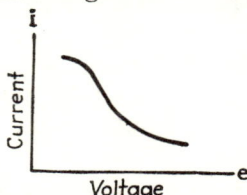

Fig. 8-2.—Current-voltage characteristic of a negative-resistance element.

L, r, and C represent the inductance, resistance, and capacitance of the resonant circuit, usually called the *tank circuit*. (Losses in the condenser are assumed to be negligible.) Although the a-c resistance, as defined by the reciprocal of the slope of the current-voltage curve of Fig. 8-2, is not constant, it may be assumed to be constant in the range of operation if the current variations are not too large. Then the negative resistance is

$$\rho = \frac{de}{di} = \text{const.} \tag{8-1}$$

Application of Kirchhoff's laws to the circuit of Fig. 8-1 gives the following differential equation for the current through the inductance:

$$\frac{d^2i}{dt^2} + \left(\frac{r}{L} + \frac{1}{\rho C}\right)\frac{di}{dt} + \frac{r + \rho}{L\rho C}\, i = 0 \tag{8-2}$$

Solution of Eq. (8-2) gives the following expression for the current:[1]

$$i = A\epsilon^{-\frac{1}{2}(r/L + 1/\rho C)t} \sin(\omega t + \alpha) \tag{8-3}$$

in which A and α are constants, and the angular frequency of oscillation is

$$\omega = \sqrt{\frac{r + \rho}{\rho}\frac{1}{LC} - \frac{1}{4}\left(\frac{1}{\rho C} + \frac{r}{L}\right)^2} \tag{8-4}$$

[1] Cohen, A., "Differential Equations," Chap. VII, D. C. Heath & Company, Boston, 1906.

Since the numerical value of ρ is negative, it follows that if the magnitude of ρ is less than L/rC, the exponential factor of Eq. (8-3) increases with time, showing that the amplitude of oscillation builds up; if ρ is greater than L/rC, on the other hand, the amplitude decreases with time, and oscillation will eventually cease. In the critical case for which ρ is just equal to L/rC, the exponential factor is unity, indicating that oscillation neither builds up nor dies down but, once started, maintains constant amplitude. Thus the criterion for oscillation is

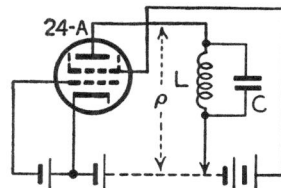

Fig. 8-3.—Dynatron oscillator circuit.

$$|\rho| \lessgtr \frac{L}{rC} \qquad (8\text{-}5)$$

Under the threshold condition, when $|\rho| = L/rC$, Eq. (8-4) reduces to

$$\omega = \sqrt{\frac{r+\rho}{\rho}\frac{1}{LC}} \qquad (8\text{-}6)$$

Inasmuch as r, the a-c resistance of the inductance coil and leads, is ordinarily only a few ohms, whereas the negative resistance ρ is seldom less than 2 or 3 thousand ohms, the frequency is practically equal to $1/2\pi\sqrt{LC}$, and small changes in ρ, such as might result from the variation of battery voltages, have a negligible effect upon the oscillation frequency if the threshold condition can be maintained.

The current represented by Eq. (8-3) is sinusoidal only when ω is a real quantity. When ω is imaginary the current varies exponentially until it reaches critical values at which it changes abruptly, as shown in Figs. 8-17 and 8-19. Oscillation is then said to be of the *relaxation* type. Relaxation oscillators will be discussed in Sec. 8-10. An analysis of Eq. (8-4) indicates that relaxation oscillations should occur at large values of L/rC. This prediction is verified in practice. When the tuning capacitance is simply the distributed coil capacitance, for instance, the current is usually not sinusoidal in form.

The amplitude of oscillation of any oscillator containing a nonlinear circuit element should be kept small in order to prevent excessive harmonic generation. The fact that this may readily be done with practical negative-resistance oscillators constitutes one of the principal advantages of this type of oscillator. A second important advantage is the excellent frequency stability. A third advantage is the ease with which the frequency range may be altered by changing the size of the single inductance.

Three practical negative-resistance oscillator circuits are shown in Figs. 8-3, 8-4, and 8-5. That of Fig. 8-3, called the *dynatron*

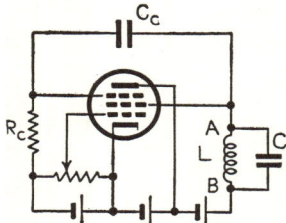

Fig. 8-4.—Negative-trans-conductance (transitron) oscillator.

oscillator, makes use of the negative-resistance portion of a tetrode plate characteristic (see Sec. 3-8).[1] The *negative-transconductance* or *transitron* oscillator of Fig. 8-4 makes use of the fact that increase of negative suppressor voltage of a pentode causes more electrons to go to the screen, instead of to the plate, and thus increases the screen current, *i.e.*, that the screen-plate transconductance is negative.[2] Both in the circuit of Fig. 8-4 and in the *push-pull* negative-resistance oscillator of Fig. 8-5[3] a negative resistance may be shown to exist between the points *A* and *B*. This may be done either by the use of equivalent circuits (see Probs. 4-3 to 4-5) or by physical analyses of the actual circuits. The amplitude of oscillation of all three circuits may be controlled by means of the control-grid bias. The reactance of the coupling condensers C_c should be small in comparison with the coupling resistors R_c in the circuits of Figs. 8-4 and 8-5.

In using the circuits of Figs. 8-3, 8-4, and 8-5, the output voltage may be taken from across the resonant tank circuit or, preferably, from a separate coil coupled to the tank inductance *L*.

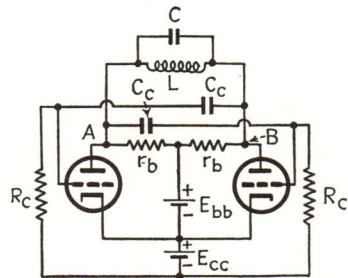

Fig. 8-5.—Push-pull negative-resistance oscillator.

8-3. Feedback Oscillators.—A feedback oscillator can be considered as a tuned feedback amplifier in which the amplitude and phase angle of the feedback voltage are such as to cause

[1] Hull, A. W., *Proc. I.R.E.*, **6**, 535 (1918).

[2] Herold, *loc. cit.*

[3] Reich, H. J., *Proc. I.R.E.*, **25**, 1387 (1937).

oscillation.[1] Suppose that a voltage e_i is applied to the input of an amplifier and that the resulting output voltage is e_o. If a portion of the output voltage is applied to the input, in addition to e_i and in phase with it, this feedback
voltage will act in the same manner as e_i. If
the magnitude of the feedback voltage is
exactly equal to e_i, then it can replace e_i,
and the amplifier will continue to deliver the
original output e_o, if e_i is removed. In other
words, the amplifier will oscillate at constant
amplitude. If the feedback is increased, the

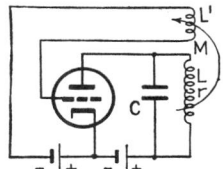

Fig.   8-6.—Tuned-plate oscillator.

amplitude will build up; if it is decreased, the amplitude will die
down. Among the simpler types of feedback oscillators are
the tuned-plate oscillator of Fig. 8-6 and the tuned-grid oscillator
of Fig. 8-7, in which a portion of the voltage developed in the plate
circuit is introduced into the grid circuit by
means of magnetic coupling. In the Hartley
oscillator, shown in Fig. 8-8, feedback results
from both magnetic and capacitive coupling.

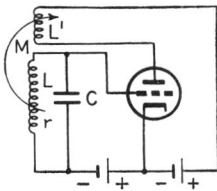

Fig.   8-7.—Tuned-grid oscillator.

Feedback oscillators are usually analyzed
by use of the equivalent plate circuit, even
though the amplitude of oscillation may be so
high that the path of operation is far from
linear. Although this method of analysis
gives no indication of the production of harmonics, it yields considerable valuable information concerning the fundamental frequency of oscillation and the conditions which must be satisfied

in order that sustained oscillations may be
produced. In order to simplify the analysis, it is customary to neglect the effect of
grid current. Although grid current cannot be neglected in a rigorous treatment,
it is usually satisfactory to make use of the
simpler analysis and to bear in mind that
the results must be modified to take grid
current into account. Losses resulting
from the flow of grid current have the

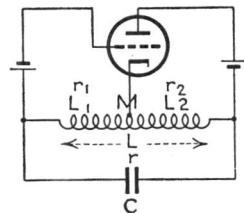

Fig. 8-8.—Hartley os-cillator.

same effects upon the operation of the circuit as an equivalent

---

[1] For an analysis of phase relations in oscillators, see C. K. Jen, *Proc.
I.R.E.*, **19**, 2109 (1931). See also footnote, p. 171.

loss in the tuned circuit.   Reduction of plate current resulting from diversion of electrons to the grid increases the curvature of the dynamic transfer characteristic and thus tends to increase harmonic content.   It will be seen that advantage may be taken of the flow of grid current to limit the amplitude of oscillation by automatically increasing the grid bias.

Figure 8-9 shows the equivalent plate circuit for the tuned-plate oscillator under the assumption that condenser losses are negligible.   The alternating grid voltage E_g is induced in the grid coil by virtue of magnetic coupling to the plate coil.   If M is assumed to be positive when an increase of I results in a positive induced voltage, then

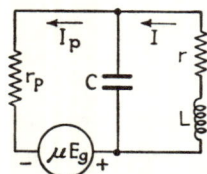

FIG. 8-9.—Equivalent plate circuit for tuned-plate oscillator.

$$E_g = j\omega MI \qquad (8\text{-}7)$$

Summation of voltages in the circuits of Fig. 8-9 gives the following equations:

$$I_p r_p + I(r + j\omega L) = \mu E_g = \mu j\omega MI \qquad (8\text{-}8)$$

$$\frac{I_p}{j\omega C} - I\left(r + j\omega L + \frac{1}{j\omega C}\right) = 0 \qquad (8\text{-}9)$$

The solution of these three simultaneous equations gives the equation

$$j\omega(Crr_p + L - \mu M) - \omega^2 r_p LC + r_p + r = 0 \qquad (8\text{-}10)$$

Equation (8-10) is an identity that can hold only if the sums of the real and of the imaginary terms are each zero.   Equating the imaginary terms to zero gives the criterion for sustained oscillation of constant amplitude

$$r_p rC + L - \mu M = 0 \qquad (8\text{-}11)$$

This can be satisfied only if M is positive and if

$$|\mu M| = r_p rC + L \qquad (8\text{-}12)$$

or

$$g_m| = \left|\frac{rC}{M} + \frac{L}{Mr_p}\right| \qquad (8\text{-}13)$$

If g_m exceeds the value given by Eq. (8-13), the circuit oscillates with increasing amplitude.   It follows from Eqs. (8-7) and (8-11) that, in order for sustained oscillation to take place, the coupling not only must equal or exceed a critical magnitude, but must also be of such sign as to result in a positive increment of grid voltage when the current through the plate inductance increases.

Equating the real terms of Eq. (8-10) to zero gives an expression for the frequency of oscillation. Under the threshold condition, for which $r_p r C + L - \mu M = 0$, the frequency of oscillation is

$$f = \frac{1}{2\pi\sqrt{LC}} \sqrt{\frac{r + r_p}{r_p}} \tag{8-14}$$

When no power is being drawn from the oscillating circuit, r is small in comparison with r_p, and the frequency of oscillation is practically the natural frequency of the resonant circuit, $1/2\pi\sqrt{LC}$.

Similar analyses for the tuned-grid (Prob. 8-1) and Hartley circuits show that the frequency of oscillation approximates $1/2\pi\sqrt{LC}$ when no power is drawn from the circuits.

The three feedback oscillator circuits that have been discussed, as well as a number of other singly and doubly tuned circuits, may be derived from the generalized circuit of Fig. 8-10 by eliminating one or two of the condensers or by making M zero. The interelectrode capacitances of the tube and the distributed winding capacitances may serve as the condensers of the circuit of Fig. 8-10 and circuits derived from it.

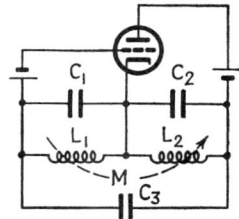

FIG. 8-10.—Generalized feedback oscillator circuit.

The Hartley oscillator has long been a favorite circuit. One reason for this is that the criterion for oscillation is not critical. L_1 and L_2 are usually the two portions of a tapped coil, and the position of the tap may be used to control the amplitude of oscillation. The circuit will oscillate most readily when the ratio of L_2 to L_1 lies in the range from approximately 0.6 to 1, the ratio increasing with amplification factor. Because the tuning condenser shunts both the grid and plate coils, the Hartley oscillator gives a lower frequency for a given total inductance than either the tuned-plate or tuned-grid oscillators and is therefore particularly suitable for the production of low audio frequencies when the necessity for good wave form prevents the use of iron-core inductances.

8-4. Push-pull Oscillators.—The basic feedback oscillator circuits may be modified to use two tubes in push-pull. As in amplifiers, the use of push-pull circuits increases the power output and decreases the harmonic content. The frequency stability of push-pull circuits is also higher than that of single-sided circuits. They are used principally at high and ultrahigh frequencies.

Series and Parallel Feed.—Circuits in which the plate-supply voltage is connected in series with the plate inductance, as in Figs. 8-6, 8-7, 8-8, 8-10, and 8-11*a*, are called *series-feed* circuits. In practice it may be desirable or necessary to connect the plate to the oscillating circuit through a condenser of low reactance and to apply the direct voltage to the plate through a choke, the reactance of which is so high that it does not appreciably affect the oscillating circuit. Air-core chokes are used in radio-frequency circuits, iron-core chokes in audio-frequency circuits. An example of this method of applying the direct plate voltage, called *parallel feed*, is given by the circuit of Fig. 8-11*b*. The objection to the use of parallel feed is that parasitic oscillations may take place in the feed condenser and choke.

Oscillator Output.—As in negative-resistance oscillators, the output voltage of feedback oscillators may be taken from across the tank circuit or, preferably, from a separate coil coupled to the tank inductance.

8-5. Use of Self-bias to Limit Amplitude of Oscillation.—For the purpose of simplicity, fixed biasing voltages have been indicated in the basic circuits of Figs. 8-6, 8-7, 8-8, and 8-10. Fixed bias is rarely used, however, in practical oscillators. In order to prevent excessive distortion and to aid in obtaining frequency stabilization, it is necessary to limit the amplitude of oscillation. In feedback oscillators the criterion for oscillation involves the transconductance of the tube, and the amplitude builds up until the average (dynamic) transconductance (see Sec. 3-25) drops to the critical value below which oscillation cannot take place. Unfortunately, the average transconductance first increases with amplitude, and so the amplitude may increase to a high value before the average transconductance again falls sufficiently to result in equilibrium. If the circuit is adjusted to give small equilibrium amplitude, then it will not start of its own accord.   A similar difficulty may be experienced with some negative-resistance oscillators.   This difficulty may be prevented by causing the grid bias to increase automatically with amplitude.

The most common method of limiting the amplitude of oscillation is the use of a grid-blocking condenser and grid leak, as shown in Fig. 8-11.   The initial bias is zero, but, as soon as oscillation commences, the grid is driven positive during a portion of the cycle and so electrons flow from the cathode to the grid.   During the remainder of the cycle these electrons cannot return to the cathode but can only leak off the condenser and grid through the grid leak R_c.   The trapped electrons make the potential of the grid negative with respect to the cathode, thus pro-

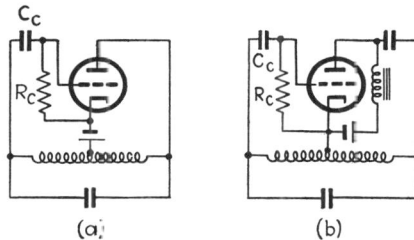

Fig. 8-11.—Use of grid condenser and leak to limit amplitude of oscillation.

viding a bias.[1]   The greater the amplitude of oscillation, the more positive the grid swings, and the greater is the average grid current.   Thus the bias builds up with oscillation amplitude, causing the transconductance to fall until equilibrium is established.   In this manner the amplitude may be prevented from becoming too high without making the quiescent transconductance so low as to prevent oscillation from starting spontaneously.   Under equilibrium conditions grid current flows during only a very small fraction of the cycle, and the grid bias is very nearly equal to the amplitude of the alternating grid voltage.

Low power loss in the resistor, high frequency stability, and good wave form call for the use of high grid-leak resistance; but it is found that, if the resistance is too high, oscillation is not continuous.   After a number of cycles of oscillation the bias becomes

---

[1] The bias may also be considered to result from the flow of current through the grid leak.

so high that the circuit stops oscillating. Because oscillation starts at a lower bias than that at which it stops, some time elapses while the condenser discharges sufficiently to allow oscillation to recommence, and so periods of oscillation alternate with periods of rest. This phenomenon is termed *motorboating*.[1] The period of motorboating depends upon the time required for the condenser to discharge, which increases with the product of the grid condenser capacitance and the grid-leak resistance.

Another factor that limits the size of the grid resistor is danger of cumulative increase of positive grid voltage and plate current as the result of primary and secondary grid emission.[2]

8-6. Figure of Merit of Oscillator Tubes.—The form of Eq. (8-13) and of similar equations derived for other feedback oscillator circuits shows clearly the importance of high transconductance in tubes used in feedback oscillators. These equations also show that, for a given transconductance, oscillation will take place more readily the higher the plate resistance. Since at a given transconductance the amplification factor is proportional to the plate resistance, it follows that the "figure of merit" of a tube for use in a feedback oscillator is the product μg_m. As this is also the figure of merit of a power tube, power tubes are in general good feedback oscillator tubes.

8-7. Frequency Stability.—Undesired changes of frequency result from three major causes: changes in the mechanical arrangement of the elements of the oscillating circuit; in the values of the circuit parameters; and in the amplification factor, grid and plate resistances, and interelectrode capacitances of the tube.[3] Changes in the mechanical arrangement of the circuit elements may be produced by vibration; by mechanical, electrostatic, or electromagnetic forces; or by temperature changes. They can be minimized by careful mechanical and electrical design and by temperature control.

[1] BEATTY, R. T., and GILMOUR, A., *Phil. Mag.*, **40**, 291 (1920). RSCHEWKIN, S., and WWEDENSKY, B., *Physik. Z.*, **23**, 150 (1922). TAYLOR, L. S., *J. Opt. Soc. Am.* and *Rev. Sci. Instruments*, **11**, 149 (1926); *J. Franklin Inst.*, **203**, 351 (1927); **204**, 227 (1927); *Phys. Rev.*, **29**, 617 (1927).

[2] REICH, H. J., "Theory and Applications of Electron Tubes," pp. 184–185.

[3] See, for instance, F. B. Llewellyn, *Proc. I.R.E.*, **19**, 2063 (1931), and R. Gunn, *Proc. I.R.E.*, **18**, 1560 (1930).

Variations in the values of the circuit parameters result from changes in temperature of inductances and condensers and from variation of load, which alters the effective a-c resistance r of the tuned circuit. Changes of inductance and capacitance can be minimized by: temperature control; the use of thermally compensated inductances[1] and temperature-controlled compensating condensers;[2] and the careful choice of apparatus and the judicious location of component parts. The most common method of preventing the load from affecting the frequency is to take the required power from a "buffer" amplifier that is excited by the oscillator, rather than from the oscillator directly.

Tube factors and electrode capacitances are dependent upon operating voltages, upon cathode emission, and upon electrode spacing. Operating voltages can be stabilized by the use of voltage-regulating devices. Variation of cathode emission is probably the least important factor and can be reduced by the maintenance of rated cathode temperature. Electrode spacing, which depends to some extent upon tube temperature, affects the interelectrode capacitances. The dependence of frequency upon interelectrode capacitances and upon stray circuit capacitance can be minimized by the use of a high ratio of tuning capacitance to inductance and by the use of circuits in which the tuning capacitance shunts the grid-plate capacitance.

Dependence of frequency upon plate resistance may be minimized by the use of resistance-stabilized circuits, in which a high resistance in series with the plate reduces the percentage change of total plate-circuit resistance.[3] The most effective method of frequency stabilization, however, is the use of vibrating mechanical elements electrostatically or magnetically coupled to the oscillating circuit. At radio frequencies this is accomplished by the use of quartz crystals, in which compression or expansion results in the production of a potential difference between opposite faces and, conversely, application of a potential difference results in an elongation or contraction.[4] At audio

[1] Griffiths, W. H., *Wireless Eng.*, **11**, 234 (1934).

[2] Gunn, R., *Proc. I.R.E.*, **18**, 1565 (1930).

[3] Horton, J. W., *Bell System Tech. J.*, **3**, 508 (1924); Terman, F. E., *Electronics*, July, 1933, p. 190.

[4] Cady, W. G., *Proc. I.R.E.*, **10**, 83 (1922). For additional references see H. J. Reich, "Theory and Applications of Electron Tubes," p. 335.

frequencies it is accomplished by the use of magnetostrictive rods, which expand or contract when magnetized.[1] In quartz-crystal oscillators the frequency variation may be made less than 2 parts in a million; in magnetostriction oscillators it may be limited to 1 part in 30,000.

8-8. Beat-frequency (Heterodyne) Oscillators.[2]—An entirely different type of audio-frequency oscillator which has rapidly gained in popularity during recent years is the beat-frequency oscillator. In an oscillator of this type, shown

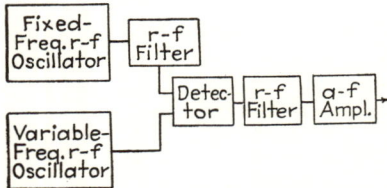

Fig. 8-12.—Schematic diagram of heterodyne oscillator.

schematically in Fig. 8-12, the outputs of two radio-frequency oscillators of slightly different frequencies are applied simultaneously to a detector.   The output of the detector contains, in addition to the impressed radio frequencies, their sum and difference. By means of a filter the fundamental radio frequencies and their

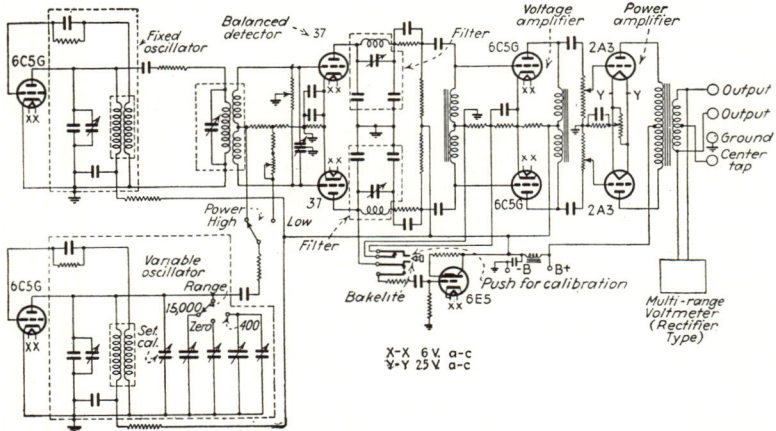

Fig. 8-13.—Circuit diagram of heterodyne oscillator. (*Courtesy of Clough Brengle Company.*)

sum are removed, leaving only the difference frequency in the output, which may be suitably amplified by audio-frequency

---

[1] Pierce, G. W., *Proc. I.R.E.*, **17**, 42 (1929); Salisbury, W. W., and Porter, C. W., *Rev. Sci. Instruments*, **10**, 142 (1939).

[2] See bibliography, H. J. Reich, "Theory and Applications of Electron Tubes," p. 364.

amplifiers.   The popularity of the heterodyne oscillator is due
principally to the fact that the whole range of audio frequencies,
from 15,000 cycles, or higher, down to as low as 1 cycle, may be
covered with a single dial.   Other advantages that may be
obtained with careful design include good wave form, constant
output level, lightness, and compactness.   By proper variable
condenser design a logarithmic frequency scale may be obtained,
a considerable advantage when the oscillator is to be used
in obtaining amplifier-response curves.   Unless extreme care
is taken in the design and construction, however, this type of
oscillator is likely to have relatively poor frequency stability,
which necessitates frequent setting against a standard frequency
during the period of use, particularly during the time required to
establish temperature equilibrium.   The circuit diagram of a
typical beat-frequency oscillator is shown in Fig. 8-13.

8-9. Resistance-tuned Oscillators.—Comparison of Fig. 4-18
with Fig. 8-4 shows that the circuit of Fig. 4-18 is the basis of
the oscillator of Fig. 8-4.   Solution of Probs. 4-2, 4-3, and 4-4
indicates that, unless the reactance of C_c is negligible in comparison with R_c, the effective negative resistance between points
A and B is shunted by an effective inductive reactance.   For this
reason sinusoidal oscillations may be produced in the circuit of
Fig. 8-4 even when the inductance L is omitted, provided that a
path is furnished for the steady component of screen current
by the use of resistance R in place of L.[1]   The expressions for
the frequency of oscillation and for the criterion of oscillation
involve R_c, C_c, R, and C, as well as the tube factors.[1]   Similarly,
sinusoidal oscillations are obtained in the circuit of Fig. 8-5
without the inductance L when R_c, C_c, and C are properly
chosen.[1]

Another method of producing sinusoidal oscillations without
the use of inductance is by means of the circuit shown in basic
form in Fig. 6-38.   As pointed out in Prob. 6-10, between
the input terminals this circuit acts like a negative resistance in
parallel with an inductance.   If the circuit constants are properly
chosen, sinusoidal oscillations are produced when a condenser C_2
is connected between the terminals.   In order to ensure the correct bias for the grid of the first tube of the amplifier, C_2 must be

[1] DeLAUP, P. S., *Electronics*, January, 1941, p. 34 (see bibliography).

shunted by a resistance R_2. The criterion for oscillation may be shown to be that μ' must exceed $R_1/R_2 + C_2/C_1 + 1$, and the frequency of oscillation to be $1/2\pi\sqrt{R_1R_2C_1C_2}$ (see Prob. 8-2). Figure 8-14 shows a practical form of this circuit used in one of the most successful commercial resistance-tuned oscillators.[1] The ballast lamp R_3, in combination with the resistance R_4, provides inverse feedback that makes the amplification and phase shift of the two-stage resistance-capacitance-coupled amplifier independent of variable circuit parameters, supply voltage, and tube characteristics and at the same time affords a method of stabilizing the amplitude of oscillation. Increase of amplitude

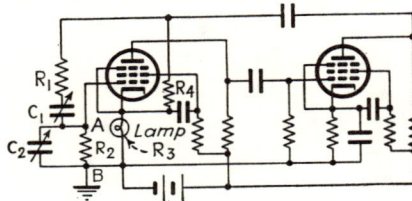

Fig. 8-14.—Circuit diagram of resistance-tuned oscillator.

raises the current through the lamp and thus increases its resistance. This in turn increases the feedback, which decreases μ' and hence decreases the amplitude of oscillation. If

$$R_1C_1 = R_2C_2,$$

the frequency of oscillation is $1/2\pi R_1C_1$. The fact that the frequency may be thus made inversely proportional to the capacitance, instead of to the square root of the capacitance, makes it possible to cover a 10 to 1 frequency range with ganged condensers of the type used in broadcast receivers.

When a conventional resistance-coupled amplifier is used in the circuit of Fig. 6-38, an even number of stages is required. Because the mu-factor relating the suppressor and screen grids of a pentode is negative, however, a single pentode may be used in this circuit, as shown in Fig. 8-15. The purpose of the resistance R_f and condenser C_f is to provide inverse feedback in order to improve wave-form and stability. The frequency is varied by means of C_1, C_2, and R_2.

[1] Terman, F. E., Buss, R. R., Hewlett, W. R., and Cahill, F. C., *Proc. I.R.E.*, **27**, 649 (1939).

Another type of resistance-tuned oscillator consists essentially of an inverse-feedback amplifier in which the feedback network is a resistance-capacitance bridge of such form that the feedback is a minimum, and the amplification of the amplifier therefore a maximum, at one frequency.[1] If a small amount of the output voltage of the amplifier is fed back directly to the input, in phase with the input voltage, oscillation takes place at this frequency. The frequency of oscillation is controlled by means of the resistances of the bridge circuit used to provide inverse feedback.

8-10. Relaxation Oscillators. In almost all of the tuned oscillators discussed up to this point the production of oscillations requires the presence of both inductance and capacitance, the frequency of oscillation being dependent upon the product of

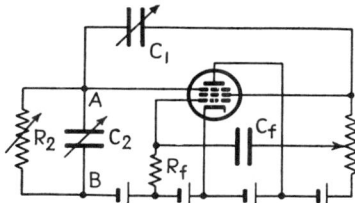

FIG. 8-15.—Circuit diagram of resistance-tuned oscillator.

L and C and the oscillations being approximately sinusoidal. In these oscillators the phenomenon of oscillation is associated with the periodic transfer of energy from the inductance to the capacitance and vice versa. There is another important group of oscillators, known as *relaxation oscillators*, in which either capacitance or, more commonly, inductance may be absent.[2] Relaxation oscillations are produced when the electric or magnetic field of a capacitance or an inductance is built up until a set of limiting conditions is reached, the field then being dissipated until a second set of limiting conditions causes the field to be built up again. The limiting conditions may be caused in a number of ways, such as the closing of relay contacts, the breakdown and extinction of glow- or arc-discharge tubes, or the abrupt change of current to an electrode of a high-vacuum trigger tube when the electrode voltages assume critical values. For certain applications, relaxation oscillators are of great value and have a number of advantages over tuned oscillators. Among these advantages are the number and amplitude of harmonics present in the output; the ease with which the frequency may be stabilized

[1] SCOTT, H. H., *Proc. I.R.E.*, **26**, 226 (1938); *General Radio Experimenter*, **13**, April, 1939, p. 1; **14**, January, 1940, p. 6.

[2] VAN DER POL, B., *Phil. Mag.* **2**, 978 (1926).

by the introduction into the oscillating circuit of small voltages whose frequency is a multiple or submultiple of the oscillator frequency; the wide range of frequency that can be obtained in a single oscillator; and the compactness, simplicity, and low cost.

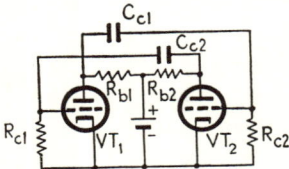

Fig. 8-16.—Circuit diagram of multivibrator.

For other applications on the other hand, the high harmonic content of relaxation oscillators makes them of little or no value.

Glow- and arc-discharge tubes are often used in relaxation oscillators. The operation of glow and arc relaxation oscillators is so closely associated with the theory of glows and arcs that they can be discussed best in Chap. 9, which deals with glow- and arc-discharge tubes and circuits.

Relaxation oscillators using high-vacuum tubes are based upon the high-vacuum trigger circuits discussed in Chap. 6, Sec. 6-18. Condensers are incorporated in these circuits in such a manner that the assumption of either set of equilibrium

Fig. 8-17.—Wave form of condenser current of symmetrical multivibrator.

tube currents is followed by the flow of current into the condensers through resistances. As the condenser voltages change, a critical point is reached at which the tube currents change abruptly to the other equilibrium values.

The first type of relaxation oscillator to be developed was the

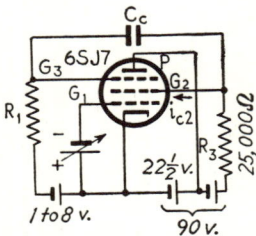

Fig. 8-18.—Van der Pol relaxation oscillator.

multivibrator, described in 1919 by Abraham and Bloch.[1] Many modifications and applications have been discussed since by other writers. The basic multivibrator circuit is shown in Fig. 8-16. Comparison with the Eccles-Jordan trigger circuit of Fig. 6-26 shows that the multivibrator may be derived from the Eccles-Jordan circuit by replacing the resistors R_c of Fig. 6-26 by condensers, C_c.

The output voltage may be taken from any of the circuit elements, or the current of either tube may be used. The

[1] Abraham, H., and Bloch, E., *Ann. Physik,* **12,** 237 (1919).

wave form of the condenser current and of the grid and plate voltages for a symmetrical circuit is shown in Fig. 8-17. If the circuit is not symmetrical, the two halves of the wave are dissimilar. The frequency of oscillation increases with decrease of resistances and capacitances.

FIG. 8-19.—T y p i c a l wave form of condenser current or suppressor voltage for the circuit of Fig. 8-18.

Figure 8-18 shows a type of relaxation oscillator first described by van der Pol,[1] and later improved by others.[2] This circuit may be derived from the trigger circuit of Fig. 6-27 by replacing the 50,000-Ω grid-coupling resistor by the condenser C_c. The

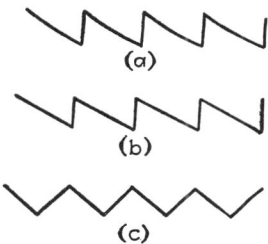

FIG. 8-20.—T y p i c a l waves of condenser voltage in the circuits of Figs. 8-18 and 8-21.

frequency of oscillation increases with decrease of R_1 and C_c and is also dependent upon R_3. Figure 8-19 shows a typical curve of condenser current or suppressor voltage; Fig. 8-20 shows typical waves of condenser voltage. Waves of the form of Fig. 8-20b are useful in the operation of cathode-ray oscillographs (see Sec. 12-5) and cathode-ray television equipment. Figure 8-21 shows another circuit, also based upon the pentode trigger circuit of Fig. 6-27, with which a wave of the form of Fig. 8-20b can be more readily obtained. The output voltage is taken from across the condenser C. The frequency is varied by means of R and C.

8-11. Use of Relaxation Oscillators in Frequency Transformation. Relaxation oscillators are of great value in frequency transformation. Introduction into the oscillator circuit of a small voltage having a multiple or submultiple of the oscillation frequency causes the relaxation oscillator to "lock in." With

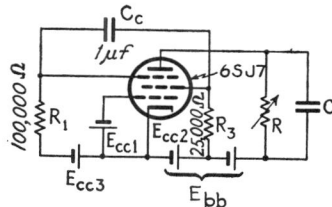

FIG. 8-21.—Relaxation oscillator for the production of a sawtooth voltage wave. The output voltage is taken from across the condenser C.

reasonable care in circuit adjustment, relaxation oscillators may be controlled when the frequency ratio is as great as 50,

---

[1] VAN DER POL, *loc. cit.*

[2] HEROLD, E. W., *Proc. I.R.E.*, **23**, 1201 (1935).

but usual ratios do not exceed 10. The fundamental output of one controlled oscillator may be used to control a second relaxation oscillator, which may in turn control a third, etc. By this means it is possible to obtain an audio-frequency voltage of great stability from the final relaxation oscillator when the first one is controlled by a crystal-controlled radio-frequency oscillator. The audio-frequency output may be used to drive a synchronous clock.[1] By observation of the clock over a long period of time a very accurate determination may be made of the frequency of the crystal-controlled oscillator or of any lower frequency controlled by it. By separating and amplifying the various harmonics of the controlled relaxation oscillators, a large number of frequencies of high constancy may be obtained from one crystal oscillator. The multivibrator has proved to be the most satisfactory type of relaxation oscillator for use in frequency conversion.[2] The usual method of introducing frequency-control voltage into relaxation-oscillator circuits is by means of transformer or condenser coupling to one or more grid circuits.

Problems

8-1. *a.* Show that the frequency of oscillation of the tuned-grid oscillator of Fig. 8-7 is

$$f = \frac{1}{2\pi\sqrt{\dfrac{C(Lr_p + L'r)}{r_p}}} \tag{8-15}$$

b. When no power is drawn from the circuit, Lr_p greatly exceeds $L'r$. Simplify Eq. (8-15) under this assumption.

c. Under the same assumption, show that the criterion for sustained oscillation of constant amplitude is

$$g_m = \frac{rC}{M} + \frac{M}{Lr_p} \tag{8-16}$$

8-2. Derive the criterion for oscillation and the frequency of oscillation of the circuit formed by connecting a parallel combination of R_2 and C_2 between the input terminals of the circuit of Fig. 6-38. (Hint: For oscillation of constant amplitude to take place, the susceptance of C_2 must be equal in magnitude and opposite in sign to the susceptance between the terminals, and the conductance of R_2 must be equal in magnitude and opposite in sign to the conductance between the terminals.)

[1] Horton, J. W., and Marrison, W. A., *Proc. I.R.E.*, **16**, 137 (1928).

[2] Abraham and Bloch, *loc. cit.;* Mercier, M., *Compt. rend.*, **174**, 448 (1922); Clapp, J. K., *J. Opt. Soc. Am.* and *Rev. Sci. Instruments*, **15**, 25 (1927); Marrison, W. A., *Proc.*, *I.R.E.*, **17**, 1103 (1929).

CHAPTER 9

GLOW- AND ARC-DISCHARGE TUBES

Preceding chapters have dealt only with electron tubes in which the gas density is so low that the probability of collision of electrons with gas molecules is small and relatively few ions are present. This chapter will deal with the flow of current through regions of comparatively high gas density, in which the probability of ionizing collisions of electrons with molecules is comparatively high and many ions are consequently present in the gas, and with the construction, characteristics, and applications of practical gaseous conduction tubes. The student should review Chap. 1.

The early experiments on gas-filled tubes were performed years before the discovery of thermionic emission, but the development of useful gas-filled tubes, particularly of the grid-controlled type, lagged far behind that of high-vacuum tubes. It was not until careful experiments suggested the fundamental laws and processes governing the phenomena involved that great strides were made in the design, manufacture, and application of gaseous tubes. A knowledge of these laws is important in the understanding of gaseous tube operation.

9-1. Current-voltage Characteristics of Glows.—A gas or vapor containing no ions would be a perfect insulator. No current could flow as the result of a potential applied between two nonemitting electrodes immersed in such a gas. Ion-free gases are hypothetical only, for cosmic rays, radioactive materials in the walls of containers, photoelectric emission, and other ionizing agents ensure the presence of some "residual" ions. In an actual gas the application of potential between electrodes will cause a migration of the residual ions and give the effect of current flow.

The magnitude of the current associated with the drift of residual ions evidently depends upon the rate of production of ions and upon the rate at which ions are swept away, which depends

233

in turn upon the applied voltage. This current is sometimes called the *dark current* because it is not accompanied by appreciable radiation. The relation between voltage and dark current under static conditions is shown graphically by the portion *oab* of the typical characteristic curve of Fig. 9-1. That the increase of voltage over the range *ab* causes no increase in the current indicates that residual ions are being swept out of the gas by the electric field at the same rate as they are being created. The dark current is usually of the order of a microampere.

As the voltage is increased, a value is reached, as at *b*, at which the current again begins to rise   The increase of current above the saturation value maintained from *a* to *b* is the result

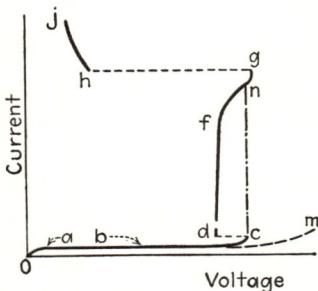

FIG. 9-1.—Current-voltage characteristic of a typical gas-filled cold-cathode diode.

of ionization of gas molecules by collision with electrons that have been accelerated by the applied electric field and of secondary emission from the cathode caused by positive-ion bombardment. If the electrode spacing is very close and the gas pressure low, the likelihood is small that an electron in moving from the cathode to the anode will strike and ionize a neutral gas molecule. The current can then be increased beyond *b* only by increase of voltage and the characteristic is of the form shown by the dashed curve *bm*. With electrode spacing and gas pressure used in most glow-discharge tubes, on the other hand, an electron may make many ionizing collisions in moving from the cathode to the anode and the electrons released near the cathode as the result may in turn produce other ions in moving to the anode. The positive ions are drawn to the cathode, where they may liberate secondary electrons. The number of secondary electrons released for each initial electron that leaves the cathode increases with the applied voltage. Because each secondary electron can in itself cause further ionization, the rate at which the current rises with voltage increases with voltage. A critical point is finally reached at which one secondary electron is released for each initial electron. Since each secondary electron will in turn cause, through ionization, the release of still another secondary electron, the current continues to increase without further increase of voltage. In fact, as shown in Fig. 9-1, the voltage actually falls. The increase of current without increase of voltage is called *breakdown*, and the voltage at which it commences is called the *breakdown voltage*. The current that flows just prior to breakdown is called the *threshold current*. In Fig. 9-1, breakdown occurs at the point *c*. The breakdown voltage depends upon the cathode material, the tube and electrode structure, the kind or kinds of gas used, and upon the gas pressure. In many tubes it is also reduced by illumination of the cathode.[1] Low breakdown voltage is attained by treating the cathode with barium.

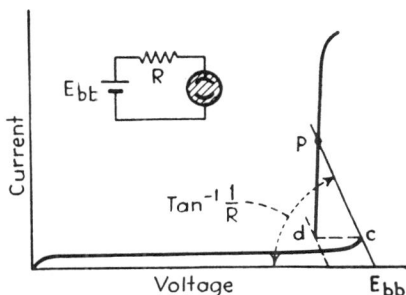

FIG. 9-2.—Anode diagram of a glow-discharge tube.

Appreciable ionization by collision does not take place until the electrode voltage greatly exceeds the ionization potential of the gas, and so the breakdown voltage in practical tubes is rarely less than 70 volts, and may range to hundreds of volts. The threshold current is of the order of 1 or 2 μa. The behavior of the tube subsequent to breakdown is dependent to such a great extent upon the characteristics of the external circuit that it is difficult to determine with complete assurance the characteristics of the tube itself. Experiments appear to indicate, however, that if the terminal voltage could be reduced rapidly enough by increase of circuit resistance or decrease of applied voltage, the voltage would change from *c* to *d* without change in current. Normally, however, the applied voltage and the circuit resistance remain constant, and so the tube voltage falls only as the result of circuit *IR* drop. The current increases abruptly

[1] OSCHWALD, U. A., and TARRANT, A. G., *Proc. Phys. Soc. London*, **36**, 241 (1924); REICH, H. J., *J. Opt. Soc. Am.*, **17**, 271 (1928).

and the tube voltage falls to values determined by the intersection of the characteristic with a load line corresponding to the circuit resistance, as shown in Fig. 9-2 by point p. After breakdown the current can be increased to values above p by increasing the applied voltage or by decreasing the circuit resistance; conversely, it can be reduced by decreasing the voltage or by increasing the resistance. If the current is reduced below the value at d, however, it falls abruptly to a value in the dark-current range. The voltage at d is, therefore, called the *extinction voltage*. The extinction voltage ranges from about 60 volts to several hundred volts in practical tubes and is usually from 10 to 100 volts less than the breakdown voltage.

Between d and f, the current increases with very little change in voltage. The current range covered by this portion of the characteristic depends upon the area of the cathode, and may extend to values of 50 ma or more. In order to indicate the difference in magnitude of the very small currents below c and the relatively large currents above d, a gap is shown in the curve. A value of current is reached, at f, beyond which a much larger increase of voltage is required to produce a given change in current.   In the vicinity of g, however, the current is so high that if it is maintained for an appreciable time the cathode becomes hot enough to emit electrons. The thermionic emission reduces the voltage drop through the tube in a manner that will be explained (Sec. 9-11), causing further increase of current and greater emission.   The cumulative action may result in an abrupt decrease of potential to about the ionization potential of the gas, at point h, and, unless limited by circuit resistance, the current may rise to destructive values.   In the region from b to g, the discharge is characterized by comparatively low current density and high voltage drop and is called a *glow*.   Beyond h, the discharge is characterized by high current density and low voltage drop and is called an *arc*. Actually, as will be explained in a later section, the fundamental distinction between an arc and a glow does not lie so much in the current density and electrode voltage, as in the fact that in an arc there exists at the cathode some copious source of electron emission other than secondary emission.

If the circuit resistance is small, the current jumps directly from the threshold value at c to a high value at n. In some tubes the current at n may be so high as to cause a very rapid rise in cathode temperature to a value sufficient to cause thermionic emission. The time taken may be so short that breakdown appears to be accompanied by the immediate formation of an arc. In other tubes, on the other hand, several seconds may elapse between breakdown and the formation of an arc.

A characteristic obtained with steady voltages, of which the curve of Fig. 9-1 is a typical example, is called a *static* characteristic. The shape of such a characteristic depends upon the kind of gas; the gas pressure; electrode material, structure, and temperature; tube age; and initial cathode emission, which in turn varies with cathode illumination and with the strength of other ionizing agents in the gas, electrodes, or tube walls. Characteristics obtained with varying voltages and currents are called *dynamic* characteristics. Because of the time required for ionization to build up to an equilibrium value when the current is increased and for deionization to take place after the current is interrupted or decreased, the voltage corresponding to an instantaneous value of varying current depends not only upon that current and upon the factors just listed, but also upon the current that flowed at previous instants. It is evident that a particular glow-discharge tube has not a single current-voltage characteristic, but an infinite number of such characteristics, and that the breakdown and extinction voltages depend upon the manner in which the tube is used. For this reason, the predetermination of the behavior of a glow tube in a given circuit is difficult, if not impossible.

9-2. Physical Aspects of the Glow Discharge.—Ionization following breakdown is accompanied by excitation of some of the gas molecules. In transitions to states of lower internal energy these molecules emit visible radiation in the form of a soft glow that gives the name to this type of discharge. The glow is made up of a number of distinct regions. The general form of a glow at gas pressures of the order of 1 mm or less of mercury[1] is shown in Fig. 9-3a.[2] In the vicinity of the cathode is a relatively dark region, called the *cathode dark space*, or, in honor of two of the early workers in the field of glow discharges, the

---

[1] 1 atm   = 760 mm Hg
  1 micron of Hg = 0.001 mm Hg

[2] SLEPIAN, J., and MASON, R. C., *Elec. Eng.*, **53**, 511 (1934).

Crookes or *Hittorf dark space*. The brightness of the cathode dark space increases toward the cathode, culminating sometimes in a luminous layer very close to the cathode, called the *cathode glow*. In hydrogen and the noble gases there is a much darker layer immediately adjacent to the cathode, usually not more than 1 mm in length, called the *primary dark space*. Toward the anode, the cathode dark space terminates quite sharply

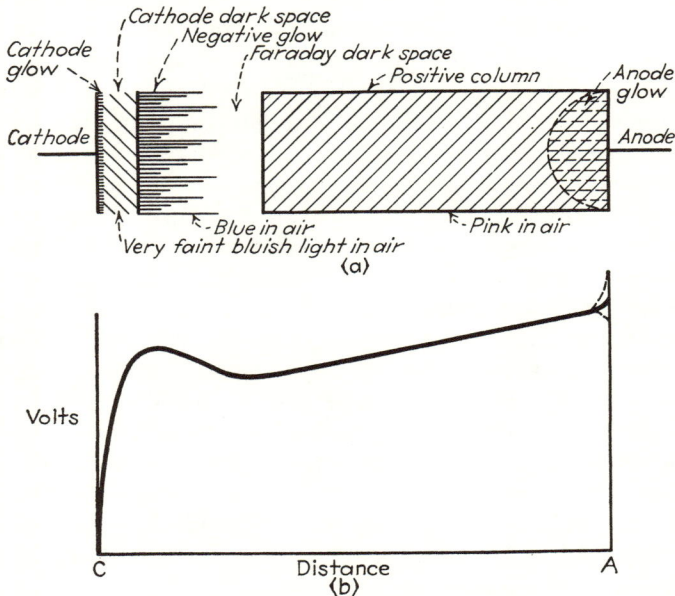

Fig. 9-3.—(*a*) Appearance of the glow discharge between plane-parallel electrodes; (*b*) potential distribution in the glow discharge between plane-parallel electrodes.

and distinctly in a luminous region called the *negative glow*. The brightness of the negative glow decreases toward the anode, and the glow gradually merges into another relatively dark region, the *Faraday dark space*. Beyond the Faraday dark space is the *positive column*, a fairly luminous region which may contain striations and which extends to the anode. Sometimes the surface of the anode is covered by a luminous layer called the *anode glow*.

If the anode is moved toward the cathode while the tube is glowing, the various regions of the discharge remain fixed relative to the cathode, and the positive column and the Faraday dark space in turn appear to move into the anode. If the current is maintained constant during this experiment, the voltage across the tube falls slowly. As the anode enters the negative glow, the voltage begins to rise rapidly with further movement of the anode until it equals the supply voltage and the tube goes out. If the electrode spacing is kept constant on the other hand, and the pressure is lowered, the cathode dark space increases in thickness, appearing to push away the negative glow, Faraday dark space, and positive column, which disappear into the anode in turn. As the cathode dark space expands, the outer boundary becomes less distinct. When the cathode dark space reaches the anode, the voltage must be raised in order to maintain the discharge. At extremely low pressures, at which the dark space fills the whole interelectrode space, the walls of the tube fluoresce. This phenomenon is caused by the impact upon the walls of high-speed electrons (cathode rays), which have been accelerated throughout the interelectrode space without suffering loss of energy by collision with gas molecules. In most practical glow-discharge tubes, the pressure is in the range from 0.1 to 50 microns.

9-3. Potential Distribution in the Glow Discharge.—Experiments have shown that the potential distribution between cathode and anode is of the form shown in Fig. 9-3b. The greatest part of the applied potential appears across the cathode dark space, a region in which positive space charge predominates. Preponderance of positive ions is caused by the fact that positive ions move toward the cathode, and electrons away. It is accentuated by the large mass and consequent low velocities of the positive ions. The fall in potential through the cathode dark space is called the *cathode fall of potential,* or *cathode drop.*

The potential maximum in the negative glow is caused by positive-ion space charge, in a manner analogous to the production of a potential minimum by electrons near the surface of a thermionic emitter in vacuum.

Measurements show that if there are no striations the field in the positive column is small and practically constant, indicating that the electron and positive-ion densities are approximately equal. The potential gradient (field) in the positive column must be great enough to supply the energy that is lost through diffusion of ions to the walls. The ratio of the diffusion current to the anode current at constant current density increases with decrease of tube radius, and hence the gradient varies inversely with the tube radius. This is an important consideration in the design of small-diameter tubes of the type used in neon signs. The gradient also decreases with increase of current and with decrease of pressure.

Adjacent to the anode there is usually a jump in potential, which may be either positive or negative, depending upon whether the current is high or low and the electrode area small or large. At some value of anode current the anode drop is zero for an electrode of given area.

9-4. Normal and Abnormal Glow.—When the glow current is limited to a sufficiently low value by means of external resistance, the discharge covers only a portion of the cathode. An increase of current causes the discharge to spread over a greater portion of the cathode, the current density, cathode drop, and the thickness of the cathode dark space remaining constant. When the cathode is not completely covered by the glow, the discharge is said to be *normal* and the current density, cathode drop, and dark-space thickness are designated by the same terms. The *normal* cathode drop is a function of the gas used and the material of which the cathode is made, and is independent of gas pressure. It is small in the noble gases and is usually smaller in gas mixtures than in pure gases. It decreases with decrease of electron affinity of the cathode material. The normal cathode drop usually exceeds 100 volts and may be as high as 400 volts or more but by proper choice of gases and cathode material may be made as low as 37 volts.[1] The "normal" current density (current per unit area of the cathode covered by glow) and the thickness of the dark space depend not only upon the gas and the cathode material but also upon the gas pressure.

When the whole surface of the cathode is covered by glow, the cathode drop and the current density increase with increase of current, and the thickness of the cathode dark space decreases.[2]

[1] Slepian, and Mason, *loc. cit.;* Thomson, J. J., and Thomson, G. P., "Conduction of Electricity through Gases," Vol. II, pp. 231–232, Cambridge University Press, London, 1928.

[2] If one makes the assumption that the current through the dark space

The discharge is then said to be *abnormal*. The terms *normal* and *abnormal* are, unfortunately, misleading, inasmuch as the abnormal type of discharge is fully as common as the normal, both in experimental and in practical tubes. To avoid possible ambiguity, quotation marks will be placed about these terms when they are used to differentiate between the two types of discharge. In Fig. 9-1 the "normal" range of current extends from *d* to *f*; the "abnormal" range from *f* to *g*.

9-5. Applications of Glow Tubes.—Applications of glow-discharge tubes include the production of light, voltage stabilization, generation of nonsinusoidal voltages, control of current or power, rectification, protection of apparatus or circuits, and

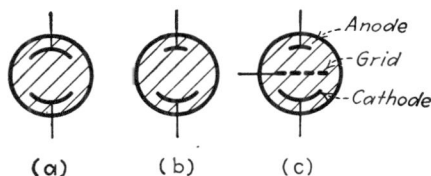

(a)   (b)   (c)
Fig. 9-4.—Symbols for glow-discharge tubes.

amplification. For most of these applications special types of tubes have been developed.

Glow tubes are unquestionably used most extensively in the form of the familiar neon sign, in which the light is emitted from an extended positive column. Various colors are obtained by the use of different gases and of fluorescent glass tubing. Although principles discussed in the foregoing sections are applicable to such tubes, the particular requirements of this field make it a specialty best discussed in books devoted to the subject.[1] Because of the limited use of glow tubes in rectification, amplification, and apparatus protection, no further space will be devoted to these applications. Figure 9-4 shows symbols that will be used for glow-discharge tubes. Symbol (*a*) represents a two-element tube in which the electrodes are of equal area, symbol (*b*) one in which the area of one electrode exceeds

---

is limited by space charge, then a derivation similar to that which gives Child's law (see Sec. 2-10) shows that the dark space should decrease in thickness as the current density increases.

[1] See, for instance, S. C. Miller and D. G. Fink, "Neon Signs," McGraw-Hill Book Company, Inc., New York, 1931.

that of the other, and (c) a grid-controlled glow tube. In such a tube the larger electrode ordinarily serves as cathode. The shading indicates that the tube contains gas or vapor in sufficient quantity to allow the formation of a glow or an arc. The electrode structure of glow tubes is determined by such factors as the desired values of current capacity, breakdown voltage, and light-emitting area.

9-6. The Glow-discharge Tube as a Voltage Stabilizer.—

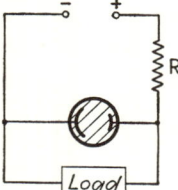

Fig. 9-5.—Circuit diagram of a glow-tube voltage regulator.

Because a large increase of current in the "normal" range is accompanied by only a small increase of tube voltage, a glow tube may be used as a simple voltage stabilizer. The circuit is that of Fig. 9-5. The resistance R is high enough to limit the tube current to the "normal" range when the load current is zero. Load current increases the voltage drop in the resistance and so reduces the tube voltage. A small reduction of tube voltage in the "normal" current range, however, results in a comparatively large decrease in tube current, which decreases the IR drop. Small variations of load current therefore cause compensating variations of tube current, the voltage across the tube remaining essentially constant. A tube designed for this purpose should have large cathode area in order to give a large range of "normal" current. The 874 neon or argon-filled tube, which has a "normal" voltage of approximately 90 volts, an ignition voltage of approximately 120 volts, and a maximum current rating of 50 ma, was designed for this service.[1]

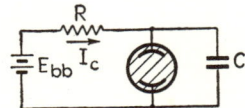

Fig. 9-6.—Basic circuit of the glow-tube relaxation oscillator.

9-7. The Glow-tube Relaxation Oscillator.—A useful application of the glow-discharge tube is made in the glow-tube relaxation oscillator, the simplest circuit of which is shown in Fig. 9-6. A glow tube, shunted by a condenser C, is connected to a d-c supply through a high resistance R (usually not less than 1 megohm). When the circuit is first closed, the condenser charges

---

[1] The current-limiting resistors mounted in the bases of some types of small glow tubes must be removed if the tubes are to be used as voltage stabilizers.

through the high resistance. The condenser voltage rises exponentially, as indicated by the relation

$$V = E_{bb}(1 - \epsilon^{-t/RC}) \tag{9-1}$$

The curve of condenser voltage is shown in Fig. 9-7. When the condenser voltage becomes equal to the firing (breakdown) voltage V_f of the tube, the tube breaks down, and the condenser discharges through the tube. Since negligible resistance is ordinarily used between the condenser and the tube, the initial discharge current approximates the relatively high value corresponding to point n of the characteristics of Fig. 9-1. The condenser discharges very quickly to a voltage equal to the extinction potential V_e, at which the tube goes out and the condenser commences recharging. The condenser voltage varies periodically between the voltages V_e and V_f at a frequency determined by these voltages and by the circuit constants.

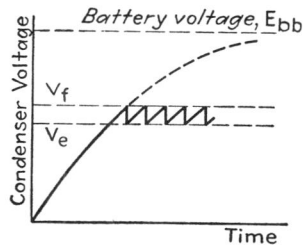

Fig. 9-7.—Variation of condenser voltage in the glow-tube relaxation oscillator of Fig. 9-6.

The time of discharge is so short that the frequency of oscillation depends almost entirely upon the time taken to charge the condenser from the extinction potential to the breakdown potential. The frequency decreases with increase of the difference between the breakdown and extinction voltages, of the capacitance of the condenser, and of the resistance. It decreases with increase of applied voltage.[1] It is not possible to predict exact values of frequency from known circuit constants because the breakdown and extinction voltages are themselves complicated functions of the frequency, the tube temperature, illumination of the electrodes, and the magnitude of the discharge current.

Frequencies as low as 1 cycle in 15 min may be readily obtained. The chief difficulty encountered in obtaining such a low frequency results from the increase of condenser leakage with

[1] Righi, A., *Rend. accad. Bologna*, **6**, 188 (1902); Pearson, S. O., and Anson, H. S., *Proc. Phys. Soc. London*, **34**, 175, 204 (1922). For bibliography, see F. Bedell and H. J. Reich, *J. Am. Inst. Elec. Eng.*, **46**, 563 (1927).

condenser capacitance. The upper frequency limit, which usually does not exceed 10,000 cycles, is attained without the use of a condenser, the electrodes and leads furnishing the required capacitance. The upper frequency limit results because there is a lower limit to the resistance, below which the tube glows permanently. Some change in oscillation frequency with illumination of the cathode is sometimes noted.[1]

Like other types of relaxation oscillators, discussed in Chap. 8,

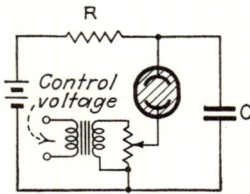

FIG. 9-8.—Glow-tube oscillator stabilized by control voltage.

the glow-tube oscillator can be locked into step with a frequency equal, or very nearly equal, to the oscillator frequency or a multiple or submultiple of that frequency. The control voltage is best introduced through a transformer in series with the terminal of the tube that does not connect to the resistance, as shown in Fig. 9-8.

The wave form of the condenser voltage is shown by Fig. 9-7. The wave shape is virtually that of a right triangle, except that the hypotenuse is curved because of the exponential rise of voltage. For given ignition and extinction voltages the curvature decreases with increase of battery voltage, and may be made very small. A true saw-tooth wave of voltage in which the hypotenuse of the triangle is straight is obtained if the charging current is maintained constant, so that the condenser charge and voltage increase linearly with time. Under the assumption of instantaneous condenser discharge, the oscillation frequency is then

$$f = \frac{I}{C(V_f - V_e)} \tag{9-2}$$

in which I is the constant charging current in amperes, C is the condenser capacitance in farads, and V_f and V_e are the firing and extinction voltages. Since these voltages are complicated functions of the frequency of oscillation (Sec. 9-1), Eq. (9-2) cannot be used in the exact predetermination of frequency. It is of value only in indicating the manner in which the various factors affect the frequency.

[1] OSCHWALD, U. A., and TARRANT, A. G., *Proc. Phys. Soc. London*, **36**, 241 (1924); REICH, H. J., *J. Opt. Soc. Am.*, **17**, 271 (1928).

The best method of obtaining nearly constant charging current is by the use of a voltage pentode, as shown in Fig. 9-9, in place of the resistance R of Fig. 9-6.

At the very small currents (microamperes) required for charging the condenser, the plate current of a pentode is practically independent of plate voltage over a large range of voltage. An additional advantage of the pentode is the ease with which the plate current, and hence the frequency,

6 SJ7

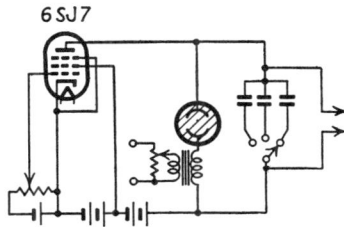

Fig. 9-9.—Circuit of a glow-tube oscillator in which the condenser voltage rises linearly with time.

can be controlled by means of the grid and screen voltages.

9-8. Applications of the Glow-tube Oscillator.—The glow-tube oscillator can serve as a convenient generator of audio-fre-

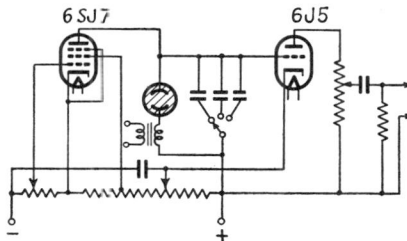

Fig. 9-10.—Glow-tube oscillator and direct-coupled amplifier.

quency voltage for applications in which high harmonic content is desirable, or at least not objectionable.[1]   Since resistance across the tube changes the frequency, distorts the wave form, and may even stop oscillation, the oscillator must be followed by a capacitance-coupled or, preferably, direct-coupled amplifier if it is necessary to vary the output voltage or if current or power output is required.   A typical circuit is shown in Fig. 9-10.

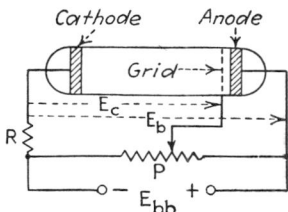

Fig. 9-11.—Basic form of grid-controlled glow-discharge tube.

9-9. Grid Control of Glow Discharge.—The voltage at which breakdown occurs can be controlled by means of a grid placed between the cathode

[1] Kock, W. E., *Electronics*, March, 1935, p. 92.

and the anode, as illustrated in principle by the sketch of Fig. 9-11. This tube is assumed to be of such construction that the entire cathode surface is shielded from the anode by the grid before breakdown. The grid is so close to the anode that the grid-anode breakdown potential greatly exceeds the grid-cathode breakdown potential, and the grid-anode discharge, if it does form, is of the stable type corresponding to the dotted curve bm of Fig. 9-1.

In the use of a grid-controlled glow-discharge tube the anode supply voltage E_{bb} exceeds the cathode-anode breakdown potential. If the grid voltage E_c is zero, no discharge can take place between grid and cathode. The anode is positive with respect to the grid by the entire supply voltage E_{bb}, but breakdown between anode and grid is prevented by their close spacing. Breakdown does not occur between anode and cathode because the field of the anode terminates on the grid, rather than on the cathode. If the grid voltage E_c is gradually raised, breakdown occurs between grid and cathode when the grid voltage equals the grid-cathode breakdown potential. If the anode is sufficiently more positive than the grid, the discharge at once transfers to the anode. The anode voltage at which the transfer occurs decreases with increase of grid-cathode current. Resistance in the cathode lead limits the grid and anode currents to their rated values.

After breakdown the grid has no further control over the discharge. If the grid is made negative with respect to the region of the discharge in which it is situated, then positive ions are drawn toward the grid wires, and electrons are repelled from them. In the immediate vicinity of the grid wires, therefore, positive-ion space charge predominates. The resulting positive-ion *sheath*, illustrated in Fig. 9-12, builds up to such a thickness that at its outer boundary the negative field caused by the voltage applied to the grid is just balanced by the positive field from the sheath.[1] Beyond the boundary of the sheath, in

[1] LANGMUIR, I., *Science*, **58**, 290 (1923); LANGMUIR, I., and MOTT-SMITH, H. M., JR., *Gen. Elec. Rev.*, **27**, 449, 538, 616, 762, 810 (1924); TONKS, L., MOTT-SMITH, H. M., JR., and LANGMUIR, I., *Phys. Rev.*, **28**, 104 (1926); MOTT-SMITH, H. M., JR., and LANGMUIR, I., *Phys. Rev.*, **28**, 727 (1926); TONKS, L., and LANGMUIR, I., *Phys. Rev.*, **34**, 876 (1929); LANGMUIR, I., *Phys. Rev.*, **33**, 964 (1928).

the main part of the discharge, the discharge is completely shielded from the grid by the sheath, so that electrons and positive ions are not influenced by the grid. If the grid is positive with respect to the discharge in its vicinity, then electrons are drawn toward the grid and positive ions are repelled from it. An electron sheath forms of sufficient thickness to shield the main body of the discharge from the positive grid. Although the space charge within a sheath is constant for any value of grid voltage and anode current, the charges that constitute the sheath move in response to the field produced by the impressed grid voltage. Current, therefore, flows to the grid.

If the spacing between the grid wires can be made sufficiently small so that the sheaths surrounding adjacent wires overlap, then the anode will be completely shielded from the cathode by the sheath, and the discharge will stop.[1] Unfortunately, however, the thickness of the sheath, like that of the

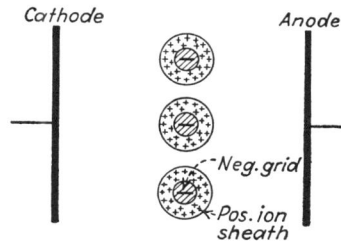

FIG. 9-12.—Formation of a positive-ion sheath around a negative grid in an ionized gas.

cathode dark space, decreases with increase of density of the anode current. At values of anode current density that are high enough to be of practical value, the sheath thickness is usually too small to make complete grid control possible. The only external effect of variation of grid voltage after the tube has broken down is change in the grid current. Because electrons are more readily accelerated than the more massive positive ions, the electron grid current that flows when a positive voltage is applied to the grid is considerably greater than the positive-ion current that flows when an equal negative voltage is applied. Since a grid-controlled glow-discharge tube has some of the characteristics of the high-vacuum trigger circuits discussed in Chap. 6, it is classified as a *trigger tube*.

The grid also prevents the tube from breaking down if it is unconnected, or "floats." If electrons and positive ions are in temperature equilibrium, the electrons have a much higher average velocity than the more massive positive ions. When an

[1] LÜBCKE, E., *Z. tech. Physik*, **8**, 445 (1927).

insulated electrode is immersed in an ionized gas, therefore, many more electrons than positive ions strike it per second. The positive ions recombine with electrons at the surface, but the excess' electrons, which cannot leak off the insulated electrode, charge it negatively. In vacuum, or if the electrode were struck by equal numbers of electrons and positive ions, it would assume a potential equal to the space potential at that point, which is intermediate between the potentials of the cathode and the anode. The negative charge acquired by the electrode lowers its voltage relative to the space until the negative field which it produces attracts additional positive ions and repels electrons in such numbers that as many positive ions as electrons strike the electrode per second   If the grid of the tube of Fig. 9-11 is left unconnected and the gas is ionized, the grid assumes a potential that may be only slightly positive with respect to the cathode. The small dark current, which must flow between anode and cathode before breakdown can occur, results in sufficient ionization to charge the grid in this manner and thus prevent breakdown. When this charge is allowed to leak off the grid so rapidly that the resulting grid current is at least equal to the threshold grid-cathode current, then grid-to-cathode breakdown takes place, and the current may transfer to the anode if the anode voltage is somewhat higher than the grid voltage after breakdown. One of the simpler methods of causing breakdown is to touch a conductor connected to the grid or suddenly to bring a large conductor close to a metal surface connected to the grid.

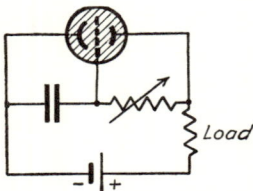

Fig.   9-13.—Circuit for grid-controlled glow tube.

Figure 9-13 shows a modification of the basic circuit of Fig. 9-11. Dark current that flows through the high grid-circuit resistance prior to breakdown reduces the grid voltage to a value less than the breakdown value. Decrease of the resistance raises the grid voltage. Anode-cathode breakdown does not necessarily occur when the grid voltage equals the breakdown value, but when the grid current that flows subsequent to grid-cathode breakdown becomes large enough to allow transfer of the discharge from the grid to the anode at the prevailing anode voltage. The condenser ensures transfer by providing a large surge of grid current when grid-cathode breakdown occurs. A phototube may be used in place of the grid resistor in the circuit of Fig. 9-13 or in place of the left-hand portion of the voltage divider *P* in the circuit of Fig. 9-11.

When direct voltages are used, the anode current of a grid-controlled glow tube can be stopped only by reducing the anode voltage below the extinction value, or by opening the anode circuit completely. For the grid to regain control, the grid voltage must also be reduced below the extinction value at least momentarily, and kept below the breakdown value until breakdown is again desired. If one main electrode is very much smaller than the other, then appreciable anode current can flow only when the large electrode is used as the cathode, and rectification will result when alternating supply voltage is used. The grid then regains control at the end of each conducting half cycle, and the rectified current can be interrupted by means of the grid voltage. A practical tube constructed in this manner, the *grid-glow tube*, is illustrated in Fig. 9-14.[1]

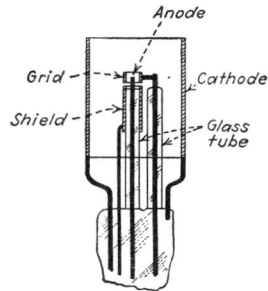

FIG. 9-14.—Electrode structure of the grid-glow tube.

The use of a small anode in the grid-glow tube not only results in rectification, but also accentuates the negative charging of the grid when it is free. During the flow of dark current between anode and cathode before breakdown occurs, the large number of electrons formed in the large volume outside of the grid are drawn toward the anode, and many of these strike the grid. The only positive ions that can strike the grid, on the other hand, are the relatively few formed in the small volume of gas between the grid and the anode. Thus the number of electrons that strike the grid exceeds the number of positive ions both because of the greater speed of the electrons and because the grid is placed at a point where large numbers of electrons are converging. Thus the grid is always only slightly positive relative to the cathode when the grid is free, and grid-to-cathode breakdown cannot occur.

[1] KNOWLES, D. D., *Elec J.*, **27**, 232 (1930); KNOWLES, D. D., and SASHOFF, S. P., *Electronics*, July, 1930, p. 183.

The close spacing of the grid and anode prevents grid-to-anode breakdown.

9-10. Starter-anode Glow Tubes.—A different method of controlling anode-cathode breakdown is used in the OA4 "gas triode." This tube uses a *starter anode* in place of a grid.[1] The tube is designed so that breakdown does not occur directly between the main anode and the cathode unless the anode voltage is at least 225 volts. Breakdown occurs between the starter anode and the cathode, on the other hand, when the starter anode voltage is 90 volts or less. Starter-anode breakdown is followed by breakdown to the main anode if the starter-anode current and main-anode voltage are sufficiently great. The required value of starter-anode current increases from zero to approximately 250 ma with decrease of main-anode voltage from its breakdown value to a value equal to the starter-anode breakdown voltage. Since the main anode is very small in comparison with the cathode, the tube rectifies and may be used on alternating supply voltage. The tube can carry 25 ma continuously, which is ample for the operation of relays. Because of the very small current required in the starter-anode circuit, the tube may be controlled by voltages in tuned radio-frequency circuits.[1] It has other applications as a control device.

Advantage of Glow Tubes.—The principal advantage of glow tubes over high-vacuum thermionic tubes and hot-cathode arc-discharge tubes is that no source of cathode heating power is required. In the control of power and of large currents, however, the lower voltage drop and higher current capacity of arc tubes make them superior to glow tubes.

9-11. Arc Discharges.—So far in this chapter the discussion has related to glow discharges, which are characterized by comparatively small currents and by voltages considerably greater than the ionization potentials of the gases. The high voltage drop in the glow discharge is accounted for mainly by the fall in potential across the cathode dark space. The high cathode drop is necessary in order to maintain the current flow, for in this region the positive ions are given the requisite energy to eject electrons from the cathode by bombardment. The increase of cathode drop with current in the "abnormal" range of current

[1] BAHLS, W. E., and THOMAS, C. H., *Electronics*, May, 1938, p. 14; INGRAM, S. B., *Trans. A.I.E.E.*, **58**, 342 (1939).

may be explained by the greater energy required to eject the additional electrons involved in the increase of current.

That this explanation of the cathode drop in potential is valid appears to be proved by the use of a cathode which can be heated to a temperature high enough to cause thermionic emission. It is found that, when the cathode is heated, the voltage drop across the discharge falls. If the thermionic emission is sufficient to supply all of the electrons required to carry the anode current, the potential across the tube drops to a value that is usually approximately equal to the ionization potential of the gas or vapor.

Discharges in which current density is high and the voltage drop is of the order of the ionization potential are commonly called *arcs*. As stated in Sec. 9-1, distinction between glows and arcs on the basis of voltage drop and current density is not a fundamental one. The essential distinction lies in the copious emission of electrons at the cathode of an arc by some process other than positive-ion bombardment. Possible emission processes include thermionic emission or emission resulting from the intense electric field caused by positive-ion space charge at the cathode. Glow currents are normally limited to low densities because of heating of the cathode and subsequent change to an arc when the density is high. High–current-density glows may be maintained for time intervals that are too short to allow the cathode to heat to the temperature required for emission (as in the discharge of a large condenser through a glow tube). Likewise, low–current-density arcs may be maintained if the cathode is heated by external means.

The transformation of a glow into an arc does not afford a satisfactory method of forming an arc in cold-cathode tubes with ordinary solid metallic cathodes because the resulting high temperature usually destroys the cathode. By the use of a special cathode made in the form of a cup containing a cesium compound, enough emission can be obtained at low cathode temperature to allow an arc to be maintained without damage to the cathode (see Sec. 9-42).[1] Although the peak current that can be handled by such a cathode may be of the order of several hundred amperes, the average current is usually a fraction of an

[1] GERMESHAUSEN, K. J., and EDGERTON, H. E., *Elec. Eng.*, **55**, 790 (1936).

ampere.   More commonly used is the mercury pool type of cold-cathode arc, in which electron emission from the cathode is probably obtained because of high positive-ion space-charge field at the surface of the mercury cathode.   In mercury pool tubes, the arc is started by making and breaking contact between the anode and the mercury cathode, or between an auxiliary anode and the cathode.   After the tube fires, discharge takes place between the anode and a luminous area on the mercury surface, called the *cathode spot*, which furnishes electrons for the discharge.   The area of the cathode spot is very small, and the current density[1] at the spot is of the order of 1000 to 5000 amp/sq cm.   Because of positive-ion bombardment, the surface of the mercury is depressed in the vicinity of the cathode spot.   The tendency of the spot to climb the sides of the depression, and consequent displacement of the depression, causes the spot to skim over the surface unless means are provided to fix its position.[2]   Very large currents can be carried by mercury pool tubes.   A third type of practical arc-discharge tube is that in which copious electron emission is obtained by the use of a cathode of high emission efficiency, heated by a separate electrical source.

9-12. Arcs with Separately Heated Cathodes.—Usually, practically the entire voltage impressed between the electrodes of an arc is accounted for by the cathode drop, which is approximately equal to the ionization potential.   The low cathode drop that distinguishes an arc from a glow is maintained only as long as an emission current equal to the anode current is obtained without the need of a higher drop.   When the arc current in a tube with separately heated cathode exceeds the thermionic current from the cathode, a positive-ion space charge develops near the cathode that raises the cathode drop sufficiently to supply the required additional electrons by positive-ion bombardment.   Although the secondary emission from the cathode or the increased thermionic emission resulting from the rise in cathode temperature may not be harmful to the cathode, oxide-coated cathodes disintegrate under positive-ion bombardment

---

[1] There appears to be evidence that, when the current is large, it may divide among a large number of spots, each of which carries from 5 to 15 amp. See H. W. Lord, *Electronics*, May, 1936, p. 11.

[2] Wagner, C. F., and Ludwig, L. R., *Elec. Eng.*, **53**, 1384 (1934).

when the ion velocity exceeds a critical value. The value of the *disintegration voltage* above which the positive-ion velocity becomes so high as to deactivate or destroy coated cathodes lies between 20 and 25 volts for the inert gases and mercury vapor.[1] The ionization potentials of some of the noble gases and of mercury vapor are sufficiently lower than the disintegration voltage to make it possible to design hot-cathode arc-discharge tubes in which the cathode does not disintegrate if the average anode current is kept below the value corresponding to the electron emission from the cathode. Such tubes will pass currents considerably in excess of the emission current for periods of time that are too short to allow much rise in temperature of the cathode.

In tubes with separately heated cathodes the arc voltage is usually nearly independent of current in the working range of current. For this reason the current is determined practically entirely by the applied voltage and the circuit impedance, which must always be chosen so that the average current does not exceed the emission current.

Hot-cathode arc diodes (rectifiers) are of two types: high-pressure, which carries the trade name *tungar* or *rectigon;* and low-pressure, designated by the trade name *phanatron.* Grid-controlled hot-cathode arc tubes are known as *thyratrons.* This was originally also a trade name but has now been released for general use.

9-13. Tungar Rectifier.—The first type of hot-cathode arc rectifier to be developed was the tungar.[2] One of the principal functions of the argon gas or mercury vapor used in this tube is to protect the oxide-coated cathode against evaporation of the barium so that the cathode can be operated at high temperature and hence high emission efficiency. To accomplish this the pressure of the gas or mercury vapor must be about 1 mm. Glow breakdown voltage at this relatively high pressure is so low that the tubes cannot be used at high voltage, and satisfactory grid control cannot be attained. The principal application of tungar rectifiers has been in battery charging.

[1] HULL, A. W. *Trans. Am. Inst. Elec. Eng.*, **47**, 753 (1928); *Gen. Elec. Rev.*, **32**, 213 (1929).

[2] HULL, A. W., *Trans. Am. Inst. Elec. Eng.*, **47**, 753 (1928).

9-14. Cathode Structure of Low-pressure Hot-cathode Arc Tubes.[1]—At low gas or vapor pressures, such as must be used in grid-controlled arc tubes and high-voltage arc rectifiers, the gas does not exert a protective action upon the cathode. Since the cathode cannot be operated at high temperature, as in the tungar, high cathode efficiency must be attained by the use of special cathodes that have low heat loss. This is made possible by the characteristics of the arc discharge. In high-vacuum tubes the electrons that leave the cathode must follow the electric field, and any emitting surface to be of value must be placed so that some lines of force from the anode will terminate upon it. In the arc tube, on the other hand, as soon as the tube fires, the whole tube is filled with large, and practically equal, numbers of positive ions and electrons. The flow of current consists of a relatively slow drift of electrons toward the anode and of positive ions toward the cathode. Electrons in the immediate vicinity of the anode are drawn toward it, leaving excess positive charge behind them which immediately causes the advance of other electrons that are nearer the cathode. At the cathode, electrons that drift away are replaced by those emitted from the cathode. This drift is superimposed upon the high random velocity due to the temperature of the gas and need not take place along the initial field from cathode to anode. In effect, the presence of the ionized gas enables the electrons to move in curved paths which do not coincide with the field, so that portions of the cathode surface that are not subject to the initial field set up by the anode voltage are effective in supplying electrons as soon as the tube is allowed to break down. Hence cathodes may be made up in forms that greatly reduce the loss of heat.

High emission efficiency is attained at the expense of rapid heating, since the greater heat capacity and reduced heating energy increase the time taken to establish thermal equilibrium. In practice a compromise must be made between high efficiency

---

[1] Hull, *loc. cit.;* Hull, A. W., *Gen. Elec. Rev.*, **32,** 213 (1929). Hull, A. W., and Langmuir, I., *Proc. Nat. Acad. Sci.*, **15,** 218 (1929). Hull, A. W., *Physics*, **2,** 409 (1932), **4,** 66 (1933). Lowry, E. F., *Electronics*, October, 1933, p. 280; December, 1935, p. 26; *Elec. J.*, April, 1936, p. 187. Knowles, D. D., Lowry, E. F., and Gessford, R. K., *Electronics*, November, 1936, p. 27.

and short heating time. In small arc tubes the heating time of indirectly heated high-efficiency cathodes usually ranges from 1 to 5 min.

In Fig. 9-15a is shown the type of filamentary cathode originally used in the FG-27 thyratron. Heat that is radiated

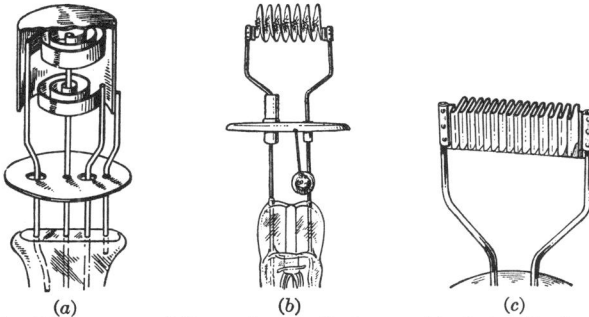

(a)   (b)   (c)

FIG. 9-15.—Three types of filamentary cathodes used in hot-cathode arc tubes.

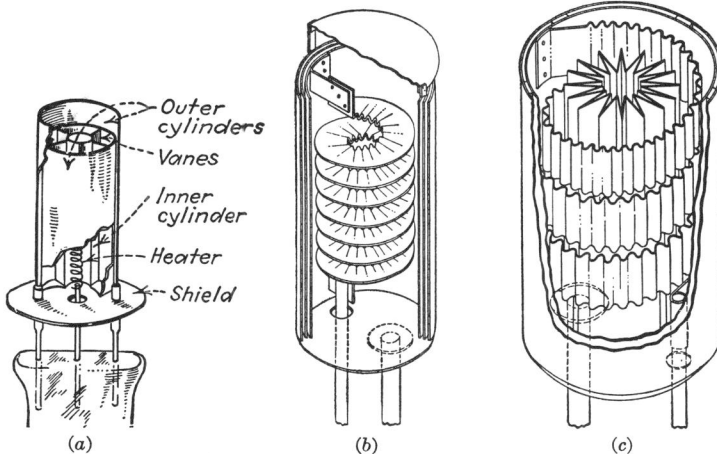

Outer
cylinders

Vanes

Inner
cylinder

Heater

Shield

(a)   (b)   (c)

FIG. 9-16.—Typical indirectly heated cathodes used in hot-cathode arc tubes.

by any of the inner turns of the spiral filament is absorbed by adjacent turns. Radiation from the outer surface is reduced by the bright nickel cap which surrounds the filament. Heat loss may also be reduced by crimping the ribbon, as in the filament of Fig. 9-15b, or by folding it, as in the filament of Fig. 9-15c.[1] Figure 9-16a shows the construction of the indirectly

[1] LOWRY, *loc. cit.*

heated cathode used in the FG-67 and other types of thyratrons. Heat loss is greatly reduced by reflection from the outer concentric cylinders. The active coating covers the outside of the inner cylinder which surrounds the heater, the inner surface of the first outer cylinder, and the connecting vanes. Figures 9-16*b* and 9-16*c* show two cathodes that combine direct and indirect heating.[1] The cathode of Fig. 9-15*a* has an average emission current rating of $2\frac{1}{2}$ amp at a power consumption of 35 watts, that of Fig. 9-15*c* a peak current rating of 65 amp at 200 watts, and that of Fig. 9-16*a* an average emission current rating of $2\frac{1}{2}$ amp at $22\frac{1}{2}$ watts.

The difference in potential between the ends of the filament or heater of a grid-controlled hot-cathode arc tube must be less than the ionization potential of the gas or vapor. Otherwise discharge takes place and produces a continuous supply of ions that prevent the grid from controlling the anode current. In filamentary cathodes the crest potential drop through the filament must be less than the difference between the ionization and disintegration potentials. If the filament voltage is higher than this, the anode potential relative to the negative end of the filament exceeds the disintegration potential when the anode voltage relative to the positive end is equal to the ionization potential. Special care must be taken in preventing discharge between the ends of 110-volt heaters. Five-volt cathode heaters or filaments are usually used.

9-15. Choice of Gas or Vapor.—Either mercury vapor or the inert gases may be used in hot-cathode arc-discharge tubes but mercury vapor is used in most types. The inert gases have the advantage of not being greatly affected by changes of temperature. Because the vapor pressure of mercury is dependent upon the temperature, mercury vapor tubes are very susceptible to small changes of tube temperature such as may result from air currents or changes of cathode temperature. The disadvantages of the rare gases are their higher ionization potentials, which result in higher tube drop than with mercury; their very much lower ignition voltages, which greatly reduce the maximum alternating voltage that can be applied to the anode without breakdown in the reverse direction and without loss of control by the grid; and their likelihood of being "cleaned up" as the

[1] Lowry, *loc. cit.*

result of absorption by the walls and electrodes. The tube drop under load is about 10 or 11 volts in mercury vapor tubes and about 16 volts in argon tubes. Only a small quantity of mercury, usually not more than a few drops, is sufficient to supply ample vapor. The vapor pressure is controlled by the temperature of the tube, and usually lies in the range from 1 to 50 microns. In this range of vapor pressure, any glow that may form when the cathode is cold, or when the anode is negative, is of the stable type, illustrated by the dotted characteristic *bm* of Fig. 9-1. Such a stable glow is followed only rarely by arc breakdown.

9-16. Grid Control of Arcs.—The most commonly used method of controlling the firing of hot-cathode arc tubes is by means of a grid. The grid acts primarily as a shield between the anode and the cathode, preventing electrons emitted by the cathode from moving into the accelerating field between the grid and the anode. Inasmuch as only a few electrons in the grid-anode space are enough to start the discharge, the effectiveness of the grid depends upon how completely the grid shields the cathode. Hence, the largest hole in the grid structure is the determining factor, rather than the average mesh as in high-vacuum tubes. By proper design of electrode shape and spacing, the grid may be made to shield the cathode so completely that a positive grid voltage is required to start the arc. The performance of a grid-controlled arc tube as a control device is specified by its *grid-control characteristics*. These are curves of anode voltage *vs.* critical grid voltage below which the tube fires. Grid-control characteristics for several types of thyratrons are shown in Figs. 9-19, 9-21, 9-23, and 9-25.

The critical grid voltage depends not only upon the electrode structure and the anode voltage, but also upon the pressure, which, in mercury vapor tubes, is a function of the temperature of the condensed mercury. The vapor pressure not only affects the critical grid voltage directly, but at high temperature the grid-anode glow breakdown potential may be so low that a glow may form between the grid and the anode at relatively low anode voltage, and the grid thus lose control. At low temperature, on the other hand, the vapor density may be too low to make possible sufficient ionization for the neutralization of negative space charge near the cathode. The voltage therefore cannot fall to the low value that is characteristic of an arc, and the current is limited by space charge.

Experiments have shown that the time required for complete breakdown of grid-controlled arc tubes is of the order of a few microseconds.[1] No study appears to have been made of the mechanism of breakdown. The following is a possible theory. Electrons that pass beyond the grid are accelerated by the field between the grid and the plate and cause ionization in the grid-anode region, the resulting positive ions being drawn to the grid. Because the positive ions are greater in number than the initial electrons that pass through the grid, a positive-ion sheath is formed adjacent to the grid. As the grid is made less negative, or more positive, more initial electrons enter the grid-anode space, and the ionization increases. The resulting increase of charge density in the sheath strengthens the field in the vicinity of the grid. At some critical grid voltage the field strength becomes great enough to cause glow breakdown. This is immediately followed by arc breakdown to the cathode. In negative-grid tubes another possible factor in the breakdown process is the shielding of the grid by positive-ion space charge, which causes the grid to become ineffective in holding back electrons from the cathode. Transfer of the discharge from the grid to the cathode is probably caused by the high voltage drop through the dark space that forms at the grid when glow breakdown occurs, the number of electrons from the cathode that pass beyond the grid being insufficient to neutralize the positive-ion space charge. In positive-grid tubes the transfer is favored by the greater voltage that exists between the cathode and the anode than between the grid and the anode. In some tubes the critical grid voltage at low anode voltage may be so positive that the initial breakdown is between grid and cathode. In order that the discharge may transfer to the anode the grid current must then exceed a minimum value which decreases with increase of anode voltage.

Although experimental arc tubes have been built in which large currents can be interrupted by a grid,[2] in practical tubes

---

[1] NOTTINGHAM, W. B., J. Franklin Inst., 211, 271 (1931); HULL, A. W., and SNODDY, L. B., Phys. Rev., 37, 1691 (1931) (abstr.); SNODDY, L. B., Physics, 4, 366 (1933).

[2] LÜBCKE, E., Z. tech. Physik, 8, 445 (1927); KOBEL, A., Schweiz. elektrotech. Verein Bull. 24, 41 (1933); RISCH, R., Schweiz. elektrotech. Verein Bull.

only very small anode currents can be stopped by the grid.[1] For all practical purposes, therefore, it is correct to say that in thyratrons the grid loses control of the anode current after firing. The anode current is determined by the applied voltage, the circuit impedance, and the essentially constant voltage drop through the tube.

9-17. Grid Current Previous to Firing.—One very important factor in the application of thyratrons is the grid current that flows prior to firing. Grid current is particularly objectionable in tubes used in control circuits in which the grid current must flow through a very high resistance such as a phototube or a coupling resistance. The resulting voltage drop may prevent firing of the tube.[2] By supplying electrons to the region between the grid and the anode even when the grid is negative, grid emission may also result in loss of grid control.

Grid current results from five principal causes: (1) electrons attracted to the grid from the cathode, (2) positive ions attracted to the grid, (3) electrons emitted by the grid, (4) capacitance between the grid and other electrodes, and (5) internal or external leakage between the grid and other electrodes. Electron flow from cathode to grid is obtained only when the grid is positive or insufficiently negative to counteract the initial velocities of electrons emitted by the cathode. When the grid is negative, the grid current results both from positive ions drawn to the grid and from electrons emitted by the grid as the result of emitting material deposited upon the grid. The closer the grid is to the cathode, the greater is the amount of emitting material that is condensed upon the grid, and the higher is the grid temperature during operation. The grid current resulting from grid emission, therefore, increases with decrease of spacing between the grid and the cathode. It also increases with the grid surface available for the depositing of emitting material and for subsequent electron emission. Because positive-ion bombardment tends to remove active material deposited upon the grid, grid emission is

26, 507 (1935); BOUMEESTER, H., and DRUYVESTEYN, M. K., *Philips Tech. Rev.,* **1,** 367 (1936); LÜDI, F., *Helvetica phys. Acta,* **9,** 655 (1936); *Electronics,* May, 1937, p. 66 (abstr.).

[1] REICH, H. J., *Elec. Eng.,* **55,** 1314 (1936).

[2] FRENCH, H. W., *J. Franklin Inst.,* **221,** 83 (1936).

less with tubes designed to operate with a negative grid.[1] Current caused by capacitance between the grid and other electrodes naturally increases with decrease of electrode separation.

9-18. External Grid Control.—An electrode on the outside of the tube, in contact with the glass, can induce a charge on the inner surface of the wall or change the charge that collects from the ionized gas.   If the electrode structure is such that negative charge on the walls of the envelope can prevent emitted electrons from leaving the cathode, then such an external grid can be used to control firing of a hot-cathode arc.[2] Because charge induced on the inside of the glass wall rapidly becomes neutralized by charge of opposite sign from the ionized gas, the external grid voltage is effective only for short time intervals, and the external grid is of principal value in a-c operation.

9-19. Control by Magnetic Field.—Another type of control of breakdown of thyratrons is by means of magnetic fields.[3] A field at right angles to the line between anode and cathode raises the anode firing voltage, whereas a field parallel to the anode-cathode axis usually lowers the firing voltage. The control results from deflection of electrons leaving the cathode. A field normal to the axis deflects the electrons in such a manner as to reduce the number passing through the grid into the region between grid and anode. A field parallel to the axis, on the other hand, increases the number of electrons that enter the region between the grid and the anode (see Sec. 1-21).   Strong radio-frequency fields, especially at very high frequencies, also affect the firing of grid-controlled arcs.[4]

9-20. Deionization.—The application of discharge tubes, particularly of the grid-controlled type, is limited by time taken for deionization after interruption of the anode current.   In order

[1] MORACK, M. M., *Gen. Elec. Rev.*, **37**, 288 (1934).

[2] CRAIG, PALMER H., *Electronics*, March, 1933, p. 70; WATANABE, Y., and TAKANO, T., *J. Inst. Elec. Eng. Japan*, **54**, 131 (1934); CRAIG, P. H., and SANFORD, F. E., *Elec. Eng.*, **54**, 166 (1935).

[3] SAVAGNONE, R., *Elettrotecnica*, **19**, 689 (1932).   REICH, H. J., *Rev. Sci. Instruments*, **3**, 580 (1932); *Electronics*, February, 1933, p. 48.   WATANABE, Y., and TAKANO, T., *J. Inst. Elec. Eng. Japan*, **53**, 62 (1933).   KANO, I., and TAKAHASHI, R., *J. Inst. Elec. Eng. Japan*, **53**, 83 (1933).   McARTHUR, E. D., *Electronics*, January, 1935, p. 12.   PENNING, F. M., *Physica*, **3**, 873 (1936). JURRIAANSE, T., *Physica*, **4**, 23 (1937).

[4] REICH, *loc. cit.*

that the grid shall be able to prevent firing when the anode voltage is reapplied it is necessary that the ions remaining in the interelectrode space shall be so few that anode-to-grid breakdown cannot take place and positive-ion sheaths cannot shield the grid.   The completeness of deionization necessary to reestablish grid control increases with anode voltage.   For this reason the time required for the grid to regain control increases with anode voltage.   Although a single nominal value of deionization time is often given, it may not adequately indicate the performance of the tube.   The behavior of the tube can be specified completely by means of curves of voltage necessary to cause reignition

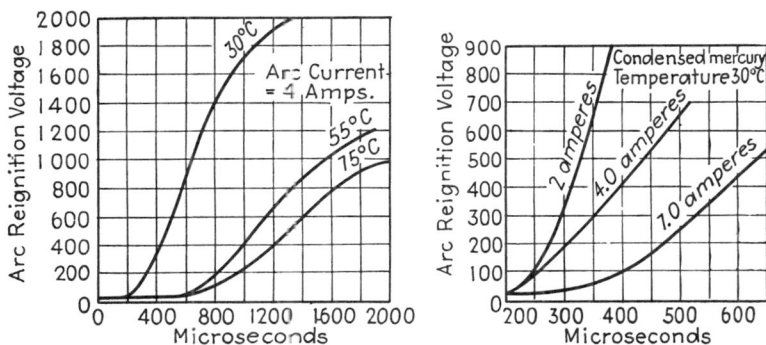

FIG. 9-17.—Typical curves of arc reignition voltage of grid-controlled hot-cathode arc tubes as a function of time after extinction.

as a function of time after extinction, for given values of grid voltage, temperature or pressure, and current previous to extinction.   Typical curves of reignition voltage *vs.* time are shown in Fig. 9-17.[1]

The most effective method of deionization in discharge tubes is by recombination at electrodes and walls (see Sec. 1-11), and so deionization is favored by reducing the distance that ions must travel to walls and electrodes.   Experimental curves such as those of Fig. 9-17 show that pressure, magnitude of anode current, and potential of the grid relative to the surrounding space also affect the rate of deionization.[2]   Because of increase of ion density, the deionization time increases with increase of current

[1] BERKEY, W. E., and HALLER, C. E., *Elec. J.*, **31**, 483 (1934).

[2] HULL, A. W., *Gen. Elec. Rev.*, **32**, 222 (1929); BERKEY and HALLER, *loc. cit.*   See also S. S. Mackeown, J. D. Cobine, and F. W. Bowden, *Elec. Eng.*, **53**, 1081 (1934); J. D. Cobine, *Physics*, **7**, 137 (1936); J. D. Cobine, and

previous to extinction. Negative grid or anode voltage pulls the positive ions out of the interelectrode space, and so speeds up deionization. Resistance in the grid circuit causes a lowering of negative grid voltage as the result of flow of positive-ion grid current and thus slows down deionization. Increase of gas pressure retards diffusion to the walls, increasing the deionization time. Since the vapor pressure in mercury vapor tubes increases with condensed mercury temperature, the rate of deionization decreases with increase of tube temperature.

9-21. Voltage and Current Ratings of Phanatrons and Thyratrons.[1]—Because of the possibility of the formation of a glow discharge between the anode and the grid and resultant loss of grid control, there is a limiting value of positive anode voltage above which a grid cannot prevent an arc tube from firing. This is called the *peak forward voltage*. Likewise, there is a limiting negative anode voltage, called the *peak inverse voltage*, above which a glow discharge may form between the anode and the grid or cathode. There is then the possibility of *arcback*, which is the flow of arc current in the reverse direction to the normal flow. When arcback occurs, the tube ceases to rectify. Both the peak forward voltage and the peak inverse voltage depend upon the material of which the electrodes are made (or with which they become coated), upon the kind of gas or vapor, and upon the gas or vapor pressure. In vapor tubes, the large change of vapor pressure with temperature makes these voltages dependent upon tube temperature. The peak forward voltage is greatly lowered if the grid becomes hot enough to give appreciable thermionic emission. Similarly, the peak inverse voltage is lowered by undue heating of the anode. In periodic operation of the tube, the peak forward and peak inverse voltages are also dependent upon the time intervening between extinction of the tube and reapplication of anode voltage and upon the magnitude of the anode current previous to extinction. Because of danger of excessive anode heating and of destructive positive-ion bom-

---

R. B. Power, *J. Applied Physics*, **8**, 287 (1937); C. Concordia and W. F. Skeats, *Trans. A.I.E.E.*, **58**, 371 (1939).

[1] General Electric Company *Bull.* GET-426. See also H. C. Steiner, A. C. Gable, and H. T. Maser, *Elec. Eng.*, **51**, 312 (1932); O. W. Pike and D. Ulrey, *Elec. Eng.*, **53**, 1577 (1934); Standards on Electronics, p. 4, Institute of Radio Engineers, New York, 1938.

bardment of the cathode, current limitations also exist. The *maximum instantaneous anode current* is the highest instantaneous periodic current that the tube can stand under normal operating conditions without damage to the anode because of overheating or to the cathode because of positive-ion bombardment. The length of time during which a given tube can stand this instantaneous current or the frequency with which it can stand an instantaneous current surge of a given duration depends upon tube heating.

The *maximum average anode current* is a rating based upon tube heating. It represents the highest average anode current that can be carried continuously through the tube. In the case of a rapidly repeating cycle of operation, this may be measured on a d-c meter. Otherwise, it is necessary to calculate the average current over a period not to exceed a definite interval of time which is specified for each design of tube. For instance, a tube with a maximum instantaneous anode current rating of 15 amp, a maximum average anode current rating of 2.5 amp, and an integration period of 15 sec could carry 15 amp for 2.5 sec out of each 15 sec or 7.5 amp for 5 sec out of every 15 sec.

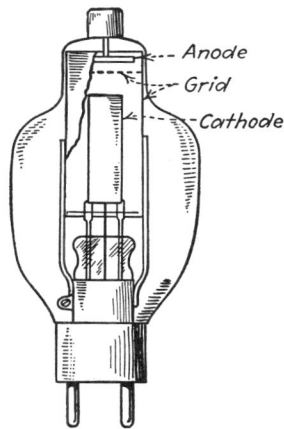

FIG. 9-18.—Electrode structure of the type FG-67 thyratron.

The grid current ratings are given in terms of the *maximum instantaneous grid current* and the *maximum average grid current,* and the integration period is the same as for the anode current.

The *tube voltage drop* is the anode-to-cathode voltage under normal anode current flow. It will be represented by the symbol E_a. The extinction voltage is equal to E_a.

9-22. Electrode Structure and Characteristics of Thyratrons.— In most applications in which thyratrons are operated with direct anode voltage, or in which the frequency of the alternating voltage is high, it is necessary to use tubes that deionize as rapidly as possible. Figure 9-18 shows the construction of a typical tube of this type, the FG-67. Rapid deionization is achieved by the use of close spacing and small volume between the grid "baffle" (dotted in Fig. 9-18) and the anode and cathode, small distance between the back of the anode and the glass bulb, close spacing between the glass bulb and the upper part of the grid cylinder, and small holes in the grid baffle. The rated deionization time of the FG-67 thyratron is 100 microseconds. The grid-control characteristics are shown in Fig. 9-19. Because of the high shielding by the grid and the closeness of the grid to the cathode, the grid current previous to breakdown is high,

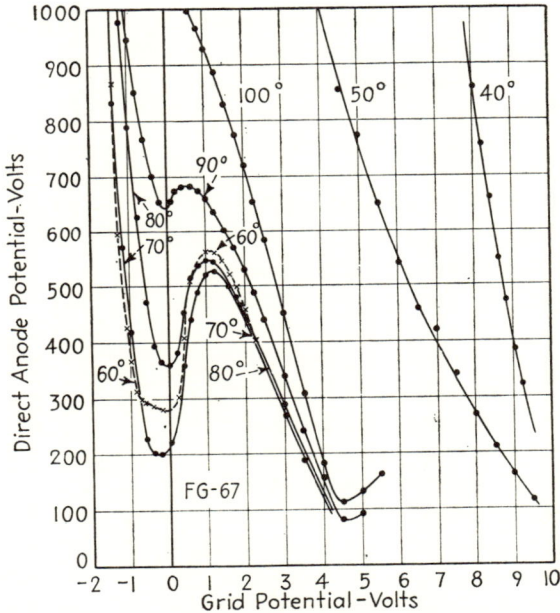

Fig. 9-19.—Grid-control characteristics of a type FG-67 thyratron. (*From data obtained by Robert Gibson for Master's thesis, University of Illinois, June, 1940.*)

and the tube is not suitable for use in circuits in which the grid current must flow through a high resistance.

In three-electrode thyratrons designed for control circuits with high grid-circuit resistance, the grid current is kept small by the use of adequate spacing between electrodes; by designing and placing the grid so as to reduce depositing of emitting material evaporated from the cathode, as well as heating of the grid by the cathode; and by making the shielding action of the grid small enough so that a negative voltage must be used on the grid to prevent firing.   Figure 9-20 shows the electrode structure of a typical heater-cathode thyratron triode of the negative-grid type,

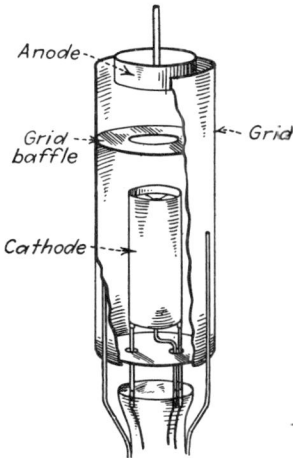

FIG. 9-20.—Electrode structure of the type FG-57 negative-grid thyratron.

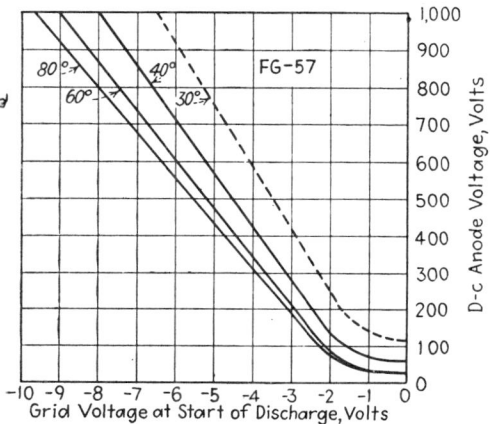

FIG. 9-21.—Grid-control characteristics of the type FG-57 thyratron.

the FG-57.   The grid-control characteristics of this tube are shown in Fig. 9-21.   The rated deionization time of this tube is 1000 microseconds.

In some control circuits it is advantageous or necessary to use a tube in which a positive grid voltage is required to start the arc. Positive grid control can be attained at the expense of increased grid current by making the shielding action of the grid so effective that the field from the anode cannot penetrate to the cathode.   This is accomplished by the use of three baffles in the grid structure, in place of the single baffle used in negative-grid tubes.   The holes in the grid baffles are also much smaller than the single hole used in the grid of the negative-grid tube.   Figures 9-22 and 9-23 show the electrode structure and grid-control characteristics of the type FG-33 positive-grid thyratron, which has a rated deionization time of 1000 microseconds.

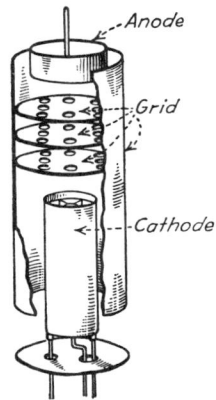

FIG. 9-22.—Electrode structure of the type FG-33 positive-grid thyratron.

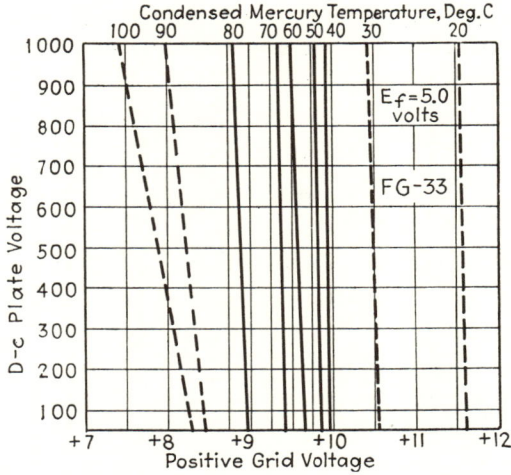

Fig. 9-23.—Grid-control characteristics of the type FG-33 thyratron.

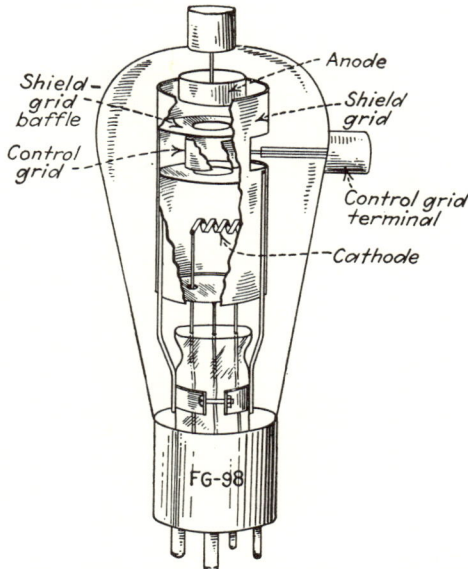

Fig. 9-24.—Electrode structure of the type FG-98 shield-grid thyratron.

Even with the most careful design, the grid current of three-electrode thyratrons previous to firing may be so great as to give difficulty when the grid circuit contains very high resistance. Furthermore, the changes in grid current as the tube warms up or ages may necessitate frequent readjustment of the circuit constants or voltages. These difficulties may be avoided by the addition of a fourth electrode, which acts as a shield.[1]

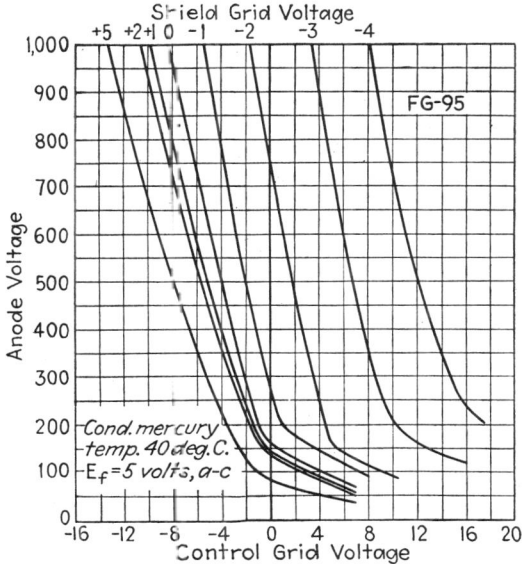

FIG. 9-25.—Grid-control characteristics of the type FG-95 shield-grid thyratron.

The construction of a typical shield-grid thyratron, the FG-98, is shown in Fig. 9-24. In this tube the shield grid consists of a structure intermediate in form between the grids of negative- and positive-grid three-electrode thyratrons, two baffles being used. The control grid consists of a short cylinder whose diameter is somewhat larger than the holes in the grid baffles, and the grid is placed between the two baffles. It can be seen that the form and position of the control grid are such as to prevent the depositing of appreciable amounts of emitting material from the cathode or the absorption of much heat

[1] LIVINGSTON, O. W., and MASER, H. T., *Electronics*, April, 1934, p. 114; JACOBI, W., and KNIEPKAMP, H., *E.T.Z.*, **58**, 1233 (1937).

radiated by the cathode or anode. Moreover, this grid is out of the direct path of the arc, so that the grid current when the tube conducts is also reduced and the grid receives little heat from the arc. The small size of the control grid minimizes the grid current resulting from electrons or ions drawn to the grid or reaching the grid from the cathode as the result of initial velocities. The small size of the grid and the grid lead, in conjunction with the shielding afforded by the shield grid, also results in low capacitance between the grid and the anode and cathode. The short and direct grid lead minimizes both the internal and the external leakage.

Another very important advantage of the shield-grid thyratron is that the tube can be made to have either positive or negative control characteristics by adjusting the voltage of the shield grid. This is indicated by the characteristics of the type FG-95 thyratron, shown in Fig. 9-25.

9-23. Comparison of Thyratrons and High-vacuum Tubes.— Thyratrons differ from high-vacuum tubes in more respects than they resemble them. The similarity consists mainly of the dependence of current in both types of tubes upon thermionic emission and upon movement of electrons from cathode to anode. The differences between the two types, in addition to those involving the structure of the electrodes and envelopes, the presence of gas or vapor and of positive ions in thyratrons, and the emission of light from thyratrons, are shown in Table 9-I.

The high anode and emission efficiencies of hot-cathode arc tubes make possible the control of large currents and high power by means of relatively small tubes. The FG-57 thyratron, for instance, has a maximum average anode current rating of $2\frac{1}{2}$ amp and a peak anode voltage rating of 1000 volts and can, therefore, control 2500 watts of power. This tube is only slightly larger than the type 50 high-vacuum triode, which has a maximum operating plate current of 55 ma and a power output that cannot exceed about 20 watts, even in class C operation.

Hot-cathode arc tubes have been built in sizes ranging from 10 watts to 100 kw (load power). Current ratings range up to 100 amp average current, and voltage ratings up to 1500 volts. There is a corresponding variation in tube structure and design, ranging from small glass-enclosed argon-filled tubes to large water-cooled metal-enclosed mercury vapor tubes.

TABLE 9-I.—COMPARISON OF THYRATRONS AND HIGH-VACUUM TUBES

Thyratron	*High-vacuum*
Grid loses control after the tube fires.	Grid has complete control of anode current.
Anode and grid currents are determined by the applied voltage and the circuit resistance. Circuit resistance is essential.	Anode current is determined by the electrode voltages. No circuit resistance needed.
Essentially a high-current, low-voltage tube. Because of low tube drop, anode-circuit efficiencies may exceed 98 per cent.	Essentially a low-current, high-voltage tube. Plate-circuit efficiency may approach 85 per cent in class C operation, but is usually less than 50 per cent.
Anode voltage is constant after the tube fires.	Anode voltage may vary.
Cathode emission efficiency may be high.	Cathode emission efficiency is relatively low.
Cathode heating time is high in types using high-efficiency heater-type cathodes. Tube heating time may also be high in mercury vapor tubes.	Except in large power tubes, heating time is short.
Cathode may be damaged if operated at low temperature or if the anode current exceeds the thermionic emission current for any other reason.	Cathode temperature may be reduced without damage to the tube. The cathode is not ordinarily damaged by currents exceeding rated values.
Characteristics of mercury vapor tubes are affected by tube temperature.	Characteristics are independent of tube temperature.
Grid current flows when the grid is negative.	Negligible grid current flows when the grid is more than approximately $\frac{1}{2}$ volt negative.
Deionization time limits frequency of operation to several thousand cycles or less.	The frequency of operation may exceed 100 Mc.
Arcback may occur.	Tube conducts in one direction only.

Special Precautions in the Use of Arc Tubes.—Before proceeding to a discussion of circuits for hot-cathode arc tubes it seems advisable to list special precautions that must be observed in the use of these tubes. They are as follows:

1. The cathode should be brought to normal operating temperature before anode voltage is applied. Failure to observe this precaution results in excessive cathode drop and in cathode disintegration.

2. Mercury vapor tubes should be heated for a sufficient time to allow the vapor pressure to assume its normal value.   Greater heating time is required if the mercury has been scattered about the tube walls and electrodes than is otherwise needed.

3. Enough anode resistance must be used to limit the maximum instantaneous and average anode currents to their rated values.   Failure to observe this precaution results in cathode disintegration and over-heating of the anode.

4. Sufficient resistance must be used in the grid circuit to limit the maximum instantaneous and average grid currents to their rated values. Excessive grid current may cause damage because of heating of the grid or the grid-lead wires.   If the grid resistance is omitted and an arc forms to the grid, the current may rise to such a high value that the grid wires may melt or the heating of the grid lead shatter the seal and allow air to enter the tube.

9-24. Applications of Hot-cathode Arc-discharge Tubes.— Applications of hot-cathode arc tubes include light production, rectification, current and power control, oscillation (inversion), commutation, and amplification.   Some of these applications will be discussed in the following sections.

Hot-cathode Arc Tube as a Light Source.—The use of arcs as light sources is one of the early practical applications of electricity.   Arc-discharge tubes such as the mercury vapor and sodium vapor lamps are efficient sources of light, for they have the advantage of producing visible radiation in the manner of the glow tube and have a much smaller voltage drop.[1] Recently the fluorescent vapor lamp has taken its place among practical high-efficiency light sources.   Except during starting, the filamentary cathodes in this type of tube are heated by positive-ion bombardment.   The light emanates mainly from a fluorescent coating on the inner surface of the glass tube, a great variety of colors being obtained by the use of different fluorescent materials.   For details of the design and operation of arc lamps the reader will find it instructive to refer to the technical literature on the subject.[2]

Thyratrons may be used as a stroboscopic light source. Usually, however, the production of light of sufficient intensity

---

[1] DUSHMAN, S., *Elec. Eng.*, **53**, 1283 (1934).

[2] MAILEY, R. D., *Elec. Eng.*, **53**, 1446 (1934); BUTTOLPH, L. J., *Elec. Eng.*, **55**, 1174 (1936); McKENNA, A. B., *Elec. J.*, **33**, 439 (1936); HAWKINS, L. A., *Trans. Am. Illuminating Eng. Soc.*, **32**, 95 (1937).

for the observation of rapidly moving objects requires such high values of peak current that cold-cathode tubes stand up better. A second advantage of cold-cathode arc tubes for this purpose is the more rapid deionization, which makes possible a light flash of extremely short duration. Stroboscopes will, therefore, be discussed in a later section dealing with cold-cathode arc tubes.

9-25. Hot-cathode Arc Diode as a Rectifier.—Like its high-vacuum counterpart, the hot-cathode arc tube is essentially a rectifier. At voltages for which the tube is designed, current flows in only one direction. There are, however, two essential differences, which have been noted before. The tube voltage drop is only from 10 to 20 volts, and the voltage is almost independent of the current passed by the tube. Hence the arc tube acts like a switch of zero resistance in series with a counter-e.m.f. of from 10 to 20 volts. Figure 9-26 shows the construction of the type FG-166 phanatron.

Rectifier circuits using hot-cathode arc tubes are the same as those using high-vacuum tubes, but provision must be made to ensure that the tube is brought to rated temperature before the anode voltage is applied. The advantages of arc tubes over high-vacuum tubes in rectification will be discussed in Sec. 11-3. Circuits and filters for rectifiers will also be taken up in that chapter.

Fig. 9-26.—Cutaway view of the type FG-166 phanatron rectifier. (*Courtesy of General Electric Company.*)

9-26. Arc Tube as a Control Device. D-c Operation.—In most applications of thyratrons to the control of direct current and power it is essential not only to control the firing of the tube but also to stop the anode current at a subsequent time. Since the grid usually has little or no effect upon the anode current after the tube fires, it is necessary to find some other means of stopping the current. The simplest method is, of course, to open

the circuit, but this is usually not feasible, especially when the anode current is large. Furthermore, convenience and flexibility of control demand that the current should be interrupted by electrical, rather than mechanical, means. Four circuits, called the *parallel, series, relaxation,* and *counter-e.m.f.* circuits, have been devised for this purpose. Because of its many applications, the parallel circuit will be treated in detail.

9-27. Parallel Control.—The basic *parallel* circuit for the control of direct current is shown in Fig. 9-27.[1] Closing switch S_1 reduces the negative bias on the grid (or applies a positive bias) and causes the tube to fire. The grid no longer has control, and the switch S_1 may be opened without affecting the anode current. The potential drop across the load R_L charges the condenser C to a voltage equal to the supply voltage less the tube

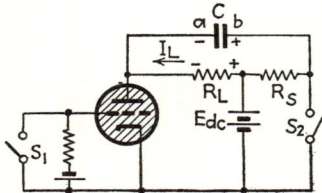

Fig. 9-27.—Basic parallel d-c thyratron control circuit.

drop. The polarity is such that terminal b of the condenser is positive relative to terminal a. If the switch S_2 is closed, the positive terminal b of the condenser is connected to the cathode, and, since the negative terminal is already connected to the anode, the anode is made negative with respect to the cathode. The arc current stops, and the current through the load is diverted to the charging of the condenser. As the condenser charges, the anode voltage rises. If the grid is negative and the tube deionizes so rapidly that the anode voltage never becomes equal to the tube reignition voltage (see Sec. 9-20), then the arc stays out and the grid regains control. This is usually expressed somewhat less precisely by stating that the grid regains control if the deionization time is shorter than the time required for the anode voltage to reach the value corresponding to the normal tube drop. The rate of rise of anode voltage decreases with increase of condenser capacitance and of load resistance. The rapidity of deionization, on the other hand, decreases with increase of load current. The capacitance necessary to ensure that the grid shall regain control, therefore, increases with load current. The purpose of the resistance R_s is to prevent a short circuit of the battery when S_2 is closed.

[1] Hull, A. W., *Gen. Elec. Rev.*, **32**, 390 (1929).

A much more useful circuit is obtained by replacing S_2 in Fig. 9-27 by a second thyratron, as shown in Fig. 9-28.[1] When either tube is conducting, the condenser charges to such polarity that the terminal connected to the anode of that tube is negative with respect to the other terminal. Firing of the other tube by a positive grid impulse applies a negative voltage, equal to the supply voltage less twice the tube voltage drop, to the anode of the first tube, causing it to be extinguished. Similar action is obtained if the resistors are adjacent to the cathodes and the condenser is connected between the cathodes, as in Fig. 9-29. The firing impulses may be applied to the grids directly, as in Fig. 9-28, through resistance-capacitance networks, as in Fig. 9-29, or through one or two transformers, as in Fig. 9-30.

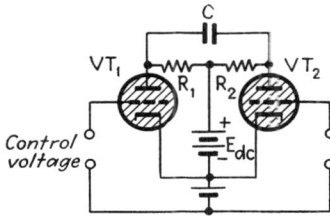

Fig. 9-28.—Two-tube parallel d-c control circuit.

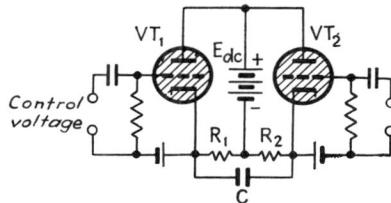

Fig. 9-29.—Alternative form of two-tube parallel d-c control circuit.

From the theory of operation of the circuits of Figs. 9-28 and 9-29 it follows that it is necessary to have rapid rise of arc reignition voltage in order to ensure that one tube extinguishes when the other fires. For this reason tubes with short rated deionization time should be used in these circuits and their derivatives. This is especially important when the circuits are used as the basis of inverters or other types of oscillators. The FG-67 and FG-43 thyratrons and other types having equal or shorter deionizing time are suitable for this kind of service.

The circuits of Figs. 9-28 and 9-29 are the basis of many interesting and useful circuits. One of these is the parallel type of thyratron inverter.

9-28. Thyratron Inverters.—The use of direct current in place of alternating current in the transmission of power has a number of advantages, the most obvious of which is that direct current involves only voltage and polarity, whereas alternating

[1] Hull, A. W., *Gen. Elec. Rev.*, **32**, 399 (1929).

current involves voltage, frequency, phase, phase sequence, and power factor. From an economic point of view the advantage of d-c transmission arises from the higher voltage which can be used without danger of corona. The maximum r-m-s alternating voltage that can be transmitted is less than the maximum direct voltage because the crest voltage determines the magnitude of corona effects. Other advantages of d-c transmission are elimination of dielectric losses and line reactance and reduction of insulation stresses at a given effective voltage. Disadvantages of d-c transmission are the greater likelihood of insulator flashover and resultant power arc, and the greater difficulty of interrupting an arc when it does occur. Because of the difficulty of generating high direct voltage and the impossibility of transforming direct voltages, d-c power transmission necessitates the use of rectifiers at the transmitting end of the line and of equipment for changing back to alternating current of suitable wave form at the receiving end.[1] An arc-tube oscillator capable of changing appreciable d-c power into a-c power at commercial frequencies is called an *inverter*. Four types of single-phase inverters have been developed. These are based upon the parallel, series, relaxation, and counter-e.m.f. control circuits.

Another field of application of inverters may be developed in the speed control of synchronous and induction motors. Since the frequency of the a-c output of the inverter is easily controlled by the grid excitation, speed control of motors connected to the inverter may thus be obtained.

9-29. The Parallel Inverter.—The parallel type of inverter is essentially the parallel d-c control circuit of Fig. 9-28, with the anode resistors replaced by a center-tapped transformer.[2] In the simplest form of parallel inverter the grids are excited from an external source of voltage of desired frequency through a center-tapped grid transformer, as in Fig. 9-30. Each tube conducts during one-half of the cycle of grid excitation voltage. Commutation is obtained by use of the commutating condenser C, as explained in Sec. 9-27. The output voltage wave form is depend-

[1] WILLIS, C. H., BEDFORD, B. D., and ELDER, F. R., *Elec. Eng.*, **54**, 102 (1935); BEDFORD, B. D., ELDER, F. R., and WILLIS, C. H., *Gen. Elec. Rev.*, **39**, 220 (1936); ALEXANDERSON, E. F. W., *Electronics*, June, 1936, p. 25.

[2] PRINCE, D. C., *Gen. Elec. Rev.*, **31**, 347 (1928); HULL, *loc. cit.*

ent upon the magnitude of the load current, the power factor of the load, the leakage inductance of the transformer, and the inductance in series with the d-c supply, and upon the capacitance of the condenser. If the coupling of the transformer is close, as is usually true, the wave form of the output voltage is approxi-

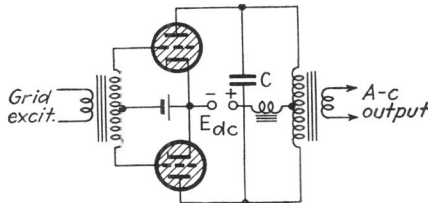

Fig. 9-30.—Circuit of separately excited parallel inverter.

mately that of the condenser voltage.   Figure 9-31 shows typical waves of output voltage.[1] Waves of the form of (*a*) or (*b*) are likely to be obtained when the load is nonreactive; waves of the form of (*c*) are obtained when the ratio of the total effective inductance to the total effective resistance of the circuit, including the load, is high. The dotted lines indicate instants at which the tubes fire.

An analysis of commutation in the parallel inverter indicates that the size of the condenser must be carefully determined. The type and magnitude of the load, as well as the constants of the inverter circuit itself, must be taken into consideration.

The grids of a parallel inverter may be excited from the output or from the anode circuit of one of the tubes. When this is done, it is essential that the

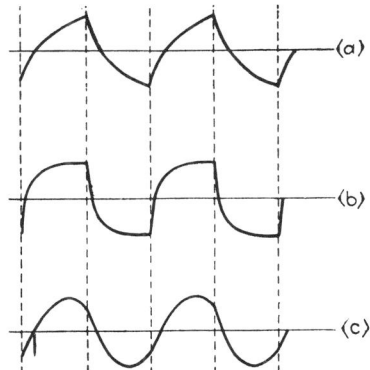

Fig. 9-31.—Typical parallel-inverter voltage wave forms: (*a*) light nonreactive load; (*b*) heavy nonreactive load; (*c*) inductive load.

exciting voltage should have the proper phase relation to the output voltage.   The phase of the grid voltage may be con-

[1] TOMPKINS, F. N., *Trans. Am. Inst. Elec. Eng.*, **51**, 707 (1932); SCHILLING, W., *Arch. Elektrotech.*, **27**, 22 (1933); RUNGE, I., and BECKENBACH, H., *Z. tech. Physik* **14**, 377 (1933); WAGNER, C. F., *Elec. Eng.*, **54**, 1227 (1935); **55**, 970 (1936).

trolled by means of combinations of capacitance and resistance. Figure 9-32 shows one form of self-excited circuit.[1] The frequency is controlled by the constants of the grid and anode circuits. The frequency varies with d-c line voltage and with load current and power factor. To prevent excessive

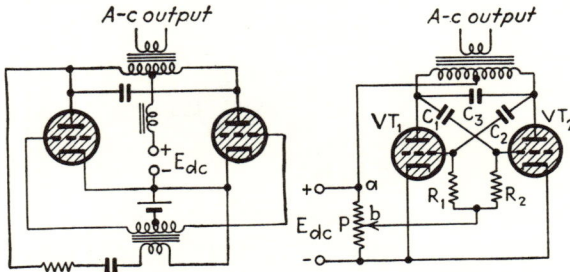

FIG. 9-32.

FIG. 9-33.

FIGS. 9-32 and 9-33.—Self-excited parallel inverters.

frequency variation and to ensure that incorrect phase relation between grid and output voltages will not cause the operation to become unstable and both tubes to fire simultaneously, considerable care is necessary in the design of the grid circuit. A type of self-excited parallel inverter in which excitation involves grid rectification is shown in Fig. 9-33.[2]

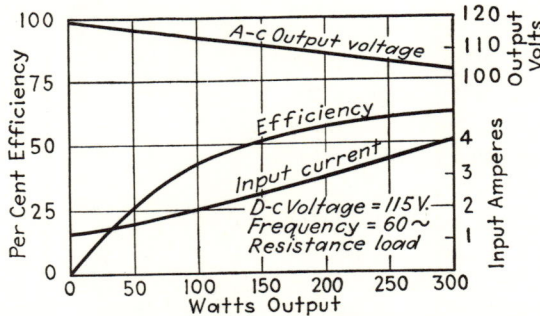

FIG. 9-34.—Performance curves for a parallel inverter.

Figure 9-34 shows curves of output voltage and efficiency for a parallel inverter operating from a 115-volt d-c supply.[3]

[1] BAKER, W. R. G., FITZGERALD, A. S., and WHITNEY, C. F., *Electronics*, April, 1931, p. 581.

[2] STANSBURY, C. C., *Elec. Eng.*, **52**, 190 (1933).

[3] BAKER, W. R. G., and CORNELL, J. I., *Electronics*, October, 1931, p. 152.

The low efficiency is caused by the comparatively small direct supply voltage and the consequent high ratio of the tube drop to the supply voltage. Both the efficiency and the output are increased by raising the direct voltage.

9-30. The Thyratron as a Saw-tooth-wave Generator.— Thyratron inverters are designed primarily for the generation of large amounts of a-c power in applications in which sinusoidal wave form is desirable. Thyratrons are used also in the production of low-power alternating voltages of saw-tooth and rectangular wave form. A rectangular voltage wave may be obtained across the load resistors in the circuit of Fig. 9-28 when the grids are excited with alternating voltage of the desired frequency, as in the parallel inverter of Fig. 9-30.

As generators of saw-tooth voltage, thyratrons are used in a manner similar to that of glow tubes, but have a number of advantages. Dependence of firing voltage upon grid voltage makes possible simple control of amplitude. Because of the amplifying property of the grid, smaller voltage is required to synchronize the oscillator to a control frequency, and there is less likelihood of distortion of the voltage wave than when the control voltage is introduced in series with a glow tube. The lower tube drop allows the use of smaller supply voltage and, in conjunction with the use of negative grid bias to obtain high firing voltage, results in large amplitude of oscillation. The high instantaneous current that the tube will pass results in shorter discharge time than with glow tubes and makes possible the increase of amplitude of oscillation by the use of inductance in series with the condenser. Shorter deionizing time allows oscillation to take place at much higher frequency. Finally, the presence of an ample supply of electrons at the cathode makes the firing potential independent of cathode illumination and of cosmic radiation and other random ionizing agents. The frequency is, therefore, much more constant than with glow tubes. The dependence of firing voltage of mercury vapor tubes upon tube temperature makes it advisable to use gas-filled tubes when frequency stability is important.

The circuit of Fig. 9-35 oscillates when the grid voltage is insufficiently negative (or too positive) to prevent the tube from firing at the maximum voltage to which the condenser charges. The condenser charges exponentially, and the condenser voltage is of the form shown in Fig. 9-36. Because of the action of the inductance L, the condenser discharge is nearly sinusoidal and the condenser polarity reverses during discharge.[1] The total change in condenser voltage is approximately equal to twice the firing voltage V_f minus the tube drop E_a. The inductance should be large enough to limit the discharge current to the rated

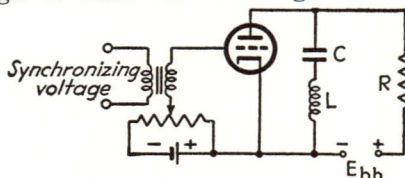

FIG. 9-35.—Basic circuit of the thyratron relaxation oscillator.

maximum instantaneous anode current. The frequency of oscillation is approximately

$$f = \frac{1}{R_L C_1 \log_\epsilon \dfrac{E_{bb} + V_f - E_a}{E_{bb} - V_f}} \tag{9-3}$$

The circuit also oscillates when L is replaced by a resistance, the behavior being similar to that of the glow-tube oscillator of Fig. 9-6. The change in condenser voltage is equal to the difference between the ignition and extinction voltages,[2] and the frequency of oscillation is

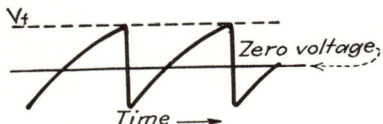

FIG. 9-36.—Wave form of the condenser voltage of the circuit of Fig. 9-35.

$$f = \frac{1}{RC \log_\epsilon \dfrac{E_{bb} - E_a}{E_{bb} - V_f}} \tag{9-4}$$

If the resistance R is replaced by a voltage pentode operated on the flat portion of the plate characteristic, the charging current is nearly constant, and the condenser charges practically linearly, as in the glow-tube oscillator of Fig. 9-9. A type 885 or 884 argon-filled tube is commonly used in this circuit. The extinction voltage of this tube is only about 15 volts, and the firing voltage may be as high as 300 volts (with -30 volts on the grid). Because of the large difference between V_f and E_a, the amplitude of the condenser voltage is much greater than in the glow-tube

[1] Note that L may be merely the inductance of leads between the condenser and the tube.

[2] The extinction voltage is equal to the tube drop E_a.

oscillator. When the inductance L is used, the condenser voltage may vary between the maximum limits of -300 and $+300$ volts. The frequency of oscillation is approximately

$$f = \frac{I}{(2V_f - E_a)C} \tag{9-5}$$

where I is the constant charging current, V_f is the firing voltage, E_a is the tube drop, and C is the total capacitance, including that of the tube and wires. In the derivation of Eq. (9-5), it is assumed that the inductance L has negligible resistance and that the condenser discharge is instantaneous. When L is replaced by a current-limiting resistance, the frequency is given approximately by Eq. (9-2), in which V_e equals E_a.

Since V_f and E_a are independent of frequency in arc tubes, Eqs. (9-2) and (9-3) to (9-5) may be used in predetermining the frequency of oscillation or in designing an oscillator for a desired frequency range. As in glow-tube oscillators, very low frequency of oscillation may be attained by the use of large condensers. Because of the greater difference between ignition and extinction voltages, the condenser capacitance required for a given frequency is lower in the arc-tube oscillator than in the glow-tube oscillator. Frequencies higher than $20,000 \sim$ may be attained with the arc-tube oscillator, the upper limit of frequency resulting partly from failure of the tube to extinguish when the period of oscillation approaches the deionization time.

In order to protect the tube against damage as the result of excessive peak current, resistance or inductance must be used in series with the tube. For a maximum condenser voltage of 300 volts, the type 884 tube requires a current-limiting resistance of $1000\ \Omega$, or an inductance equal in henrys to the condenser capacitance in microfarads.[1]

A typical circuit using a pentode to control the charging current is shown in Fig. 9-37. P_1 adjusts the charging current by varying the control-grid voltage of the pentode and thus controls

---

[1] When a condenser of capacitance C, initially charged to a voltage E_0, is discharged through an inductance L, and the ratio of inductance to resistance is high, the peak discharge current is approximately equal to $E_0\sqrt{C/L}$. Thus, if the inductance in henrys is equal to the capacitance in microfarads, the peak current is approximately $E_0/1000$ amp, which is the same as would be obtained if the condenser were discharged through a $1000\text{-}\Omega$ resistance.

the frequency. P_2 adjusts the 884 bias and thus the ignition voltage. Since the ignition voltage affects both the amplitude and the frequency of oscillation, P_2 changes the amplitude and frequency simultaneously. P_3 varies the amplitude of the output voltage. The principal application of this and similar circuits is in providing a linear time axis for cathode-ray oscillographs (see Sec. 12-5).

9-31. A-c Operation of Thyratrons. Phase Control.—When a thyratron is operated on alternating voltage, the tube extinguishes near the end of the positive half cycle, and the grid regains control without the use of special circuits for interrupting the anode current. By controlling the time in the cycle at which the

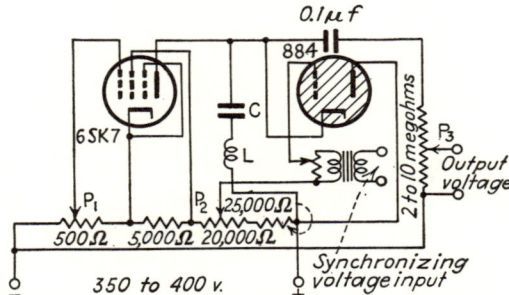

Fig. 9-37.—Thyratron relaxation oscillator in which the condenser charging current is controlled by a pentode.

tube fires, the grid can vary the average anode current. This type of control may be attained by varying the phase of the grid voltage with respect to the anode voltage.[1] The principle of operation can be explained by the aid of the diagrams of Fig. 9-38, which apply to resistance load. The solid curve v_p represents the sinusoidal applied voltage in the anode circuit, which is equal to the instantaneous anode voltage e_p, up to the time of firing. The other solid curve v_g represents the instantaneous applied voltage in the grid circuit. Under the assumption that no grid current flows previous to firing, the grid voltage e_g is equal to v_g up to the instant of firing. The dotted curve indicates the critical grid voltage at which the tube would fire at the instantaneous anode voltage given by the curve of v_p. The critical–grid-voltage curve is derived from the grid-control characteristic.

[1] TOULON, P., U. S. Patent 1654949.

The tube fires at the instant in the cycle when the **grid voltage** becomes less negative (or more positive) than the critical grid voltage.   The anode voltage then becomes equal to the normal tube drop, and, with resistance load, the anode current rises abruptly to a value equal to the applied anode voltage less the

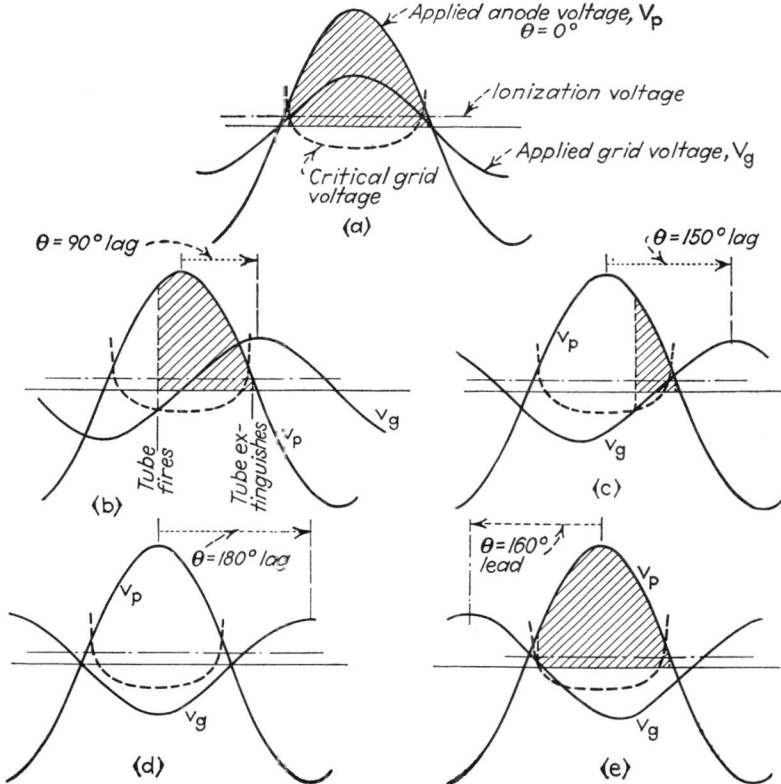

FIG. 9-38.—Variation of the firing period of a thyratron by change of phase angle between grid voltage and anode voltage.

tube drop, divided by the load resistance.   Current continues to flow until the anode supply voltage falls below the ionization potential toward the end of the positive half cycle.   The wave of tube current during the conducting portion of the cycle is of nearly the same shape as the wave of applied anode voltage.   To avoid needless complication of the diagrams, the current waves are not shown, but the portion of the cycle during which current

flows is indicated by shading.   The instant in the cycle at which
the tube fires is that at which the intersection of the applied–
grid-voltage curve crosses the curve of critical grid voltage from
below.[1]   Diagrams *a*, *b*, *c*, and *d* correspond respectively to 0-,
90-, 150-, and 180-deg lag of grid voltage relative to anode voltage.   Inspection of these diagrams shows that the instant of
firing is retarded by increase of angle of lag θ and that the portion
of the cycle during which current flows is decreased, becoming
zero when θ is slightly less than 180 deg.   The average anode
current therefore decreases progressively with increase of angle
of lag.

The reader can readily show by means of similar diagrams that
if the grid excitation voltage leads the anode excitation voltage
by any angle up to about 170 deg, the tube fires as soon as the
anode voltage exceeds the ionization potential, near the beginning
of the cycle.   Since the grid has no control after the tube fires,
current flows during practically the entire positive half cycle.
Diagram *e* corresponds to a 160-deg angle of lead.   When the
angle θ approaches 180-deg lead, however, a value is reached at
which the grid voltage is more negative (or less positive) than the
critical value throughout the positive half cycle.   For values of θ
greater than this, no current flows.   Thus a small change of θ
in the vicinity of 170-deg lead causes an abrupt change of anode
current from full average value to zero.   This will be termed
on-off control, in contrast to the *gradual* or *progressive* control
obtained when the grid voltage lags the anode voltage.

When the load contains inductance, the anode current wave
differs in shape from that of the applied anode voltage.   The
current rises gradually after firing and continues to flow after the
anode supply voltage falls below the ionization potential,
the shape of the wave depending upon the ratio of inductance
to resistance in the load.

Figure 9-39 shows the manner in which the average anode
current varies through a resistance load as the phase angle θ is
varied from 180-deg lag to 180-deg lead.   This diagram is
derived under the assumption that the amplitude of the applied
grid voltage greatly exceeds the maximum critical grid voltage.

[1] Since the grid has no control after the tube fires, nothing happens at an
instant in the cycle when the wave of applied grid voltage crosses the wave
of critical grid voltage from above.

The fairly wide range of phase angle in the vicinity of 180 deg throughout which the anode current is zero results from failure of the tube to conduct at anode voltages lower than the ionization potential. Because of reduction of the fraction of the cycle during which the anode voltage is less than the ionization potential, the zero-current range of the control characteristic of Fig. 9-39 decreases with increase of anode voltage amplitude.

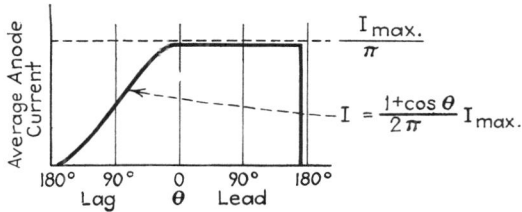

Fig. 9-39.—Theoretical curve of average anode current of a thyratron as a function of the phase angle θ of the grid voltage relative to the anode voltage.

A similar type of control is effected by keeping the phase of the grid voltage constant and varying the amplitude. If v_g lags v_p by slightly less than 180 deg, as shown in Fig. 9-40, the variation of anode current is gradual. If the angle of lag is 180 deg, on-off control is obtained. Phase control can also be used with tubes controlled by external grids[1] or magnetic fields[2] or with the ignitron (see Sec. 9-40).

The anode current can be varied gradually over a smaller range when alternating voltage is used in the anode circuit and direct voltage in the grid circuit. If the grid voltage is insufficiently negative (or too positive) to prevent the tube from firing at the

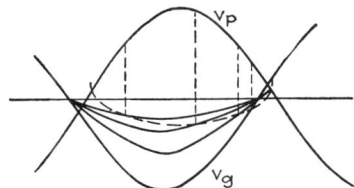

Fig. 9-40.—Wave diagram showing the variation of firing period by change of amplitude of grid voltage.

beginning of the cycle, then anode current flows during nearly the whole positive half cycle. Increase of negative grid voltage (or decrease of positive voltage, in the case of a positive-grid tube) makes the tube fire later in the cycle. When the grid voltage is only slightly less than that required to prevent firing at the crest of the applied anode voltage, the tube conducts for approximately a quarter of the cycle. Further increase of

[1] See footnote 2, p. 260.
[2] See footnote 3, p. 260.

negative grid voltage prevents the tube from firing at all. The current can be decreased continuously from a value corresponding to half-wave rectification to half this value. A serious disadvantage of this type of circuit is that its behavior is influenced by small changes of anode supply voltage. This type of control is not applicable to external grid tubes but can be used with magnetic control.

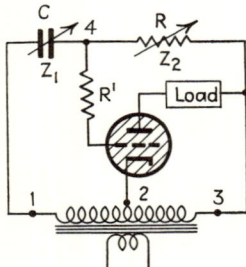

FIG. 9-41.—Simple type of practical phase-control circuit.

9-32. Phase-control Circuits.—Any convenient method can be used to shift the phase of the grid voltage. A simple method is the use of a phase shifter (a transformer having a single-phase secondary winding that can be turned through 360 electrical degrees within a polyphase winding arranged to produce a rotating field) as in Fig. 9-50a. A series combination of resistance and reactance is the basis of a number of practical phase-control circuits, of which Fig. 9-41 is a typical example. The phase of the grid voltage is varied by changing R or C. The function of R' in series with the grid is to limit the grid current to a safe value after the tube fires. The required value depends upon the minimum values of the two phase-shifting impedances. It may be omitted if both impedances are at all times large enough to limit the grid current to the maximum average value.

With tubes in which appreciable grid current flows previous to firing, the voltage drop through this resistor may affect the phase control adversely. For this reason, this resistor should in general not be much larger than necessary to limit the grid current after firing. The resistor has little effect, how-

FIG. 9-42.—Vector diagram fo rthe circuit of Fig. 9-41 previous to firing.

ever, in circuits using shield-grid thyratrons, which pass negligible grid current previous to firing.

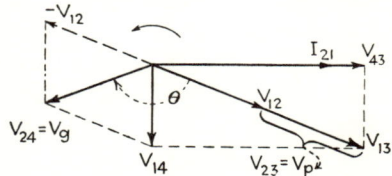

The vector diagram representing the voltages of the circuit of Fig. 9-41 up to the time that the tube fires is shown in Fig. 9-42. The current I_{21} is used as reference, and the grid current is assumed to be negligible previous to firing. The voltage V_{43}

across the resistance is in phase with the current, whereas the voltage V_{14} across the condenser lags the current by 90 deg. The secondary voltage V_{13} is the vector sum of V_{14} and V_{43}. The grid voltage V_g is equal to V_{24}, which is the vector sum of V_{14} and V_{21}, or the vector difference of V_{14} and V_{12}. The impressed anode voltage V_p is equal to V_{23}.

A vector diagram that is more susceptible to analysis may be derived from that of Fig. 9-42 by application of the theorem that the significance of a vector diagram is unchanged by displacing the vectors without altering their magnitudes or the angles between them.[1] The resulting diagram for the special case in which the secondary is center-tapped is that of Fig. 9-43. Since V_{14} and

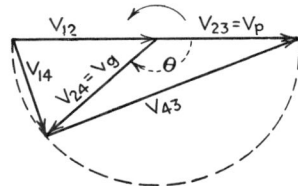

FIG. 9-43.—Circle vector diagram equivalent to the vector diagram of Fig. 9-42.

V'_{43} are perpendicular and their sum is always equal to the secondary voltage V_{13}, which is assumed to be constant, it follows from a theorem of plane geometry that their intersection must lie on the circumference of a circle, the diameter of which is V_{13}. It can be readily seen from this diagram that decreasing R, or increasing the capacitive reactance by decreasing C, decreases θ, the angle of lag of the impressed grid voltage relative to the impressed anode voltage, and thus produces a gradual increase of average anode current.

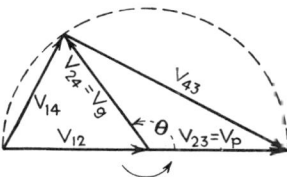

FIG. 9-44.—Circle vector diagram for the circuit obtained by interchanging C and R in the circuit of Fig. 9-41.

When the resistance and condenser are interchanged, the vector diagram becomes that of Fig. 9-44.[2] The angle θ is now measured in the opposite direction, showing that the grid voltage leads the anode voltage by the angle θ. If θ is made to approach 180 deg by the use of very small resistance or capacitance, then the current is zero, as shown by Fig. 9-39. A slight increase in either R or C retards the phase of the grid voltage and causes

[1] WEINBACH, M. P., "Alternating Current Circuits," p. 98, The Macmillan Company, New York, 1933.

[2] Note that transposing C and R is equivalent to changing the connection of the anode circuit from terminal 3 to terminal 1 of the transformer.

the average current to increase suddenly to full value.   This circuit evidently gives on-off control.

An inductance can be used in place of the condenser in the circuit of Fig. 9-41.   Since it is impossible, however, to construct an inductance coil that does not have appreciable resistance, the voltage across the inductance will not be 90 deg out of

TABLE 9-II

z_2 (adjacent to load)	z_1	Manner of varying resistance	Manner of varying reactance	Manner in which current increases
Resistance........	Capacitance	Decrease	Increase	Gradually
Capacitance......	Resistance	Increase	Decrease	Suddenly
Resistance........	Inductance	Decrease	Increase	Suddenly
Inductance........	Resistance	Increase	Decrease	Gradually

phase with the current, and the vectors representing the voltages across the inductance and the resistance will not be perpendicular.   The general behavior can, however, be determined from a diagram in which the vectors are assumed to be perpendicular. The reader will find it instructive to construct these diagrams for the circuit obtained by replacing C in Fig. 9-41 by an induct-

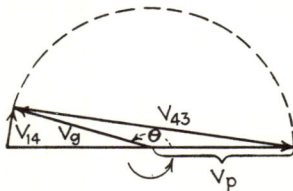

Fig.   9-45.—Circle vector diagram for a phase-control circuit in which increase of resistance causes an abrupt increase of average anode current.

ance and for the circuit in which the inductance and resistance are transposed.   Table 9-II, is convenient in determining the circuit to be used for a particular application.   [In Table 9-II, z_2 refers to the impedance adjacent to the load, and z_1 to the impedance between the grid and the side of the transformer to which the load is not connected (see Fig. 9-41).]

It is a simple matter to determine, without reference to this table, the correct circuit to produce a desired result.   Suppose, for instance, that it is desired to increase the current suddenly by an increase of resistance.   Figure 9-39 shows that sudden increase of average current requires that the angle of lead of the grid voltage relative to the anode voltage should be reduced by a small amount from a value somewhat less than 180 deg.

The grid voltage must lie in the second quadrant of the circle vector diagram, and so the diagram must be that of Fig. 9-45.   If increase of resistance is to de-
crease the lead of V_g, V_{14} must be the voltage across the resistance, and V_{43}, which lags V_{14} by 90 deg, must be the voltage across a con-denser.   Thus the impedance ad-jacent to the load must be a capacitive reactance, and the other must be the resistance.

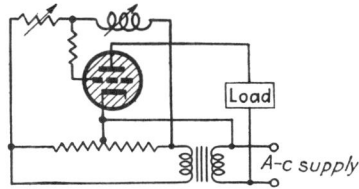

FIG. 9-46.—Variant of the circuit of Fig. 9-41 in which the load current is taken directly from the line.

When the line voltage is high enough to give the required load current, some reduction in cost may be effected by drawing the load current directly from the line.   The center-tapped trans-former may then be replaced by an untapped transformer shunted by a center-tapped resistance as in Fig. 9-46.   This transformer need have only sufficient current capacity to carry the voltage-divider current and the grid cur-

FIG. 9-48.—Form of phase-control circuit in which the load current is taken directly from the line.

rent after firing.   To ensure the proper phase relations of the voltages, the resistance of the voltage divider should be small in comparison with the phase-shifting im-pedances.   A somewhat similar circuit is shown in Fig. 9-47.   It should be noted that the circuits of Figs. 9-41, 9-46, and 9-47 are suitable only for use with loads that will operate on direct or pulsating current.

Another modification of the circuit of Fig. 9-41 that is particularly useful when the load current or voltage exceeds the rated value for the tube is shown in Fig. 9-48.[1]   When the phase of the grid voltage is adjusted so that the tube does not conduct, the current through the load cannot exceed the normal

FIG. 9-48.—Phase-control circuit useful when the current or voltage of the load exceeds the rated value for the tube.

[1] CRAIG, P. H., *Electronics*, March, 1933, p. 70; **10,** 26 (1937).   KNOWLES, D. D., LOWRY, E. F., and GESSFORD, R. K., *Electronics*, November, 1936, p. 27.

exciting current of the transformer. As the average tube current is increased, the primary current also increases, both because of the alternating component of secondary current and because of the saturating effect of the direct component of secondary current. If a step-up transformer is used, the load current exceeds the tube

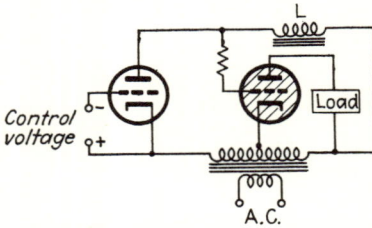

Fig. 9-49.—Phase-control circuit in which the use of a vacuum tube as resistance makes control by direct voltage possible.

current. In this manner a tube can be made to control load current many times as great as the rated maximum average anode current. The turn ratio, and hence the load current, is limited because the secondary voltage must not exceed the rated maximum peak inverse or forward voltages. If a step-down transformer is used, on the other hand, the tube can be used with a supply voltage greatly in excess of the rated maximum peak voltage, the turn ratio and voltage being limited by the allowable average tube current. This circuit is suitable only for loads that operate on alternating current.

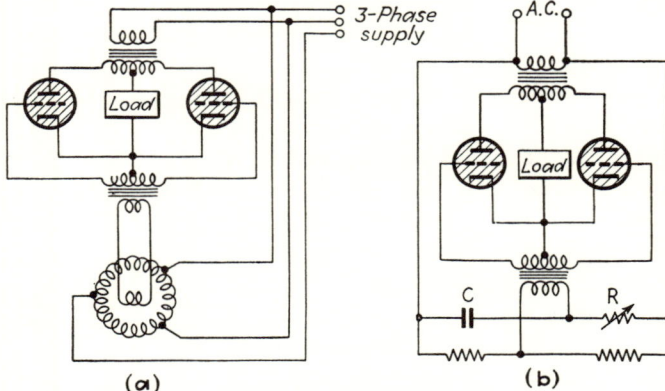

Fig. 9-50.—Full-wave phase control circuits with (a) phase shifter and (b) phase-shifting network.

A high-vacuum amplifier tube may be used in place of the resistance in phase-control circuits. By this means a very small direct voltage in the grid circuit of the high-vacuum tube can control large amounts of current and power. Figure 9-49 shows one method of connecting the vacuum tube.

The load current can be doubled by the use of two thyratrons in a full-wave circuit such as that of Fig. 9-50a.[1] This circuit also illustrates the use of a phase shifter, which may be replaced by a combination of resistance and reactance as in Fig. 9-50b.[1]

The field of application of most phase-control circuits in which a very high resistance may be used as the controlling element can be greatly extended by replacing the resistance by a phototube (see Sec. 10-11).

9-32A. Use of Saturable Reactor in Phase-control Circuits.— Sometimes it is necessary to apply phase control to loads that require alternating current. Although this can be accomplished by means of the circuits of Figs. 9-48 and 9-50, the fact that the anode current in general consists of periodic pulses lasting only a portion of the cycle causes the wave form of the load current to be poor even in full-wave circuits. This difficulty can be avoided by using the thyratron current to saturate the core of a reactor, the reactance of which controls the load current. This

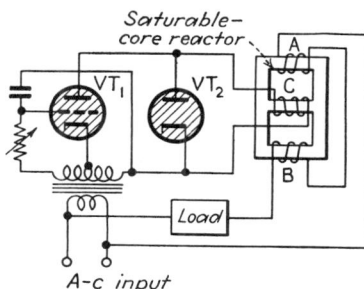

Fig. 9-51.—Phase-control circuit using saturable reactor.

method has the additional advantage of making possible the control of larger load currents at higher voltages.

A typical control circuit incorporating a saturable reactor is shown in Fig. 9-51. The load current is limited by the reactance of the coils A and B. These coils are of equal dimensions and are connected so that the fluxes that they produce add in the outer arms of the core but cancel in the center arm, which holds the winding C. For this reason no alternating voltage is induced in coil C. The anode current of the thyratron VT_1 flows through coil C, producing a d-c flux which divides equally between the outer arms of the core and thus reduces the reactance of A and B. When the average anode current is zero, the load current cannot exceed the exciting current of the reactor. If the maximum average anode current is sufficient to saturate the core, the resulting reactance is so small as to have very little effect upon the

---

[1] Baker, W. R. G., Fitzgerald, A. S., and Whitney, C. F., *Electronics*, January, 1931, p. 467.

load current.   The function of the rectifier VT_2 is to provide a path for the direct current in coil C during the portion of the cycle when VT_1 does not conduct.[1]   If VT_2 were omitted, the voltage induced in coil C would tend to maintain current flow in VT_1 during the whole cycle and thus prevent the variation of saturating current by phase control of VT_1.

9-33. Tubes for Phase-control Circuits.—In most phase-control circuits the grid-circuit resistance or impedance is high. For this reason these circuits function best with low grid-current tubes, preferably of the shield-grid type.

Applications of A-c–operated Control Circuits.—Phase-control circuits are used for the control of illumination, for the control and stabilization of alternating load current and voltage, for the control and stabilization of the voltage and frequency of alternators, for temperature control and stabilization, for the control of rectifier output voltage, and for many other purposes. In the control of current, the advantage of phase-control thyratron circuits over variable resistance lies in the great reduction of power loss and heat generation and in the possibility of using small variable condensers or low-current variable resistances as the control units.   As a switch the a-c–operated thyratron has found its greatest application in the control of spot welders. For a comprehensive treatment of commercial and laboratory applications of thyratrons the reader should refer to other texts.[2]

9-34. Welding Control.[3]—In electric welding it has been found to be advantageous to use a series of equally spaced spot welds, rather than a continuous weld.   In order to accomplish this, the welder must be switched on and off periodically. Because of the heavy currents, mechanical switches are unsatisfactory.   The value of the thyratron in this service arises from the ability of the grid to control large currents without in itself requiring large current, from the consistency with which the

[1] Babat, G., *Proc. I.R.E.*, **22**, 314 (1934).

[2] Henney, K., "Electron Tubes in Industry," 2d ed., McGraw-Hill Book Company, Inc., New York, 1937; Gulliksen, F. H., and Vedder, E. H., "Industrial Electronics," John Wiley & Sons, Inc., New York, 1935.

[3] Griffith, R. C., *Gen. Elec. Rev.*, **33**, 511 (1930); Martin, S., Jr., *Welding*, **3**, 293, 361 (1932); Lord, H. W., and Livingston, O. W., *Electronics*, July, 1933, p. 186; Chambers, D. E., *Elec. Eng.*, **54**, 82 (1935); Palmer, H. L., *Gen. Elec. Rev.*, **40**, 229, 321 (1937).   See also footnote 2, p. 302.

grid can control the welding time, and from the absence of large current transients when tube control is used.

Figure 9-52 shows one form of thyratron switching circuit for welding control.[1]   The operation is in some respects similar to that of the circuit of Fig. 9-48.   The thyratron grids are biased negatively by the auxiliary rectifier tubes, so that no anode current flows when the control switch is open.   The current through the welding transformer then cannot exceed the exciting current of the series transformer.   When the switch is closed, there is applied to the thyratron grids an alternating voltage

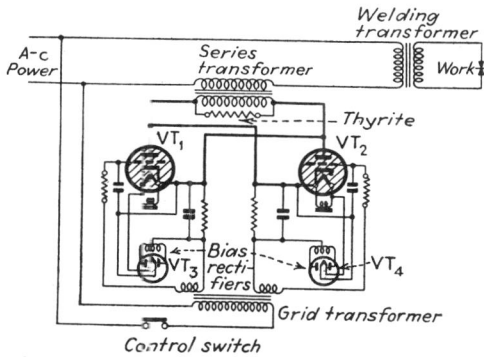

Fig. 9-52.—Thyratron welding control circuit.

that is in phase with the anode voltage and thus causes the flow of full average anode current.   When the thyratrons conduct, the effective primary impedance of the series transformer is reduced to a very low value, and practically full line voltage is applied to the primary of the welding transformer. The thyrite resistor across the primary of the series transformer prevents dangerous surges of voltage.   The control switch of the circuit of Fig. 9-52 is usually replaced by an intermediate control circuit, which is in turn operated by the voltage from a thyratron relaxation oscillator of the type discussed in Sec. 9-30.   Adjustment of the circuit constants of this oscillator and of the bias applied to the intermediate control circuit makes it possible to vary the frequency of the welding cycle and the portion of the cycle during which welding current flows.   Because the oscillator is controlled by 60-cycle synchronizing voltage (see Fig. 9-35), the timing is very accurate.

[1] CHAMBERS, *loc. cit.;* PALMER, *loc. cit.*

In another type of circuit the welding time is limited to half a cycle or less.[1] The portion of the cycle during which current flows is controlled by the use of phase control.

9-35. Mercury Pool Arc-discharge Tubes.—Mercury pool arc-discharge tubes may, in general, be used in the circuits and

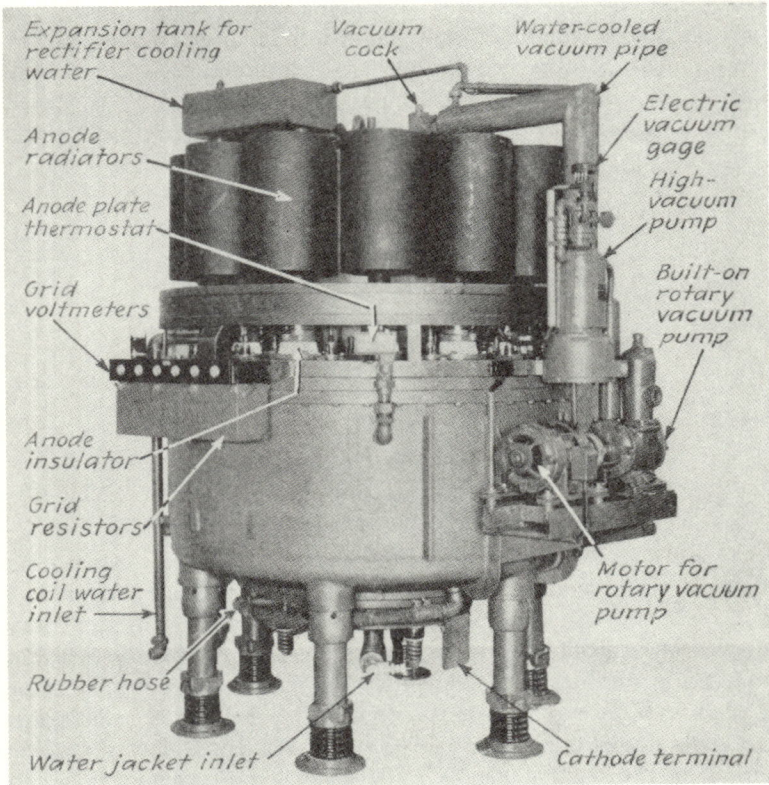

FIG. 9-53.—Typical grid-controlled multi-anode tank rectifier. This rectifier is approximately 9 ft high and can handle 2750 kw at 625 volts. (*Courtesy Allis-Chalmers Manufacturing Company.*)

applications treated under hot-cathode arc tubes. Mercury pool tubes are much more rugged than hot-cathode arc tubes, and are designed for types of service requiring high currents, measured in tens and hundreds or even, instantaneously, thousands of amperes. The fact that the cathode need not be heated results

[1] GRIFFITH, *loc. cit.;* LORD and LIVINGSTON, *loc. cit.*

in three other advantages over the thyratron: (1) the over-all efficiency is higher, (2) the tube is instantly available for operation, and (3) freedom from danger of cathode deactivation or destruction gives increased reliability in industrial service.

As rectifiers, mercury pool tubes have been used for many years, first in glass envelopes, later in metal tanks continuously evacuated, and finally, in small sizes, in sealed metal envelopes.

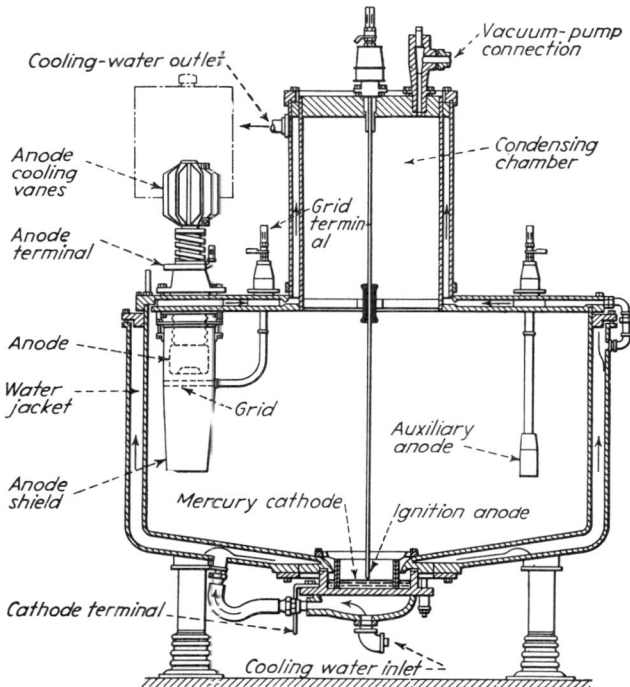

Fig. 9-54.—Cross section through typical Allis-Chalmers mercury-arc power rectifier of the multianode type. Main anode, at left, is shown air-cooled. The broken line indicates optional radiator for water-cooling.

For a detailed discussion of constructional and operational features of these rectifier tubes the reader should refer to books on the subject of commercial power rectification.[1]

[1] Prince, D. C., and Vogdes, F. B., "Principles of Mercury Arc Rectifiers and Their Circuits," McGraw-Hill Book Company, Inc., New York, 1927; Marti, O. K., and Winograd, H., "Mercury Arc Rectifiers—Theory and Practice," McGraw-Hill Book Company, Inc., New York, 1930; Jolley, L. B. W., "Alternating Current Rectification," John Wiley & Sons, Inc., New York, 1931. See also bibliography at the end of Chap. 11.

Grid-controlled mercury pool rectifiers provided with keep-alive anodes are used as power rectifiers, phase control affording a simple method of varying or regulating the output voltage. (See Sec. 11-3.) The grids, which surround the anodes, also serve to prevent mercury from depositing on the anode and causing arcback. A typical high-power, grid-controlled tank rectifier is shown in Figs. 9-53 and 9-54. Tubes of this type have relatively long deionizing time and are not convenient for use in the control of small amounts of power. The field of application of mercury pool arcs has been greatly extended by the development of igniter-controlled tubes.[1]

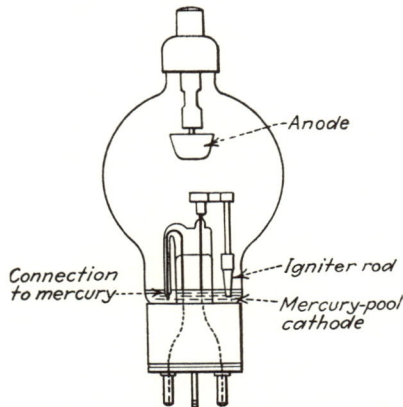

Fig. 9-55.—Structure of typical glass thyratron. (*Courtesy of Westinghouse Electric and Manufacturing Company.*)

9-36. Igniter Control.—The igniter is a high-resistance refractory rod which dips into the mercury pool, as shown in Fig. 9-55. If the potential applied to the rod is such that the gradient along the rod exceeds a critical value of about 100 volts/cm, an arc forms between the rod and the mercury pool.[2] This arc constitutes a source of electrons for the anode-cathode system, and the main arc then strikes between anode and cathode. It has been found by experiment that the main arc strikes within a few microseconds of the igniter arc.[3]

---

[1] Slepian, J., and Ludwig, L. R., *Trans. Am. Inst. Elec. Eng.*, **52**, 693 (1933); Knowles, D. D., *Electronics*, June, 1933, p. 164.

[2] Slepian and Ludwig, *loc. cit.*

[3] Dow, W. G., and Powers, W. H., *Elec. Eng.*, **54**, 942 (1935).

The igniter rod is made of a crystalline material that is not wet by mercury, such as boron carbide or silicon carbide. Consequently, contact with the mercury is made at a large number of small points. The small area of these points, together with the relatively high resistance of the rod material, results in such a high potential gradient at the points of contact that either electrons are drawn from the mercury or thermal explosion occurs, resulting in the formation of tiny arcs. The action is s milar to the formation of an arc between separating contacts. The currents in these minute arcs rapidly rise. If the resistivity of the rod is not too great, the resulting electron emission from the cathode spots becomes adequate to allow the formation of the main arc between the mercury and the anode. In order to limit the energy required to initiate the arc, the rod diameter and the shape of the end of the rod must be properly chosen.[1] The starting current increases with rod diameter. In practice the igniter arc may be formed by discharging a condenser through the igniter and by other methods that will be discussed.

As in thyratrons, the anode current after firing is determined by the applied voltage, the anode-circuit impedance, and the constant tube drop. To prevent destructive rise of current, anode-circuit impedance is essential.

9-37. Ignitron Construction.—A typical air-cooled ignitron, the KU-637, is shown in Fig. 9-55. The capacity of air-cooled tubes is limited by the allowable rise in temperature of the anode and of the tube as a whole. The use of metal construction and water cooling has resulted in tubes of greatly reduced size and with smaller probability of arcback. It has been found that tendency toward arcback in mercury pool tubes is favored by the positive-ion *back* current that flows during the negative half-cycle before deionization is complete.[2] Since the deionizing time is reduced by lowering the temperature (see Sec. 9-20), the efficient cooling attainable in water-jacketed metal ignitrons is conducive to freedom from arcback.

The important features of construction of water-cooled ignitrons may be discerned from Figs. 12-56 and 12-57, which show a

[1] SLEPIAN, and LUDWIG, *loc. cit.;* CAGE, J. M., *Gen. Elec. Rev.*, **38**, 464 (1935); TOEPFER, A. H., *Elec. Eng.*, **56**, 810 (1937).

[2] LUDWIG, L. R., MAXFIELD, F. A., and TOEPFER, A. H., *Elec. Eng.*, **53**, 75 (1934).

drawing of the type WL-651 ignitron and a cut-away view of the type FG-258A ignitron. The shell is not insulated from the mercury cathode and is, therefore, at cathode potential. The igniter and anode leads are insulated from the envelope by means of glass bushings. If the conducting time of the tube

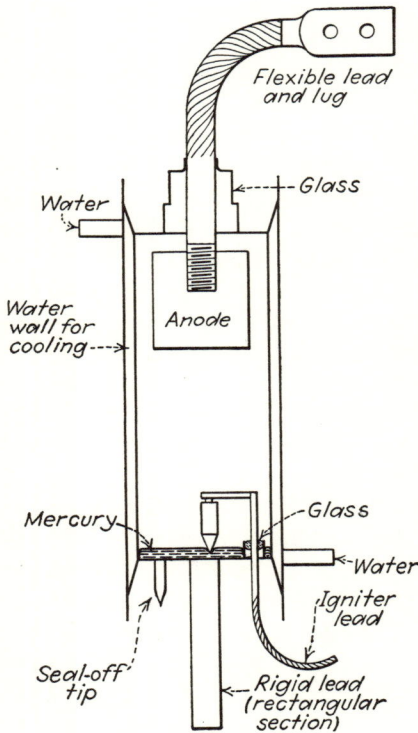

FIG. 9-56.—Structure of type WL-651 water-cooled metal ignitron. (*Courtesy of Westinghouse Electric and Manufacturing Company.*)

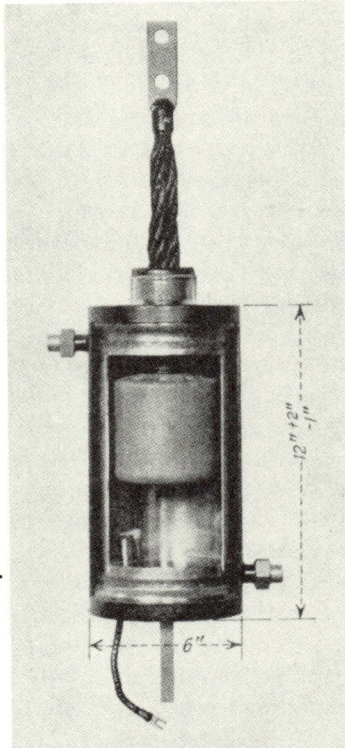

FIG. 9-57.—Cut-away view of type FG-258A water-cooled metal ignitron. (*Courtesy of General Electric Company.*)

exceeds the time in which the spot can move to the edge of the pool, it may anchor to the envelope and cause material to be sputtered from the metal wall. For this reason, some ignitrons are provided with a *spot-fixer*.[1] This is a metal strip at the

---

[1] WAGNER, C. F., and LUDWIG, L. R., *Elec. Eng.*, **53**, 1384 (1934); TONKS, L., *Physics*, **6**, 294 (1935); SLEPIAN, J., and TOEPFER, A. H., *J. Applied Physics*, **9**, 483 (1938).

surface of the mercury pool, which prevents the cathode spot from moving about.

9-38. Comparison of Igniter and Grid Control.—There are two fundamental differences between the hot-cathode thyratron and the cold-cathode ignitron. The first is the mechanism of electron emission at the cathode. In the cold-cathode arc, emission probably results from the formation by space charge of very high fields at the surface of the cathode, rather than from thermionic emission, as in the hot-cathode arc. The second difference, the method of controlling the formation of the arc, is in reality the result of the first. In a hot-cathode arc tube the continuous ample emission of electrons at the cathode makes it possible for the arc to form when the anode voltage exceeds the ionization potential of the gas or vapor. The function of·the grid in a thyratron is to prevent formation of the arc. Before the grid can regain control after arc extinction, it is necessary that deionization shall be so complete that the arc cannot form between the grid and cathode and that the grid is not surrounded by an ion sheath which prevents it from holding back electrons emitted by the cathode. This may require as much as 1000 μsec. In the cold-cathode arc tube, on the other hand, the emission mechanism is such that high current density and high ion density in the vicinity of the cathode are necessary for its maintenance. Within a few microseconds after extinction, the deionization in the vicinity of the cathode is great enough so that the required emission is not reestablished by reapplication of anode voltage.[1] Furthermore, even if the anode voltage is high enough to cause a glow, breakdown into an arc occurs only rarely and at random intervals. The function of the control electrode in a mercury pool tube is not, therefore, to prevent formation of the arc, but to initiate the arc by producing ionization of density comparable with that maintained by the arc. A heavy current from igniter to pool causes the formation of an auxiliary arc which is followed within a microsecond by the formation of the main arc.[2]

9-39. Comparison of Thyratron and Ignitron Characteristics.—Because of the great rapidity with which control is reestablished, the certainty of control is greater for the ignitron than for the

---

[1] KNOWLES, D. D., and BANGRATZ, E. G., *Elec. J.*, **30**, 501 (1933).

[2] Dow, W. G., and POWERS, W. H., *Elec. Eng.*, **54**, 942 (1935).

thyratron. Arcbacks may occur occasionally, but it has been shown that arcback is essentially a random phenomenon and that the probability of its occurrence can be reduced to as low as one arcback in a month of use.[1] Other advantages of the ignitron were discussed in Sec. 9-35. A serious disadvantage of the ignitron is the necessity for a large pulse of energy to initiate the arc. An igniter current of the order of several amperes for a time of about 100 μsec may be required. During this time the anode voltage must remain about 25 volts above the normal tube drop of 10 volts in order that the tube shall fire. In contrast to the hot-cathode arc tube, which will operate at small anode currents, the mercury pool type of arc tube requires an anode current of the order of 1 or 2 amps in order to maintain the arc. This is sometimes a disadvantage but may, on the other hand, assist in the extinction of the arc in d-c operation. The maximum peak voltages at which ignitrons can be operated are in general lower than those of thyratrons.

9-40. Ignitron Control Circuits.—The methods used in stopping the anode current of thyratrons are applicable to ignitrons. The arc may also be extinguished by reducing the current for an instant below the value necessary to maintain the cathode spot.

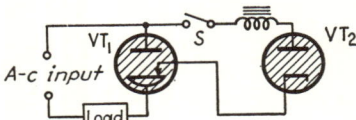

Fig. 9-58.—Ignitron firing circuit.

Because of the relatively high energy required to fire the ignitron, the simple phase-control circuits discussed earlier in the chapter cannot be applied directly to ignitron control. A phase shifter capable of supplying the necessary power may be used. Several circuits have been developed that allow the tube to be fired by energy supplied by the line.[2]

Figure 9-58 shows the basic form of one type of ignitron firing circuit. The rectifier tube VT_2 serves the dual function of preventing the flow of igniter current during the negative half of the cycle of applied voltage and of interrupting the igniter current after the anode fires in the positive half cycle. After the anode fires, the voltage applied to the igniter circuit is the ignitron tube drop, which is approximately equal to the rectifier

[1] Slepian, J., and Ludwig, L. R., *Trans. Am. Inst. Elec. Eng.*, **51**, 92 (1932). See also D. C. Prince, *J. Am. Inst. Elec. Eng.*, **46**, 667 (1927).

[2] Knowles and Bangratz, *loc. cit.*

tube drop.   The igniter current therefore falls to zero.   Substitution of a thyratron in place of the rectifier, as in Fig. 9-59, makes possible the control of the time in the cycle at which the ignitron is fired.

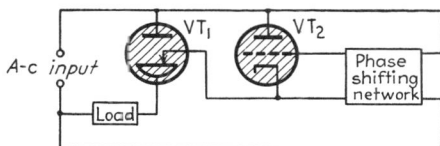

FIG. 9-59.—Ignitron phase-control circuit incorporating a thyratron.

In the circuits of Figs. 9-58 and 9-59 the igniter current flows through the load.   For this reason there is likely to be some variation of the time in the cycle at which the anode fires.   This difficulty is avoided in the circuit of Fig. 9-60, in which the con-

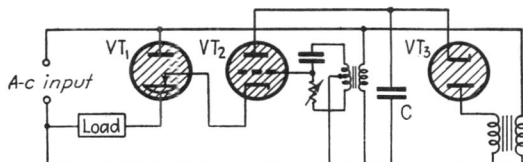

FIG. 9-60.—Phase-control circuit in which the ignitron is fired by energy stored in the condenser *C*.

denser *C* is charged through the rectifier VT_3 and discharged through the thyratron VT_2 at a time determined by the phase-shifting network.   Oscillograms show that with this circuit the ignitron fires with regularity at a predetermined point of the cycle of alternating supply voltage.[1]   The rectifier circuit is

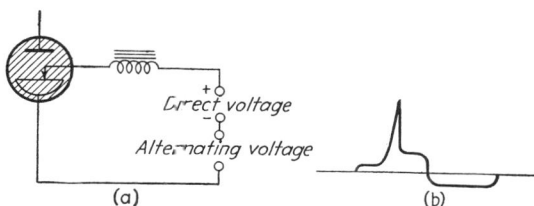

FIG. 9-31.—Ignitron firing circuit.

designed so that the charging current of the condenser is less than that required to maintain the arc of the thyratron VT_2.

Because of the high peak currents to which the thyratrons are subjected in the circuits of Figs. 9-59 and 9-60, particularly

[1] KNOWLES and BANGRATZ, *loc. cit.*

if anode breakdown fails to occur, the life of the thyratrons is relatively short. The need for thyratrons is avoided in the circuit of Fig. 9-61a, in which direct and alternating voltages are impressed simultaneously in the igniter circuit, which contains an iron-core choke.[1] As the result of core saturation, a high pulse of igniter current flows during the positive crest of impressed alternating voltage, as shown in Fig. 9-61b. The average igniter current and the reverse current during the negative half cycle are, however, small. Phase control may be obtained by shifting the phase of the impressed alternating igniter voltage relative to the anode voltage.

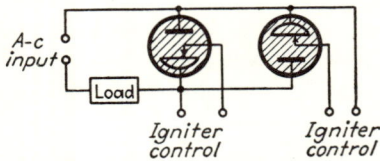

FIG. 9-62.—Full-wave ignitron circuit.

The circuits of Figs. 9-59, 9-60, and 9-61 can be readily converted into full-wave circuits. Figure 9-62 shows a full-wave ignitron circuit that permits current to start flowing at a predetermined point in each half cycle.[2]

Ignitron Applications.—The applications of the ignitron are in general the same as those of the thyratron. They include spot-welding control, inversion and frequency transformation, illumination control, and motor commutation.[3] At present spot-welding control is by far the most important application of ignitrons.

9-41. Externally Controlled Mercury Pool Arc Tube.—Breakdown of a glass mercury pool tube containing a small amount of inert gas may be initiated by means of an external electrode in contact with the glass wall. The sudden application of high voltage between the external electrode and the cathode causes the formation of a glow, with subsequent formation of an arc between the anode and the cathode. The objection to this type of control lies in the lowering of the anode-cathode glow breakdown voltage by the use of gas, but it has found application in stroboscopes.

[1] KLEMPERER, HANS, *Electronics*, December, 1939, p. 12.

[2] STODDARD, R. N., *Elec. Eng.*, **53**, 1366 (1934).

[3] WAGNER, C. F., and LUDWIG, L. R., *Elec. Eng.*, **53**, 1384 (1934); LUDWIG, L. R., MAXFIELD, F. A., and TOEPFER, A. H., *Elec. Eng.*, **53**, 75 (1934); SILVERMAN, D., and COX, J. H., *Elec. Eng.*, **53**, 1380 (1934); DAWSON, J. W., *Elec. Eng.*, **55**, 1371 (1936); PACKARD, D., and HUTCHINGS, J. H., *Elec. Eng.*, **56**, 37, 875 (1937).

9-42. The Strobotron.—Another type of cold-cathode arc tube has been developed by Germeshausen and Edgerton.[1]

The electrode structure of this tube is illustrated in Fig. 9-63. The cathode consists of a cup containing a cesium compound that liberates free cesium under the action of the cathode spot. The cathode is surrounded by a ceramic insulator which concentrates the discharge on the active portion of the cathode and serves as a support for the inner grid. This grid is a wire-mesh screen directly above the cathode. During the operation of the tube, the inner grid becomes coated with cesium, which lowers

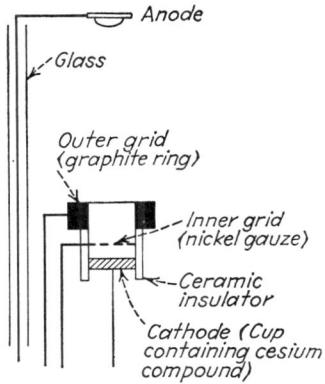

FIG. 9-63.—Strobotron electrode structure.

the breakdown voltage when this grid acts as a cathode. A second or outer grid, a graphite ring, is mounted above

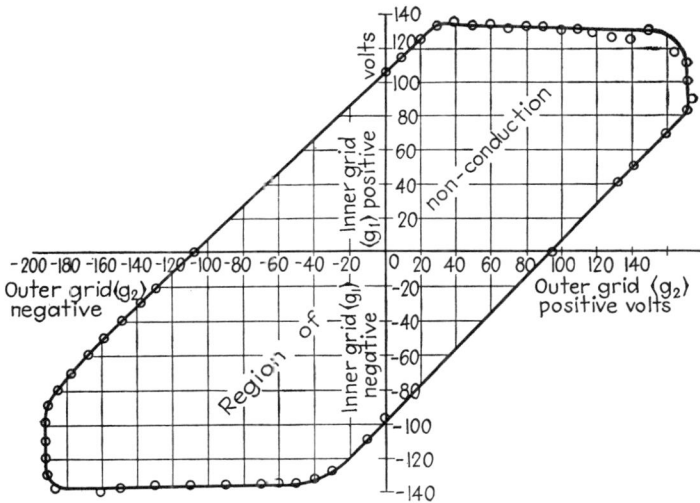

FIG. 9-64.—Strobotron control characteristic. The tube does not fire at combinations of grid voltages lying within the characteristic.

the ceramic insulator. Graphite is used because the cesium

[1] GERMESHAUSEN, K. J., and EDGERTON, H. E., *Elec. Eng.*, **55**, 790 (1936).

which condenses on it does not lower the breakdown voltage between it and the cathode.   The anode is about an inch above the grid, the anode support wire being insulated by means of a glass shield in order to prevent the discharge from taking the shorter path to the support.   One of the noble gases, usually neon or argon, is used in the tube.

Breakdown is initiated as a glow discharge between two of the electrodes, usually the two grids.   If the glow current exceeds a certain value and the anode source is capable of supplying sufficient current to maintain an arc, a cathode spot immediately forms, and the discharge changes into an arc.   Because either grid may be made either positive or negative relative to the cathode, there is considerable latitude in the operating voltages that may be used.   A typical control characteristic is shown in Fig. 9-64.   By proper choice of grid voltages, the glow current required to initiate arc breakdown may be made as small as 2×10^{-9} amp.[1]   The tube will carry a peak current of 200 to 300 amp and an average current of 50 ma.

Developed primarily as a stroboscopic light source, the strobotron has other applications.[2]   It may, for instance, be used to fire an externally-controlled mercury pool arc tube.   Its advantages as a stroboscopic light source result in part from the large peak current that can be carried without damage to the cathode.

9-43. Stroboscopes.—An important industrial and scientific application of the arc tube is as a stroboscope.   If an intermittent source of light is synchronized to the frequency of rotation or vibration of a mechanical device or to a multiple or submultiple of the frequency, the moving object will appear to be stationary when examined by the light.   The requirements of such a light source are (1) easily controlled frequency of illumination, to allow synchronization of light and motion over a large frequency range; (2) extremely short duration of light flash, so that the moving part under observation will not appear to move while it is illuminated; and (3) light of great brightness, so that the moving part will be clearly seen despite the short time of illumination. By acting as a shutter of extremely high speed, the stroboscopic

---

[1] WHITE, A. B., NOTTINGHAM, W. B., EDGERTON, H. E., and GERMESHAUSEN, K. J., *Electronics*, March, 1937, p. 18.

[2] GERMESHAUSEN, K. J., and EDGERTON, H. E., *Electronics*, February, 1937, p. 12; GRAY, T. S., and NOTTINGHAM, W. B., *Rev. Sci. Instruments*, **8**, 65 (1937).

light source also makes possible the photographing of rapidly moving objects.

One type of stroboscopic tube, the strobotron, has already been discussed. Where small il-lumination suffices, thyratrons may be used as the light source. Ordi-nary thyratrons are not designed to be efficient light sources, however, and the production of intense illu-mination necessitates the use of such large peak currents that the life of a hot-cathode tube is shortened. Mercury pool tubes are therefore usually used in preference to thy-

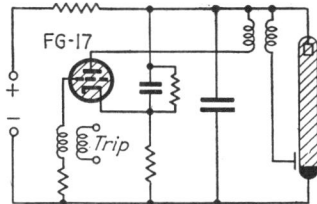

FIG. 9-65.—Stroboscope in which the discharge of a con-denser through a cold-cathode arc tube is controlled by a thyratron.

ratrons. The tubes may be constricted where the discharge takes place. The constriction not only concentrates the light-emitting region, but the prox-imity of the walls also speeds deionization of the gas and thus prevents serious afterglow.

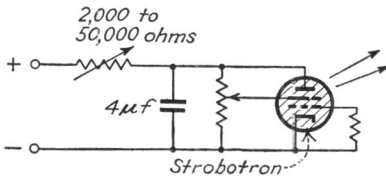

FIG. 9-66.—Self-excited strobotron stroboscope.

To produce a sharply de-fined flash of light, a condenser is discharged through the stroboscopic tube. Discharge may be initiated by a voltage impulse applied to an external electrode or an internal grid or by firing an auxiliary thyratron which is in series with the tube and a source of limited current, so connected that

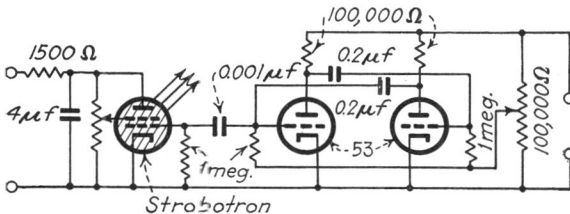

FIG. 9-67.—Strobotron stroboscope controlled by a multivibrator.

the condenser discharges only through the main tube. The inert gas which is essential to the use of external arc initiation is not objectionable in stroboscopic tubes because the relatively small diameter and large electrode spacing prevent the glow breakdown voltage from being too low.   The complete circuit of a stroboscope is complicated by the necessity of tripping the tube by an impulse of steep wave front in order to ensure accurate adjustment and synchronization, especially in the observation of rapidly moving objects.   Figure 9-65 shows a typical circuit in which a thyratron controls the tripping impulse applied to the external grid of a mercury pool arc tube.[1]   Figure 9-66 shows a simple self-excited strobotron circuit.[2]   A circuit using a strobotron controlled by a multivibrator is shown in Fig. 9-67.[1]

Problems

9-1. *a.* Design a circuit in which a glow- or arc-tube oscillator causes the periodic opening and closing of a relay.   The frequency of operation and the fraction of the cycle during which the relay is energized are to be adjustable.   All voltages except for cathode heating should be derived from a single 220-volt d-c supply.   The relay closes on 7 ma and opens on 6 ma. Specify all tubes, circuit constants, and operating voltages.

b. By constructing a curve of plate current *vs.* time, on which the critical relay currents are shown, prove that the percentage of the cycle during which the relay is energized cannot be varied progressively from zero to 100 per cent.

9-2. Derive Eqs. (9-1) to (9-5).

9-3. By means of a circle vector diagram, determine which of the impedances of Fig. 9-41 should be a resistance and whether the other should be inductive or capacitive in order that increase of resistance may produce progressive increase of average anode current.

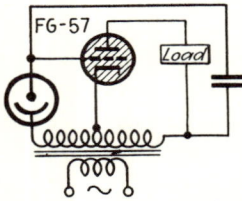

Fig. 9-68.—Circuit diagram for Prob. 9-5.

9-4. *a.* Draw waves of anode voltage *vs.* electrical degrees for sinusoidal anode voltages of 200 volts and 800 volts crest value; and, by the use of the grid-control characteristics of Fig. 9-21, construct corresponding waves of critical grid voltage for a type FG-57 thyratron.

b. Use the curves of (*a*) to derive curves of average anode current *vs.* phase angle θ between grid and anode voltages, for crest grid voltage equal to twice and to ten times the maximum critical grid voltage.

9-5. The operation of the phase-control circuit of Fig. 9-68 is erratic, regardless of the size of the condenser used.   The phototube is found to be good, and all tube voltages are correct.   Suggest a probable cause of this difficulty, and a remedy.

[1] EDGERTON, H. E., and GERMESHAUSEN, K. J., *Rev. Sci. Instruments*, **3**, 535 (1932).   See also H. E. Edgerton, *Elec. Eng.*, **50**, 327 (1931) and *Electronics*, July, 1932, p. 220; R. C. Hitchcock, *Elec. J.*, **32**, 529 (1935); H. E. Kallmann, *Proc. I.R.E.*, **27**, 690 (1939); C. C. Street, *Electronics*, April, 1940, p. 36.

[2] GERMESHAUSEN and EDGERTON, *Elec. Eng.*, *loc. cit.*

CHAPTER 10

LIGHT-SENSITIVE TUBES AND CELLS

In all tubes discussed in preceding chapters the flow of current is controlled by means of voltages applied to the electrodes. There is another very important class of tubes or cells, in which the current and the output voltage are controlled by incident energy radiant, and the operation of which depends upon some form of the photoelectric effect. These devices have made possible sound pictures, television, and many kinds of commercial and laboratory control and measuring equipment.

10-1. Types of Photoelectric Phenomena.—The control of current by light may be accomplished by the application of three types of photoelectric phenomena: (1) the photoemissive effect, or emission of electrons from metallic surfaces as the result of incident radiation; (2) the photoconductive effect, or change of resistance of semiconductors by the action of incident radiation; and (3) the photovoltaic effect, or production of a potential difference across the boundary between two substances that are in close contact, by illumination of the boundary. The best known of these phenomena, the photoemissive effect, appears in practical form in the *phototube* (*photocell*). The phototube is an electron tube in which one of the electrodes is irradiated for the purpose of causing electron emission.

10-2. Historical Survey.—The photoemissive effect was discovered by Heinrich Hertz in 1887. In the course of his classical experiments on electric oscillations and electric waves, Hertz noticed that the maximum length of a spark that could be made to jump across a small spark gap was increased when light from another spark was allowed to fall upon it. By means of a series of experiments he showed conclusively that the effect was caused by ultraviolet light and that it was greatest when the light fell upon the negative electrode of the spark gap. Subsequent contributions to knowledge concerning the photoemissive effect were made by Wiedemann and Ebert, Hallwachs,

305

Righi, Stoletow, Elster and Geitel, J. J. Thomson, Lenard, and others.[1]

Hallwachs proved that the photoemissive effect involved the loss of negative electricity from the illuminated surface. Righi connected two electrodes to an electrometer, by means of which he observed the flow of current when the surface of one electrode was illuminated. Stoletow added an external source of voltage and measured the current by means of a galvanometer. Elster and Geitel predicted and proved that the alkali metals should be the most sensitive photoelectric emitters of all the metals and found that sodium and potassium respond not only to ultraviolet radiation, but also to visible light. Lenard measured the ratio of the charge to the mass of the particles that carry the photoelectric current and showed them to be the same particles as those which Thomson had previously proved to carry the current in a beam of cathode rays, and which were subsequently called *electrons*.

10-3. Laws of Photoelectric Emission.—The early experiments resulted in the formulation of two laws relating photoelectric emission with the rate at which radiant energy strikes the emitting surface and with the wave length of the incident energy. The rate at which the radiant energy strikes is specified in terms of *radiant flux* (intensity of radiation), which is defined as the time rate of flow of radiant energy and is usually expressed in ergs per second or watts. The two laws of photoemission are:

1. The number of electrons released in unit time at a photoelectric surface by radiation of constant spectral distribution is directly proportional to the incident radiant flux.

2. The maximum energy of electrons released at a photoelectric surface is independent of the amount of radiant flux incident upon the surface but varies linearly with the frequency of the radiation.

The first law was one of the factors that led to the formulation of the quantum theory of radiation. This law is of practical importance because of the desirability of a linear relation between anode current and incident flux in applications of phototubes.

The second law was explained in 1905 by Einstein, who assumed that incident radiant energy could be transferred to the electrons only in quanta of magnitude $h\nu$ and that a portion of

_____
[1] See references at the end of this chapter.

this energy was used in removing the electrons from the emitter, the remainder appearing as kinetic energy of the emitted electrons. This is stated mathematically by Einstein's equation,

$$h\nu = w + \tfrac{1}{2}mv^2 \tag{10-1}$$

in which ν is the frequency of the incident radiation, w is the electron affinity of the emitter, v is the maximum velocity of the emitted electrons, h is Planck's constant, and m is the mass of an electron. Equation (10-1) holds only for the fastest electrons, which are removed from the atoms at the surface of the emitter. Some radiation penetrates through the outer layers of atoms, liberating electrons within the emitter. These electrons may lose energy in moving to the surface, so that their velocities after emission are less than that indicated by Einstein's equation. It can be seen from Eq. (10-1) that there is a minimum value of ν below which the energy of the incident photon is less than the electron affinity and no emission can take place. This limiting frequency is called the *threshold frequency* and is indicated by the symbol ν_0. Substituting $v = 0$ and $\nu = \nu_0$ in Eq. (10-1) shows that

$$\nu_0 = \frac{w}{h} \tag{10-2}$$

The wave length corresponding to the threshold frequency is termed the *long-wave limit*, λ_0. Einstein's equation was verified experimentally in 1916 by Millikan,[1] who determined the maximum velocities of emitted electrons for various frequencies of incident radiation by measuring the retarding potential necessary to reduce the anode current to zero. Einstein's equation is of practical importance because it indicates that the electron affinity of the emitter must be small in order that the emitter may be sensitive to visible radiation.

10-4. Current-wave-length Characteristics.—Photoelectric tubes and cells, like the human eye, are not equally responsive to equal amounts of radiant flux of different wave lengths. For this reason the response of a phototube to a given amount of radiant flux depends upon the manner in which the energy of the incident radiation is distributed in regard to wave length, which in turn depends upon the source of the radiation. In

---

[1] Millikan, R. A., *Phys. Rev.*, **7**, 355 (1916).

order to indicate fully the manner in which a phototube responds to radiation it is necessary to indicate not only the sensitivity to radiation of specific energy distribution, but also the manner in which the current varies with wave length at constant incident

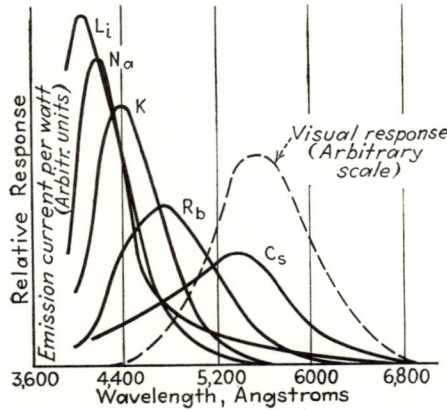

Fig. 10-1.—Current–wave-length characteristics for the alkali metals.

energy.   For this reason, tube manufacturers usually specify the performance of phototubes for illumination from a tungsten-filament lamp operated at a temperature of 2870°K, and furnish a *current–wave-length characteristic*, which is a graph showing the relation between direct anode current per unit energy of incident radiant flux, and the wave length of the incident steady radiant flux.

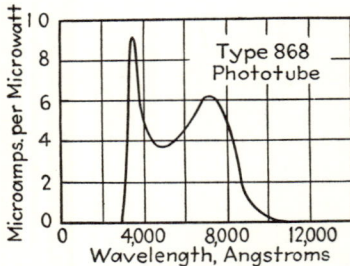

Fig. 10-2.—Current–wave-length characteristic for the type 868 phototube.

Current–wave-length characteristics for the alkali metals are shown in Fig. 10-1.   Comparison of these curves with the dotted curve, which shows the visual sensitivity of the human eye, clearly indicates that cesium is by far the most satisfactory of the alkali metals for use with visible radiation.

Equation (10-2) suggests that the long-wave limit can be pushed farther toward the red end of the visible spectrum by reduction of the electron affinity.   The electron affinity of photoelectric emitters, like that of thermionic emitters, can be lowered by the use of composite films made up of consecutive layers of different metals, of metals on oxides, and of metals on a monatomic layer of oxygen. The use of composite emitters results not only in response at much longer wave lengths, but also in a marked increase of sensitivity over the whole visible range of wave length. At present the most satisfactory type of cathode for use with visible radiation consists of a thin layer of cesium deposited upon a layer of cesium oxide formed upon a silver surface. The sensitivity of cesium oxide tubes extends well into the infrared band of radiation. This is shown, in Fig. 10-2, by the current–wave-length characteristic of a typical cesium-oxide tube, the type 868. The sharp cutoff at the ultraviolet end of the spectrum is caused by absorption of the shorter wave lengths of the radiation by the glass envelope. High sensitivity in the ultraviolet region may be obtained by use of a pure sodium cathode enclosed in an envelope of quartz or special glass such as *nonex*, which transmits ultraviolet radiation. By the proper choice of cathode materials, the use of color filters, and the combination of two or more tubes of different color response, it is possible to adjust the resultant characteristic curve to meet special requirements.

10-5. Light Units.—Radiant flux incident upon a phototube is ordinarily measured in *lumens*, and the illumination or flux density in *foot-candles*. The *lumen* is defined as the flux through a unit solid angle from a point source of one candle. The *foot-candle* is the illumination on a surface 1 sq ft in area on which there is a uniformly distributed flux of 1 lumen. When the flux is uniform, the illumination in foot-candles equals the flux in lumens divided by the area in square feet.

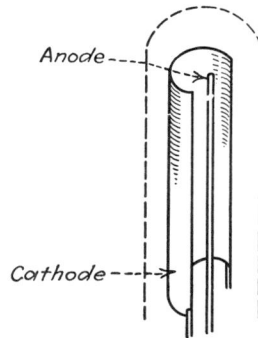

FIG. 10-3.—Electrode structure of a typical phototube.

10-6. The Vacuum Phototube.—Phototube cathodes usually consist of a half cylinder of silver or silver-plated copper covered with a composite film. The shape of the anode is not critical, the most important requirement being that it should intercept as little light as possible. A common form of anode in tubes with cylindrical cathodes is a wire located at the axis of the cylinder, as shown in Fig. 10-3. In such a tube the initial velocities of only relatively few electrons are such as to carry them to the anode. Voltage must, therefore, be applied in order to draw all emitted electrons to the anode.

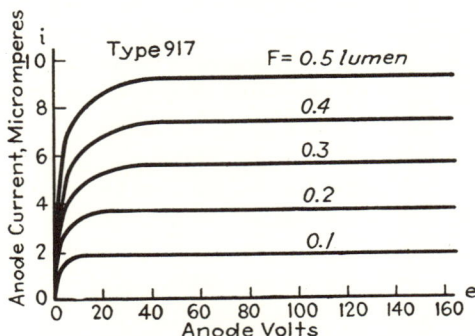

Fig. 10-4.—Current-voltage characteristics for the type 917 vacuum phototube.

Phototubes may be classified as *vacuum phototubes* and *gas phototubes*. A *vacuum phototube* is one that is evacuated to such a degree that its electrical characteristics are essentially unaffected by gaseous ionization. A *gas phototube* is one into which a quantity of gas has been introduced, usually for the purpose of increasing its sensitivity.

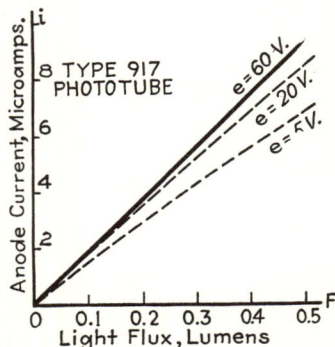

Fig. 10-5.—Static curves of anode current *vs.* luminous flux for the type 917 vacuum phototube.

Static current-voltage curves for a typical cesium oxide vacuum phototube, the 917, are shown in Fig. 10-4, and static curves of anode current *vs.* luminous flux in Fig. 10-5. The solid curve of Fig. 10-5 applies to all anode voltages above saturation; the dotted curves, which are ordinarily of no great practical interest, are for anode voltages below saturation. Curvature of the dotted curves is probably the result of space charge. It should be emphasized that the curves of Figs. 10-4 and 10-5 apply only to light from a tungsten filament at a color temperature of 2870°K. Curves obtained with radiation of different energy distribution are of similar form, but the current range may be different.   Such curves may be derived by means of the following procedure:

1. Multiply ordinates of the current–wave-length characteristic by the corresponding ordinates of the curve of Fig. 10-6, which shows the relative energy distribution of radiation from a tungsten filament at 2870°K, and plot these products as a function of wave length.

2. Plot a similar curve of the products of ordinates of the current–wave-length characteristic and those of the energy distribution curve for the given source.

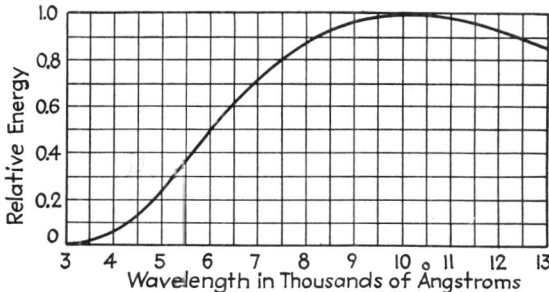

Fig. 10-6.—Relative energy distribution for radiation from a tungsten filament at a color temperature of 2870°K.   [*From data by W. E. Forsythe and E. Q. Adams, Denison University Bulletin, J. of the Scientific Laboratories,* **32,** 70 (1937).]

3. Multiply the current scale of the current-voltage characteristics by the ratio of the area under the second product curve to the area under the first product curve.   For approximate results, the ratio of the sums of 15 or 20 uniformly spaced ordinates of the product curves may be used in place of the ratio of the areas, and so the product curves need not be drawn.

10-7. Phototube Sensitivity.—*Static sensitivity* of a phototube is the ratio of the direct anode current at a specified steady anode voltage to the incident constant radiant flux of specified value. It is usually expressed in microamperes per microwatt.   When the radiant flux is confined to a single frequency or a very narrow band of frequencies, the ratio is called the *monochromatic sensitivity.*[1]

Variational sensitivity of a phototube is the ratio of the change in anode current at a specified steady anode voltage to the change

[1] 1933 and 1938 reports of the Standards Committee of the Institute of Radio Engineers.

in the total luminous flux entering the tube.   As most precisely used, the term refers to infinitesimal changes, as indicated by the defining equation[1]

$$s = \frac{\partial i}{\partial F} \tag{10-3}$$

It is evident that the variational sensitivity is the slope of the curve of current *vs.* flux at the given values of anode voltage and flux.   It may also be found from the family of current-voltage characteristics by the use of small increments.

10-8. The Gas Phototube.—It can be seen from the curves of Figs. 10-4 and 10-5 that the currents that are obtained from a

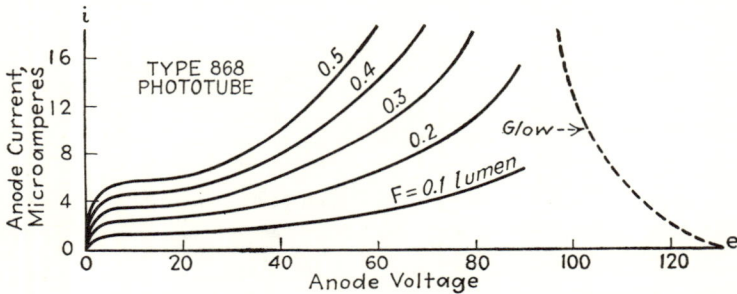

Fig. 10-7.—Current-voltage characteristics for the type 868 gas phototube.

vacuum phototube are very small even with cathodes of high sensitivity.   The sensitivity of the tube can be greatly increased by introducing a small quantity of gas.   The increase of current results mainly from ionization of gas by the emitted electrons in moving to the anode.   Ionization by collision takes place in a gas phototube when the anode voltage approaches the ionization potential of the gas.   The new electrons thus released pass to the anode, and the positive ions are drawn to the cathode.   The current is increased at every point between the cathode and anode by an amount corresponding to the number of ionizing collisions per second between the cathode and anode.   Increase of anode voltage increases the number of primary electrons that make ionizing collisions.   When the voltage becomes sufficiently high, then, after a primary electron makes one ionizing collision, both it and the new electron may make one or more other

[1] 1933 and 1938 reports of the Standard Committee of the Institute of Radio Engineers.

ionizing collisions in moving toward the anode. Some increase of current also results from secondary emission produced when positive ions strike the cathode. A tenfold increase of anode current may be attained by the use of gas, the current increasing rapidly as the voltage is raised above the ionization potential. Figures 10-7 and 10-8 show static curves of anode current *vs.* anode voltage and of anode current *vs.* luminous flux for the type 868 gas phototube. Below 15 volts the current-voltage curves are of the same general form as those of a vacuum phototube, since little ionization takes place below this voltage.

The gas that is used in phototubes must meet a number of requirements. It must not react with the electrodes or be absorbed by the electrodes or the tube walls, it should have a low ionization potential, and it should have a low molecular weight in order that the positive ions may be quickly accelerated. The only gases that do not react with the alkali metals used in the cathodes are the inert gases, helium, neon, argon, krypton, and xenon. The ionization potential of these gases decreases in the order in which they are listed, whereas the atomic weight increases. Argon gives a satisfactory compromise as regards these factors and is relatively inexpensive. Neon and helium are used in some tubes, but the use of argon is more common.

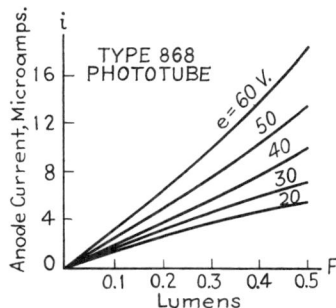

Fig. 10-8.—Static curves of anode current *vs.* luminous flux for the type 868 gas phototube.

The ratio of the sensitivity of a gas phototube at a given voltage and flux to the sensitivity obtainable at the same voltage and flux without ionization resulting from presence of gas is called the *gas amplification factor*. This factor depends upon the gas pressure. If the pressure is too low, the spacing between the gas molecules is relatively so great that there is slight probability that an emitted electron will strike a gas molecule in moving from the cathode to the anode. If the pressure is too high, on the other hand, the probability is great that an electron will be stopped by a gas molecule before it has been accelerated far enough to have acquired sufficient energy to cause ionization. As the pressure is increased from a very low value, the number of collisions made by an electron in moving from the cathode to the anode increases, but the kinetic energy acquired between collisions with molecules decreases. It is not surprising, therefore, that there is an optimum gas pressure. This is found to be about 0.2 mm Hg for the noble gases.

The gain in sensitivity resulting from the use of gas is partly offset by a number of disadvantages. One, shown by Fig. 10-8, is the loss of linearity between anode current and flux. A second disadvantage is that a glow discharge may take place at voltages above about 90. The breakdown voltage falls with increase of flux, in a manner indicated roughly by the dotted curve in Fig. 10-7. Glow is objectionable not only because it causes the current to be independent of illumination, but also because it may permanently reduce the sensitivity of the tube.

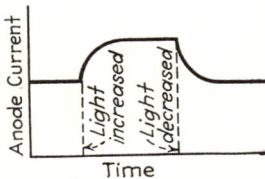

Fig. 10-9.—Lag in the response of a gas phototube.

The anode voltage must, therefore, be kept below the value at which glow breakdown can occur. Limitation of supply voltage to 90 volts makes the maximum output voltage that can be obtained less than that attainable with vacuum phototubes. To prevent destructive rise of anode current in the event that glow breakdown does occur, a resistance of 100,000 Ω or more must always be used in series with a gas phototube. Since a high resistance is also necessary in order to produce high voltage output, the need of such a resistance is not a disadvantage.

The third disadvantage resulting from the use of gas in phototubes is caused by the relatively large mass of positive ions. Because the time taken for a positive ion to pass from the vicinity of the anode to the cathode is appreciable, there is a perceptible time lag in the response to a change in flux. The manner in which a gas phototube responds to an abrupt increase and decrease of flux is shown in Fig. 10-9. The effect of the time lag is similar to that of inductance in the phototube circuit, as it tends to prevent changes of anode current and produces a phase difference between sinusoidal periodic light fluctuations and the resulting alternating component of anode current. It also causes the variational sensitivity of the tube to decrease with increase of modulation frequency of the light.[1] This is illustrated by the *dynamic response curve* of Fig. 10-10, which shows the relative variational sensitivity of a type 868 gas phototube as a function of modulation frequency. When a gas phototube is used in conjunction with an amplifier to convert changes of light into sound, the effect of a drooping dynamic response curve can be offset by the use of an amplifier that has a rising frequency characteristic.

10-9. Phototube Circuits.—Phototube currents are so small that a galvanometer is the only current-operated device that they can operate directly.   One or more stages of amplification must

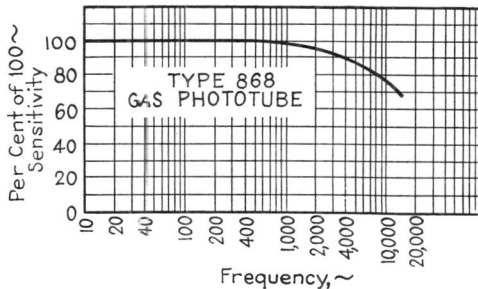

FIG. 10-10.—Dynamic response curve for the type 868 gas phototube.

be used in practical applications of the phototube. Since vacuum-tube amplifiers are voltage-operated devices, the changes of phototube current must be converted into voltage changes by means of impedance in series with the tube.   Because the currents are very small, the impedance must be high, usually from 1 to 25 megohms.   Although transformers have been designed for use with phototubes, the difficulty of obtaining adequate primary reactance at the lower audio frequencies makes it simpler and cheaper to use resistance or resistance-capacitance coupling between the phototube and the amplifier.

In order to simplify diagrams of circuits discussed in this chapter, all tubes are shown as triodes, and all direct voltage sources as batteries. Tetrodes and pentodes of proper characteristics (Sec. 10-14) may be used in place of triodes, and batteries may be replaced by other types of power supplies.

When a relay or other current-operated electrical device is to be controlled by changes of steady or average flux, a direct-coupled

[1] Modulation frequency, the frequency at which the illumination varies, should not be confused with the radiation frequency of the incident light.

amplifier must be used.   A circuit in which increase of illumination causes an increase in plate current of the amplifier tube is termed a *forward circuit;* one in which increase of illumination causes a decrease of plate current is called a *reverse circuit.*   Figure 10-11 shows a simple forward circuit in which increase of illumination causes a relay to be energized.   Figure 10-12 shows a similar reverse circuit.   The forward circuit of Fig. 10-13 is operated

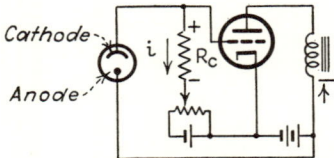

Fig. 10-11.—Forward d-c photo-tube circuit.

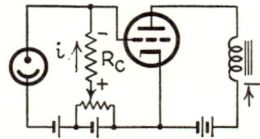

Fig. 10-12.—Reverse d-c phototube circuit.

entirely from a single source of direct voltage.   If the relay is shunted by a condenser in order to by-pass the alternating component of plate current, or if a slow-acting relay is employed, this circuit can also be used on an alternating voltage supply.   The phototube and amplifier then pass current during only one-half of the cycle.

Improved forward and reverse a-c–operated circuits are shown in Figs. 10-14 and 10-15.[1]   The purpose of the grid condensers is to eliminate the difference in phase between grid and anode voltages resulting from the capacitance of the phototube and amplifier electrodes.   The sensitivity of these a-c circuits is less than half that of the corresponding d-c circuits at the same voltages.   The illumination at which the relay closes is adjusted in the circuits of Figs. 10-11 to 10-15 by variation of grid bias of the amplifier tube.

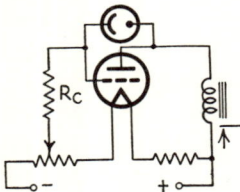

Fig. 10-13.—Forward phototube circuit operated from a single voltage source.

Another a-c–operated circuit is that of Fig. 10-16.   The action is as follows: During the half of the cycle in which the anode and the amplifier plate are negative, a positive voltage is applied

[1] Although the phototube is shunted between the amplifier grid and plate in Figs. 10-13 and 10-14, the only actual difference in the phototube connection from that in the circuit of Fig. 10-11 is that the phototube current flows through the relay.   The voltage drop through the relay is small and so does not affect the operation.

to the grid through the condenser *C*. The flow of grid current charges the condenser to a voltage approximately equal to the peak voltage between *A* and *B*, the side of the condenser adjacent to the grid being negative. During the half of the cycle that

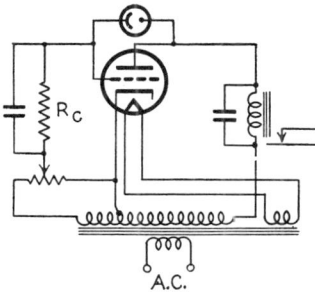

Fig.   10-14.—A–c–operated forward phototube circuit.

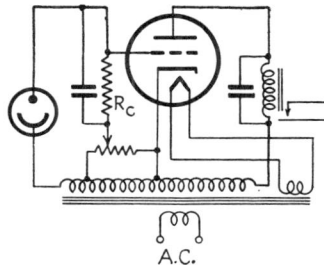

Fig.   10-15.—A–c–operated   reverse phototube circuit.

makes the plate and the anode positive, the grid is negative with respect to the cathode of the amplifier by an amount equal to the sum of the condenser voltage and the instantaneous voltage between *A* and *B*. If the phototube is dark, the charge on the condenser cannot leak off; but if the phototube is illuminated, the charge flows off through the phototube, lowering the negative voltage of the grid and increasing the plate current. Adjustment of the potentiometer varies the average grid bias and thus changes the illumina-tion at which the relay closes. It should be noted that the circuit is in effect a bridge, the voltage of the grid during the negative half of the cycle depending upon the relative size of *C* and the sum of the phototube and amplifier grid-to-plate capacitances. If *C* is too small, no charge is stored during the negative half cycle. If *C* is too large, on the other hand, the reduction of

Fig. 10-16.—A–c–operated
forward phototube circuit.

condenser voltage during the positive half cycle, caused by the phototube current, is too small and the sensitivity is low. A 0.0005-μf condenser gives satisfactory results with a type 6J5 amplifier tube and a 0.00025-μf condenser with a type

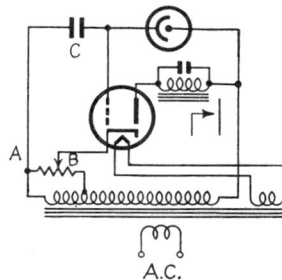

6SK7 amplifier.   The over-all sensitivity is considerably higher with the 6SK7 than with the 6J5 amplifier tube.

10-10. Circuits for Measurement of Illumination.[1]—The foregoing circuits may be used for measuring illumination if the relay is replaced by a meter.   Because the variation of plate current may be only a small fraction of the operating plate current of the amplifier, it is usually necessary to balance out the steady component of plate current in order to obtain accurate readings.   This may be accomplished by the circuit of Fig. 10-17.   The voltage divider P is adjusted so that there is no difference of potential across the meter and all the plate current flows through the resistance.   Any change in plate current results in the flow of current through the meter.   For high sensitivity the resistance R must be large as compared with the meter resistance, but increase of resistance necessitates an increase of plate supply voltage.   Steady current can also be eliminated from the meter by the use of the two-tube balanced circuit of Fig. 10-18.[2]   This circuit is unaffected by fluctuations of battery voltage and reads linearly over a wide range of illumination.   The meter in the circuits of Figs. 10-17 and 10-18 may be replaced by other types of current-operated devices.

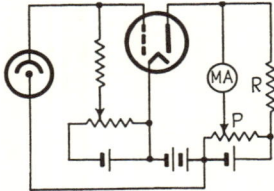

FIG.   10-17.—Phototube circuit for the measurement of illumination.

10-11. Use of Phototubes in Phase-control and Trigger Circuits. Phototubes can be incorporated in the thyratron phase-control circuits of Figs. 9-41 to 9-51, thus making possible the control of load current by light.   The phototubes are used as the variable resistance elements in the phase-shifting circuits, being

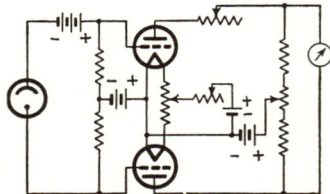

FIG. 10-18.—Balanced circuit for the measurement of illumination.

connected so that the phototube and thyratron anodes are posi-

[1] For more complet treatments of this subject, see W. E. Forsythe (editor), "Measurement of Radiant Energy," McGraw-Hill Book Company, Inc., New York, 1937; also Keith Henney, "Electron Tubes in Industry," McGraw-Hill Book Company, Inc., New York, 1937.

[2] EGLIN, J. M., *J. Opt. Soc. Am.*, **18**, 393 (1929); KOLLER, L. R., *J. Western Soc. Eng.*, **36**, 15 (1931).

tive during the same half of the cycle.   Because of the very high resistance of phototubes and the difficulty of obtaining comparable reactance at commercial frequencies by means of an inductance, a condenser must be used as the reactive element in the phase-shifting circuit.   Two typical circuits are shown in Fig. 10-19.   The function of the resistance R in circuit b is to provide a leakage path for electrons that collect on the grid side of the condenser.

Phototubes may also be used to control the trigger circuits of Figs. 6-26 and 6-27.   Phototubes in series with or in place of the resistances R_c of Fig. 6-26 allow the current transfer to be initiated by the interruption of light beams.   Phototubes in

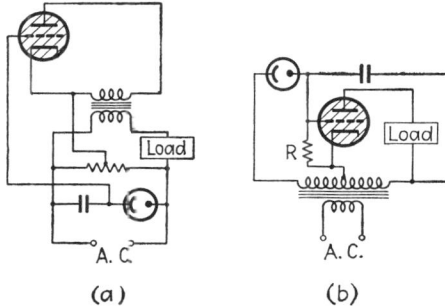

FIG. 10-19.—Thyratron phase-control circuits incorporating phototubes, by means of which large currents may be controlled by illumination.

parallel with or in place of the resistances R_c' allow the circuit to be tripped by increase of illumination.

10-12. Limitations of Direct-coupled Circuits.—The circuits of Figs. 10-11 to 10-18 respond both to periodically repeated changes of illumination and to sustained changes of steady illumination.   Greater sensitivity may be obtained by the use of an additional stage of amplification, directly coupled to the first; but it is then difficult to adjust the circuit to operate at different illumination levels, and small variations in the illumination level alter the bias of the second stage.   The difficulty of obtaining high amplification in direct-coupled circuits imposes a lower limit to the change in illumination that can be used to operate circuits of this type.   Aside from their relatively low sensitivity, these circuits are unsatisfactory for the amplification of modulated light because they are thrown out of adjustment by changes of average illumination.

10-13. Circuits for Use with Modulated Light.—To amplify only the varying component of anode current produced by fluctuating or modulated light, as in the reproduction of sound recorded on film, the phototube is usually coupled to the first amplifier tube by means of resistance-capacitance coupling, as shown in Fig. 10-20. The coupling condenser prevents the variation of amplifier bias with changes of average illumination. After the first stage, any type of amplifier having the desired characteristics may be used.

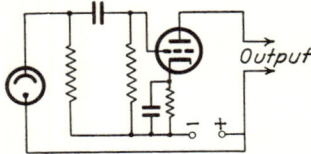

Fig. 10-20.—Circuit for converting modulated light into alternating current or voltage.

10-14. Sensitivity of Phototube and Amplifier.—The theoretical sensitivity, or change of plate current per lumen change in light flux, of the circuits of Figs. 10-11, 10-12, and 10-13 can be readily determined. For a vacuum phototube the change in voltage across the coupling resistor per lumen change of flux is equal to the product of the tube sensitivity in microamperes per lumen by the coupling resistance in megohms, or

$$\frac{\Delta e_c}{\Delta F} = sR_c \qquad \text{volts/lumen} \tag{10-4}$$

If the change of voltage is not too great, the resulting change of plate current is

$$\Delta i_b = \frac{\mu\Delta e_c}{r_p + R_b} \qquad \text{amp} \tag{10-5}$$

and

$$\frac{\Delta i_b}{\Delta F} = \frac{s\mu R_c}{r_p + R_b} \qquad \text{amp/lumen} \tag{10-6}$$

in which the resistances r_p and R_b are measured in ohms. The resistance of milliammeters and of relays suitable for use in the plate circuit of an amplifier tube is usually negligible in comparison to the plate resistance of the tube, so that Eq. (10-6) may be simplified to

$$\frac{\Delta i_b}{\Delta F} = sg_mR_c \times 10^{-3} \qquad \text{ma/lumen} \tag{10-7}$$

in which s is the phototube sensitivity in microamperes per lumen, g_m is the amplifier tube transconductance in micromhos, and R_c is the coupling resistance in megohms.[1] If the cathode is uniformly illuminated, or if the light is concentrated upon the cathode by means of a uniformly illuminated lens, the sensitivity can be expressed also in milliamperes per foot-candle change in illumination and is equal to $sg_mR_cA \times 10^{-3}$ ma/ft-candle, where A is the effective cathode area or the area of the lens. It is important to note that the sensitivity is proportional to the transconductance of the amplifier tube.

If the changes of flux are very large, the value of the transconductance of the amplifier tube may vary considerably over the range of operation. A more accurate determination of the sensitivity of the circuit can then be made by using in place of g_m the ratio of the change in plate current to the change in grid voltage, as determined from the plate diagram or the transfer characteristic of the amplifier tube. If a gas phototube is used in place of a vacuum phototube, the phototube sensitivity is not constant, and the ratio of the actual change of anode current to the change in flux should be used in place of s. This may be determined from the anode-circuit diagram.

10-15. The Anode Diagram.—Anode diagrams similar to the plate diagrams of amplifier tubes are often of value in determining the performance of phototubes. An anode diagram for a vacuum phototube is illustrated in Fig. 10-21. The load line passes through the point on the voltage axis corresponding to the anode supply voltage and makes an angle with the voltage axis whose tangent is equal to the reciprocal of the load resistance (expressed in volts per ampere). Above

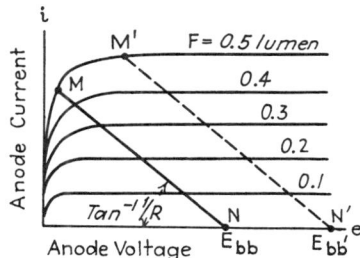

Fig. 10-21.—Anode diagram for vacuum phototube.

saturation the characteristic curves of Fig. 10-21 corresponding to equal increments of flux are practically horizontal, equidistant, straight lines, and therefore intersect the load line at equidistant points. This shows that if the anode voltage of a vacuum phototube is always sufficiently high to give saturation current, the

---

[1] Note that r_p, μ, g_m, and s must be determined for the given operating points.

current and the voltage across the load resistor are essentially proportional to the flux.

Except over a very small range of voltage, the characteristics of gas phototubes are not equidistant, parallel, straight lines, and so the anode current and output voltage are not proportional to

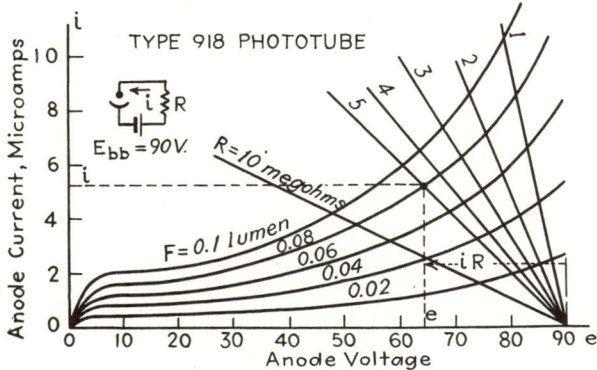

FIG. 10-22.—Anode diagram for the type 918 gas phototube.

flux. The anode current may be expanded in an infinite series similar to the plate-current series for an amplifier tube. It is difficult, however, to evaluate the coefficients of such an expansion in the solution of problems. It is more practical to deter-

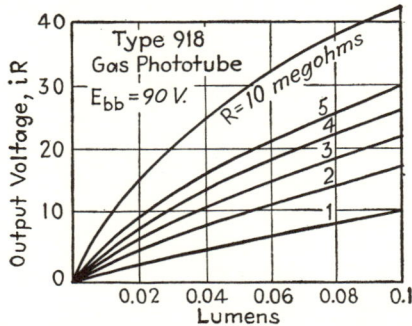

FIG. 10-23.—Curves of output voltage *vs.* luminous flux for the type 918 gas phototube with load, derived from the anode diagram of Fig. 10-22.

mine the output voltage and harmonic content by means of the anode diagram. Figures 10-22 and 10-23 show the anode-circuit diagram of the type 918 phototube and the curves of output voltage *vs.* luminous flux which are derived from it. Harmonic content can be determined from the anode diagram of Fig. 10-22 or the voltage-flux curves of Fig. 10-23 by the use of equations given in Chap. 4, in the same manner as for amplifier tubes.

10-16. Design of Phototube Circuits.—The fact that the anode current of a vacuum phototube is practically independent of anode voltage above saturation means that the anode current is also independent of coupling resistance if the anode voltage is always above saturation. The output voltage, therefore, increases linearly with coupling resistance. If the coupling resistance is made very large, however, the anode voltage may fall below saturation at high values of flux, destroying the linearity between current and flux, as shown by the load line MN in Fig. 10-21. This difficulty can be remedied by increasing the anode supply voltage, as indicated by the load line M'-N'. The size of the coupling resistance that can be satisfactorily used at a given maximum flux is limited by the maximum allowable anode voltage (usually not less than 250 volts in vacuum phototubes), by tube and circuit leakage conductance, and by resistor "noise." With special care in the elimination of circuit and tube leakage it is possible to use properly designed coupling resistors as large as 100 megohms, but ordinarily it is not advantageous to exceed 25 megohms. When extreme sensitivity is essential, as in the measurement of minute quantities of light, leakage in the phototube and phototube socket should be minimized by the use of a phototube in which the anode terminal is at the top of the tube, and of low anode voltage. If the anode voltage is kept below 20 volts, the danger of ionization of residual gas in vacuum phototubes is avoided. Grid leakage in the amplifier tube is reduced by the use of low screen and plate voltage and low cathode temperature. High sensitivity may be attained without the need of high anode supply voltage by using a pentode[1] (see Fig. 6-6) or a second phototube[2] in place of the coupling resistor.

When gas phototubes are used in the conversion of modulated light into alternating voltage or current, the harmonic content of the output increases with coupling resistance. Allowable amplitude distortion, therefore, usually limits the coupling resistance to 1 or 2 megohms. In control circuits, however,

[1] SHEPARD, F. H., JR., *RCA Rev.*, **2**, 149 (1937); BULL, H. S., and Lafferty, J. M., *Electronics*, November, 1940, p. 31 and December, 1940, p. 71.
[2] SHEPARD, *ibid*.

large values of coupling resistance can also be used with gas phototubes.

Danger of cumulative increase of plate current as the result of primary and secondary grid emission and of ionization of residual gas imposes a limit on the grid-circuit resistance that can be used with many amplifier tubes at rated plate voltages.[1] To make use of the large values of coupling resistance that are desirable in order to give high sensitivity, it is necessary, therefore, to use low values of plate and screen operating voltage. This is normally not a disadvantage, since enough plate current to operate small relays may be readily obtained with most tubes at plate voltages of 100 or less. A second amplifier stage, operated at normal voltages, may be used if necessary. Care must also be taken to ensure that the allowable amplifier plate dissipation is not exceeded for any value of light flux at which the phototube is operated. Since IR drop in the grid resistor prevents the application of appreciable positive voltage to the grid, ample protection is usually afforded by the use of sufficiently low plate and screen supply voltages so that the allowable plate dissipation is not exceeded when the grid voltage is zero.

10-17. Photoconductive Cells.—The photoconductive effect was discovered in 1873 by Willoughby Smith, who observed a change in the resistance of the crystalline form of selenium with illumination. Although a number of semiconducting substances are now known to be photoconductive, selenium is still used in most photoconductive cells. Early selenium cells were made by covering two closely spaced conductors with a thin coating of amorphous selenium, which was subsequently converted into crystalline selenium by heat treatment. The conductors were commonly made in the form of interlocking metallic combs, or of two wires wound close together on a nonconducting frame, as shown in Fig. 10-24. Modern

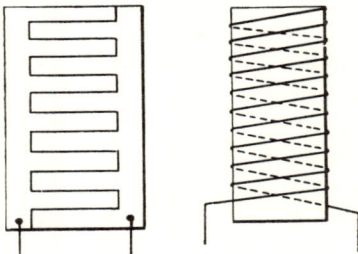

Fig. 10-24.—Two forms of grids used in selenium cells.

[1] Reich, H. J., "Theory and Applications of Electron Tubes," pp. 184–185.

cells are made by condensing selenium vapor in a thin film upon a double grid of gold or platinum fused to or sputtered upon a glass plate. The glass is maintained at the proper temperature so that the film is deposited in the crystalline form.

The photoconductive effect is thought to be caused by the emission of electrons within the material. In their motion under the influence of applied voltage, these photoelectrons produce other ionization. Equilibrium is established when the rate of recombination becomes equal to the rate of ion formation. This theory is in agreement with experimentally observed laws. It is found experimentally that (1) for a short time after the light is applied, before much displacement of positive ions or appreciable secondary ionization takes place, the change in current resulting from illumination is proportional to the incident flux; (2) for exposures of sufficient length to enable the current to reach equilibrium, the current is proportional to the square root of the incident flux; (3) with rapidly fluctuating light the alternating current is proportional to the incident flux and inversely proportional to the frequency of fluctuation. The lag in the response of a selenium cell is caused mainly by the low velocity of the relatively heavy positive ions. The dependence of current upon time of illumination and the related falling dynamic response curve make the photoconductive cell unsatisfactory for the undistorted conversion of modulated light into voltage or current.

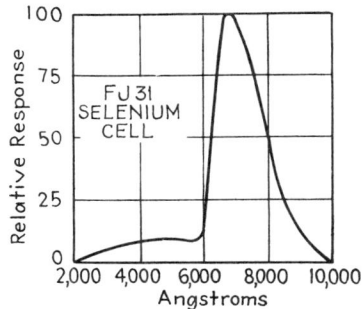

Fig. 10-25.—Relative response of the type FJ-31 selenium cell, in per cent of maximum response, as a function of wave length.

Unlike the phototube, the photoconductive cell passes appreciable current when it is dark, the *dark resistance* of commercial cells ranging from about 100,000 Ω to 25 megohms. The ratio of *light* to *dark* currents may be as high as 25 but is more commonly about 8 or 10. The current capacity does not usually exceed a few milliamperes, but by proper design may be increased to as much as $\frac{1}{4}$ amp. The sensitivity is directly proportional to the voltage across the cell, and consequently cells are usually operated at as high voltage as possible without overheating and subsequent breakdown. In Figs. 10-25 and 10-26 are shown the current–wave-length characteristic curve and the dynamic response curves of a typical selenium cell, the General Electric type FJ-31. The peak of the spectral sensitivity curve is in the red, which makes the cell suitable for use with artificial illumination and infrared radiation.

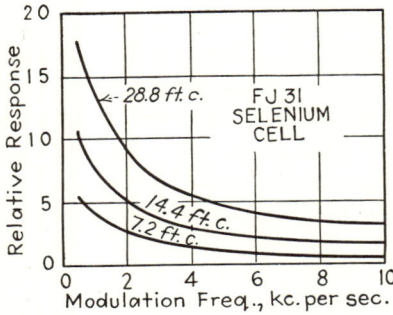

FIG. 10-26.—Dynamic response curves for the type FJ-31 selenium cell.

Expressions for the voltage sensitivity of selenium cells and of the ampere-turn sensitivity of selenium cells used to operate relays may be derived.[1] It is generally simpler, however, to make use of a current-voltage diagram in the same manner as with phototubes and amplifiers. Because the cell resistance at a given

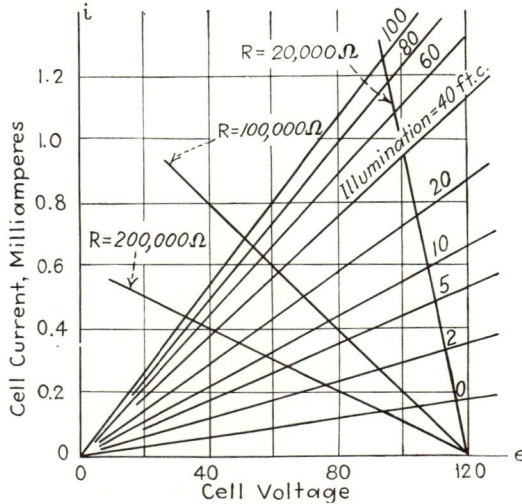

FIG. 10-27.—Typical current-voltage diagram for a selenium cell.

value of illumination is independent of cell voltage, the current-voltage curves are straight lines and may be readily

[1] ZWORYKIN, V. R., and WILSON, E. D., "Photocells and Their Applications," 2d ed., John Wiley & Sons, Inc., 1934, pp. 175–180.

derived from a single static curve of current *vs.* illumination at any voltage. A family of current-voltage characteristics, together with a number of load lines for 120-volt supply voltage, is illustrated in Fig. 10-27. It can be seen from this diagram that the change in current per foot-candle change in illumination, and hence the current sensitivity, is a maximum for zero load resistance, and decreases rapidly as the load resistance is increased. The change in voltage across the load resistance per foot-candle change in illumination, and hence the voltage sensitivity, passes through a maximum as the load resistance is increased. With small changes of illumination, maximum voltage sensitivity is obtained when the load resistance is approximately equal to the average resistance of the cell in the range of operation.

10-18. Photovoltaic Cells (Barrier-layer Cells).—The photovoltaic effect was first observed by Becquerel,[1] who discovered

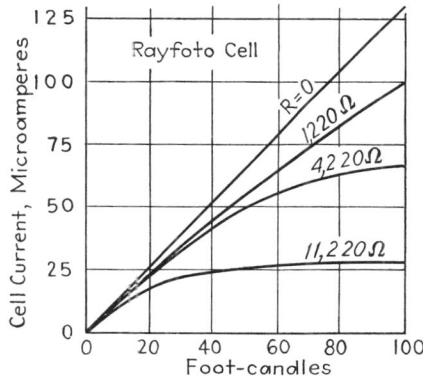

FIG. 10-28.—Curves of current *vs.* illumination for the Rayfoto cell.

that an e.m.f. is set up between two electrodes immersed in an electrolyte when one of the electrodes is illuminated. Two cells based upon the Becquerel effect were the Rayfoto cell, which employed a cathode of cuprous oxide on copper and an anode of lead in an electrolyte of lead nitrate; and the Photolytic cell,[2] which was similar in construction but which employed

[1] BECQUEREL, E., *Compt. rend.*, **9**, 144, 561 (1839).
[2] Although these cells are no longer on the market, they are still of theoretical interest.

cuprous oxide on copper for both electrodes, thus eliminating voltage when the cell was dark. Curves for the Rayfoto type of cell, taken from an article by Fink and Alpern,[1] are shown in Figs. 10-28 and 10-29. It can be seen that when the cell is short-circuited the current is proportional to the illumination but that external circuit resistance destroys the linearity and also results in considerable reduction of current sensitivity. The response of this cell to fluctuating light falls rapidly with increase of light-modulation frequency, so that it is not satisfactory for converting modulated light into sound.

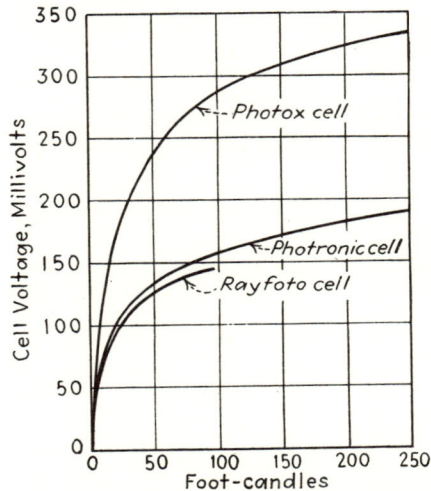

FIG. 10-29.—Curves of generated voltage *vs.* illumination for three types of photovoltaic cells.

A more recent type of photovoltaic cell, the *barrier-layer* cell, is made of a layer of cuprous oxide in very close contact with a metal, usually copper, gold, or platinum, or of a thin layer of iron selenide on iron. It is found that illumination of the boundary or *barrier plane* between the compound and the metal sets up an e.m.f. and that current flows if the compound and the metal are connected through an external circuit. The phenomenon, which is now known to be caused by the emission of electrons from the compound into the metal, was first observed

[1] FINK, G., and ALPERN, D. K., *Trans. Am. Electrochem. Soc.*, **58**, 275 (1930).

by Fritts in 1884 in the course of experiments on selenium cells.[1] Improvements in design and manufacture have resulted in selenium[2] and cuprous-oxide[3] barrier-layer cells capable of producing currents of 100 μa or more per lumen.

There are two forms of barrier-layer cells. In the first, called the *back-effect* cell, the cuprous oxide or iron selenide is deposited upon the metal in the form of a thin layer. The light passes through the compound to the metal, as shown in Fig. 10-30a, the photoelectric action taking place at the boundary between them. Electrons flow across the boundary from the oxide or selenide to the metal, and the conventional direction of current in the external circuit is from the compound to the metal.

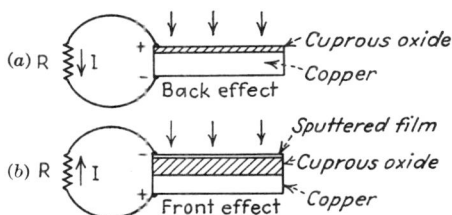

FIG. 10-30.—Arrangement of electrodes in front-effect and back-effect barrier-layer cells.

Contact to the compound is made by means of a conductor pressed against the compound or by means of a thin layer of metal sputtered on the compound near the outer edge of the surface. Because of absorption of the light of shorter wave lengths in the oxide, the current–wave-length characteristic of a cuprous oxide back-effect cell shows a maximum at the red end of the spectrum.

The second form of cell, called the *front-effect cell*, is made by sputtering a thin film of silver, gold, or platinum on the exposed surface of the cuprous-oxide or selenide layer, which is formed on the metal as in the back-effect cell. Light enters the cell through the sputtered film, as shown in Fig. 10-30b. Emission of electrons takes place at both surfaces of the oxide or selenide but is greater at the front surface, causing the sputtered film to become negatively charged with respect to the metal and resulting in

[1] FRITTS, C. F., *Proc. Amer. Asso. Adv. Science*, **33**, 97 (1884); ADAMS, W. G., and DAY, R. E., *Proc. Royal Soc. London*, **25**, 113 (1877).

[2] BERGMANN, *Physik. Z.*, **32**, 286 (1931).

[3] LANGE, B., *Physik. Z.*, **31**, 139 (1930).

current in the conventional sense from the metal to the sputtered film through the external circuit. Absorption of light by the sputtered film is small, and the peak of the spectral sensitivity curve is at the blue end of the visible spectrum.

The short-circuit current of a barrier-layer cell, like that of an electrolytic cell, is directly proportional to the total flux incident upon the surface and is independent of the area illuminated. The introduction of external resistance destroys the linearity between current and flux and reduces the current sensitivity, the curves of current *vs.* illumination being similar to those of Fig. 10-28. The internal resistance of the cell results almost entirely

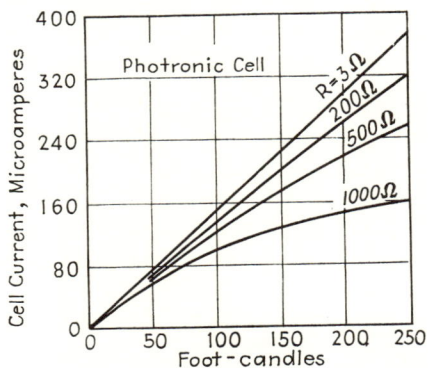

Fig. 10-31.—Curves of current *vs.* illumination for the Photronic cell.

from the fact that the emitted electrons must pass along the poorly conducting layer of cuprous oxide or iron selenide from the point of emission to the external contact. The response of barrier-layer cells to fluctuating light falls rapidly with increase of modulation frequency because of the relatively high capacitance between the two surfaces.

The Photox cell is an example of a front-effect cuprous-oxide cell. It has a current sensitivity of 100 μa/lumen, a cathode area of 0.02 sq ft, and produces a voltage of 0.2 volt with 50–ft-candle illumination. A curve between cell voltage and illumination is shown in Fig. 10-29.

The Photronic cell is an iron selenide cell. The characteristics of the Photronic cell are shown in Figs. 10-29, 10-31, 10-32, and 10-33. The manufacturers state that the response of the cell does not vary over long periods of time. It does, however, show a certain amount of fatigue, as shown by Fig. 10-33, and is sensitive to temperature changes. The response to modulated light is poor. For 100 per cent response at 60 cycles, the response is 58 per cent at 120 cycles, 30 per cent at 240 cycles, and 6.4 per cent at 1000 cycles. The cell is unsuited, therefore, to the conversion of modulated light into alternating current. The internal

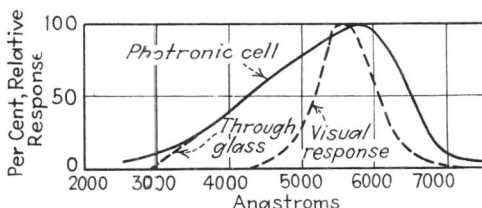

FIG. 10-32.—Curve of relative response *vs.* wave length for the Photronic cell.

resistance of the Photronic cell differs from that of the Photox cell, necessitating differences in the design of circuits.[1]

The chief advantage of photovoltaic cells lies in the fact that they require no external voltage supply.[2] Relays have been designed to operate directly from photovoltaic cells, but, because the resistance of the relay reduces the current sensitivity, it is difficult to obtain high armature torque. The generated voltage is so small that an amplifier of high current sensitivity is required

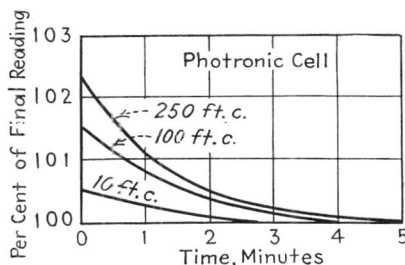

FIG. 10-33.—Curves showing fatigue in the Photronic cell.

if an amplifier is used between the cell and the relay. A single-stage amplifier is ordinarily inadequate. Even for small values of flux, for which the voltage sensitivity is high, the Photronic cell has a sensitivity of only about 25 mv/lumen, and the Photox cell about 50 mv/lumen. This is very small as compared with

[1] BARTLETT, C. H., *Rev. Sci. Instruments*, **3**, 543 (1932).

[2] LAMB, A. H., *Instruments*, **5**, 230 (1932).

the 500-volt/lumen sensitivity obtainable even with the vacuum type of phototube. The voltage sensitivity of photovoltaic cells may be increased by series operation of units, and the current sensitivity by parallel operation. The photovoltaic cell finds one of its principal applications in photometry. In combination with a low-resistance microammeter it makes a simple and rugged foot-candle meter.

10-19. Comparison of Phototubes, Photoconductive Cells, and Photovoltaic Cells.—From the point of view of linearity of response, absence of time lag, and freedom from fatigue and temperature effects, the phototube is far superior to either the photoconductive or the photovoltaic cell. It gives the highest voltage output of the three types but has low current output and low current sensitivity. Because of its high voltage output, however, it may be efficiently used with an amplifier in the operation of current-controlled apparatus. The poor dynamic response of photoconductive and photovolta c cells makes them unsuitable for the conversion of modulated light into sound, but they have the advantage of ruggedness and relatively high current output, which makes possible the direct operation of relays or meters if relatively large changes of illumination are available. The photovoltaic cell has the additional advantage of not requiring an external voltage source. Since the voltage output of a photovoltaic cell is small, and independent of load resistance, the current sensitivity of a single-stage amplifier is insufficient to increase the current change available to operate a relay. Because of the inconvenience and expense involved in the use of a two- or three-stage d-c amplifier, it is usually not advantageous to use an amplifier in conjunction with a photovoltaic cell. Low-resistance relays and comparatively large changes of illumination are consequently required. The over-all voltage or current sensitivity of a photoconductive-cell circuit may be increased by the use of an amplifier.

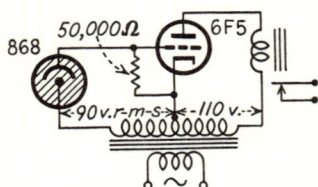

Fig. 10-34.—Circuit diagram for Prob. 10-1.

Problems

10-1. Criticize the circuit of Fig. 10-34. (Six errors.)

10-2. The following data apply to a photoelectrically controlled relay:

Phototube sensitivity...................... 7 μa/lumen
Phototube cathode area.................. 1 sq in.
Amplifier tube........ .... Type 6J5
Coupling resistor.......................... 8 megohms
Relay operating currents.................. $\begin{cases} 8 \text{ ma, closing} \\ 7 \text{ ma, opening} \end{cases}$
Relay resistance...... .... 1000 Ω

a. Draw the diagram of a circuit in which increase of illumination will cause the relay to be opened. All phototube and amplifier voltages are to be derived from a single 220-volt d-c supply.

b. Specify values of resistance that will provide the correct filament current and suitable values of plate voltage and adjustable biasing voltage.

c. Specify the value and polarity of the C supply voltage that will just open the relay at a phototube illumination of 72 ft-candles. The source of light is a tungsten filament operated at 2870°K.

d. How much must the illumination be decreased to cause the relay to close?

10-3. The following data apply to a phototube-amplifier-relay circuit:

Phototube............................... Type 868 (see Fig. 10-7)
Phototube cathode area.................... 0.9 sq in.
Amplifier tube............................ Type 6J5
Coupling resistance........ .... 1 megohm
Relay resistance.......................... 1000 Ω
Relay closing current..................... 6 ma
Relay opening current..................... 4 ma
Phototube anode supply voltage............ 90 volts
Amplifier plate supply voltage............. 90 volts
Light source.............. .... Tungsten filament at 2870°K

a. Show the circuit diagram for a circuit in which increase of illumination causes the relay to close.

b. From the plate characteristics of the type 6J5 tube find the grid voltages at which the relay will open and close.

c. From the characteristic curves of the type 868 phototube (Fig. 10-7), plot a curve of voltage across the coupling resistor as a function of light flux.

d. From the curve of (c) determine the grid supply voltage necessary to open the relay when the incident flux is 0.2 lumen.

e. Determine the change in illumination, in foot-candles, necessary to close the relay after the circuit is adjusted as in (d).

10-4. a. Plot curves of per cent second and third harmonic in the voltage output of a type 918 phototube operated from an 80-volt supply with a 7-megohm load, as a function of incident light flux for 80 per cent and 100 per cent modulation of incident light.

b. Repeat for a load having a d-c resistance of 10 megohms and an a-c resistance of 7 megohms at signal frequency.

10-5. Determine the factor by which the current scale of the current-voltage characteristics of a type 868 gas phototube must be multiplied in order that the characteristics shall hold for a light source whose energy distribution is given by the following table:

Wave length, angstroms	Relative energy	Wave length, angstroms	Relative energy	Wave length, angstroms	Relative energy
3000	0	5500	42	8000	15
3500	1	6000	65	8500	6
4000	6	6500	93	9000	2
4500	14	7000	100	9250	0
5000	25	7500	55		

Bibliography

The literature on the scientific aspects of photoelectricity is very extensive. More complete treatments of the subject than that given in this chapter will be found in the following books and articles:

HUGHES, A. L., and DuBRIDGE, L. A.: "Photoelectric Phenomena," McGraw-Hill Book Company, Inc., New York, 1932.

ZWORYKIN, V. K., and WILSON, E. D.: "Photocells and Their Application," John Wiley & Sons, Inc., New York, 1934.

WALKER, R. C., and LANCE, T. M. C.: "Photo-electric Cell Applications," 3d ed., Sir Isaac Pitman & Sons, Ltd., London, 1939.

FIELDING, T. J.: "Photo-electric and Selenium Cells," Chapman & Hall, Ltd., London, 1935.

KOLLER, L. R.: "The Physics of Electron Tubes," McGraw-Hill Book Company, Inc., New York, 1937.

ALLEN, H. S.: "Photoelectricity," Longmans, Green & Company, New York, 1913.

HUGHES, A. L.: "Photo-Electricity," Cambridge University Press, London, 1914.

CAMPBELL, N. R., and RITCHIE, D.: "Photoelectric Cells," Sir Isaac Pitman & Sons, Ltd., London, 1934.

HUGHES, A. L.: "Report on Photoelectricity," National Research Council.

BARNARD, G. P.: "The Selenium Cell," Archibald Constable & Co., Ltd., London, 1930.

BENSON, T. W.: "Selenium Cells," Spon & Chamberlain, New York, 1919.

LANGE, B.: "Photoelements and Their Application," Reinhold Publishing Corporation, New York, 1938.

HUGHES, A. L.: Fundamental Laws of Photoelectricity, *Elec. Eng.*, **53**, 1149 (1934).

NIX, F. C.: Photo-conductivity, *Rev. Modern Phys.*, **4**, 723 (1932).

GRONDAHL, L. O.: The Copper Cuprous Oxide Rectifier and Photoelectric Cell, *Rev. Modern Phys.*, **5**, 141 (1933).

The following partial list of books and articles covers applications of light-sensitive tubes and cells:

Henney, Keith: "Electron Tubes in Industry," McGraw-Hill Book Company, Inc., New York, 1937.

Gulliksen, F. H., and Vedder, E. H.: "Industrial Electronics," John Wiley & Sons, Inc., New York, 1935.

Breisky, J. V., and Erikson, E. O.: *J. Am. Inst. Elec. Eng.*, **48**, 118 (1929).

Vedder, E. H.: *Elec. J.*, **27**, 152 (1930).

Romain, B. P.: *Rev. Sci. Instruments*, **4**, 83 (1933).

Chambers, D. E.: *Elec. Eng.*, **54**, 82 (1935).

Gulliksen, F. H., and Stoddard, R. N.: *Elec. Eng.*, **54**, 40 (1935).

Wilson, E. D.: *Electronics*, April, 1935, p. 118.

Shepard, F. H., Jr.: *Electronics*, February, 1935, p. 59; June, 1936, p. 34; *Proc. I.R.E.*, **24**, 1573 (1936); *RCA Rev.*, **2**, 149 (1937).

Powers, R. A.: *Electronics*, September, 1935, p. 11; June, 1936, p. 22.

Vedder, E. H.: *Elec. J.*, **32**, 425 (1935).

Lamb, A. H.: *Elec. Eng.*, **54**, 1186 (1935).

Holmes, R. M.: *Electronics*, April, 1937, p. 33.

CHAPTER 11

RECTIFIERS AND FILTERS

The practically universal use at the present time of alternating current in the transmission and distribution of electric power necessitates the use of some means for converting into direct current in certain applications of electric power. Although this may be accomplished by rotary converters or motor-generator sets, it is often simpler, cheaper, and more efficient to use electronic rectifiers. Other advantages of electronic rectifiers include quiet operation, ease and speed of starting and, in mercury pool types, long life, high momentary overload capacity, and immunity to frequency short-circuits. Outstanding applications of electronic rectifiers are made in supplying direct voltages for electric railways, for electrolytic plants, and for the operation of electron tubes.

Since the output of a rectifier is pulsating, and the voltage used in most tube circuits must be nearly free of pulsation, rectifiers that supply direct voltages to tubes must be followed by smoothing filters. In order to prevent interference in adjacent communication lines, it is also important to keep the ripple small in the distribution of rectified currents. Because of the many factors involved in rectification and filtering, only the principal aspects of the subject will be presented in this chapter.

11-1. Definitions.—A *rectifier* is a device having an asymmetrical conduction characteristic which is used for the conversion of an alternating current into a current having a unidirectional component. Such devices include vacuum-tube rectifiers, gaseous rectifiers, oxide (barrier-layer) rectifiers, and electrolytic rectifiers. A *half-wave rectifier* is a rectifier that changes alternating current into pulsating current, utilizing only one-half of each cycle. A *full-wave rectifier* is a double-element rectifier arranged so that current is allowed to pass to the load circuit in the same direction during each half cycle of the alternating supply voltage, one element functioning during one half cycle and another during the next half cycle.

The alternating component of unidirectional voltage from a rectifier or generator used as a source of d-c power is called *ripple voltage*. The ripple voltage is not generally sinusoidal and may, therefore, be analyzed into fundamental and harmonic components.

The importance of the ripple voltage relative to the d-c component of the rectifier or filter output voltage is often specified by means of the *per cent ripple*, which is defined by the Standards Committee of the Institute of Radio Engineers[1] as the ratio of the r-m-s value of the ripple voltage to the algebraic average value of the total voltage, expressed in percentage. The effectiveness

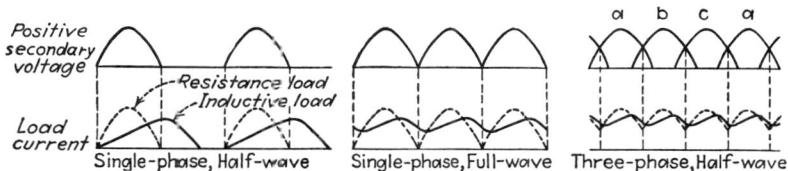

Fig. 11-1.—Curves of positive secondary voltage and load current for single-phase and three-phase rectifiers.

of a smoothing filter increases, however, with the frequency of the voltage input to the filter. Furthermore, in all but the half-wave single-phase rectifier, the amplitudes of the ripple harmonics decrease rapidly with increase of the order of the harmonics. For these reasons, if a filter is designed to produce adequate filtering at the fundamental ripple frequency, the ripple harmonics will usually be reduced to negligible values, and so only the fundamental component of ripple voltage need be considered in designing the filter. The ratio of the amplitude of the fundamental component of ripple voltage to the average (direct) value of the total voltage will be called the *ripple factor*.

The effectiveness of a smoothing filter in removing a component of ripple voltage of any frequency may be indicated by the effect that it would have upon a sinusoidal voltage of that frequency. The ratio of the amplitude of a sinusoidal voltage of given frequency impressed upon the input of a filter to the amplitude of the resulting sinusoidal output voltage will be termed the *smoothing factor* at that frequency.

The following symbols will be used:

[1] 1933 Report of I.R.E. Standards Committee.

Supply frequency.................................... f

Fundamental ripple frequency........................ f_r

Amplitude of fundamental component of ripple voltage at
   filter input....................................... E_{r1}

Average value of total output voltage................. E_{dc}

Ripple factor at input to filter, E_{r1}/E_{dc}............... ρ

Smoothing factor at any frequency.................... α

Smoothing factor at fundamental ripple frequency....... α_1

Primed symbols will be used to indicate the ripple voltage and its components and the ripple factors at the output of the filter (across the load).

11-2. Current Wave Form.—In Fig. 11-1 are shown curves of positive anode voltage and of load current in a single-phase half-wave rectifier, in a single-phase full-wave rectifier, and in a three-phase half-wave rectifier, with resistance and inductance loads, under the assumption that tube and transformer voltage drops are zero. When the load (including the filter) is nonreactive, current flows in each phase only when that phase has the highest induced voltage, and the instantaneous current is proportional to the instantaneous voltage. The current waves are shown by

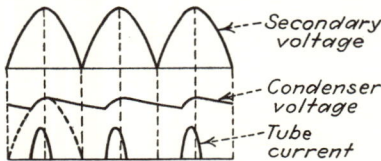

Fig. 11-2.—Approximate wave form of load voltage and tube current in a full-wave single-phase rectifier with resistance-capacitance load.

the dotted curves. (The effect of the constant voltage drop in an arc rectifier tube is to prevent the flow of current when the induced voltage is less than the normal tube drop.) The presence of inductance in the load tends to prevent the current from building up and dying down, and thus changes the forms of the current waves to those shown by the solid curves. If the inductance is made sufficiently large, the load current becomes practically constant, and so the current in each phase is very nearly a square-topped pulse.

When a resistance load is shunted by a condenser, current flows through the rectifier only when the induced voltage exceeds the condenser voltage. If the condenser is large and the resistance high, current flows just for a short time at the peaks of the induced voltage. The approximate forms of typical voltage and current waves with resistance-capacitance load are shown in Fig. 11-2.

When the load is such that current flows in each phase during the entire time in which its induced voltage exceeds those of the other phases (inductive or nonreactive load), then the voltage wave across the rectifier load consists of the portions of the phase voltage waves lying between the intersections of waves of the different phases. The voltage waves for different numbers of phases are shown by the solid curves of Fig. 11-3. The form of the corresponding current wave can be determined by analyzing the voltage wave into its Fourier components, dividing each component by the impedance of the load (including the filter) at the corresponding frequency, and adding the component currents obtained in this manner.[1] If the presence of capacitance

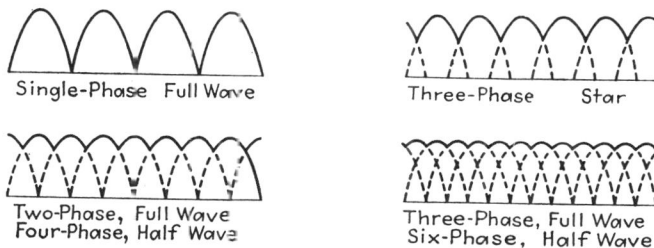

Single-Phase Full Wave

Three-Phase Star

Two-Phase, Full Wave
Four-Phase, Half Wave

Three-Phase, Full Wave
Six-Phase, Half Wave

FIG. 11-3.—Wave form (solid lines) of load voltage for resistance or inductance load.

in the rectifier load causes each tube to pass current during only a portion of the possible firing period, then the load voltage during the nonconducting portion of the cycle depends upon the parameters of the load. Under these conditions the determination of the current wave form becomes difficult and necessitates the use of successive approximations.[2] Considerations of efficiency and voltage regulation recommend, however, that enough inductance should be used in the load to cause current to flow during the maximum firing period of each tube.

11-3. Choice of Rectifier Tubes and Circuit.—The choice of rectifier tubes and circuit involves a number of factors, of which the following merit special consideration:

1. *Type of Rectifier Tubes.*—The low voltage drop of mercury vapor tubes results in higher efficiency of operation than with high-vacuum tubes and, because the drop is practically constant

[1] STOUT, M. B., *Elec. Eng.*, **54**, 977 (1935).
[2] STOUT, *ibid.*

throughout the working range of current, the voltage regulation is better than with high-vacuum tubes. For a tube of given size and given filament power the mercury vapor tube will pass higher current than the high-vacuum tube. The peak voltage of the mercury vapor rectifier is limited, however, because of danger of glow and subsequent breakdown into an arc during the half of the cycle when the anode is negative. The hot-cathode mercury vapor rectifier is much more subject to damage due to overload or low cathode temperature, and adequate provision must be made to ensure that the anode voltage will not be applied before the cathode has reached operating temperature. Another disadvantage of mercury vapor rectifiers is that the abrupt changes of anode current that occur when the arc fires and extinguishes produce objectionable transient and high-frequency disturbances. Provision must be made to prevent these disturbances from affecting apparatus connected to the power supply or from being transferred to the a-c line or radiated.

Grid-controlled arc rectifiers are advantageously used in large power supplies.[1] The use of phase control affords a simple method of reducing the direct voltage. In power supplies for radio transmitters, gradual increase of voltage in starting prevents damage to the transmitter tubes and also prevents failure of filter condensers as the result of large current surges.[2] The grids may be used to provide high-speed automatic regulation of the direct voltage. Grid control also makes possible interruption of the anode current within one cycle of the supply frequency when a short circuit or other overload occurs. The circuit may be designed so that the energy stored in the filter is returned to the line by inverter action, instead of being dissipated in a flashover arc. The likelihood of arcback (current flow in the reverse direction) is reduced by the use of grids in mercury arc rectifiers.

2. *Transformer Design.*—The design of the transformer, or transformers, is dependent upon the type of circuit and tubes. Factors that must be taken into consideration are the primary

---

[1] BROWN, H. D., *Gen. Elec. Rev.*, **35**, 439 (1932); Foos, C. B., *Elec. Eng.*, **53**, 568 (1934); KIME, R. M., *Electronics*, August, 1933, p. 219; JOURNEAUX, D., *Elec. Eng.*, **53**, 976 (1934); DURAND, S. R., and KELLER, O., *Proc. I.R.E.*, **25**, 570 (1937).

[2] DURAND AND KELLER, *ibid.*

and secondary volt-amperes, the secondary voltages, and insulation required between windings.

3. *Efficiency.*—The efficiency of operation depends upon the transformer and tube efficiencies. Tube efficiency, as already stated, is greater for mercury arc rectifiers than for high-vacuum rectifiers. The efficiency of both the tubes and the transformer increases with the percentage of the cycle during which anode current flows. For this reason, if a filter is used, it is advisable to design it so that current flows in each tube during its maximum firing period. In some rectifier circuits, current flows in only one direction in each leg of the transformer. The resulting d-c component of flux saturates the core, reducing the efficiency by increasing the magnetizing current and hysteresis loss and by introducing harmonics into the secondary voltage.

4. *Filament Supply.*—In certain rectifier circuits the cathodes are at the same potential and may be operated from the same heating transformer; in others, on the other hand, it is necessary to use either separate filament supplies or heater-type tubes with adequate insulation between cathodes and heaters.

5. *Ripple Frequency and Amplitude.*—The size and cost of a filter capable of reducing the ripple factor to a given value at the load decrease with increase of ripple frequency and with decrease of ripple amplitude at the filter input. The allowable ripple factor at the load depends upon the type of service for which the power supply is designed. In the microphone circuit of a radio transmitter the ripple factor must be less than 0.005 per cent. In audio-frequency amplifiers not followed by high-gain radio-frequency amplifiers, ripple factors may range from 0.01 to 0.1 per cent without causing objectionable hum, and even 1 per cent may sometimes be tolerated. About 1 per cent represents the upper limit in voltages used for cathode-ray oscillographs. In industrial applications and in control devices of the type discussed in Chaps. 9 and 10, the allowable ripple may sometimes be so high that the smoothing filter may be omitted.

In general, the ripple frequency increases and the ripple amplitude decreases with increase of the number of phases. The wave form of the rectified voltage for different numbers of phases is shown by the solid lines in Fig. 11-3.

11-4. Characteristics of Rectifier Circuits.—Table 11-I lists important information concerning some of the more common

TABLE 11-I (See first paragraph of Sec. 11-4 for explanation of items listed.)

Type of circuit	Single-phase half-wave — Inductance in series with load	Single-phase half-wave — Resistance load, without choke	Single-phase full-wave	Single-phase bridge	Two-phase full-wave (four-phase star) — 2-phase supply	Three-phase star — 3-phase supply	Three-phase double star (six-phase star full-wave) — 3-phase supply	Three-phase star full-wave — 3-phase supply	Double three-phase with balance coil — 3-phase supply
Secondary volts per leg ÷ direct voltage	2.22	2.22	1.11	1.11	0.785	0.855	0.740	0.428	0.855
Primary volts per leg ÷ direct voltage	2.22	2.22	1.11	1.11	0.785	0.855	0.740	0.428	0.855
Primary current per leg ÷ direct current	0.707	1.57	1.0	1.0	0.707	0.471	0.577	0.816	0.408
Secondary current per leg ÷ direct current	0.707	1.57	0.707	1.0	0.500	0.577	0.408	0.816	0.289
Primary kva ÷ d-c watts	1.57	3.49	1.57	1.11	1.57	1.48	1.81	1.05	1.48
Secondary kva ÷ d-c watts	1.57	3.49	1.11	1.11	1.57	1.21	1.28	1.05	1.05
Peak inverse tube voltage	3.14	3.14	3.14	1.57	2.22	2.09	2.09	1.05	2.42
Average tube current ÷ direct current	0.707	1.57	0.707	0.707	0.50	0.577	0.408	0.577	0.289
Peak tube current ÷ direct current	1.00	π	1.00	1.00	1.00	1.00	1.00	1.00	0.50
Fundamental ripple frequency f_r in terms of supply frequency	f	f	$2f$	$2f$	$4f$	$3f$	$6f$	$6f$	$6f$
Ripple factor ρ_c	1.77*	1.57	0.667	0.667	0.150	0.25	0.057	0.057	0.057
Second-harmonic ripple factor ρ_2	1.54**	0.667	0.133	0.133	0.030	0.057	0.014	0.014	0.014
Third-harmonic ripple factor ρ_3		0	0.057	0.057	0.016	0.025	0.006	0.006	0.006

* Values change with ratio of load resistance to series inductance.

types of rectifier circuits.[1] It should be noted that all voltage, current, and volt-ampere values in this table are given with respect to the average values of direct voltage, direct current, and d-c power, respectively. The values listed are derived under the assumption that tube and transformer voltage drops are negligible and that the transformer is perfect. In deriving the current relations it is furthermore assumed that each tube conducts during the entire time in which the induced voltage in its phase is positive and exceeds the positive voltages of the other phases. An examination of this table discloses the advantages of certain circuits over others.

The single-phase half-wave rectifier has as its chief merits its simplicity and low cost. These advantages are offset, however, by the high ripple amplitude and low ripple frequency, which in some applications necessitate the use of a comparatively expensive smoothing filter; by low voltage output; and by low transformer efficiency. The low transformer efficiency results partly from the high effective alternating voltages and currents and partly because the rectified direct current flows through the secondary and saturates the core. Core saturation increases the magnetizing current and the hysteresis loss and introduces harmonics into the secondary voltage. It is impractical to use sufficient filter inductance to cause current to flow during the whole cycle. In fact, in order to raise the output voltage and assist in removing ripple, a condenser is usually shunted across the output of the rectifier. This reduces still further the time during which secondary current flows, and so decreases the transformer efficiency. The single-phase half-wave rectifier is now used comparatively little.

The single-phase full-wave rectifier is the most commonly used type of rectifier at voltages below 1000 volts and currents of 1 amp or less. The ripple frequency is twice that of the a-c supply, and the ripple amplitude is sufficiently small so that smoothing is not difficult. The circuit is simple and requires only one two-anode (full-wave) rectifier tube. The single-phase bridge circuit subjects the tubes to a lower peak inverse voltage than the single-phase full-wave circuit and requires smaller transformer primary volt-ampere rating. It has the disadvantages that three separate filament transformers must be used,

[1] ARMSTRONG, R. W., *Prcc. I.R.E.*, **19**, 78 (1931).

that the circuit requires three tubes (one two-anode and two single-anode rectifiers) instead of one, and that the efficiency is somewhat lower because of increased tube loss.

The ripple amplitude is much lower in polyphase rectifiers, and the ripple frequency higher than in single-phase rectifiers. The three-phase star connection has the disadvantage that current flows in each leg of the secondary in one direction only, causing core saturation. This difficulty does not occur in the other polyphase circuits that are listed in Table 11-I. The three-phase star full-wave connection requires low transformer volt-ampere rating and subjects the tubes to low peak inverse voltage but requires four filament transformers. In the double three-phase rectifier with balance coil, induced voltages in the balance coil cause equal currents to flow simultaneously in two phases, one in each wye. This results in low average and peak tube currents, but the peak inverse tube voltage is comparatively high. Many other connections are possible, some of which give increased efficiency or improved voltage regulation.[1] There appears to be a trend toward the use of a large number of phases (30 or more) in large commercial tank rectifiers.[2]

11-5. Smoothing Filters.—Three types of filters are commonly used in power supplies. These are (1) a condenser shunted across the rectifier output, as in Fig. 11-4*a*; (2) one or more sections, each of which consists of a series inductance followed by a shunt capacitance, as in Fig. 11-4*b*; and (3) a combination of 1 and 2, as in Fig. 11-4*c*. The use of a single condenser across the rectifier output is of principal value when the load current is small, as in voltage supplies for cathode-ray oscillographs. The multisection inductance-condenser filter is in general the most satisfactory, since it results in good voltage regulation, low peak anode current, and high tube and transformer efficiency. The multisection inductance-condenser filter with condenser input is used mainly in small single-phase power supplies. It has a higher smoothing factor than a multisection filter without input condenser that has the same total inductance and capacitance, and it results in higher direct voltage. The direct voltage at light load approximates the crest alternating secondary voltage E_m, as compared with $0.318E_m$ in a half-wave single-phase rectifier

---

[1] ARMSTRONG, *loc. cit.*

[2] MARTI, O. K., *Elec. Eng.*, **59**, 218 (1940).

without the input condenser and $0.636E_m$ in a full-wave single-phase rectifier (see Table 11-I). The rise of direct voltage at light load causes the voltage regulation to be greater than when the condenser is omitted. Other disadvantages resulting from the use of a condenser in the input to the filter are increased peak anode current, particularly in mercury vapor tubes, and higher peak inverse voltage. The peak inverse voltage is the crest secondary voltage plus the condenser voltage at the instant of crest secondary voltage. Since the condenser voltage approximates the crest secondary voltage under light load, the peak inverse voltage may approach twice the crest secondary voltage.

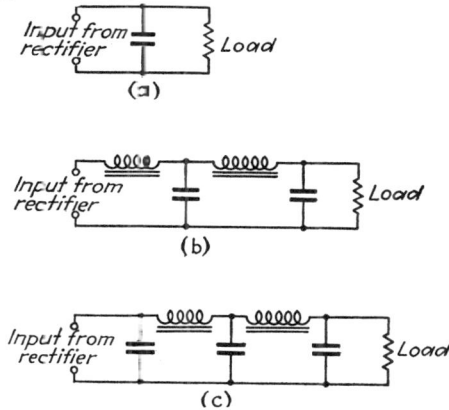

FIG. 11-4.—Three types of smoothing filters: (*a*) condenser; (*b*) choke-condenser (L-section); (*c*) choke-condenser with condenser input (pi-section).

The chokes of the circuits of Figs. 11-4*b* and *c* may be replaced by resistances. The d-c resistance of resistance-condenser filters is much higher than that of inductance-capacitance filters using the same size condensers and having the same smoothing factor. Hence the voltage regulation, the loss in direct voltage, and the heat dissipation are greater. Furthermore, they result in higher peak anode current and lower transformer efficiency. The development of small, low-cost electrolytic condensers of high capacitance has, however, made feasible the use of resistance-condenser filters when the requirements of low cost, lightness, and small size outweigh the desirability of high quality.

11-6. Analysis of Condenser Filter.—When the rectifier output is shunted by a condenser, as in Fig. 11-4*a*, the tubes pass current only when the induced voltage exceeds the condenser voltage.

Since the charging current of the condenser is limited only by the transformer reactance and the tube drop, the condenser voltage builds up nearly as fast as the induced secondary voltage until the crest induced voltage is attained. Beyond the crest of the induced voltage, unless the load current is very large, the

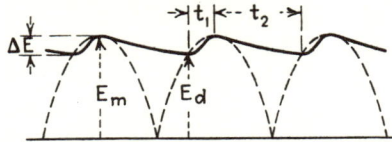

FIG. 11-5.—Wave form (solid line) of the condenser and load voltage in the circuit of Fig. 11-4a under light load.

induced voltage falls more rapidly than the condenser voltage, and so the tube ceases to conduct. The condenser discharges through the load, and the terminal voltage falls exponentially at a rate that is determined by the condenser capacitance and the load resistance, until the induced voltage again exceeds the condenser voltage. The wave of condenser voltage is of the general form shown in Fig. 11-5. At light loads the ripple factor is given approximately by the relation

$$\rho = \frac{1}{\pi f_r R C} \qquad (11\text{-}1)$$

11-7. Voltage Doubler.—A useful form of the rectifier with condenser-shunted output is the voltage-doubling circuit shown in Fig. 11-6. In this circuit two condensers are charged in alternate halves of the cycle through two rectifier tubes. The condensers are connected in series, so that their voltages add, giving a load voltage that approaches twice the crest secondary voltage at light loads. The average terminal voltage is twice the average voltage of each condenser, and the variation of terminal voltage is equal to the voltage variation of each condenser. The ripple frequency is twice that of each condenser, or twice the supply frequency. At light loads the ripple factor is approximately

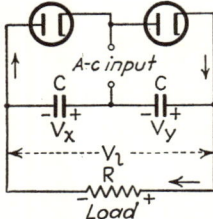

FIG. 11-6.—Voltage-doubler circuit.

$$\rho = \frac{1}{\pi f R C} \qquad (11\text{-}2)$$

where f is the supply frequency and C is the capacitance of each condenser.

For some applications the voltage doubler can furnish the required high direct voltage without the use of a transformer between the supply and the rectifier. The advantage of high direct voltage is offset by the requirement of two filament transformers or of a full-wave rectifier tube with two independent cathodes. The 25Z5 tube is a heater-type rectifier tube designed for this circuit By the use of more complicated circuits it is possible to obtain a direct output voltage approximately equal to four times the crest alternating voltage.[1] Voltage doublers, like the simple condenser filter, may be followed by choke-condenser filters for further smoothing.

11-8. Choke-condenser (L-section) Filters.—From Fig. 11-7 it can be seen that the smoothing factor for a single-section choke-condenser filter is equal to the total input impedance of the filter divided by the impedance of the parallel combination of the condenser and the load resistance. With values of C that are sufficiently large to give adequate filtering, the vector sum of the condenser and load admittance is approximately equal to the condenser admittance alone. Since the resistance of the choke is small in comparison with the inductive reactance, the smoothing factor is approximately

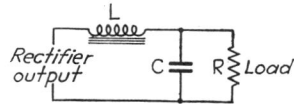

FIG. 11-7.—Single-section choke-condenser (L-section) filter.

$$\alpha = \frac{x_l - x_c}{x_c} = \omega^2 LC - 1 \tag{11-3}$$

The required value of the product LC to give a smoothing factor of value α is

$$LC = \frac{\alpha + 1}{\omega^2} \tag{11-4}$$

Under the assumption that the inductive reactance is large in comparison with the capacitive reactance, the required value of LC for each stage of a filter having n similar sections is approximately

$$LC = 0.0253 \frac{\sqrt[n]{\alpha_1} + 1}{f_r^2} \tag{11-5}$$

[1] GARSTANG, W. W., *Electronics*, February, 1932, p. 50; WAIDELICH, D. L., *Electronics*, May, 1941, p. 28.

where α_1 is the required smoothing factor at the ripple frequency f_r.[1]

It is evident from Eq. (11-5) that a given smoothing factor may be obtained with one stage or with two or more stages. Furthermore, the required value of the product LC may be obtained with an infinite number of combinations of L and C. Choice of the best number of stages and of the individual values of L and C to give the necessary product LC is governed in part by such considerations as cost of chokes and condensers, available sizes of chokes and condensers, and voltage regulation resulting from choke resistance. Usually it is satisfactory to make all sections of a multisection filter identical. There may, however, be a lower limit to the amount of inductance that it is advisable to use in the first stage.

It may be shown both theoretically[2] and experimentally[3] that the terminal voltage rises markedly when the inductance of the first choke is reduced below the value necessary to maintain continuous flow of anode current. Continuous flow of anode current is also desirable from the standpoints of tube and transformer efficiency and minimization of peak anode current. Continuous flow of anode current, low peak anode current, and low voltage regulation may be ensured by making the inductance L_1 of the first choke greater than the value

$$L_0 = 0.18 \frac{\rho R_t}{f_r} \qquad (11\text{-}6)$$

at minimum load and twice this value at full load, where R_t is the total resistance of the load, including the chokes.[3] The desired variation of choke inductance from minimum load to full load is accomplished by proper choice of air gap.[3] For a 60-cycle, single-phase, full-wave rectifier, Eq. (11-6) reduces to[3]

$$L_0 = \frac{R_t}{1000} \qquad (11\text{-}7)$$

To prevent resonance effects, the natural frequency of each filter section should be less than the ripple frequency. In

---

[1] Lee, Reuben, *Elec. J.*, **29**, 186 (1932).

[2] Reich, H. J., "Theory and Applications of Electron Tubes," Sec. 14-10.

[3] Dellenbaugh, F. S., Jr., and Quinby, R. S., *QST*, February, 1932, p. 14; March, 1932, p. 27; April, 1932, p. 33.

order to avoid the possibility of amplifier motorboating as the
result of common plate-circuit impedance in a number of stages
(see Sec. 6-14), the reactance of the final filter condenser should
be small at the low-frequency end of the frequency band for
which the amplifier is designed.

Figure 11-8 shows the complete circuit of a single-phase, full-
wave power supply with a two-section choke-condenser filter.
One function of the "bleeder" resistance is to prevent excessive
transient voltages in the filter condensers when the power

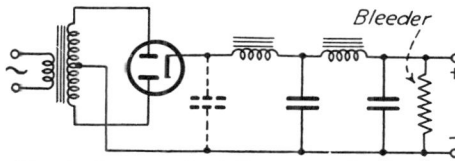

FIG. 11-8.—Circuit diagram of a full-wave single-phase power supply.

supply is turned on under light load. It may also serve as a
voltage divider.

11-9. Voltage Stabilizers.—In certain applications of electron
tubes, notably in oscillators and measuring instruments, it is
necessary to provide direct voltage that remains essentially
constant in spite of fluctuations of line voltage. A number of
voltage stabilizers using high-vacuum tubes have been devised
(see also Sec. 9-6).[1] Three basic circuits are shown in Fig. 11-9.

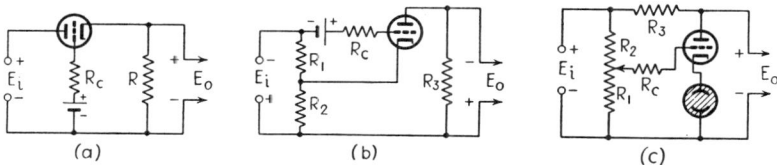

FIG. 11-9.—Basic stabilizer circuits: (a) degenerative type; (b) amplification-
factor–bridge type; (c) transconductance-bridge type using glow-tube bias.

In the degenerative circuit a, increase of current through R, which
may be the load, causes an increase of negative grid bias, which
tends to prevent increase of current and hence of voltage across

[1] GRAMMER, G., *QST*, August, 1937, p. 14; BOUSQUET, A. G., *Electronics*,
July, 1938, p. 26; WALTZ, W. W., *Electronics*, December, 1938, p. 34; RCA
Application Note 96; HUNT, F. V., and HICKMAN, R. W., *Rev. Sci. Instru-
ments*, **10**, 6 (1939) (with 13 references); NEHER, H. V., and PICKERING,
W. H., *Rev. Sci. Instruments*, **10**, 53 (1939) (with bibliography); COOMBS,
J. N., and NIMS, P. T., *Electronics*. January, 1940, p. 40.

R.   The function of R_c is to prevent the flow of high grid current in the event of removal of E_i.   Analysis of the equivalent plate circuit shows that best stabilization is obtained with tubes having high amplification factor.   Loss of output voltage as the result of tube drop is minimized by the use of a high-current power tube.

In circuit b, the ratio of R_2 to R_1 is made equal to the amplification factor.   When the input voltage changes, the change of plate voltage is then μ times the change of grid voltage, and so the plate current and the voltage across R_3, which may be the load, remain unchanged.   Good stabilization is obtained over a range of input voltage throughout which the amplification factor remains approximately constant.   The output voltage may be made to increase with decrease of input voltage by making R_2/R_1 less than μ. R_c serves the same function as in circuit a.   The output voltage in this circuit is less than the input voltage by the sum of the voltage across R_1 and the drop through the tube.   Since $R_1 = R_2/\mu$ for balance, the voltage loss in R_1 may be minimized by the use of a high-mu tube.   The tube drop is least for a given load (plate) current in power tubes.

In circuit c, the glow tube, which may be replaced by a battery if a resistance is added in series with the grid, maintains the cathode of the triode at a constant positive voltage relative to the negative side of the input.   The negative bias of the triode, therefore, decreases with rise of input voltage.   Analysis of the equivalent plate circuit shows that when $R_3 = R_2/R_1 g_m$ the output voltage is independent of input voltage throughout a range of input voltage and plate current in which g_m is essentially constant.   Since R_3 should be small in order to prevent unnecessary loss of voltage, a tube used in this circuit should have high transconductance.

In some applications of voltage compensators, internal resistance (change in output voltage with change in load current) is objectionable.   It is reduced in the circuits of Fig. 11-9 by reduction of plate resistance, but is relatively high even when power triodes are used.   Improved circuits having low internal resistance and giving high stabilization over wide ranges of input voltage and load current have been developed.   Two such circuits that incorporate an amplifier in the basic circuit of Fig. 11-9a are shown in Fig. 11-10.[1]   Although the tubes indicated in Fig. 11-10 are suitable for a general-purpose unit, they may be replaced by other types to meet various requirements. The coupling resistor R_2 should be large in comparison with the plate resistance of the amplifier tube. R_3 should limit the glow-tube current to the "normal" range. The performance

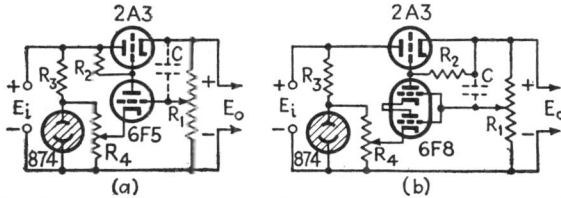

FIG. 11-10.—Degenerative type stabilizers incorporating an amplifier. The condenser C serves to eliminate ripple and surges.

of the circuit of Fig. 11-10b was reported by Hunt and Hickman[1] to be equivalent to that of storage cells of about 15 amp-hr capacity.

11-10. Illustrative Problem.—This chapter will be concluded with a typical problem of power-supply design. The required power supply is to be single phase and full wave and must be able to furnish a d-c output of 200 ma at 350 volts with a ripple factor that does not exceed 0.1 per cent. To prevent excessive voltage regulation a choke-input filter should be used.

Examination of the operating characteristics of the 5U4-G high-vacuum rectifier (see page 378) shows that this tube will furnish the required current and voltage. Assume that the output will be shunted by a 20,000-Ω voltage divider (bleeder), which will draw $17\frac{1}{2}$ ma at 350 volts. Table 11-I gives 120 $\sim$ and 0.667 for the values of f_r and ρ. Since the allowable value of ρ', the ripple factor at the output of the filter, is 0.001, $\alpha_1 = 0.667/0.001 = 667$. Substitution of these values of f_r and $\sim_1$ in Eq. (11-5) gives the following values of LC:

Single-section filter .... 1174×10^{-6} henry $\times$ farad
Two-section filter.............. 47.1×10^{-6} henry $\times$ farad
Three-section filter............ 17.1×10^{-6} henry $\times$ farad

At full load L_1 should not be smaller than $R_t/500$. Choke resistance neglected, R_t at full load is equal to the full-load voltage divided by the total full-load current, or

[1] HUNT and HICKMAN, *loc. cit.*

$$\frac{350}{0.200 + 0.0175} = 1610 \ \Omega.$$

Therefore L_1 should not be less than 3.22 henrys. At minimum load L_1 should exceed $R_t/1000 \cong 20{,}000/1000 = 20$ henrys. A first choke having an inductance of 25 henrys at a current of $17\frac{1}{2}$ ma should satisfy this requirement. If the inductance falls to half this value at full load, the required capacitance for each filter section is

      Single-section filter.............................. 93.9 μf
      Two-section filter................................. 3.77 μf
      Three-section filter............................... 1.37 μf

A two-section filter using two 4-μf condensers, or a three-section filter using three 1.5- or 2-μf condensers, will give the required filtering. For the two-section filter the resonant frequency of one section is $1/2\pi \sqrt{12.5 \times 4 \times 10^{-6}} = 22.5 \sim$ at full load. The resonant frequency of one section of the three-section filter is 31.8 $\sim$. Both of these values are far below the fundamental ripple frequency and are, therefore, satisfactory.

Although an approximate value of the required transformer voltage, under the assumption that the tube drop is negligible, could be found from Table 11-I, the required voltage can be found more accurately from the operating characteristics of the 5U4-G rectifier. If each choke has 75 ohms resistance, the voltage drop through two chokes is approximately 32.5 volts at full load and the transformer secondary voltage should be 500 volts each side of center to give the 350-volt output. The output voltage rises to approximately 440 volts when the external load is removed.

The values of L and C chosen above in both the two- and the three-section filter are enough larger than the values that just give the maximum allowable ripple so that it is unnecessary to recheck the computations, taking into account the resistance of the chokes in finding L_1.

It is interesting to compute the ripple factor that would be obtained if the above two-section filter were used with a three-phase rectifier. For a three-phase rectifier $f_r = 180 \sim$. Substituting $f_r = 180 \sim, C = 4 \times 10^{-6} \mu$f and $L = 12.5$ henrys in Eq. (11-5) gives 3960 for α_1. Since $\rho = 0.25$ for the three-phase rectifier, $\rho' = 0.0063$ per cent. This clearly shows the improvement in filtering resulting from an increase in the number of phases.

Problems

11-1. Design a B supply to meet the following specifications:

Output voltage............ ..... 300 volts
Maximum load current..... 100 ma
Ripple factor........ ..... Not to exceed 0.0005
Supply............... ..... 110 volts, 60 cycle, single phase

Impedance presented to the load at 50 cycles must not exceed 1000 Ω. Voltage regulation should be small.

11-2. Show that a rectifier tube must be able to withstand a peak inverse voltage of twice the crest secondary voltage when an input condenser is used in the filter.

11-3. By means of the equivalent plate circuit, show that the effectiveness of the circuit of Fig. 9-11a increases with μ.

11-4. By means of the equivalent plate circuit, show that the circuit of Fig. 11-9b should be adjusted so that $R_2/R_1 = \mu$.

11-5. By means of the equivalent plate circuit, show that the circuit of Fig. 11-9c should be adjusted so that $R_3 = R_2/R_1 g_m$.

Supplementary Bibliography

PRINCE, D. C., and VOGDES, F. B.: "Principles of Mercury Arc Rectifiers and Their Circuits," McGraw-Hill Book Company, Inc., New York, 1927.

JOLLEY, L. B. W.: "Alternating-current Rectification," John Wiley & Sons, Inc., New York, 1931.

MARTI, O. K., and WINOGRAD, H.: "Mercury Arc Power Rectifiers," McGraw-Hill Book Company, Inc., New York, 1930.

Additional references on the subject of power rectifiers and filters will be found throughout and at the end of Chap. 14 of "Theory and Applications of Electron Tubes," by H. J. Reich. The following references cover recent work:

KILGORE, L. A., and COX, J. H.: *Trans. A.I.E.E.*, **56**, 1134 (1937); **57**, 168 (1938).

McDONALD, G. R.: *Trans. A.I.E.E.*, **58**, 563 (1939).

LEE, REUBEN: *Electronics*, April, 1938, p. 39.

DEELEY, P. M.: *Communications*, April, 1938, p. 19.

SCOTT, H. J.: *Electronics*, June, 1938, p. 28.

TRUCKSESS, D. E.: *Bell Lab. Rec.*, **17**, 24 (1938).

WALLIS, C. M.: *Electronics*, October, 1938, p. 12.

HUNTOON, R. D.: *Rev. Sci. Instruments*, **10**, 176 (1939).

SCOTT, H. H.: *Electronics*, August, 1939, p. 42.

STOUT, M. B.: *Electronics*, September, 1939, p. 32.

MERRILL, F. D., JR.: *Electronics*, November, 1939, p. 16.

HONNELL, M. A.: *Communications*, January, 1940, p. 14.

WALLIS, C. M.: *Electronics*, March, 1940, p. 19.

WITTING, E. G.: *Rev. Sci. Instruments*, **11**, 182 (1940).

RICHTER, W.: *Electronics*, June, 1940, p. 20.

WAIDELICH, D. L.: *A.I.E.E. Tech. Paper* 41–105, presented at A.I.E.E. Summer Convention, Toronto, June, 1941.

CHAPTER 12

ELECTRON-TUBE INSTRUMENTS

Important applications of electron tubes are made in the field of measurement. Measuring instruments incorporating electron tubes include voltmeters, ammeters, wattmeters, ohmmeters, time and speed meters, frequency meters, wave analyzers, and oscillographs. This final chapter will deal with the two of these instruments that are most frequently used, vacuum-tube voltmeters and cathode-ray oscillographs.

12-1. Vacuum-tube Voltmeters.[1]—The advantages of vacuum-tube voltmeters over electromagnetic meters are their high input impedance, wide frequency range, and high sensitivity. Although vacuum-tube measuring instruments usually embody electromagnetic meters, the required sensitivity of the latter is generally small enough so that the cost of a complete electronic instrument is considerably less than that of an electromagnetic or electrostatic meter of comparable sensitivity. The vacuum-tube voltmeter is of particular value in the measurement of voltage in circuits in which the flow of meter current would appreciably alter the voltage, as in radio-frequency circuit measurements, the measurement of amplifier output voltage, or the measurement of the voltage of a charged condenser.

Although there are many types of vacuum-tube voltmeters, only the three types that are most commonly used will be discussed in this book. These are plate-detection, diode, and slide-back voltmeters.

12-2. Plate-detection (Transrectification) Voltmeters.[2]—The basic circuit of the plate-detection voltmeter is shown in Fig. 12-1.

---

[1] For a general discussion of vacuum-tube voltmeters covering developments through 1932, see T. P. Hoar, *Wireless Eng.*, **10**, 19 (1933). See also August Hund, "High-frequency Measurements," pp. 136–161, McGraw-Hill Book Company, Inc., New York, 1933.

[2] MOULLIN, E. B., and TURNER, L. B., *J. Inst. Elec. Eng.* (*London*), **60**, 706 (1922); MOULLIN, E. B., *J. Inst. Elec. Eng.* (*London*), **61**, 295 (1923) and *Wireless World*, **10**, 1 (1922).

Alternating voltage applied to the grid circuit is measured by the change in reading of the d-c milliammeter in the plate circuit. Because of curvature of the transfer characteristic, the amplitude of the positive half cycle of plate current exceeds the amplitude of the negative half cycle. The average plate current, therefore, exceeds the quiescent plate current, as shown in Fig. 3-19 (see Secs. 3-15, 3-19, and 7-7), the change in current being a function of the impressed alternating voltage. The meter must be calibrated by the application of known voltages. The condenser, whose reactance is small at the lowest input frequency, prevents variation of load impedance with frequency and thus eliminates a possible cause of dependence of calibration upon frequency.

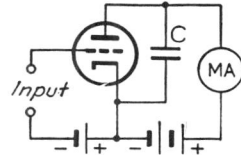

Fig. 12-1.—Basic circuit of plate-detection vacuum-tube voltmeter.

The voltmeter may be calibrated by the application of known sinusoidal voltages. Negligible current is drawn from the circuit under measurement if the crest voltage is less than the grid bias.

The reading of a plate-detection meter in the measurement of nonsinusoidal voltages is affected by the shape of the transfer characteristic and by the magnitude of the grid bias. An analysis based upon the first two terms of the series expansion for plate current shows that in class A operation the reading is proportional to mean-square signal voltage if the transfer characteristic is parabolic. The meter may then be calibrated to read r-m-s voltage. In practice it is difficult to obtain a transfer characteristic that approaches closely to parabolic form and, therefore, the change in average plate current is not strictly proportional to mean-square voltage and the change in current will be affected by the wave form of the impressed voltage. A close approach to a parabolic characteristic can be attained by the use of the balanced triode circuit of Fig. 12-2, but this circuit has the disadvantage of drawing a small current from the circuit whose voltage is being measured.

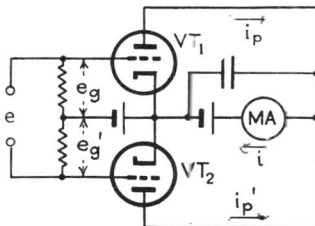

Fig. 12-2.—Balanced plate-detection vacuum-tube voltmeter.

When the tube of Fig. 12-1 is biased to cutoff, plate current flows only during the positive half cycle of the impressed voltage.

If the shape of the transfer characteristic is made to approach linearity by the use of high load resistance, the average plate current is proportional to the average value of the positive half cycle of impressed voltage. When the load resistance is small, however, curvature of the transfer characteristic causes the reading in class B operation to be more nearly proportional to mean-square positive input voltage than to average positive input voltage, particularly when the input voltage is small.

Since high input impedance can be obtained only if the grid is negative throughout the cycle of input voltage, voltages of amplitude greater than the cutoff grid voltage can be read only if the tube is biased beyond cutoff. Current then flows during only a portion of the positive half cycle. The average plate current cannot be affected by the form of the wave during the portion of the cycle when current does not flow, and so the average plate current is not necessarily proportional to either the average positive voltage or the mean-square positive voltage, and large errors in reading are likely to result if the voltage departs materially from sinusoidal form. Class C bias is sometimes used, however, in multirange meters.

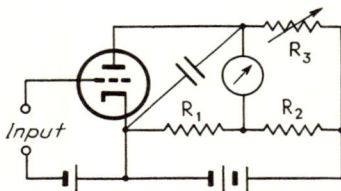

Fig. 12-3.—Plate-detection vacuum-tube voltmeter with zero balance.

Because the change in average plate current when the input voltage is impressed may be small in comparison with the total average plate current, considerable gain in sensitivity, as well as convenience in reading, is attained by balancing out the zero-signal plate current. A common method of doing this is shown by the circuit of Fig. 12-3, in which the tube forms one arm of a Wheatstone bridge.[1] The circuit may be balanced by varying any of the resistances. To avoid loss in sensitivity, R_3 must be large in comparison with the meter resistance. The required B-supply voltage increases, however, with R_3. A modified form of bridge circuit, shown in Fig. 12-4, uses a second tube in

[1] HOARE, S. C., *Trans. Am. Inst. Elec. Eng.*, **46**, 541 (1927); HAYMAN, W. G., *Wireless Eng.*, **7**, 556 (1930). See also P. A. MacDonald, *Physics*, **7**, 265 (1936) (with bibliography).

place of the resistance R_1.[1] The advantage of this circuit is that two similar tubes respond in a like manner to changes of supply voltage and cathode temperature, and so the bridge is less likely to become unbalanced. It is possible to set P_1 and P_2 so that small variations of supply voltage have little or no effect upon the zero balance.

To ensure constant operating voltages, it is best to obtain the grid and plate voltages from a common supply, the voltage of which is maintained constant by means of a glow tube or other type of voltage stabilizer (see Secs. 9-6 and 11-9) or adjusted to a definite value with the aid of a voltmeter Likelihood of changes of calibration can also be reduced by deriving the grid and plate voltages from the flow of filament or heater current through fixed resistors. Adjustment of the current to a definite value then also ensures correct grid and plate voltages.

Changes of calibration with tube age are prevented to a certain extent by keeping the static operating current con-

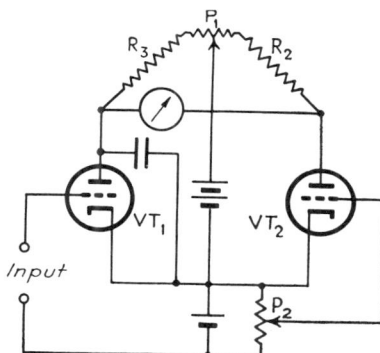

FIG. 12-4.—Circuit in which the zero-signal plate current is balanced out by the use of an auxiliary tube.

stant. It is necessary, however, to check the meter calibration from time to time regardless of the circuit used. The life of tubes of standard makes is sufficiently long so that tube deterioration is ordinarily an unimportant factor.

Dependence of calibration upon frequency, resulting from change of impedance of the electromagnetic meter used to read plate current, is prevented by the use of a shunting condenser between cathode and plate, as shown in Figs. 12-1 to 12-5. At very high frequency the reading may also be affected by imped-ance drop caused by inductance of the grid input leads and by

[1] WOLD, P. I., U S. Patent 1232879 (1916–1917). WYNN-WILLIAMS, C. E., *Proc. Cambridge Phil. Soc.*, **23**, 810 (1927); *Phil. Mag.*, **6**, 324 (1928). EGLIN, J. M., *J. Opt. Soc. Am.* and *Rev. Sci. Instruments*, **18**, 393 (1929). WINCH, G. T., *J. Sci. Instruments*, **6**, 376 (1929). NOTTINGHAM, W. B., *J. Franklin Inst.*, **209**, 287 (1930). DuBRIDGE, L. A., *Phys. Rev.*, **37**, 392 (1931).

resonance of this inductance with the capacitance of the grid circuit. Input capacitance also causes the input admittance to increase with frequency. Tubes with low effective input capacitance should be used, and the instrument should be designed so as to minimize the capacitance of all conductors connected to the control grid. For measurements at very high radio frequency it is advantageous to use an acorn tube (see Sec. 2-16) as the detector. It is also good practice to mount the tube at the end of a shielded flexible cable in order that the input voltage may be applied directly to the grid of the tube.[1]

The calibration curve of a plate-detection voltmeter may be straightened by the use of a self-biasing resistor, as in the circuit of Fig. 12-5.[2] Self-bias also increases the voltage range, since the bias increases with signal amplitude. The amplitude at which grid current starts to flow greatly exceeds the zero-signal bias.

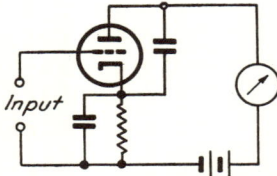

Fig. 12-5.—Self-biased plate-detection vacuum-tube voltmeter.

12-3. Diode Voltmeters.—Diode rectification can be used as the basis of vacuum-tube voltmeters that read average voltage.[3] The circuit which is shown in Fig. 12-6 is one of the simplest of all vacuum-tube voltmeter circuits. If it is assumed that the rectifier resistance is zero and that no current flows when the applied voltage is zero, then the instantaneous current is equal to the instantaneous voltage divided by the load resistance during the positive half cycle. The average current is the average voltage of the positive half cycle divided by the resistance. For a sinusoidal input voltage $E_{\max} \sin \omega t$, the average plate current is

$$I_{ba} = \frac{E_{\max}}{\pi R} = \frac{E_{rms}}{2.22R} \tag{12-1}$$

[1] BOYLE, H. G., *Electronics*, August, 1936, p. 32; RCA Application Note 47, 1935.

[2] MEDLAM, W. B., and OSCHWALD, U. A., *Wireless Eng.*, **3**, 589, 664 (1926); **5**, 56 (1928).

[3] SHARP, C. H., and DOYLE, E. D., *Trans. Am. Inst. Elec. Eng.*, **35**, 99 (1916); CHUBB, L. W., *Trans. Am. Inst. Elec. Eng.*, **35**, 109 (1916); TAYLOR, JAMES, *J. Sci. Instruments*, **3**, 113 (1925); *Wireless Eng.*, **10**, 310 (1933). DAVIS, R., BOWDLER, G. W., and STANDRING, W. G., *J. Inst. Elec. Eng.* (*London*), **68**, 1222 (1930).

For a direct input voltage E, the plate current is

$$I_b = \frac{E}{R} \tag{12-2}$$

Thus, if the diode were a perfect rectifier having zero resistance, the circuit could be calibrated on direct voltage and used to measure either direct or sinusoidal alternating voltage. Actually, curvature of the diode static characteristic and flow of plate current when the plate voltage is zero, resulting from initial velocity of electrons, cause the ratio of the alternating to the direct voltage reading to depart somewhat from the theoretical value 2.22. The error, which is most pronounced at low voltages, can be made negligible by the use of load resistances exceeding 100,000 Ω. High load resistance is also desirable in order to keep the current small. Since the average input voltage depends upon wave form, the reading of this type of meter changes with harmonic content of the impressed voltage. Although it draws

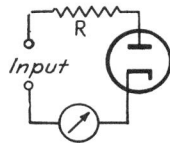

FIG. 12-6.— Simple diode voltmeter.

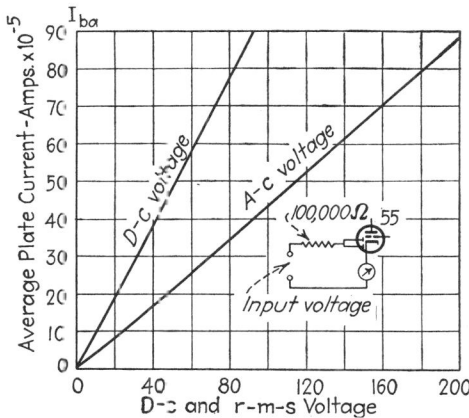

FIG. 12-7.—D-c and a-c calibration curves of the diode section of a type 6B7 (or type 55) tube used as a simple diode voltmeter.

a small current, this circuit makes possible the use of a sensitive d-c meter in the measurement of alternating voltages.

Figure 12-7 shows the direct- and alternating-voltage calibration curves of the diode sections of a type 6B7 tube used with a 100,000-Ω load. Similar curves for a 500,000-Ω load are practically straight lines through the origin, having slopes indicated by Eqs. (12-1) and (12-2).

The simple diode voltmeter is of particular value in the measurement of very high voltages when some flow of current is not objectionable.   With large values of R, the calibration curves of Fig. 12-7 are sufficiently straight, and the intercepts small enough, so that in the measurement of high voltage they may be considered to be straight lines passing through the origin and having slopes indicated by Eqs. (12-1) and (12-2).   Experimental calibration is then unnecessary.

For the measurement of small voltages the diode circuit of Fig. 12-6 may be followed by a d-c amplifier, as shown by Fig.

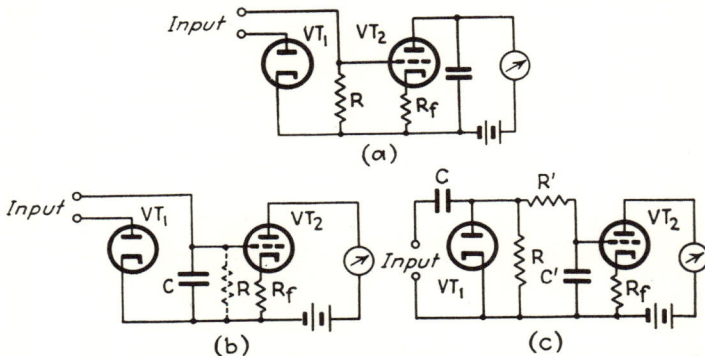

FIG. 12-8.—Diode vacuum-tube voltmeters incorporating a stage of d-c amplification.

12-8a.   Since the average plate current of VT_2 depends upon the average voltage across R, the reading of this meter, like that of Fig. 12-6, is dependent upon the average value of the positive half cycle of the applied voltage.   If R is replaced by a condenser C, as in Fig. 12-8b, the condenser charges to crest positive signal voltage.   The reading is, therefore, then a measure of the crest signal voltage.   Because C cannot discharge through either tube, a high resistance R may be shunted across C in order to allow C to discharge when the input voltage is reduced or removed.   To prevent the dependence of calibration upon frequency, the product fRC should be at least of the order of magnitude of 100 at the lowest frequency f of the input voltage.[1]   A variant of the circuit of Fig. 12-8b is that of Fig. 12-8c, in

[1] MARIQUE, JEAN, *Wireless Eng.*, **12**, 17 (1935).

which R' and C' act as a filter to keep the alternating voltage from being impressed upon the amplifier grid. The amplifier plate current in the circuits of Fig. 12-8 decreases with increase of input voltage, and so the meter cannot be damaged by excessive input voltage. If the zero-signal current is balanced out, the meter current flows in the opposite direction and cannot exceed the zero-signal plate current. Circuits a and b of Fig. 12-8 may also be used to measure direct voltage.

Inspection of the diagrams of Fig. 12-8 shows that the self-biasing resistor R_f results in inverse feedback, the circuit of the amplifier stage being of the form of the feedback circuit of Fig. 6-34c. Inverse feedback in the amplifier has four beneficial

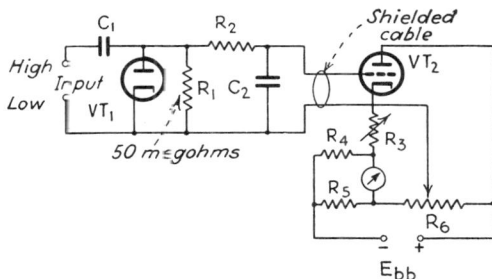

Fig. 12-9.—General Radio diode voltmeter.

effects: (1) If R_f is large, the meter reading is practically proportional to the direct grid voltage, and hence to the positive crest voltage applied to the voltmeter input. (2) Because of the opposing voltage developed across the resistor, the grid circuit can handle much larger direct voltages than the static cutoff grid voltage. Thus, much larger input voltages may be read. (3) The voltage range can be conveniently varied by changing the resistance R_f and the static biasing voltage. (4) The meter reading is practically independent of tube constants.

These facts have been employed in the design of a multirange voltmeter.[1] The circuit of this meter, shown in Fig. 12-9, incorporates the zero-balance bridge of Fig. 12-3. The sensitivity is adjusted by means of R_3, the correct amplifier bias being maintained by simultaneous adjustment of R_6. A type 955 acorn tube is used as the diode rectifier and is mounted at the end of a shielded flexible cable for high-frequency measurements.

[1] Tuttle, W. N., *Gen. Radio Experimenter*, **11**, 1 (May, 1937).

Voltage compensation in the B supply prevents change of calibration with alternating line voltage.

Figure 12-10 shows a circuit in which a single tube takes the place of the two tubes of the circuits of Fig. 12-8.[1] The function of R_f is to make the calibration linear and to increase the voltage range. The direct voltage drop through R_f is compensated by the setting of the voltage divider R_1. R_1 is adjusted so that the diode is biased negatively just enough to prevent the flow of diode current when the input is shorted. When the switch S is open, the meter reads average voltage of the positive half cycle; when S is closed, the meter reads positive crest voltage.

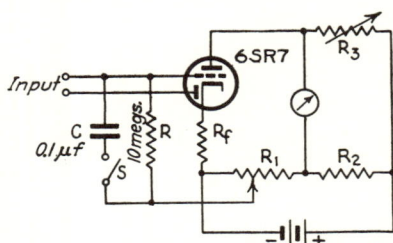

FIG. 12-10.—Diode voltmeter incorporating a d-c amplifier with zero balance.

Diode voltmeters are more sensitive than plate-detection voltmeters but have the disadvantage of lower input impedance.

12-4. Slide-back Voltmeters.—A very useful type of meter for the measurement of crest or direct voltages is the slide-back type. The original form of this type of meter is based upon the cutting off of triode plate current by negative grid voltage.[2] Just sufficient negative grid bias is applied to a triode to reduce the plate current to zero. The addition of signal voltage in the grid circuit results in the flow of current during the positive half cycles of the signal voltage, and in order to prevent the flow of plate current at any time during the signal-voltage cycle, the bias must be increased by an amount equal to the positive crest signal. In operation the bias is adjusted to reduce the plate current to zero with and without signal voltage, the difference in the two values of bias indicating the crest signal voltage of the positive half cycle. To read direct voltages, the bias is adjusted to give any convenient reading of plate current. The change in bias required to return the plate current to this value when input is applied is equal to the input voltage. One of the principal advantages of the slide-back meter is that it reads by direct

[1] A similar meter was described by A. W. Barber in *Electronics*, October, 1934, p. 322.

[2] HEISING, R. A., U. S. Patent 1232919.

comparison with a known voltage, and so does not require calibration.

In making readings of alternating voltage, difficulty arises from the fact that cutoff is not sharp. Because the transfer characteristic approaches the grid-voltage axis exponentially, the change in current corresponding to a small change in grid bias decreases with increased sensitivity of the plate-current meter. The

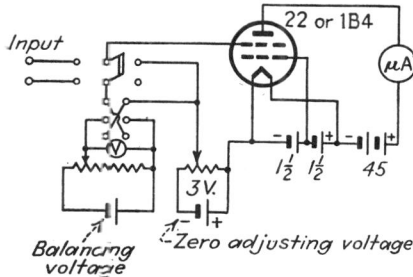

Fig. 12-11.—Slide-back voltmeter using tetrode with space-charge connection.

accuracy obtainable with a triode is rather low. Much more satisfactory results can be obtained with a tetrode or any multi-element tube in space-charge tetrode connection (see Sec. 3-9).[1] The i_b-e_{c2} curve for a positive voltage of one or two volts on the first grid approaches the voltage axis much more sharply than the transfer characteristics of triodes or the i_b-e_{c1} characteristics of multigrid tubes. Figure 12-11 shows the diagram of a meter that reads direct voltages to within 0.05 volt and alternating voltages to within $\frac{1}{2}$ per cent. To simplify operation, separate voltages are used for zero adjustment and for balancing, so that the d-c meter reads the crest voltage directly. For measuring alternating voltages the balancing voltage must always be negative. For measuring direct voltages it is advisable to apply the unknown voltage in such a direction as to make the grid negative, and so the balancing voltage must be positive.

The inaccuracy resulting from lack of sharpness of cutoff can also be overcome by working at a small value of plate current, instead of at cutoff. Because of plate detection, the change in bias required to keep the plate current constant when signal

[1] Reich, H. J., Marvin, G. S., and Stoll, K., *Electronics*, September, 1931, p. 109.

voltage is applied is not exactly equal to the crest signal voltage, and so the meter must be calibrated.[1] The calibration curve of balancing voltage *vs.* crest signal voltage approaches a straight line of unit slope through the origin as the operating plate current is reduced. Although the calibration is practically independent of plate and heater voltages and tube age, absence of the direct comparison feature is often a disadvantage of the small-current type of slide-back meter.

The use of a grid-controlled arc-discharge tube in place of a vacuum triode affords a third means of increasing the accuracy of the slide-back type of meter.[2] If care is taken to maintain the operating temperature constant, the grid voltage that prevents the firing of an arc-discharge tube at a given anode voltage is very definite. The difference in the grid bias voltages at which the tube fires with and without signal voltage in the grid circuit affords an accurate method of measuring the crest signal voltage, or an unknown direct voltage. A circuit that uses an 885 thyratron tube is shown in Fig. 12-12. R_1 and R_2 are current-limiting resistors. No anode-current meter is necessary, since firing is indicated by glow.

FIG. 12-12.—Slide-back voltmeter using a type 884 or 885 thyratron.

12-5. Cathode-ray Oscillographs.[3]—Designed originally for the study of voltage and current wave form, the cathode-ray

---

[1] MEDLAM and OSCHWALD, *loc. cit.;* AIKEN, C. B., and BIRDSALL, L. C., *Trans. Am. Inst. Elec. Eng.,* **57**, 173 (1938).

[2] HUGHES, E., *J. Sci. Instruments,* **10**, 180 (1933); RUIZ, J. J., *Rev. Sci. Instruments,* **6**, 169 (1935).

[3] RIDER, J. F., "The Cathode-ray Tube at Work," J. F. Rider, New York, 1935; MALOFF, I. G., and EPSTEIN, D. W., "Electron Optics in Television," McGraw-Hill Book Company, Inc., New York, 1938; WATSON-WATT, R. A., HERD, J. F., and BAINBRIDGE-BELL, L. H., "The Cathode-ray Oscillograph in Radio Research," H. M. Stationery Office, London, 1933; ARDENNE, M. VON, "Die Kathodenstrahlrohren," Julius Springer, Berlin, 1934; MAC-GREGOR-MORRIS, J. T., and HENLEY, J. A., "Cathode Ray Oscillography," Chapman & Hall, Ltd., London, 1936; KNOLL, M., *Arch. tech. Mess.,* **1**, 76 (1931) (summary of literature to 1931); ZWORYKIN, V. K., *Electronics,* November, 1931, p. 188 (bibliography of 12 items); BATCHER, R. R., *Proc. I. R. E.,* **20**, 1878 (1932) (bibliography of 29 items); STINCHFIELD, J. M., *Elec. Eng.,* **53**, 1608 (1934); BATCHER, R. R., *Instruments,* **9**, 6, 38, 77, 112, 140,

oscillograph finds many other useful applications. Advantages of the cathode-ray oscillograph over other types of oscillographs include its wide frequency range, which extends into the radio frequencies, its very high input impedance, its ease and convenience of operation, its portability, and its comparatively low cost.

The cathode-ray oscillograph tube, one type of which is illustrated in Fig. 12-13, consists essentially of an electron gun, two sets of electrostatic deflecting plates, and a fluorescent screen. The electron gun consists of a thermionic cathode, a grid for controlling the number of electrons that leave the cathode, and two anodes. The final velocity with which the

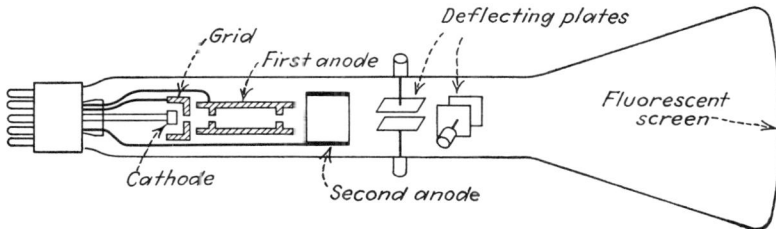

Fig. 12-13.—Electrode structure of a typical cathode-ray oscillograph tube.

electrons leave the gun is determined by the potential of the second anode. The electrostatic field between the inner and outer anodes focuses the stream of electrons in a manner somewhat analogous to the focusing of light rays by lenses.[1] If the anodes are properly shaped, the potential of the first anode, which is intermediate between that of the cathode and second anode, can be adjusted so that the beam of electrons will be brought to a sharp focus in the plane of the fluorescent screen, which consists of a coating of willemite (zinc orthosilicate), zinc sulphide, zinc phosphate, or calcium tungstate on the inner surface of the end of the glass tube. The impact of the electrons upon

---

166, 197, 231, 255, 286, 312, 341 (1936); Parr, G., "The Low Voltage Cathode Ray Tube," Chapman and Hall, Ltd., London, 1937 (extensive bibliography); Stocker, A. C., *Proc. I.R.E.*, **25**, 1012 (1937); Mayer, H. F., *Electronics*, April, 1938, p. 14; Preisman, A., *RCA Rev.*, **3**, 473 (1939); Overbeck, W. P., and Löf, J. L. C., *Rev. Sci. Instruments*, **11**, 375 (1940); Geohagen, W. A., *Electronics*, November, 1940, p. 36.

[1] Maloff, I. G., and Epstein, D. W., *Proc. I.R.E.*, **22**, 1386 (1934); **23**, 263 (1935). Epstein, D. W., *Proc. I.R.E.*, **24**, 1095 (1936).

the screen causes it to fluoresce, and so a bright spot is visible at the point where the beam strikes.[1]

The electron beam passes between the electrostatic deflecting plates. Because the electrons that comprise the beam are negative charges, the application of a potential between a set of deflecting plates causes each electron to be drawn toward the positive plate and away from the negative during its passage between the plates and thus bends the beam and displaces the fluorescent spot from its normal position on the screen (see Sec. 1-20). Because the two sets of plates are perpendicular to each other, the deflection produced by one set is at right angles to that produced by the other. Simultaneous application of direct voltage to both sets of plates produces a displacement which is the vector sum of those that result from the individual voltages. In practice the tube is mounted so that one pair of plates produces a horizontal displacement and the other a vertical. The former are often designated as the X plates and the latter as the Y plates.

Because a charge that moves in a magnetic field experiences a force at right angles to the field and to its direction of motion (see Sec. 1-21), a magnetic field may be used to deflect the luminous spot. This method is usually less convenient in oscillographic work, and requires the expenditure of appreciable power in the deflecting coils. It is used, however, with cathode-ray tubes for television.

When alternating voltage is applied to one pair of plates, the spot oscillates, and, because of persistence of fluorescence and persistence of vision, is seen as a line on the screen. Application of alternating voltage to both sets of plates causes the spot to trace a complicated path which does not in general close upon itself if the frequencies of the two voltages are different and which is, therefore, seen as a moving pattern. If the quotient of the two frequencies is rational, the path closes and the image is seen as a stationary pattern. A rational frequency

---

[1] NICHOLS, E. L., HOWES, H. L., and WILBER, D. T., "Cathodo-luminescence and Luminescence of Incandescent Solids," *Carnegie Inst. Pub.*, Washington (1928); TOMASCHEK, R., *Die Physik*, **2**, 33 (1934); PERKINS, T. B., and KAUFMANN, H. W., *Proc. I.R.E.*, **23**, 1324 (1935); LEVY, L., and WEST, D. W., *J. Inst. Elec. Eng. (London)*, **79**, 11 (1936); MALOFF, I. G., and EPSTEIN, D. W., *Electronics*, November, 1937, p. 31.

ratio can be determined by enclosing the pattern by a rectangle the sides of which are parallel to the X and Y axes and tangent to the pattern. The ratio of the Y to the X frequency equals the number of points of tangency of the curve to a horizontal side of the rectangle divided by the number of points of tangency to a vertical side. Thus, in Fig. 12-14 the ratio of the Y frequency to the X frequency is $3:2$. The form of the pattern is also affected by the harmonic content, amplitude, and phase relation of the two voltages. For sinusoidal voltages of the same frequency, that are of equal amplitude and in phase, the pattern is a straight line making a 45-deg angle with the horizontal. As the phase of one voltage is changed, the pattern becomes an ellipse which widens with increase of phase angle and becomes a circle when the phase angle reaches 90 deg. Although these patterns, called *Lissajous figures*, may be analyzed quite

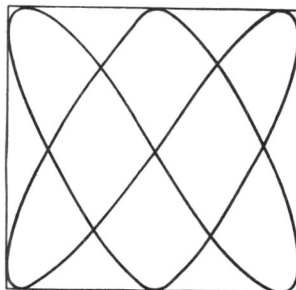

FIG. 12-14.—Lissajous figure for 3:2 frequency ratio, enclosed by a rectangle.

readily if one component is sinusoidal,[1] it is usually desirable to use an X voltage of such wave form that the unknown voltage is plotted on a time base.

In order that the image shall show the unknown voltage as a function of time, it is necessary that the spot shall periodically *sweep* across the screen horizontally with uniform velocity up to a certain point and then return instantaneously to its zero position.

FIG. 12-15.—Wave form of linear sweep voltage for cathode-ray oscillograph.

If the time taken for one timing *sweep* is equal to the period of the voltage applied to the Y plates, the pattern will consist of one cycle of the Y voltage. If the sweep frequency is equal to f_y/n, the image will show n waves of the Y voltage. The image will be stationary if n is a rational number. The required horizontal movement of the fluorescent spot can be produced by means of an X voltage that periodically increases uniformly with time and falls to zero instantaneously upon reaching a given value. The wave form of such a voltage is shown in Fig. 12-15. The earliest method of obtaining a saw-tooth voltage was

[1] KIPPING, N. V., *Wireless World*, **13**, 705 (1924).

by means of a rotating voltage divider. The usefulness of this method was limited by friction of sliding contacts and by contact resistance and other mechanical difficulties. The development of electrical methods of producing sweep voltages greatly increased the field of application of the cathode-ray oscillograph[1] and made possible the synchronization of the sweep voltage to the unknown voltage.

Methods of producing saw-tooth voltages were discussed in Chaps. 8 and 9. The circuits of Figs. 8-18 and 8-21 may be successfully used to supply sweep voltage, but the arc-tube relaxation oscillator of Fig. 9-37 is more commonly used. Many modifications of the basic glow and arc relaxation oscillator

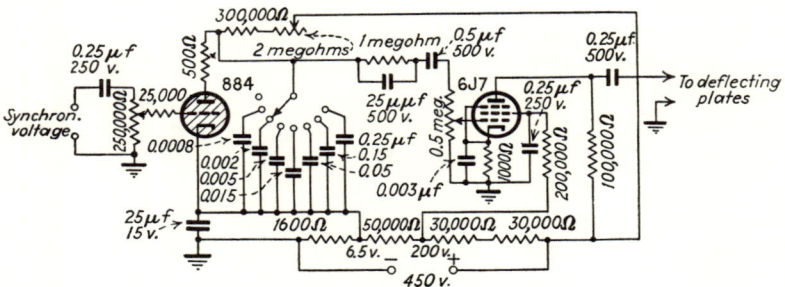

Fig. 12-16.—Sweep oscillator and amplifier.

circuits have been used as sweep oscillators.[2] A simple circuit which incorporates an amplifier for varying the sweep amplitude is shown in Fig. 12-16.[3]

It should be noted that practical sweep oscillators do not furnish a voltage that satisfies the requirements for a perfect sweep voltage, since some time is required for the voltage to fall to zero at the end of the cycle. Because of this, a portion of the observed phenomenon occurs during the return sweep. The fraction of the cycle taken by the return sweep is ordinarily negligible at low frequency, but at very high frequencies the return time may be large enough to be objectionable.

[1] Bedell, F., and Reich, H. J., *J. Am. Inst. Elec. Eng.*, **46**, 563 (1927).
[2] For a bibliography on sweep oscillators, see H. J. Reich, "Theory and Applications of Electron Tubes," p. 596.
[3] Waller, L. C., *Radio Retailing*, January, 1937, p. 65. This article gives complete specifications for the construction of an oscilloscope using a type 913 cathode-ray tube.

The ability of the grid of a cathode-ray tube to control the density of the electron beam affords a simple method of controlling the brilliance of the image without appreciably affecting the sharpness of focus. One special application of grid control of intensity is the introduction of a small voltage of known frequency into the grid circuit to produce variation of intensity of the fluorescent line by means of which time may be indicated on the pattern.[1] This is particularly helpful in the study of Lissajous figures.

In the application of cathode-ray tubes to television reception, the grid is used to vary the intensity of the spot in response to the

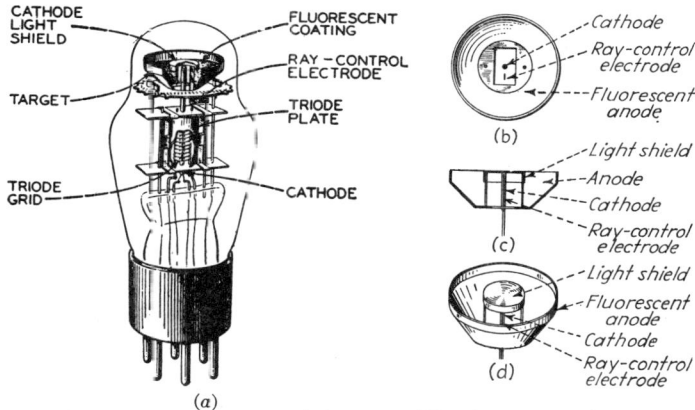

FIG. 12-17.—Structure of the type 6AB5 electron-ray tube.

received signal, so that the brightness of the image is everywhere proportional to the brightness of corresponding points of the transmitted scene or object.

12-6. Electron-ray Tube.—Another type of cathode-ray tube is the *electron-ray tube* or *magic eye*, which is used as a tuning indicator in radio receivers.[2] This tube, the construction of which is shown in Fig. 12-17, contains two sets of elements, one of which is a triode amplifier and the other a cathode-ray indicator. The latter consists of a cathode, a fluorescent anode

[1] SUNDT, E. V., and FETT, G. H., *Rev. Sci. Instruments*, **5**, 402 (1934).

[2] WALLER, L. C., and RICHARDS, P. A., *Radio Retailing*, December, 1935, p. 47; THOMPSON, H. C., *Proc. I.R.E.*, **24**, 1276 (1936); WALLER, L. C., *QST*, October, 1936, p. 35 and November, 1936, p. 23. WALLER, L. C., *RCA Rev.*, **1**, 111 (1937).

(target), and a control electrode which varies the portion of the fluorescent anode upon which the electrons strike.   The ray-control electrode is connected to the plate of the amplifier section, which is connected to the supply voltage through a high resistance, as shown in Fig. 12-18. Variation of the amplifier grid voltage changes the voltage of the ray-control electrode, and thus the portion of the target that fluoresces.

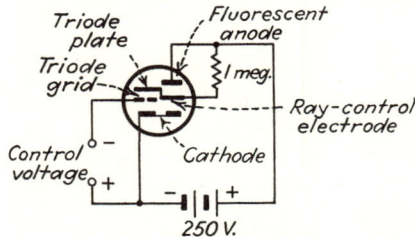

FIG. 12-18.—Electron-ray–tube circuit.

The fluorescence is observed as an annular sector of varying angular width.   The tube may be calibrated for use as a voltmeter where rough measurements suffice.

Problem

12-1. By substituting $e_g = E_1 \sin \omega t + E_2 \sin 2\omega t + E_3 \sin 3\omega t + \cdots$

in the relation $I_{ba} = \dfrac{\omega}{2\pi} \displaystyle\int_0^{\frac{\pi}{\omega}} i_b \, dt$, show that, when the transfer characteristic

is parabolic, a plate-detection voltmeter reads mean-square signal voltage and may, therefore, be calibrated to read r-m-s voltage.

APPENDIX

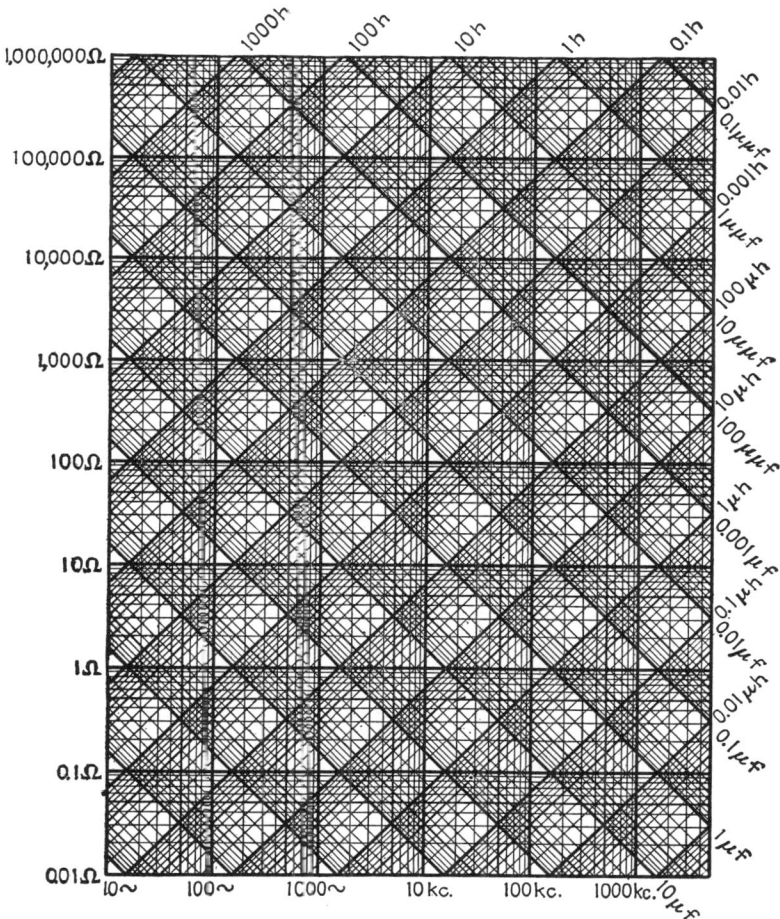

FIG. A-1.—Chart for the determination of inductive and capacitive reactance. To find reactance at any frequency, determine the intersection of the diagonal line corresponding to the given inductance or capacitance with the vertical line corresponding to the given frequency. A horizontal line through this point of intersection indicates the reactance on the scale of ohms. To find the resonant frequency for a given inductance and capacitance, find the intersection of the two corresponding diagonal lines and read the frequency on the lower scale.

371

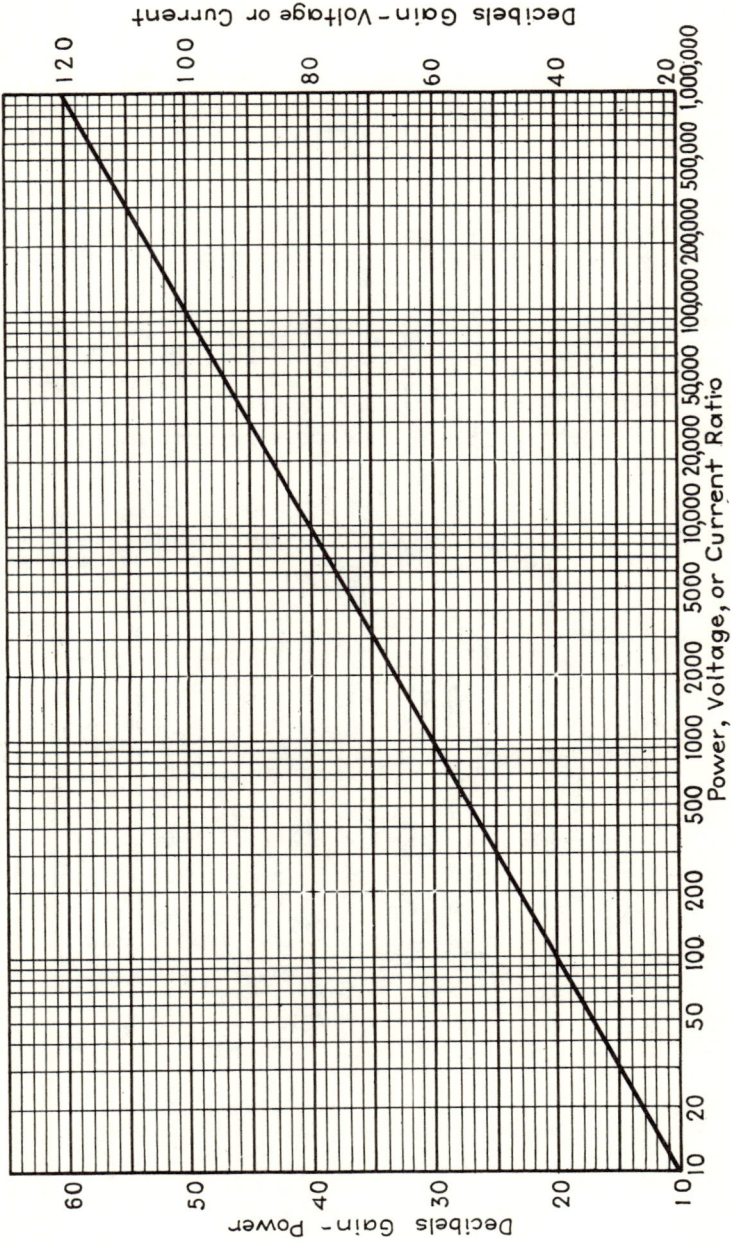

FIG. A-2.—Chart for the determination of decibel gain.

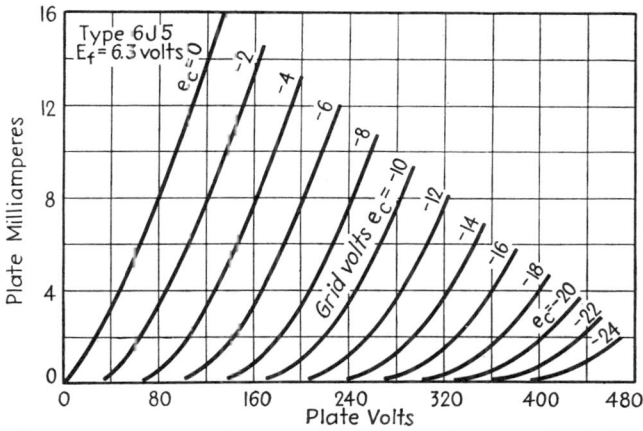

FIG. A-3.—Average plate characteristics for the type 6J5 triode.

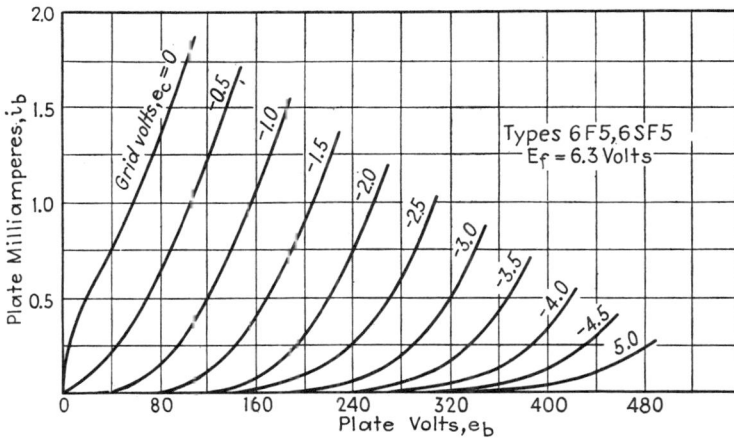

FIG. A-4.—Average plate characteristics for the types 6F5 and 6SF5 triodes.

AVERAGE PLATE CHARACTERISTICS

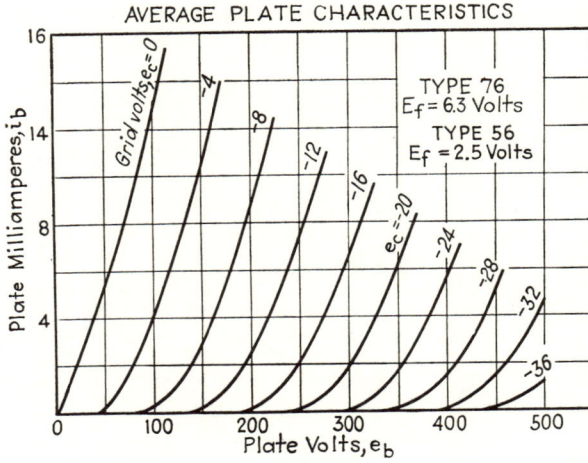

FIG. A-5.—Average plate characteristics for the types 76 and 56 triodes.

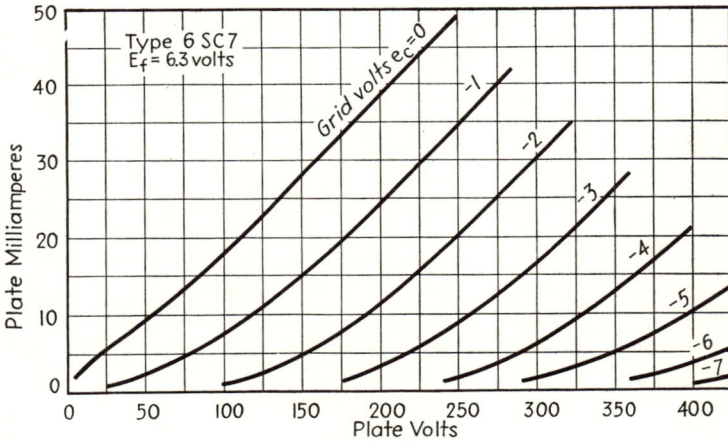

FIG. A-6.—Average plate characteristics for each unit of the type 6SC7 twin triode.

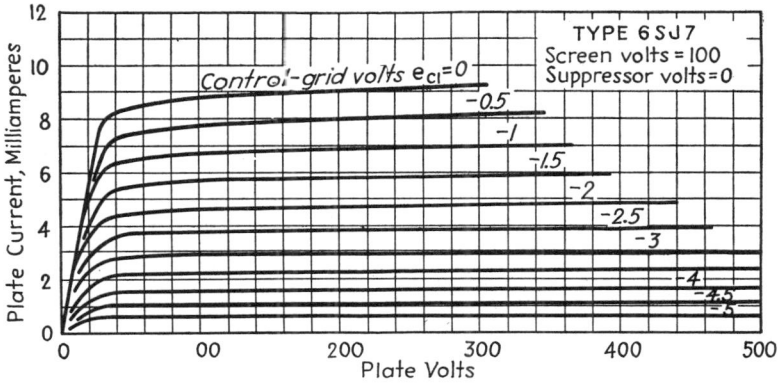

Fig. A-7.—Average plate characteristics for the type 6SJ7 pentode with 100-volt screen voltage.

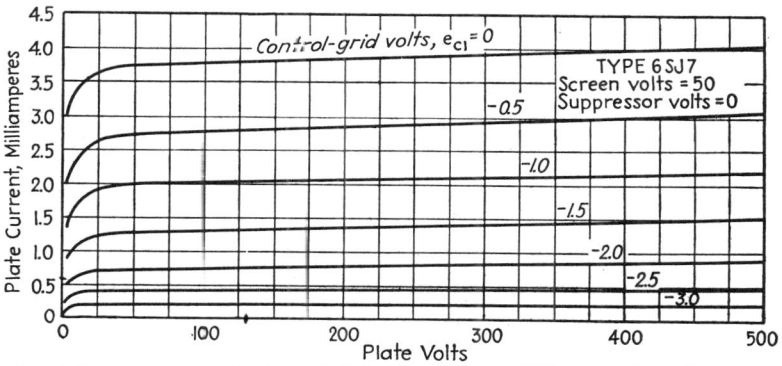

Fig. A-8.—Average plate characteristics for the type 6SJ7 pentode with 50-volt screen voltage.

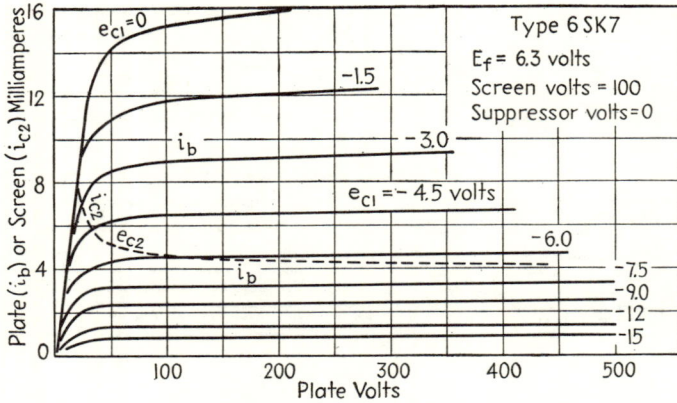

Fig. A-9.—Average plate characteristics for the type 6SK7 pentode.

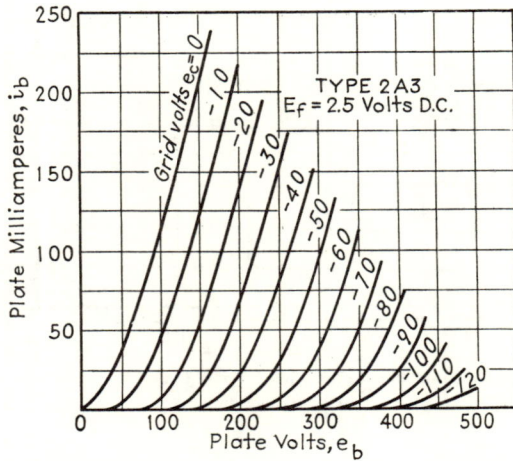

Fig. A-10.—Average plate characteristics for the type 2A3 triode.

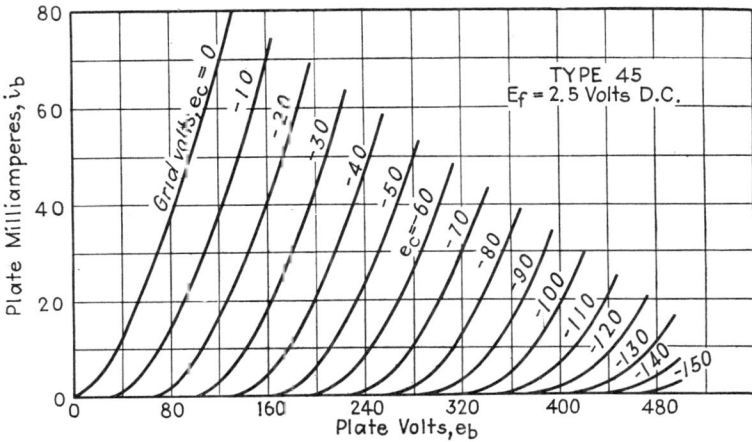

FIG. A-11.—Average plate characteristics for the type 45 triode.

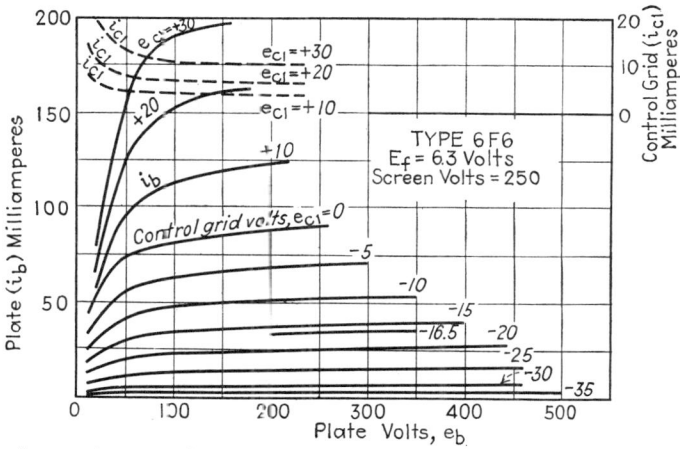

FIG. A-12.—Average plate characteristics for the type 6F6 triple-grid tube, connected as a pentode. (See Fig. 3-4 for characteristics for triode connection.)

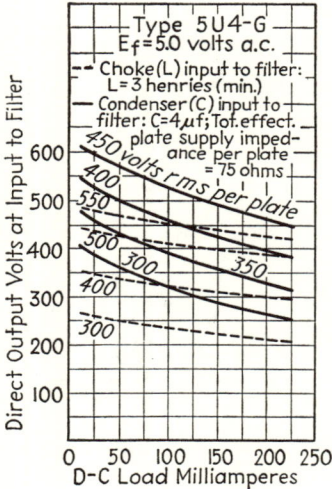

FIG. A-13.

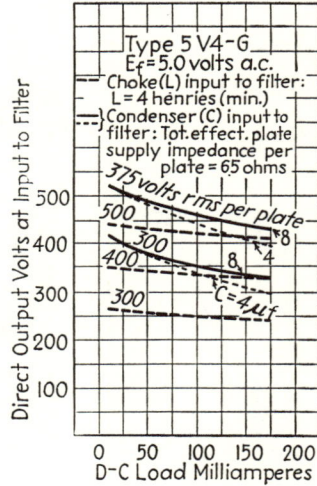

FIG. A-14.

FIGS. A-13, A-14.—Operation characteristics for the type 5U4-G rectifier.

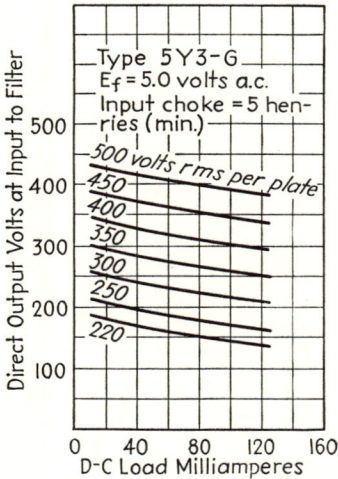

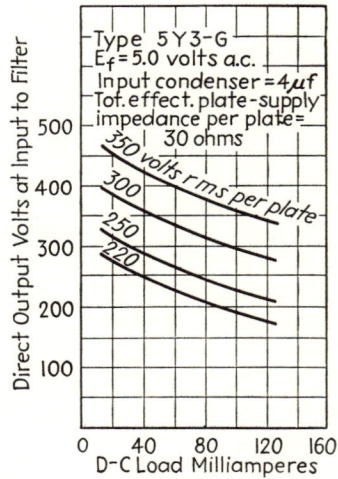

FIG. A-15.—Operation characteristics for the type 5Y3-G rectifier.

Operating Data for Typical Amplifier Tubes (Receiving Type)

Type	Classification by construction	Type of cathode	Filament or heater voltage	Filament or heater current, amp	Maximum plate voltage	Maximum screen voltage	Allowable plate dissipation, watts	Allowable screen dissipation, watts	C_{gk}*, μμf	C_{gp}, μμf	C_{pk}*, μμf	Connection and class of operation	Grid voltage	Screen voltage	Screen current, ma	Plate voltage	Plate current, ma per tube	μ	r_p, ohms	g_m, μmhos	Load resistance, ohms†	P_o watts‡	Total harmonic content, per cent
2A3	Power triode	Filament	2.5	2.5	250				9	13	4	Class A1, single tube	−45			250	60	4.2	800	5,250	2,500	3.5	5.0
												Class AB1, two tubes	−62			300	40				3,000	15.0	2.5
2A5 / 6F6	Triple-grid power amplifier	Heater	2.5 / 6.3	1.75 / 0.7	375 / 350	285	11 / 10	0.75 / 3.75				Single Class A1 pentode	−20	285	7.0	285	38	200	78,000	2,560	7,000	4.8	9.0
												Single Class A1 triode	−20			250	31	6.8	2,600	2,600	4,000	0.85	6.5
												Class AB2 triodes	−26			375	17				10,000	18.5	3.5
6J5	Detector, voltage amplifier triode	Heater	6.3	0.3	300				3.4	3.4	3.6	Voltage amplifier	−8			250	9	20	7,700	2,600			
6L6	Beam power pentode	Heater	6.3	0.9	360	270	19	2.5	3	2.4	4	Single, Class A1	−14	250	5.0	250	72	135	22,500	6,000	2,500	6.5	10.0
												Push-pull, Class A1	−16	250	5.0	250	60				5,000	14.5	2.0
												Push-pull, Class AB1	−22.5	270	2.5	360	44				6,600	26.5	2.0
6SC7	Twin high-mu triode	Heater	6.3	0.3	250				4	2.4	3.6	Voltage Amplifier	−2			250	2	70	53,000	1,325			
6SF5	High-mu triode	Heater	6.3	0.3	250				6	2.8	7	Voltage Amplifier	−2			250	0.9	100	66,000	1,500			
6SJ7	Triple-grid detector amplifier	Heater	6.3	0.3	300	125	2.5	0.3	4	0.005	11	Pentode voltage amplifier	−3	100	0.8	250	3	Greater than 1,650	Greater than 1,000,000	1,650			
												Triode voltage amplifier	−8.5			250	9.2	19	7,600	2,500			
6SK7	Triple-grid super-control (variable-mu) amplifier	Heater	6.3	0.3	300	125	4.0	0.4	6	0.005	7	Pentode voltage amplifier	−3	100	2.4	250	9.2	Approximately 1,600	Approximately 800,000	2,000			
45	Power triode	Filament	2.5	1.5	275				4	7	3	Single Class A1	−50			250	34	3.5	1,610	2,175	3,900	1.6	5.0
												Push-pull Class AB2	−68			275	14				3,200	18.0	5.0
50	Power triode	Filament	7.5	1.25	450				4.2	7.1	3.4	Single Class A1	−84			450	55	3.8	1,800	2,100	4,350	4.6	5.0
													−54			300	35	3.8	2,000	1,900	4,600	1.6	5.0

* C_{gk} and C_{pk} are total input and output capacitances (including capacitance to suppressor and screen) in the case of pentodes.
† Plate-to-plate load resistance in push-pull operation.
‡ Power output for two tubes in push-pull operation.

AUTHOR INDEX

381

H

Haeff, A. V., 71, 177
Haller, C. E., 261
Hanna, C. R., 167
Harries, J. H. O., 71
Hathaway, J. L., 213
Hawkins, L. A., 270
Hayman, W. G., 356
Heising, R. A., 362
Henley, J. A., 364
Henney, K., 290, 318, 335
Herd, J. F., 134, 364
Herold, E. W., 177, 215, 218, 231
Hewlett, W. R., 178, 228
Hickman, R. W., 349, 351
Hitchcock, R. C., 304
Hoar, T. P., 354
Hoare, S. C., 356
Holmes, R. M., 335
Honnell, M. A., 353
Horton, J. W., 134, 225, 232
Horwood, W. L., 178
Howe, G. W. O., 63
Howes, H. L., 366
Huggins, M. L., 20
Hughes, A. L., 334
Hughes, E., 364
Hughes, L. E. C., 212
Hull, A. W., 20, 64, 218, 253, 254, 258, 272, 273, 274
Hund, A., 150, 354
Hunt, F. V., 349, 351
Huntoon, R. D., 353
Hutchings, J. H., 300

I

Ingram, S. B., 250

J

Jackson, W., 85, 155
Jacobi, W., 267
Jaffe, D. L., 205
Jahnke, E., 201
Jansky, K. G., 178
Jen, C. K., 219
Johannson, H., 27
Johnson, R. P., 27
Johnston, H. R., 177
Johnstone, D. M., 176
Jolley, L. B. W., 293
Jonker, J. L. H., 113, 158, 177
Jordan, F. W., 157
Journeaux, D., 340
Jurriaanse, T., 260

K

Kallmann, H. E., 178, 304
Kano, I., 260
Kaufmann, H. W., 366
Keller, O., 340
Kellogg, E. W., 167
Kelly, R. L., 68
Kilgore, L. A., 353
Kimball, C. N., 177
Kime, R. M., 340
King, R. W., 53
Kinross, R. I., 122
Kipping, N. V., 367
Kishpaugh, A. W., 189
Kleen, W., 109
Klemperer, H., 300
Kniepkamp, H., 267
Knoll, M., 27
Knowles, D. D., 249, 254, 297, 298, 299
Kobel, A., 258
Kock, W. E., 245
Koehler, G., 144, 146
Koller, L. R., 47, 318, 334
Korff, S. A., 176
Kusunose, Y., 52

L

Lafferty, J. M., 323
Lamb, A. H., 331, 335
Lambert, R., 177
Lance, T. M. C., 334
Landon, V. D., 89, 212
Lange, B., 329, 334
Langmuir, I., 20, 26, 39, 40, 66, 246, 254
Laport, E. A., 213
Lawson, D. I., 212
Lederer, E. A., 34
Lee, R., 348, 353
Levy, L., 366
Levy, M. L., 177, 210
Livingston, O. W., 267, 290, 292
Liu, Y. J., 177
Llewellyn, F. B., 53, 81, 84, 224
Loeb, L. B., 20
Löf, J. L. C., 365
Loftin, E. H., 119
Lord, H. W., 290, 292
Loughren, A. V., 96, 167
Lowry, E. F., 254, 255, 256, 287
Lübcke, E., 247, 258
Luck, D. G. C., 199
Ludwig, L. R., 252, 294, 296, 298, 300
Luhr, O., 176

M

McArthur, E. D., 47, 260
McDonald, G. R., 353
McKenna, A. B., 270
McNally, J. O., 64
McProud, C. G., 125
MacDonald, P. A., 356

SUBJECT INDEX

A

"Abnormal" glow discharge, 240
Acorn tube, 46
Activation of emitters, 26, 29
Admittance, tube, 93–95, 136
Alkali metals, current–wave-length characteristics of, 307
Amplification, control of, 149, 151
  definition of, 117
  limit of, 153
  measurement of, 154
  mid-band, 138
Amplification factor, gas, 313
  grid, 53, 60–65, 69, 73, 379
  plate, 51–53, 56–58, 87
Amplifiers, choice of tubes for, 148, 151
  circuits, 118–126, 135 149, 153, 172
  class A, class AB, class B, class C definitions of, 127
  class AB and class B, advantages of, 170–171
  classification of, 117
  comparison of resistance-coupled and transformer-coupled, 147
  control of amplification of, 149, 151
  definition of, 114
  determination of optimum operating conditions for, 142–143, 161–165, 167–168
  direct-coupled, 118–120, 135
  distortion in, 114–117 162, 164, 136, 168
  frequency range of, 127
  graphical analysis of, 103–110, 166
  impedance-capacitance–coupled 120, 136–137
  inductance-capacitance–coupled, 148
  inverse-feedback, 171–172
  limit of amplification of, 153
  measurement of amplification of, 154
  measurement of power output of, 157–168
  noise in, 41, 153–154
  power, 110, 117, 157–168
  push-pull, 122, 169, 171
  radio-frequency, 150, 198–199
  resistance-capacitance–coupled, 137–143
  shielding of, 153
  single-tube, 132–135
  transformer-coupled, 122, 143–146
Amplitude-modulated waves, communication by means of, 198

Amplitude modulation (see Modulation)
Anode, definition of, 23
Anode current in diodes, 36–41
  (See also Plate current)
Anode current, limitation of, by space charge, 34–41
Anode diagram, 235, 321, 326
Anode glow, 238
Arc discharge, cold-cathode, 250, 300–301
  contrasted with glow discharge, 251
  definition of, 236, 251
  deionization in, 260–263
  external control of, 260, 300
  grid control of, 257–260
  hot-cathode, 252–259
  igniter control of, 260, 300
  magnetic control of, 260
  as a stroboscope, 302–304
  theory of, 250–253
Arc tubes, breakdown time of, 258
  cathode structure of, 254–256
  deionization in, 260–263
  external-grid control of, 260
  gas or vapor used in, 256
  grid-controlled, 257–260, 294
    (See also Thyratron)
  grid current in, 259
  igniter-controlled, 294–300
    (See also Ignitron)
  as a light source, 301–304
  magnetic control of, 260
  mercury-pool, 292–300
  as rectifiers, 253, 271, 339–340
  reignition voltage, 260–261
  as stroboscopes, 302–304
  strobotron, 301–302
  structure of, 254, 263–268, 271, 292–296
  tank, 292
  tungar, 253
  voltage drop in, 257, 263
    (See also Ignitron; Thyratron)
Arcback, 262, 295
Atom, excitation and ionization of, 1–3
Atom, structure of the, 3

B

Barrier-layer cells, 327–332
Beam pentode, 71–73, 171
Beat-frequency oscillators, 226

387

ANSWERS TO PROBLEMS

1-1. (a) 4.24×10^{-10} sec.   (b) 4×10^{-10} erg.

1-2. (a) Electron returns to first electrode.   It moves to a maximum distance of 0.237 cm from the first electrode.   At the instant of field reversal it is 0.118 cm from the first electrode.   (b) The energy acquired before field reversal is returned to the source of applied potential.   That acquired during the return to the first electrode is delivered to the cathode and is converted principally into heat.

1-3. (a) The energy lost by the electron in moving to the second electrode against the field is 6.4×10^{-10} erg.   As this is less than the initial energy, the electron will reach the second electrode.   (b) 6.4×10^{-10} erg is delivered to the source of applied potential.   The remainder is delivered to the second electrode and is converted mainly into heat.

3-1. $r_p = 11,600$ Ω; $\mu = 19.5$; $g_m = 1680$ micromhos.

3-2. $g_m = 1950$ micromhos (2000 micromhos from slope of transfer characteristic); $r_p = 350,000$ Ω; $\mu = 680$.

3-3. (a) $\mu \cong 8$; $g_m \cong 1700$ μmohs; $r_p = \mu/g_m \cong 4700$ Ω.

(b) $\mu \cong 15$; $r_p \cong 10,000$ Ω; $g_m = \mu/r_p \cong 1500$ μmohs.

3-4. 60, 100, 900; 120, 200, 1800; 180, 300, 2700; 160, 960, 1000; 40, 800, 840; 220, 260, 1020, 1100, 1860, 1900; 20, 140, 700, 780, 1700, 1740.

4-7. (a) $\mu = 3.5$; $r_p = 1785$ Ω; $g_m = 1960$ μmohs.

(b) $R_b = 425$ Ω.

(d) For a 50-volt grid swing, $H_1 = 24.8$ ma and $H_2 = 1.88$ ma.   For a 40-volt grid swing, $H_1 = 20$ ma and $H_2 = 1.25$ ma.

(e) $P_o = 1.54$ watts and 1.0 watt.

6-2. (c) $\mu'_1 = 7.35$ at 60 $\sim$, 10.6 at 100 $\sim$, 16.8 at 1000 $\sim$; $\mu'_2 = 17.35$; over-all gain = 42.1 db at 60 $\sim$, 45.3 db at 100 $\sim$, 49.3 db at 1000 $\sim$.

(d) $\mu'_1 = 19.85$ at 60 $\sim$, 27.7 at 100 $\sim$, 40.3 at 1000 $\sim$; $\mu'_2 = 48.4$; over-all gain = 59.6 db at 60 $\sim$, 62.6 db at 100 $\sim$, and 65.8 db at 1000 $\sim$.   (f) Use $E_c = -6$ volts, $I_{bo} = 2$ ma, $R_{cc} = 3000$ Ω.

6-3. Second stage: Use $r_o = 500,000$ Ω.   Then $r_h = 58,300$ Ω.   At 10,000 $\sim$, $\omega r_h C_2 = 0.0183$ and $\mu' = \mu'_m = 88.3$.

First stage: $C_2 = 222$ $\mu\mu$f.   If $r_1 = 50,000$ Ω and $r_2 = 250,000$ Ω, $r_h = 25,600$ Ω; then $\mu'_m = 38.4$, $\omega r_h C_2 = 0.356$ at 10,000 $\sim$; $\mu' = 0.93$ $\mu'_m = 35.7$ at 10,000 $\sim$. $r_l = 278,000$ Ω.   Make $\omega r_l C_c = 10$ at 100 $\sim$ to make $\mu' = \mu'_m$ at this frequency.   Then $C_c = 0.057$ μf.   Use $C_c = 0.06$ μf.   If $r_1 = 25,000$ Ω and $r_2 = 250,000$ Ω, $r_h = 16,900$ Ω; then $\mu'_m = 25.4$, $\omega r_h C_2 = 0.236$ at 10,000 $\sim$, $\mu' = 0.97 \mu'_m = 24.6$ at 10,000 $\sim$. $r_l = 268,000$ Ω.   If $C_c = 0.06$ μf, $\omega r_l C_c = 10$ at 100 $\sim$, and $\mu' = \mu'_m = 25.4$ at this frequency.

6-4. μ' of second stage is constant at 17.35 below 100,000 $\sim$; μ' of first stage is 16.7 at 50,000 $\sim$ and 16.0 at 100,000 $\sim$.

6-5. Crest value of fundamental component of output voltage = $(210 - 40)/2 = 85$ volts; $\mu' = 85/5.5 = 15.47$; per cent $H_2 = (250 - 164)/(2 \times 170) = 4.12$.

6-6. (a) Crest value of fundamental component of output voltage = $(208 - 90)/2 = 59$ volts; $\mu' = 59/0.75 = 78.6$; per cent $H_2 = 1.0$. (b) $r_b = r_1r_2/(r_1 + r_2) = 333,333$ Ω; $R_b = r_1 = 500,000$ Ω; crest fundamental output voltage = 53 volts; $\mu' = 70.6$; per cent $H_2 = 1.7$.

6-7. (a) Crest value of fundamental output voltage = $(188 - 38)/2 = 75$ volts; $\mu' = 75$. (b) $r_p = 208,000$ Ω; $\mu = 96$; $\mu' = 79.5$. (c) $I_{bo} = 0.125$ ma; $R_{cc} = 12,000$ Ω. (d) $\mu' = 40.5$.

6-8.

Frequency	μ'	Frequency	μ'	Frequency	μ'
20	21	550	60	10,000	102
50	40	1000	60.1	12,600	109
100	52	2000	62.5	16,500	60
200	57.5	5000	65	20,000	36
400	59.7	7000	78		

6-9. A type 2A3 triode operated at $E_{bo} = 250$ volts and $E_c = -45$ volts will deliver the 50 ma crest current.

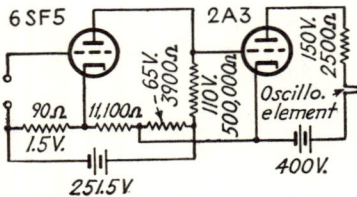

Fig. 6-39.—*Solution* for Prob. 6-9.

Crest fundamental alternating current of $(120 - 15)/2 = 52.5$ ma with 5 per cent second harmonic is obtained with a load resistance of 2500 Ω and a grid bias of -43.5 volts (-45 volts relative to mid-point of filament). $E_{gm2} = 43$ volts for 50 ma crest current. Required amplification of first stage = $\frac{43}{1} = 43$. For the first stage use 6SF6 tube with 500,000-Ω plate-coupling resistor. For $E_{bb} = 250$ volts and $E_c = -1.5$ volts, graphically determined $\mu'_1 = 71$. Input voltage to amplifier for full deflection = 0.605 volt. Use direct coupling in first stage and 2500-Ω resistor in series with oscillograph element. The circuit is shown in Fig. 6-39. A circuit of the form of Fig. 5-3b could also be used, but degeneration caused by the flow of second-stage plate current in the voltage divider would cause some loss of sensitivity.

6-11. (a) 2A3 triode or 6L6 pentode. (b) For 6L6 pentode operated on 200-volt supply with 2000-Ω load (field), plate current is 50 ma at $e_c = -16$ volts and 60 ma at -13.5 volts (determined from dynamic transfer characteristic). (c and d) Required voltage amplification for first stage = $2.5/0.05 = 50$. Use the circuit of Fig. 6-25 without the exciter. Use a 6SF5 tube in the first stage; $E_{bb} = 100$ volts, $E_c = -1.0$ volt, and 200,000-Ω coupling resistor. μ' of first stage (determined graphically) is 50. With 500,000-Ω coupling resistor, μ' of first stage is 62.

6-13. (a) $\mu = 3.6$ by graphical determination. Opt. $E_c = -0.7 \times 200/3.6 = -39$ volts. Use $E_c = -40$ volts. Zero-signal plate dissipation $= 200 \times 21 \times 10^{-3} = 4.2$ watts, which is within the allowable value. (b) Load line for 5 per cent second harmonic intersects the voltage axis at 328 volts, and the current axis at 54 ma. (c) $P_o = 0.94$ watt. (d) Opt. $r_b = 6100 \ \Omega$. (e) $r_p = 1780 \ \Omega$.

From the following graphically determined values it can be seen that some increase in power output can be obtained, at the expense of plate circuit efficiency, by changing the grid bias from -40 volts to -35 volts:

E_c volts	Zero-signal P_p, watts	P_o at 5 per cent H_2, watts	r_b ohms	r_p ohms	r_b/r_p	η_p per cent
-40	4.2	0.93	6100	1790	3.4	22.1
-37.5	5.2	0.97	4850	1600	3.03	18.6
-35	6.3	1.05	3540	1500	2.36	16.7
-32.5	7.5	1.04	2640	1400	1.89	13.9
-30	8.8	1.03	1710	1300	1.32	11.7

(f) $I_p = 0.707\mu E_c/(r_p + r_b) = 17.7$ ma for $E_c = -35$ volts; $P_o = I_p{}^2 r_b = 1.11$ watts. (g) $P_c = 1.17$ watts; (h) $P_i = 6.3$ watts; (i) See the above table. (j) P. S. $= 0.0414\sqrt{\text{mho}}$. (k) $n = 9.4$ for $r_b = 3540 \ \Omega$.

8-2. $\mu' \geqq r_1/r_2 + C_2/C_1 + 1; f = 1/2\pi\sqrt{r_1 r_2 C_1 C_2}$.

10-1. Wrong type of amplifier tube; crest phototube voltage too high for gas phototube; coupling resistance too low; relay should be shunted by a condenser; circuit should include bias adjustment; polarity of phototube is incorrect (coupling resistor should be shunted by a condenser for best results).

10-2. (a) See Fig. 10-35. (b) See Fig. 10-35. (c) For 72-ft-candle illumination, phototube flux $= 0.5$ lumen. Phototube current $= 3.5 \ \mu a$. Voltage drop across coupling resistance $= 28$ volts. Bias caused by coupling-resistance drop $= -28$ volts. For $E_{bb} = 100$ volts and $i_b = 7$ ma, $e_c = -1$ volt (determined from transfer characteristic for 1000-Ω load). Required applied biasing voltage $= +27$ volts. (d) For $E_{bb} = 100$ volts and $i_b = 8$ ma, $e_c = -0.5$ volt. $\Delta e_c = 0.5$ volt. $\Delta i = 0.0625 \ \mu a$. $\Delta L = 0.00893$ lumen. Change in illumination $= 1.285$ ft-candles.

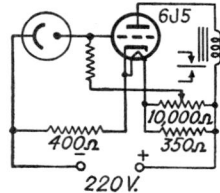

Fig. 10-35.—*Solution for Prob. 10-2.*

10-3. (a) Use the circuit of Fig. 10-11. (b) Relay closes at $e_c = -1$ volt; opens at $e_c = -2$ volts. (d) $i = 9.4 \ \mu a$ when $L = 0.2$ lumen. $E_r = +9.4$ volts. $E_{cc} = -11.4$ volts. (e) To close relay, $E_r = 10.4$ volts, $i = 10.4 \ \mu a$, $L = 0.22$ lumen, $\Delta L = 0.02$ lumen. Change in illumination required to close relay $= 3.2$ ft-candles. A common voltage supply may be used for anode and plate. C supply voltage causes the anode voltage to be one or two volts greater than 90 volts, but this will have negligible effect upon the computations.

10-5. 0.83 by planimeter; 0.85 by selected ordinates.

11-1. Use full-wave, single-phase rectifier with 5Y3G tube. For two-stage L-section filter, required $LC = 64.3$. For 20,000-Ω bleeder, $R_{min.} = 2600$ Ω, and L_1 should exceed 5.2 henrys at full load. L_1 should exceed 20 henrys at minimum load. Use 25-henry choke. If L_1 drops to 12.5 henrys at full load, required condenser capacitance per stage is 5.15 μf. Use 6 μf. Resonant frequency is 18.4 $\sim$ at full load. Voltage drop in chokes at full load is approximately 17 volts. Required secondary voltage is 425 volts each side of center. Effective output impedance of the filter at 50 $\sim$ is 560 Ω. Terminal voltage rises to about 365 volts at minimum load.